To Help Children Communicate

Mastery Performance Modules for Language Arts Teachers

Frank B. May
Portland State University

Charles E. Merrill Publishing Company
A Bell & Howell Company
Columbus   Toronto   London   Sydney

Published by
Charles E. Merrill Publishing Co.
A Bell & Howell Company
Columbus, Ohio   43216

This book was set in Oracle and Peignot.
Cover Design Coordination: Will Chenoweth
Text Designer: Ann Mirels
Production Coordination: Linda Hillis Bayma
Cover photo: Patricia Caston
Text photos: 34, 80, 369, Rich Bucurel; 2, 10, 83, 124, Celia Drake; 131, E & F
Bernstein Productions; 37, 89, Susan B. Eliot; 53, 304, Ron Engh; 5, Larry
Hamill; 49, Los Angeles Times; 35, George Morrison; 417, 421, *Resource
Teaching* (Merrill, 1978); 44, Steve Smith; 322, Ray Stanford; 2, 66, 67, 92, 100,
101, 149, 167, 196, 197, 208, 223, 240, 241, 249, 263, 270, 271, 285, 288, 310, 311,
327, 341, 354, 376, 377, 387, 391, 394, 397, 403, Dan Unkefer; 3, 142, 148, 335,
340, 402, Cynda Williams

Special thanks to the staff and students at the West Broad Elementary School,
Columbus, Ohio, whose generous assistance made most of the photos in this
book possible.

Library of Congress Catalog Card Number: 79-89098

International Standard Book Number: 0-675-08197-1

  2 3 4 5 6 7 8 9 10 — 85 84 83 82 81 80

Printed in the United States of America

Preface

This text is designed to provide preservice and experienced teachers with information and skills necessary to help children communicate. The format of this text is similar to that of *To Help Children Read,* in that performance objectives at the knowledge, simulation, and teaching levels have been provided for each module. These objectives will assist the instructor in helping students achieve mastery of concepts and procedures related to language arts instruction.

This book is equally suitable for courses using group instruction or courses in which the students proceed at their own pace. The Professional Supplement for instructors can be used with either approach and has tests for measuring students' knowledge, comprehension, and application of major ideas. Three tests are provided for each module: a practice or pretest, a parallel-form posttest, and a parallel-form repeat or retention test.

In *To Help Children Communicate,* there is an emphasis on:

- basic skills
- learning principles
- integration of the language arts

In emphasizing basic skills, however, I am extending the traditional definition (reading, writing, arithmetic) to include those skills which will eventually be necessary for finding and maintaining a job, making friends, raising children, and exhibiting similar functional and self-actualizing behaviors.

My emphasis on learning principles is the result of the belief that a great deal of teaching energy and learning time can be wasted when teachers are unaware of simple yet powerful ideas of motivation, retention, and classroom management. These ideas are introduced in Module 3 and then applied in all of the subsequent modules.

By emphasizing the integration of the language arts, I am attempting to encourage teachers to make use of the natural connections that exist in communication between reading, writing, listening, and speaking. Although the four language arts are sometimes treated separately in this text, the general theme is that communication skills are often best taught in settings that require their interaction.

Part 1 discusses three major strategies of language arts instruction: (1) using performance objectives whenever appropriate in order to determine whether "the basics" are *learned* as well as taught, (2) using children's past and present environment as a basis for planning language arts instruction, and (3) using learning principles as a guide to instructional practices.

In Part 2 the elements and methods of language arts instruction are described. Specific classroom techniques for improving children's vocabulary, grammatical fluency, speech habits, spelling, and handwriting are discussed. Ways are suggested to encourage children's creativity through spontaneous drama and personal writing while at the same time helping them make their speech and writing more communicative and interesting to others.

Part 2 also looks at ways of helping children follow both oral and written directions more closely, as well as ways of improving other reading and listening skills that lead to better comprehension. Special attention is given to those comprehension and study skills needed by students in handling required reading and listening assignments; also to those critical thinking skills required in today's mass media society.

In addition, Part 2 examines the role of children's literature in teaching and reinforcing basic language arts skills. And in the final module, various ways of individualizing a language arts program — through assessment, grouping, and the use of learning centers — are explained.

This book may be used simultaneously as a core text and as a problem-solving notebook. Each module begins with a Study Guide designed to help students prepare for a knowledge level examination. In addition, there are numerous application exercises throughout the text. This book is also designed for desktop accessibility for the busy teacher. In addition to several assessment devices that may be copied from the book, most of the modules include lists of learning activities and descriptions of games suitable for language arts instruction in the elementary classroom.

While many students and colleagues provided valuable ideas, suggestions, and contributions, a special acknowledgment is due Professor Steven Plaskon, University of Virginia; Dr. William Palmer; Dr. Johanna S. DeStefano, The Ohio State University; Dr. John M. Kean, University of Wisconsin; Professor Shirley Koeller, Texas Tech University; Professor Sheila Fitzgerald, Michigan State University; and Dr. Evelyn Wenzel, University of Florida for their helpful reviews.

CONTENTS

veloping Children's Structural Analysis Abilities | Teaching Contextual Analysis | Developing a Sight Vocabulary Through Visual Memory | Teaching Readiness Skills for Decoding

1

The Strategies of Language Arts Instruction

Planning Instruction That Emphasizes "The Basics"

There is no way to success but through a clear strong purpose.

Theodore T. Munger

Since 1964 there has been a continual decline in the United States in Scholastic Aptitude Test scores. Such a decline seems to indicate to most observers that many children in U.S. schools are not mastering the basic skills related to reading, writing, and arithmetic.

Blame for the decline has been unwillingly received by parents, teachers, school administrators, psychologists, textbook publishers, the television industry, and, of course, Dr. Spock. It has even been suggested that the decline is related to the large families created by the post World War II baby boom.

Concerned educators, parents, and business people also point to the high rate of "functional illiteracy" in the United States today. It has been estimated that at least one out of every seven youngsters seventeen years of age cannot read or write well enough to fill out job application forms. One personnel director went so far as to state that 40 to 50 percent of job applicants cannot even take the qualifying tests for jobs because of their inability to read directions, spell words, or write an understandable sentence. Experienced professors seem unanimous in their opinion that U.S. college students today cannot write, speak, or read as well as they could fifteen years ago.

A CBS News poll of parents showed that 76 percent of the parents in the United States favor a much greater emphasis in the schools on "basic skills." These are the kinds of comments concerned parents are making:

"My kid can't sound out words like I can."

"My child doesn't know how to spell anywhere near as well as I can."

"My daughter can't even punctuate a sentence."

"My son couldn't write a paragraph if he were paid to."

We could spend countless hours pinning the blame on various elements in our society. Perhaps a more useful approach, however, would be to

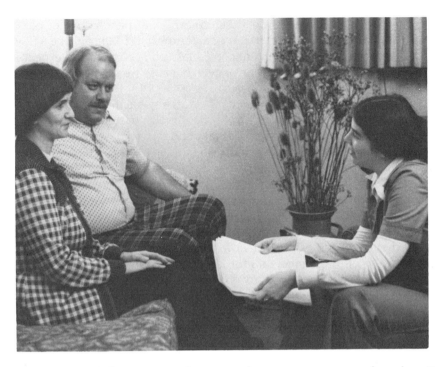

Most parents want more emphasis on "basic skills."

realize that all adults connected in even the remotest way to the education of children have a responsibility for improving it.

      This book attempts to show how teachers can emphasize basic skills without "throwing out the baby with the bathwater." It begins by redefining "the basics" in order to include other important communication skills. It explains the need and methods for establishing specific, easily evaluated objectives for language arts instruction. Then, the importance and nature of the environmental effects on children's language development is discussed in order that teachers may understand exactly what they're up against in improving basic skills. To assume that basic skills can be improved through some magical single-method approach is to ignore the teacher's "client"—namely, the individual child.

      Then, three fundamental problems facing anyone who wants to teach anything—particularly basic skills—are covered: (1) how to motivate students to learn, (2) how to help children retain what they are taught, and (3) how to deal with misbehavior that interferes with teaching and learning. Finally, the book moves on to a thorough discussion of the various elements of a language arts program and how these elements can provide opportunities not only for teaching and reinforcing the basic reading and writing skills but also for accomplishing the major aim of language arts instruction—better communication.

The Need for Specific Goal-oriented Instruction

Research on language arts instruction demonstrates that improvement in children's communication skills can best be obtained through specific instructional efforts. In other words, if we want children to exhibit a specific type of communication behavior, *we have to teach it*. We can't expect it to "unfold like a flower" simply because we have an "open concept" classroom. Nor can we expect it to emerge because we are team teaching or even because we set a good example of that particular communication skill.

All of those things—open concept, team teaching, good example—could possibly help, but they won't have the impact that direct, specific, and enthusiastic instruction can have. If we want children to have more interesting speech and writing, for instance, we must show them how to add interest appeal through conciseness, imagery, and clarity. For *most* children these qualities emerge only with specific instruction and specific reinforcement.

Module 1 shows you how to make your language arts instruction specific: how to start with a long-range goal for your students and break it down into a set of bite-sized manageable objectives, each of them suitable for a single learning experience or "lesson"; or how to start with an exciting activity and make it fit a useful long-range goal for language arts instruction.

In showing you how to do this (or in reviewing such procedures with you) I will discuss performance objectives, which are often referred to as "behavioral objectives." I believe that such objectives do have a place in a humanistic-oriented language arts program. An explanation for this belief will come at the end of the module after the nature of long-range outcomes related to the teaching of language arts has been discussed.

Special Prerequisites for Module 1

There are no special prerequisites for this module, other than those communication and thinking abilities assumed to be present among students in a college or university.

Long-range Outcomes Related to Module 1

This module should help you as a teacher to do the following:

1. Distinguish between learning activities, long-range outcomes, and performance objectives related to language arts instruction.
2. Select and create learning activities which relate to long-range outcomes of language arts instruction.
3. Select and create performance objectives which relate to long-range outcomes of language arts instruction.
4. Translate long-range outcomes and learning activities into performance objectives that accent basic skills.
5. Plan language arts programs that are balanced among (and integrated with) the four language arts of reading, writing, speaking, and listening.

Study Guide and Performance Objectives for Knowledge Level

To give yourself an overview of what is expected of you in this module, you should first scan the objectives and performance standards at all three levels—knowledge, simulation, and teaching. Then use the performance objectives for knowledge level as a study guide during your reading of the module.

Since this module has so many built-in practice exercises you have not been provided with writing space next to the performance objectives. You will find such space, however, in the practice exercises.

1.1 On a closed-book examination in which a mixed list of learning activities, long-range outcomes, and performance objectives is presented, you (the teacher-in-training) will be able to indicate by letter which are learning activities related to language arts instruction, which are long-range outcomes related to language arts instruction, which are performance objectives related to language arts instruction, and which are none of these three.

1.2 On the same examination, you will be given two lists—one of long-range outcomes related to language arts instruction and one of learning activities related to language arts instruction. You will be asked to demonstrate your ability to match the activities with the outcomes.

1.3 On the same examination, you will be given a list of performance objectives and a list of long-range outcomes related to language arts instruction. You will be asked to match the objectives with the outcomes.

1.4 On the same examination, you will be given a list of objectives related to language arts instruction and asked to check those which fulfill all the requirements for a complete performance objective.

1.5 On the same examination you should be able to change a vague and general objective into one or more specific performance objectives.

Performance Standards for Knowledge Level

A. Twenty-five minute time limit on 1.1–1.5.

B. Completion deadline: instructor will notify.

C. Recommended grading standards if grades are used: 96%: A; 92%: A—; 88%: B; 84%: B—; 80%: C; below 80%: incomplete; should be completed at 80% or better before you go on to performance objectives for simulation level. (The instructor may wish to permit a grade of A or B only the first time the test is given in order to encourage more intensive study.

Performance Objectives for Simulation Level

2.1 On a closed-book examination, you will be given a long-range outcome related to language arts instruction. You will be expected to write up a lesson plan in which you create a learning activity and at least one performance objective related to the long-range outcome. The learning outcome will be one of the following (These two outcomes are assumed to be within the range of common experience of teachers-in-training. Other outcomes may require specialized knowledge obtainable in later modules.):

1. Following oral directions.
2. Differentiating between facts and opinions presented orally. (Your instructor will either give you a choice of number 1 or 2 or determine the one you should use.)

Include the following in your written plan:
a. Approximate age level for which this activity might be appropriate: e.g., 5–7, 6–8, 11–13, etc.
b. Size of group for which this activity might be appropriate: entire class, small group, or individual.
c. Long-range outcome selected.
d. Performance objective (or objectives) you have created.
e. Prerequisite skills children might need.
f. Activity you have created—list briefly the procedural steps you might follow for the activity.
g. Materials you might need.

2.2 (Alternative objective) Same as 2.1, only a take-home examination would be given instead of a closed-book one. In this case, the instructor may wish to specify the outcome rather than give you a choice.

Performance Standards for Simulation Level

A. The performance objectives clearly state the behavior desired, the conditions under which the behavior is to be evaluated, and those performance standards which will indicate sufficient mastery of the desired behavior.

B. The performance objectives relate directly to the long-range outcome you have selected, and the learning activities relate to both your performance objectives and your long-range outcome.

*C. The activity seems appropriate to the age level of the students.
*D. The procedures seem appropriate to the size of the instructional group.
* E. Some awareness of necessary prerequisite skills is shown.

*Evaluation on the basis of these three standards should probably be less rigorous for those in pre-service training. The main criteria should probably be those emphasized in the module, namely, Standards A and B.

     F. Additional standards or modified standards may be developed by the instructor or by a committee of teachers-in-training. It is best, however, to state these *in advance* of the required performance.

     G. If a grade is given for the simulation exercise, it would of necessity be based on the subjective use of the performance standards by the instructor or a peer group. It is recommended that the simulation exercise be completed at the C level or better before the teacher-in-training moves on to the next module.

Performance Objectives for Teaching Level

No specific objectives are necessary at the teaching level for *this* module. For most of the other modules, you will be asked to apply what you have already learned at the knowledge and simulation levels by writing up plans for learning activities and carrying them out with children in an observation, micro-teaching, student teaching, intern or supervised teaching situation.

Long-range Outcomes and the Teaching of Language Arts

Mr. Hill's class was actively engaged in a creative drama experience. The children were sitting in pairs, with one child pretending to be from a foreign country and knowing only a little English. The other member of each pair was trying to explain some of the school rules, using simple words and speaking as distinctly as possible. After the activity was over, a parent who had been watching from the back of the room came up and asked Mr. Hill what his objective had been for the drama exercise.

"My objective," Mr. Hill replied, "was to provide the children with a fun experience in creative drama."

If that *was* Mr. Hill's objective, he should probably be judged not on how effective he was as a teacher but how effective he was as a baby sitter. If the children had fun—and this could probably be ascertained by the amount of smiling, giggling, and jumping up and down that occurred—Mr. Hill met his objective, *as an effective baby sitter*. However, as this module will attempt to demonstrate, there would be no way of knowing how effective he was as a *teacher* unless we knew what *long-range outcome* he had in mind and what *performance objective* he had established for this particular activity on this particular day.

Baby sitters generally seek to use up the clock in a pleasant way. Teachers, on the other hand, shouldn't be concerned *only* with providing a pleasant and "fun" environment; they should also be concerned with the development of skills, habits, and ideas—in other words, with long-range outcomes. The teacher who is concerned only with having fun with his pupils may be guilty of selling them short—and the public, too. (This is *not* meant to discourage the idea of teachers having fun with their students. Nor is it being implied that *every* activity must lead toward a definite objective.)

Most school activities should contribute toward the development of long-range skills, habits, or ideas.

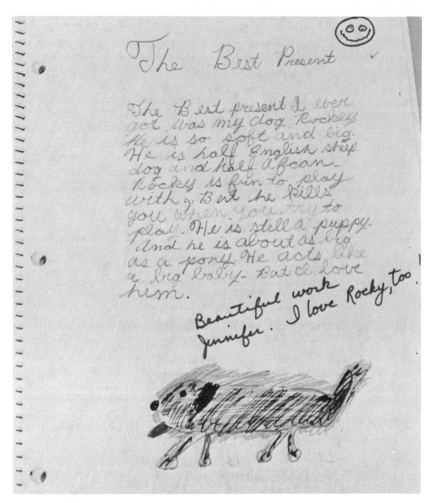

Assuming that one accepts the responsibility of teaching toward definite ends, what long-range outcomes should be considered in planning a language arts program for a group of elementary school children? Taking a very long-range view, one would have to look beyond the immediate school year for which a teacher is planning and ask what the long-range outcomes of schooling should be. Certainly *emotional maturity* would be high on the list, as would *social awareness, intellectual vigor,* and *occupational success.*

Does language arts instruction have anything to do with such idealistic outcomes? It *can* have. In fact, it can have *more* to do with them than any other area of the school curriculum, providing teachers perceive their language arts programs as means rather than as ends. Unfortunately, some teachers perceive language arts instruction as reading instruction plus some left-over hash consisting of thirty-two spelling tests, two attempts at haiku poetry, a listening game or two, one play, a badly worn workbook of "grammar exercises," and a set of 1949 elementary dictionaries.

Such a view of the language arts program is a very understandable one. Only those who have been elementary school teachers can fully understand the commitment and energy that it takes to teach at this level. Routines and subjects crowd a day that could easily be filled with nothing but answering children's eager—and sometimes frantic—questions: subjects and routines such as reading, math, social studies, milk count, lunch count, science, magazine count, more reading, p.e., music, art, Spanish. Is it any wonder that the language arts, other than reading, sometimes get ignored?

Of the four language arts—reading, writing, speaking, and listening—reading gets by far the most attention in most elementary classrooms. Yet surveys show that the time which *adults* spend on reading amounts to far less communication time than listening and speaking. This is definitely not to say that listening instruction should have the most time in the school day and reading instruction the least. Reading instruction is very exacting at the elementary school level and often more difficult than instruction in listening, speaking, and writing. It seems obvious, however, that skills which adults need to such an extent should not be treated lightly in the elementary school curriculum. Serving up reading as T-bone steak and the other language arts as left-over stew doesn't provide children with the kind of diet which will prepare them for adulthood.

Furthermore, ignoring the other language arts can be detrimental to your reading program. Later modules will explain in more detail how reading growth is enhanced by developing children's verbal fluency and by using certain writing activities in conjunction with reading instruction. These modules will attempt to show how the four language arts are interrelated and need to be taught as often as possible as integrated arts.

Now let's go back to a question asked earlier: Does language arts instruction have anything to do with long-range outcomes of schooling, such as emotional maturity, social awareness, intellectual vigor, and occupational success? In a sense, this question will be the subject of attention throughout the entire book. It is probably obvious already, however, that helping children learn to communicate better could have a vital effect on their emotional maturity and social awareness. And, certainly, since so much of children's intellectual development and social awareness is dependent on information received through listening, improving children's listening skills is likely to enhance both their intellectual and social growth.

The inability to communicate effectively can lead to emotional illness rather than maturity, to social misunderstanding and crisis rather than awareness and appreciation, to intellectual weakness, narrowness, and bigotry rather than vigor, breadth, and tolerance. A major function of formal education should be that of developing skillful communicators, people who can solve problems together and find enjoyment through relating to each other.

What do skillful communicators know how to do? We could stop with generalities and say that skillful communicators know how to listen, speak, write, and read effectively. But what we need as teachers is a set of very specific long-range outcomes. What *specific* skills do children need to develop in order to become good communicators? To answer this question, lists of specific long-range outcomes will soon follow.

Although listening, speaking, reading, and writing skills are listed separately, this is for the purpose of discussion only. In reality, it is often difficult to separate the communication abilities—a fact which we will demonstrate in later modules.

Furthermore, in the process of getting "back to the basics" we will need to expand our definition of *basics* to include listening and speaking skills as well as reading and writing skills. A child's reading and writing skills are more often than not the outward manifestations of a good or poor background in listening and speaking. Perhaps the definition of basics as "reading, writing, and arithmetic" should be supplanted with a more inclusive one: "those skills which will eventually be necessary for finding and maintaining a job, making friends, raising children, and exhibiting similar functional and self-actualizing behaviors."

Long-range Outcomes Related to Listening Skills

The following are some of the listening skills needed for effective communication:

1. Recognizing the appropriate meaning of a word used by someone else.
2. Recognizing common sentence patterns, alterations, and expansions used by a speaker.
3. Decoding a speaker's words by means of context signals, structural signals, phonetic signals, auditory memory, or a combination of signals.
4. Differentiating and interpreting pitch variations and pauses.
5. Performing literal thinking while listening.
   a. Developing associations or images.
   b. Following a sequence of events, ideas, or directions.
   c. Recognizing and recollecting significant details.
6. Performing inferential thinking while listening.
   a. Determining main ideas of speaker.
   b. Predicting events, steps, or ideas which should logically follow from what has been said.
   c. Getting meaning of new words in context.
   d. Appreciating speaker's sense of humor.
7. Performing critical thinking while listening.
   a. Distinguishing between literal and figurative expressions.
   b. Distinguishing between fact and fantasy, fact and satire, fact and opinion.
   c. Detecting propaganda techniques or speaker bias.
   d. Determining reliability of informant.
   e. Evaluating validity of premises and logic of conclusions drawn from premises.
   f. Recognizing hidden assumptions.
   g. Determining validity of inferences made by speaker.
   h. Determining validity of justifications made by speaker.

8. Responding creatively to what the listener has heard.
   a. Listening to feelings as well as words.
   b. Withholding judgments during brainstorming sessions.
   c. Translating feelings aroused by speaker into some type of art form.
   d. Sharing emotions and ideas generated by speaker.
   e. Solving a personal problem.

This list was not meant to be inclusive of all possible listening skills. One purpose in presenting it was simply to make you more aware of the nature of long-range outcomes as they apply to listening instruction. Another purpose was to show how inaccurate it is to think of listening as a single skill. It is a bit naïve to set out as a teacher to improve children's "ability to listen." Listening is obviously not a single ability but rather a large set of interrelated skills. Most of these skills will be discussed in later modules, and suggestions for helping children develop them will be provided.

Long-range Outcomes Related to Speaking Skills

The following are some of the speaking skills needed for effective communication:

1. Selecting rapidly from a large speaking vocabulary those words which communicate most effectively in a specific situation.
2. Selecting rapidly from a large reservoir of sentence patterns, alterations, and expansions those sentences which communicate most effectively in a specific situation.
3. Selecting rapidly from several dialects the dialect components which communicate most effectively in a specific situation.
4. Selecting the appropriate format for expression: description, story, dialogue, explanation, or argument.
5. Expressing ideas with self-confidence.
6. Adding interest appeal to expression:
   a. Via clarity.
   b. Via conciseness.
   c. Via energy (sincerity or enthusiasm).
   d. Via flexibility of style.
   e. Via imagery.
   f. Via naturalness.
   g. Via inventiveness.
   h. Via insight into human nature.
7. Describing events, directions, or ideas in proper sequence.
8. Enunciating clearly.
9. Articulating phonemes accurately and fluently.

10. Using pitch to signal appropriate meaning.
11. Using variation in pitch to add interest.
12. Using appropriate volume.
13. Using variation in volume to add interest.
14. Using appropriate rate.
15. Using stress to signal appropriate meaning.
16. Using pauses to signal appropriate meaning.
17. Using gestures to signal appropriate meaning.
18. Clarifying problem to be solved by a group.
19. Thinking of a variety of alternative solutions.
20. Establishing selection criteria for alternative solutions.
21. Applying selection criteria to alternative solutions.
22. Paraphrasing other people's ideas.
23. Summarizing ideas of a group.

Long-range Outcomes Related to Writing Skills

The following are some of the writing skills needed for effective communication:

1. Selecting rapidly from a large speaking vocabulary those words which communicate most effectively in a specific situation.
2. Selecting rapidly from a large reservoir of sentence patterns, alterations, and expansions those sentences which communicate most effectively in a specific situation.
3. Selecting rapidly from several dialects the dialect components which communicate most effectively in a specific situation.
4. Selecting the appropriate format for expression: description, story, dialogue, explanation, or argument.
5. Expressing ideas with self-confidence.
6. Adding interest appeal to expression.
   a. Via clarity.
   b. Via conciseness.
   c. Via energy (sincerity or enthusiasm).
   d. Via flexibility of style.
   e. Via imagery.
   f. Via naturalness.
   g. Via inventiveness.
   h. Via insight into human nature.
7. Describing events, directions, or ideas in proper sequence.
8. Producing legible handwriting through proper letter formation, alignment, spacing, slant, and size.
9. Using punctuation as a signaling device.

10. Using standard spelling (except where phonetic spelling is appropriate).
11. Using capitalization as a signaling device.
12. Determining the degree of need for high-quality spelling, handwriting, and punctuation.
13. Writing for a particular audience.

Long-range Outcomes Related to Reading Skills

The following are some of the reading skills needed by a person in order to communicate with an author (A more detailed list may be found in *To Help Children Read,* 2d ed. by Frank B. May and Susan B. Eliot.):

1. Decoding printed words by means of context, structural, and phonic signals.
2. Decoding printed words by means of visual memory.
3. Recognizing the appropriate meaning of a printed word.
4. Recognizing common sentence patterns, alterations, and expansions in print.
5. Applying appropriate pitch variations, stress variations, and pauses.
6. Developing associations or images related to passages read.
7. Following a sequence of events, ideas, or directions in print.
8. Recognizing and recollecting significant details in a passage.
9. Determining main ideas in passages read.
10. Predicting events, steps, or ideas which should logically follow from what one has read.
11. Distinguishing between literal and nonliteral passages.
12. Detecting propaganda and author bias.
13. Determining accuracy of printed information.
14. Responding creatively to what is read.

Long-range Outcomes and Related Learning Activities

Now that you have examined some of the long-range outcomes connected with language arts instruction, let's look for an answer to a practical question, What good are they? Can they help a particular teacher plan a particular learning activity for a particular group of children? Or perhaps you feel this way: Why bother thinking about long-range outcomes? They're already listed in the teachers' editions of the commercial reading and language arts programs.

It is true, of course, that authors of language arts textbooks for children usually do include a list of long-range outcomes in the teachers' editions. And it is probably true that a school principal *could* find fairly intelligent people on the streets and have them "teach" the language arts by following the teachers' editions. But ask successful language arts teachers, and they are likely to tell you that to reach many children, you must be able to depart from the commercially prepared path. *You must be able to adapt your instruction to the individual.* And this requires that you know what you're doing—that you know what the long-range outcomes of your instruction should be.

Let's return for a moment to Mr. Hill who wanted to provide his students with a "fun experience in creative drama." Mr. Hill also has a favorite activity in his spelling program. Every week he makes up a new crossword puzzle related to the words that will be on the weekly spelling test. Suppose you ask him about that. Here's the kind of conversation you might have with him:

YOU: *It seems that one of your long-range outcomes for your spelling instruction has something to do with crossword puzzles. Is that correct?*

MR. HILL: *Well, yes. That's right. What I have in mind, you see, is that the children will get better and better at crossword puzzles as the year goes on.*

YOU: *To what end?*

MR. HILL: *Pardon me?*

YOU: *Why do you want them to do better and better at crossword puzzles?*

MR. HILL: *Why? Well, uh . . . for one thing so they can enjoy crossword puzzles.*

YOU: *Is that an important skill for adults to have?*

MR. HILL: *Sure, uh . . . adults need something to do with their spare time.*

YOU: *Any other reason for having them work on crossword puzzles?*

MR. HILL: *Uh . . . yeah, sure it just makes learning to spell words a lot more fun.*

YOU: *Do you have any particular skills or concepts related to spelling you'd like the children to acquire as a result of working on crossword puzzles?*

MR. HILL: *Skills or concepts related to spelling? Uh . . . let's see, skills or concepts related to spelling. Well, now, I'm sure there are some. I just can't come up with any right at the moment. Next time I see you I'll let you know, okay?*

Let's look at what has happened to Mr. Hill. It appears that one of his favorite learning activities for spelling instruction, namely, crossword puzzles has become an end in itself, with no perceived relationship to long-range outcomes relating to spelling. In short, he's doing what many teachers find themselves doing at times—thinking of learning activities as goals in themselves rather than as means to obtain those goals.

Avoiding the Activities vs. Outcomes Confusion

There are at least two ways of avoiding this problem. One is to decide what long-range outcomes in the language arts are appropriate for the particular children you are teaching and then to create or select learning activities which show promise of moving the children toward those outcomes (see Route 1 on Figure 1.1). The other way is to select a learning activity (say, one you heard about from another teacher or one that a child suggests) and then decide how you can use that activity in such a way that one or more long-range outcomes are involved (see Route 2 on Figure 1.1). This latter approach is not so "nice" from a theoretical standpoint, but from a practical standpoint it often fits the realism of struggling classroom teachers, wracking their brains to meet the needs of too many individuals and trying to pick up crumbs of ideas wherever they fall. Whichever direction you take—from long-range outcomes to learning activities or from learning activities to long-range outcomes (and most teachers probably head both directions throughout the school year)—both routes incorporate long-range outcomes. And both ways avoid the trap of confusing ends and means.

FIGURE 1.1 The Cyclic Nature of Effective Teaching

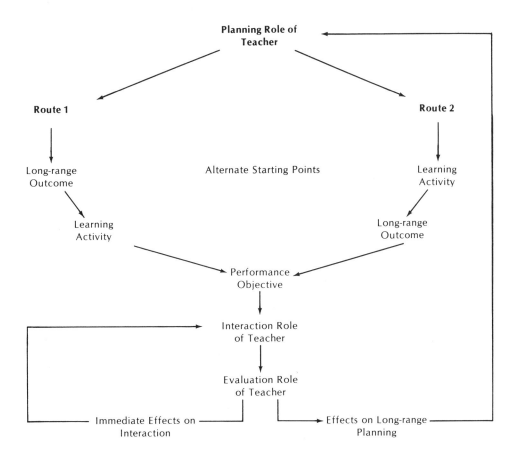

Since Mr. Hill is fond of crossword puzzles as a learning activity, he could probably take Route 2 and increase the usefulness of the activity by deciding what particular speaking, reading, listening, or writing skills he should emphasize during the time spent on the puzzles. Does he want the children to get so good at crossword puzzles that they can create their own? That might be fine for training those people who end up creating crossword puzzles for newspapers. But what long-range skill, habit, or idea does he want the children to gain from their "crosswording" experiences? What does he want them to *retain* after all those puzzles are nothing but a blurred memory?

Does Mr. Hill think that many children in the group are confused about the use of the *ite* and *ight* graphoneme? If so, then this very specific skill could become one of his long-range outcomes ("long range" in the sense that he wants them to retain this ability into adulthood). Having made it a long-range outcome, he could then design one or more crossword puzzles that would provide practice on *ite* words and *ight* words.

Suppose, on the other hand, that Mr. Hill had taken Route 1. He would have then started by assessing the children's strengths and weaknesses with respect to spelling skills. This would have allowed him to decide which long-range outcomes were the most important ones to emphasize for the year, or for the next week or month. Then, by using his list of desired outcomes as a guide, he could have selected or invented learning activities that showed promise of moving the children closer to the desired outcome. For instance, by analyzing the results of one or more spelling tests or by analyzing the spelling errors in papers children have handed in, he might have discovered that nine of his students were having difficulty spelling the /īt/ phonogram. Sometimes they used *ight* when they should have used *ite*; sometimes they used *ite* when they should have used *ight*. Thus, his long-range outcome for this group of nine children would be established: the ability to determine which one of the two graphonemes (*ite* or *ight*) is the customary one to use with various words ending with the /īt/ phonogram.

Differentiating Between Long-range Outcomes and Learning Activities

At this point you are invited to try your hand at differentiating between long-range outcomes and learning activities. Using the following list for practice, first label each one either O for outcome or A for activity. Then take the next step by trying to match each outcome with an appropriate activity. (For example, the outcome of "speaking with expression" should be matched with the activity of "choral reading.") Some suggested answers will be found at the end of the exercise. (It might be advisable to cover up the answers until you have completed the exercise.)

PRACTICE EXERCISE 1

_____ 1. choral reading

_____ 2. creative dramatics

_____ 3. following spoken directions

_____ 4. studying television ads

_____ 5. understanding feelings of others

_____ 6. speaking with expression

_____ 7. detecting propaganda devices

_____ 8. making cookies from a tape-recorded recipe

Answers to Practice Exercise 1

Distinguishing		Matching Outcome
1—A	5—O	3 with activity 8
2—A	6—O	5 with activity 2
3—O	7—O	6 with activity 1
4—A	8—A	7 with activity 4

The Need for Performance Objectives

Suppose you have decided that a long-range outcome desired for nine of your students is "determining which of two graphonemes (*ite* or *ight*) is the customary one to use with various words ending with the /īt/ phonogram." You decide to use, as one of your learning activities, an activity in which the students must select words on the chalkboard that seem to be "correct." For instance, let's say you write the following sentences on the board:

1. Bill had a *fite* with Jim.
2. Nancy turned off the *light* and went to bed.
3. Jerry liked to watch *night* baseball.
4. Barbara liked to fly her *kite*.
5. Janice watched the fish *bight* on her worm.
6. Joe threw the ball with all his *might*.
7. Sandy had all of her spelling words *rite*.
8. Phil watched the airplane go out of *sight*.
9. Sally felt that her skirt was too *tite*.

Then you ask one child in your group to put a check mark next to the number of each sentence in which the /īt/ sound is spelled correctly. Next you ask the group of nine students how to tell whether to use *ite* or *ight*. One of the children gives you the answer you're looking for, the others nod in agreement, and you send them back to their regular seats.

Have you moved the children toward the outcome you had in mind? Well, perhaps . . . but how do you know? What behavior indicates to you that your teaching was successful? The nodding of heads? Not very reliable, since children are notorious head nodders. The fact that one of the children could check the correct sentences on the board? What about the others? Could they have checked the correct sentences also? Suppose Timmy can check *some* of the sentences correctly but not all of them. How many does he have to get right before you know that he understands what you want him to understand? If

Sally can get them all right while in a group situation, can she get them all right when she's working on her own? Can she get them right when she's writing a story in which /īt/ words have to be spelled?

You can see that thinking about *long-range* outcomes is not enough. Perhaps now you also see that you need to decide on three things: (1) What behavior or performance of *each* child will demonstrate that he or she has learned what you think he or she needs to learn? (2) Under what conditions will this behavior be evaluated? (3) What quality or quantity of behavior can be reasonably expected? That is, how well does *each* child have to do it to make you satisfied that he or she really has learned something?

If you can answer those three questions, you have developed a performance objective—sometimes referred to as a behavioral or instructional objective. According to Mager (6), a performance objective is functional to the extent that you have described "what the learner will be doing when demonstrating his achievement and how you will know when he is doing it."

How to Create Performance Objectives

A well-conceived performance objective meets the following four criteria:

1. It is a statement (or thought) about the behavior of the *learner* rather than the teacher.
2. It is a statement (or thought) about *observable behavior* rather than vague and unseen improvement.
3. It includes the precise *conditions* under which the learner's behavior will be demonstrated and evaluated.
4. It includes the *standards* for the specific behavior expected (or hoped for) by the teacher.

Which of the following statements meet the first criterion? Check those which are statements about the behavior of the *learner* rather than the teacher.

PRACTICE EXERCISE 2

_____ 1. To teach the children to spell words containing the /īt/ phonogram.

_____ 2. To be able to circle all of the words containing the correct spelling of the /īt/ phonogram.

_____ 3. To write the letters of the alphabet in the correct order.

_____ 4. To explain the origin of our alphabet through the use of a film.

_____ 5. To involve the students in creating crossword puzzles.

Answers to Practice Exercise 2

Statements 1, 4, and 5 may be noble "aims," but they do *not* meet the first criterion of a performance objective. They are stated in terms of the teacher rather than the learner. Statements 2 and 3 are not complete performance objectives, but they come closer to being performance objectives than the other three, since they are statements about the learner rather than the teacher.

Which of the following statements meet the second criterion? Check those which are stated in terms of *observable behavior.*

PRACTICE EXERCISE 3

_____ 1. To understand the phonic principles involving the long vowel sound.

_____ 2. To circle those words in a list which contain vowel letters representing a long sound.

_____ 3. To know the alphabet.

_____ 4. To appreciate the value of correct spelling.

_____ 5. To read out loud from a list of words only those which contain short vowel sounds.

Answers to Practice Exercise 3

Statements 1, 3, and 4 do *not* meet the second criterion. Although statements 2 and 5 are not complete performance objectives, they come closer to being performance objectives than the other three, because they indicate the actual behavior that the teacher can observe. The problem with the first one is that the teacher hasn't yet thought of what behavior to look for that will demonstrate that the children do "understand the phonic principles involving the long vowel sound." In the third one, the teacher hasn't yet decided what performance by the children will indicate that they do "know the alphabet." What is the problem in the fourth one?

Which of the following statements meet the third criterion? Check those which include the precise *conditions* under which the learner's behavior will be evaluated.

PRACTICE EXERCISE 4

_____ 1. When given a list of words, the student will be able to circle those on the list which contain vowel letters representing the long sound without first hearing someone pronounce the words.

_____ 2. To be able to circle those words which begin with the letter *b.*

_____ 3. Given three weeks of practice, the student will be able to circle words containing vowel letters representing a short sound.

_____ 4. The student will demonstrate knowledge of the alphabet by numbering a list of words according to alphabetical order.

_____ 5. Presented with a list of words and a list of generalizations about the spelling of vowel sounds, the student will match the generalizations with the correct words.

Answers to Practice Exercise 4

Statements 2 and 3 do *not* meet the third criterion, whereas the other three do. It is true that in the second statement the expected behavior is clear: "to be able to circle those words which begin with the letter *b*." However, the conditions under which the behavior is to be demonstrated are not clear. Will the words be in list form or imbedded in sentences? Will the words be pronounced by the teacher or will the student have to pronounce them for himself? In the third statement, it is true that a *prior* condition is stated: "Given three weeks of practice," however, the conditions under which the behavior is *now* to be demonstrated are not clear. What conditions might have to be stated to make the objective clear?

Which of the following statements meet the fourth criterion? Check those which include the *standards* expected or desired.

PRACTICE EXERCISE 5

_____ 1. To write the alphabet in correct order within forty seconds.

_____ 2. To write a set of directions for a partner with sufficient clarity to enable the partner to follow the directions accurately without referring to them more than once.

_____ 3. To orally review a library book with sufficient enthusiasm and clarity that at least one person in the class raises his hand when asked immediately after the review, "Who would like to read the book?"

_____ 4. To listen to Tape #10B "Snakes" and to do the accompanying worksheet.

_____ 5. Given a list of fifteen words, the student will number them in alphabetical order.

Answers to Practice Exercise 5

Statements 4 and 5 do *not* meet the fourth criterion, whereas the other three do. Statement 4 gives a rough idea of the behavior expected—listen to the tape and do the worksheet—but does not indicate the standards of performance desired. The teacher making such a statement evidently has not thought about how well the students should listen and how well they should perform on the worksheet. In statement 5 it might be *assumed* that the student should be able to number the words in alphabetical order with 100 percent accuracy. Generally speaking, though, this is not a realistic goal—for two reasons: (1) a teacher can usually tell that children understand an idea even though they do not achieve 100 percent accuracy, and (2) it is almost impossible to avoid some ambiguity in a "test" situation.

Whatever degree of accuracy seems reasonable, whether it be 80 percent or only 60 percent. *it is probably best to decide upon the minimum acceptable standard ahead of instruction.* In this way, the teacher will have some way of determining (albeit in an arbitrary way) which children should receive additional instruction after the initial instruction has taken place. Tired teachers who have ignored this step often find themselves making statements such as this at the end of a none-too-successful lesson, "Well, some of them didn't understand that too well, but most of them got it." Or they excuse themselves by saying, "They'll get it next year." And of course, next year those children are even further behind.

Recognizing Performance Objectives

Now that you have become familiar with the four criteria of performance objectives, it is time to see if you can differentiate those statements which meet *all four criteria* from those which do not. Check each of the following statements which you consider to be complete performance objectives; that is, check only those which meet *all four* criteria. (They need not be "perfectly" written or ones you agree with.) Some suggested answers can be found at the end of the exercise. See if you can get at least seven out of ten correct.

PRACTICE EXERCISE 6

_____ 1. Given a tape recording with five brief selections, each of them followed by four numbered choices, the student will listen to the selections silently and choose the correct main idea for at least four of five selections. The student's choice of the main idea will be shown by circling the correct number.

_____ 2. Given a set of directions, the student will be able to follow them with 100 percent accuracy.

_____ 3. Using a classroom dictionary, the student will, for each word presented orally by the teacher, find the word and write down the correct page number within fifteen seconds.

_____ 4. Each student will pantomime in front of the class something the main character did as described in a book read to the students recently.

_____ 5. Given an oral list of statements, some of which are facts and some of which are opinions, the student will be able to recognize all of the statements which are opinions.

_____ 6. After finishing the story in the basal reader, each student should be able to write another ending—one which fits the rest of the story, the nature of the characters, and the nature of the setting.

_____ 7. Given ten questions on the history of the alphabet, the student will get at least seven of them right.

_____ 8. Given a good night's sleep and a hearty breakfast, each student will do well on the standardized vocabulary test tomorrow.

_____ 9. Okay, now I'd like you, Bill, to pronounce this list of words on the tape recorder; first say the number and then the word. Then I'd like you, Jim, to go back when he's finished and listen to the words. Just number your paper from one to twenty and circle the number of any word you think he didn't pronounce clearly or correctly. Then you two get together and talk about those words that Bill needs help on. Keep working on them until you think Bill can pronounce all of them correctly.

_____ 10. Given plenty of practice the student will spell fifty "Spelling Demons" with 100 percent accuracy by the end of the year.

Answers to Practice Exercise 6

1. Check.
2. No check. The conditions are not clearly stated. How are the directions to be given, orally or in writing? Behavior is also fuzzy. Does "follow them" mean to carry them out?
3. Check. (Note that the standards include both speed and accuracy, although 100 percent accuracy is *implied* (by the word "correct" and the phrase "for each word.") rather than stated. It would be better to state "100 percent accuracy is expected."
4. No check. The performance standards are not stated. To what extent should the pantomime be successfully executed? (For example: "Over half the class indicates an understanding of what event was being pantomimed by raising their hands.")
5. No check. What does it mean "to be able to recognize"? What does the student have to do to demonstrate this recognition? The behavior expected is not clear.
6. Check. (Were you fooled on this one? Notice that standards do *not* have to be thought of just in terms of accuracy or speed. Some performance by students can only be assessed in a qualitative manner.) The standards for this one are "one that fits the rest of the story. . . . "
7. No check. The behavior is not stated, nor are the conditions clear. We know the students should "get" seven out of ten, but what does the student do? Are the questions a multiple-choice type or an essay type or what?
8. No check. What does it mean to "do well"? The performance standards are not clear. Furthermore, the conditions *under which the behavior is to be evaluated* have been too simply stated as "standardized vocabulary test." The extraneous information about sleep and breakfast refers only to conditions *before* the behavior is to be evaluated.
9. Check. This is actually a complete performance objective—in this case clearly communicated to the learner himself.
10. No check. What behavior should the student demonstrate to show that she can *spell* the words? What are the conditions under which the behavior will be evaluated?

Relating Performance Objectives to Long-range Outcomes

If you got less than seven of the ten correct in Exercise 6, it would be advisable to go back to the beginning of the last section and review the four criteria of a performance objective. If you got seven or more of them correct, it would be advisable to put your knowledge to immediate use by writing a few performance objectives yourself.

Before you attempt to write your own objectives, however, you should first see if you can match some performance objectives with some long-range outcomes. Practice Exercise 7 is designed to give you appropriate practice.

Match the performance objectives with the long-range outcomes. (One of the performance objectives doesn't relate to any of the long-range outcomes.)

PRACTICE EXERCISE 7

Long-range Outcomes

_____ 1. Development of personal values.

_____ 2. Using phonic generalizations to spell new words.

_____ 3. Distinguishing between fact and opinion.

_____ 4. Ability to spell difficult irregular words.

_____ 5. Determining attitudes of speakers.

Performance Objectives

a. When presented with fifty "Spelling Demons," one at a time on flash cards, the student will write each one within two seconds. Accuracy of 90 percent desired.

b. After reading the story in the basal reader, each student will be able to write at least one sentence explaining why the main character did or did not do the right thing at the end of the story.

c. Given a list of ten words out of alphabetical order, the student will put them in the right order with 80 percent accuracy.

d. Given three editorials on the same issue to listen to on tape, the student will indicate, with at least one written sentence for each, the bias of the author. The teacher should agree with the student's judgment in at least two of the three cases.

e. Given an editorial to listen to on tape, the student will list in writing at least five factual statements made by the author. The teacher should agree with the student on at least four of the five statements.

f. When presented orally with a list of ten nonsense words, each of them spelled in a phonetically regular way, the student will write nine out of ten with the correct phonetic spelling.

Answers to Practice Exercise

1—b; 2—f; 3—e; 4—a; 5—d

If you have completed Exercise 7 and got four out of five right (or at least see why you missed what you did), you are ready to try writing some of your own performance objectives. For instance, you might take some of the long-range outcomes for language arts instruction listed previously and try creating performance objectives to go with them. For example, what might be a good performance objective related to "distinguishing between real-life stories and tales of fantasy?"

Long-range Outcome A: Distinguishing between real-life stories and tales of fantasy.

Your Performance Objective: (Hint: Before you can write a performance objective you have to imagine an activity that you will use to help students distinguish between real-life stories and tales of fantasy.)

Long-range Outcome B: (Pick one from the list of Long-range Outcomes Related to Listening Skills.)

Your Performance Objective:

Long-range Outcome C: (Pick one from the list of Long-range Outcomes Related to Speaking Skills.)

Your Performance Objective:

Long-range Outcome D: (Pick one from the list of Long-range Outcomes Related to Writing Skills.)

Your Performance Objective:

(Note: Be sure to compare your performance objectives with those of others.)

The Relationship of Performance Objectives to the Three Roles of Teaching

When you tried writing your own performance objectives, you no doubt discovered that you must have in mind not only a long-range outcome but also a related learning activity. As shown in Figure 1.1, the teacher's planning decision can move either from an idea for a learning activity to a long-range outcome or from a long-range outcome to a learning activity to a performance objective. In either case, the performance objective is a "terminal" point rather than a starting point. More accurately, the performance objective is a link or bridge between the planning role of the teacher and the interaction role.

Figure 1.1 shows how teachers can arrive at a performance objective (in thought or in writing) through one of two alternate routes. They then interact with students with intentions of carrying out the performance objective. (This interaction might be either in the form of arranging an experience for them, of participating in an experience with them, or of leading an experience.) However, almost as soon as they interact with the students, they begin to get feedback from them—in the form of puzzled looks, smiles of discovery, incorrect responses, and so on. Thus, they are moved into their role as evaluator, making temporary judgments about their own teaching and about their students' progress. These judgments have immediate effects on their interaction, *if they are flexible teachers.* Flexible teachers are free to change their tactics, if necessary, or to switch to a different activity, or to modify their standards. At the same time they are doing this, they are also making a mental note to do some more long-range planning.

Performance objectives, then, are *not* binding on either the teacher or the students. They are rough-draft proposals which bridge the gap between planning and interacting, proposals which make it possible for teachers to evaluate their own teaching and their students' growth with at least a moderate amount of precision.

Questions and Answers Concerning This Approach

QUESTION: *Do I set my standards for the group or for the individual child?*

ANSWER: *Your standards generally represent your minimum level of expectations for each child. Some teachers try to make it easier for themselves by setting group standards, such as, "I'll know whether I did a good job of teaching if 70 percent of the students get them all right." This is entirely different from saying, "I feel that every child should get at least 70 percent correct, and to any child who doesn't, I'll provide further help." A group standard ignores the responsibility a teacher has for <u>each child.</u>*

QUESTION: *Isn't this approach rather behavioristic?*

ANSWER: *Yes and no. It's based on the assumption that a learner's behavior is the only thing teachers (in contrast to mind readers) can rely upon to tell whether any learning is taking place. In that sense it is behavioristic. But it is also a humanistic approach.*

QUESTION: *How can you possibly justify this approach as a humanistic approach?*

ANSWER: *It's very easy to justify this approach as a humanistic approach. A humanist believes in the importance, the creativity, and the individuality of every person. In fact, a humanist tends to look at a group of people as separate individuals, rather than looking at the separate individuals as a group. By using behaviorally stated objectives, you are reasserting the importance of each student and what he has learned. You are not ignoring the student who doesn't "get it."*

Behavioral objectives have obtained a bad name with some people for at least two reasons (1) A behavioral objective is based on the assumption of behaviorist psychologists, who claim that people's <u>behavior</u> is all we can hope to measure; trying to measure "inside" qualities like "understanding," or "inventive insight" is essentially impossible. (2) Some programs which use behavioral objectives fail to allow enough individual choice and enough opportunities for creativity. This is not the fault of behavioral objectives but of the people who develop such programs. It's a little bit silly to blame the "behavioral objective," which is nothing more than one of many tools for the use of a skillful and sensitive teacher.

QUESTION: *This approach seems to put the teacher at the center of the stage. I thought we were trying to get away from so much of that kind of thing in teaching.*

ANSWER: *It's true that in the past teaching has often been a matter of standing up in front of the entire class and leading the orchestra or putting on a show. And some "teacher-centered" activities are highly appropriate— for inspiring children to try something new, for working with a small group having similar learning difficulties, and for any activity in which learning can be enhanced by having the experienced adult temporarily "take the wheel." The use of performance objectives, however, can help you to think more about the individual learner—about what her needs, strengths, and deficiencies are and what specific experiences might help her to grow [and not just you]. If teachers think of "planning" as something which precedes a teacher-directed show, then, of course, the perfor-*

mance objectives become mere vehicles for glorifying the teacher's role. If, on the other hand, teachers think of individual children as they plan, the performance objectives become vehicles for placing <u>children</u>, not the teacher, at the center of the stage.

QUESTION: *I don't see how the use of performance objectives gets us any closer to the basics. What do performance objectives have to do with teaching the basic skills related to reading and writing?*

ANSWER: *If you want to emphasize "the basics," you will need performance objectives to make sure the basic skills are not ignored. One <u>could </u>emphasize the basics by teaching only reading, writing, and arithmetic all day long. This approach, however, would ignore other communication skills related to speaking and listening. It would also ignore the special contributions of social studies, science, music, art, and physical education.*

A better approach is to not only teach basic skills directly but also to include basic skills in activities related to speaking, listening, social studies, and so on. To make certain, however, that the basic skills are not only "included" but learned as well, you will need to develop performance objectives for those basic skills.

Let's take, for example, some of the basic skills which will eventually be needed for filling out a job application or taking an examination for a job. Perhaps the most important basic skills in this case are those of following oral directions and following written directions. Such skills do not come naturally to most people but need to be learned. Furthermore, they are probably best learned as a basic habit starting in the early years of schooling.

Mrs. Shoemaker wanted her fifth graders to listen better, especially to follow oral directions better. She knew that she could improve their ability to follow oral directions better by having them practice this skill daily. But she also knew that she had an opportunity to include practice on some "basic" skills of reading and writing at the same time. To make sure she not only included reading and writing activities but also had the students learn the reading and writing skills connected to the activities, she developed a set of performance objectives.

Before using her performance objectives as "tests of teaching success," she provided the students with several listening exercises over a period of several days. These exercises were all designed to provide practice in following oral directions. During this time she also provided them with experiences in which they had to follow written directions. And she had them write directions as well. Her performance objectives following this series of experiences were as follows:

Performance Objective A: Given oral directions on making a paper hat, and allowed approximately ten seconds between each step, each child will be able to complete the hat exactly as directed without being given special instructions more than once.

Performance Objective B: Given written instructions on making a paper cup, with the instructions written in second grade vocabulary, each child will be able to complete the cup exactly as directed within three minutes and without any special assistance.

Performance Objective C: After completing the exercise related to Performance Objective B and without the use of the original written instructions, each child will be able to write a similar set of written instructions for making a paper cup. (The children will be told before activity B that they will be expected to also complete activity C when they are finished.) Correct spelling and legible handwriting will be expected on 90 percent of the words; the correct number and sequence of steps will also be expected.

Performance Objective D: Working in groups of three, with the first child reading a set of directions step by step, the second child writing down the directions step by step, and the third child following the written directions of the second child, the third child will be able to follow the directions and complete the project exactly according to the *original* set of directions. (Judgment of success should be made by the first child. The second child is not allowed to get help on spelling or to have the first child repeat a step. The third child must be out of hearing when the first child dictates directions to the second child.)

Now, of course, these same activities could have been carried on without the use of performance objectives. The value of performance objectives in this case, however, is to cause the teacher to think of ways of evaluating success for each activity. If teachers want to get "back to basics," then they need ways of making sure basic skills have actually been learned and not just taught.

QUESTION: *Is the performance-based approach really appropriate for the language arts? In teaching the language arts aren't we getting more into the affective domain—the domain of feelings—rather than specific measurable skills?*

ANSWER: *Yes and no. The performance-based approach is highly appropriate for the "basics": spelling, handwriting, punctuation, reading directions, and so on. Another look at the list of communication skills in this module should assure you that there are numerous opportunities for using performance objectives while teaching the language arts. On the other hand, there are some qualities in people which we seek to encourage through language arts instruction that are not readily measured—qualities such as communicative empathy, originality, and sense of humor. To try to develop performance objectives for these qualities is a little like using a yardstick to measure the beauty of a spring morning.*

When to use or not use performance objectives requires the discretion of the teacher. Experience indicates that in nine out of ten cases, performance objectives are helpful in focusing instruction and determining the degree of learning that takes place.

REFERENCES AND BIBLIOGRAPHY

1. Bloom, Benjamin S. et al. *Handbook on Formative and Summative Evaluation of Student Learning.* New York: McGraw-Hill, 1971. See Chapter 3 on "Learning for Mastery," which gives an excellent rationale for the use of performance objectives rather than the traditional system of evaluation and grading.

2. Boehnlein, Mary M. "Integration of Communication Arts Curriculum: A Review." *Language Arts* 54 (April 1977): 372–77.

3. Duffy, Gerald G. "Maintaining a Balance in Objective-Based Reading Instruction." *Reading Teacher* 31 (Feb. 1978): 519–23.

4. Fortson, Laura R. "Rethinking Curricular Integration in Terms of Child Benefits: The Role of Language Arts." *Language Arts* 54 (April 1977): 378–83.

5. Horn, Thomas D. et al. "The Basics." *Instructor* 86 (Dec. 1976): 81–88. One of a series of monthly articles on teaching the basic subjects.

6. Mager, Robert F. *Preparing Instructional Objectives.* Belmont, Calif.: Fearon, 1975. This is a short, programmed book with a simple explanation of how to write performance objectives and with many opportunities to test your knowledge as you proceed.

7. May, Frank B., and Eliot, Susan B. *To Help Children Read,* 2d ed. Columbus, Ohio: Charles E. Merrill, 1978.

8. Otto, Wayne, and Chester, Robert. *Objective-Based Reading.* Reading, Mass.: Addison-Wesley, 1976.

9. Schuster, Edgar H. "Back to Basics: What Does it Really Mean?" *Clearing House* 50 (Feb. 1977): 237–39.

10. Winterowd, W. Ross. "A Teacher's Guide to the *Real* Basics." *Language Arts* 54 (Sept. 1977): 625–30.

module

2

Understanding Environmental Effects on Majority and Minority Children

Language . . . grows out of life—out of its agonies and ecstacies, its wants and its weariness. . . .

Oliver Wendell Holmes

In Module 1 the definition of the basics was changed from "reading, writing and arithmetic" to "those skills necessary for finding and maintaining a job, making friends, raising children, and exhibiting similar functional and self-actualizing behaviors." The module then looked at the numerous skills related to both the basics and to effective communication in general. Finally, it discussed the method of using performance objectives to make sure that the basics and other communication skills are *learned* as well as taught.

Teaching the basics and other communication skills requires more, however, than the ability to develop performance objectives. In addition to this ability, the effective teacher needs, among other things, an understanding and appreciation of where her students are "coming from." What verbal environments are these students used to? How have their past verbal environments differed from the teacher's and from each other's? What effects have their past verbal environments had on their present verbal abilities? To what extent has their environment been a communicative one?

An essential ingredient of an effective language arts program is the communicative environment. In fact, this ingredient is essential from the time children are born if they are to develop their language abilities to their full potential. Not all children are so lucky.

If teachers are to work successfully with children, they need to comprehend and appreciate the various ways in which the environment has already affected (and will continue to affect) the communication abilities of those children.

The journey from babbling babies to school-age communicators has been at times a very tedious and complex one. To ensure survival during the early years, our young travelers have had to pass through a maze of personal relationships which have uniquely influenced their language patterns. And, for a steering wheel each traveler has sometimes had to rely on a very shaky self-concept—a steering wheel with a loose center hub, rickety spokes, and a slippery rim.

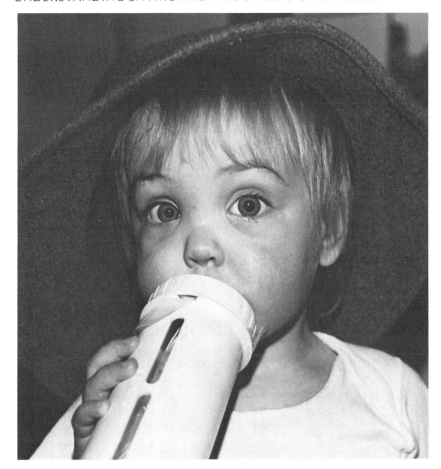

The journey from babbling babies to school age communicators has been at times a very tedious and complex one.

Language resides on the hub of the self-concept; teachers who abuse a child's language abuse the personal integrity of that child. On the other hand, teachers who help a child understand the uniqueness and power of his language help him toward greater self-understanding.

Understanding teachers need to know intimately the answers to questions such as these:

1. How influential are parents and siblings in determining a child's oral language patterns?
2. What effect does socio-economic status have on oral language growth?
3. Does our culture encourage the language development of girls more than boys?
4. Are there ways in which the school can influence the oral language of its captive learners?

Teachers who do not understand the answers to these questions, at least on a general level, cannot hope to gain the rapport necessary for effective language arts teaching.

To concern ourselves, at this point, with the development of speech is not to ignore the importance of writing, listening, and reading, but to recognize the primacy of oral language to the interrelated language arts. Not only do children learn to speak before they learn to read and write, but their speech habits also greatly influence their competencies in reading and writing. Furthermore, a large proportion of a person's communication—second only to listening—is in the form of speech.

Special Prerequisites for Module 2

There are no special prerequisites for this module other than those communication and thinking abilities assumed to be present among undergraduate and graduate students who are teachers-in-training.

Long-range Outcomes Related to Module 2

This module should enable you as a teacher to do the following:

1. Communicate with other educators concerning the influence of parents, siblings, socio-economic status, cultural expectations, and gender on the development of children's oral language behavior.
2. Communicate with parents about the influence of the home environment on their children's language behavior.
3. Communicate with other educators concerning the influence of teachers' leadership patterns and the influence of specific instructional strategies on the development of children's oral language.

Study Guide and Peformance Objectives for Knowledge Level

To give yourself an overview of what is expected of you in this module, you should first scan the objectives and performance standards at all three levels—knowledge, simulation, and teaching. Then use the performance objectives for the knowledge level as a study guide during your reading of the module.

As you find information related to each performance objective, write it down in the available blanks or on a separate sheet of paper. Then review this information shortly before your knowledge level examination.

1.1 On a closed-book examination you should be able to select the best alternative for each multiple-choice question and circle the letter of your choice. The multiple-choice questions (shown here without the alternatives) will be selected from the following. Below each one write the alternative that you think will be the correct one on the examination.

1. The range of emotional-linguistic contacts with adults varies all the way from the level of an overprotected only child to the level of:

2. What type of child would you expect to be the most mature with respect to oral language?

3. What type of child would you expect to do the best on intelligence tests?

4. How do twins usually compare to singletons in language maturity?

5. What does breakfast time have to do with language development?

6. What is the single most important cause of stuttering?

7. How do college-age stutterers tend to feel about their parents?

8. What single word would best describe the majority of parents of stutterers?

9. Children free of speech defects tend to come from what type of home?

10. About what proportion of the people in the United States does not use English as their first language?

11. Next to English what is the most common language in our country?

12. What is a major disadvantage to using an ESL (English as a Second Language) approach for helping children whose home and school languages differ?

13. At the present time, which procedure seems to be the best one for helping children whose home and school languages differ?

14. In what ways are testing procedures biased against lower SES children?

15. What is the most likely reason for low SES children demonstrating lower levels of oral language proficiency?

16. What does birth weight have to do with language development?

17. Boys tend to do better than girls on what language skill?

18. What explanation does McCarthy give for the difference in girls' and boys' performances on oral language tasks?

19. How much does the average child watch TV?

20. What is an example of effective television teaching?

21. Templin found that there was little change in the parts of speech used by children after the age of:

22. Which type of leadership pattern is most likely to influence children's speech development?

23. What is the Pygmalion effect?

24. What effect does the administrative organization of a school usually have on language development?

25. What is the main agent of change with respect to oral language development in the schools?

1.2 On the same examination, you will be given a list of statements about particular children. For each statement you should be able to write a, if it *most likely* applies to Jamie, a child raised in an orphanage; b, if it *most likely* applies to Sandy, an only child with upper-middle-class parents; c, if it *most likely* applies to Bruce, an only child who stutters; d, if it *most likely* applies to Carmen, a third grader whose parents are migrant farm workers; e, if it *most likely* applies to Dennis, who lives in the center of a large city with parents who have lower-class status; and f, if the statement applies to none of the children. The statements you will be expected to respond to will be *selected from* the following:

_____ 1. This child tends to speak more slowly than most children.

_____ 2. This child's parents maintain very high standards and are often critical.

_____ 3. This child has received insufficient attention and affection from adults.

_____ 4. He/she has highly nervous parents.

_____ 5. This child feels very little attention from his or her parents.

_____ 6. At dinner time this child is often engaged by adults in conversation.

_____ 7. This child has a higher IQ than most children.

_____ 8. He/she is bilingual.

_____ 9. This child tends to use language for solving problems only when asked to do so.

_____ 10. This child's parents tend to be quite inconsistent in their eating and sleeping requirements.

_____ 11. His/her parents rely mainly on threats as a form of discipline.

_____ 12. This child changes schools three or more times a year.

_____ 13. He/she is discouraged from speaking the home language of Spanish at school.

_____ 14. His/her mother seldom presses for verbal clarification or description.

_____ 15. His/her home consists of a two-room apartment shared by nine people in a large city.

_____ 16. This child's parents insist that he/she thinks before speaking.

_____ 17. He/she tends to use longer sentences in his/her speech than most children.

_____ 18. He/she did not receive sufficient verbal stimulation during the critical period for oral language growth.

_____ 19. This child has never been more than twenty-five blocks from home.

_____ 20. His/her parents often seem to the child to be disappointed in him/her.

_____ 21. At school, he/she is highly rewarded for his/her manner of speaking.

_____ 22. His/her parents read a lot.

_____ 23. His/her parents often disagree on techniques of discipline.

_____ 24. In school he/she tends to name or label things only when asked to do so.

_____ 25. He/she tends to speak more loudly and clearly than most children.

_____ 26. He/she speaks fluently at home but seldom communicates with teachers or peers.

1.3 On the same examination you should be able to list four specific factors in the home environment that affect the language development of children.

   1. _____

   2. _____

   3. _____

   4. _____

1.4 On the same examination you should be able to list four leadership patterns (or characteristics) of teachers that seem to encourage oral language practice.

   1. _____

   2. _____

   3. _____

   4. _____

Performance Standards for Knowledge Level

A. Twenty-five minute time limit on 1.1 through 1.4 combined.

B. Completion deadline: instructor will notify.

C. Recommended grading standards, if grades are used: 96% = A; 92% = A −; 88% = B; 84% = B −; 80% = C; below 80% = incomplete; should be completed at 80% or better before you go on to the next module. (The instructor may wish to permit a grade of A or B only the first time the test is given in order to encourage more intensive study.)

Performance Objectives for Simulation and Teaching Levels

Since this module serves as background for later modules, there are no performance objectives for the simulation and teaching levels.

Effects of the Home Environment on Language Development

Four Important Factors in the Home Environment

Teachers should be aware that many factors in the home environment affect the language development of their students:

1. The number of adults and siblings present in the home.

2. The birth order and spacing of the children.

3. The nature and the amount of conversations.

4. The interest shown in the children and the quality of affection given them.

The interaction of these factors helps to produce the variety of language strengths and weaknesses found in any classroom.

A child's language development is greatly influenced by the quantity and quality of adult contacts.

Influence of Institutionalized Environment on Language Growth

Jamie's Story

Jamie was raised in an orphanage from infancy. At the age of fourteen, he was taken into the Clunden family and began to live a more "normal" life. Although his foster parents and new siblings made his life at home quite pleasant, he found school to be a very fearful experience. Because his vocabulary was limited, he was hesitant to communicate and did so only when someone was patient enough to listen. No intensive training was given to Jamie, although it was assumed that his everyday contacts with school peers and his foster family would cause him to improve his speaking and conceptual abilities.

The assumption was an honest and understandable one, but after a year's time it proved to be fallacious. For some reason, Jamie was not making much progress. Finally, an experimentally minded teacher agreed to tutor him for a short period after school each day, and within two months Jamie had increased his vocabulary and was a little more fluent in his daily conversation. But progress after that was pitifully slow, and the tutor decided to give up the attempt. Jamie is presently sixteen and has never attended a school dance and does not participate in extracurricular activities.

Jamie's story is a fictitious one, but it demonstrates the adverse effect that some institutionalized environments can have on the development of a child's language.

What the Research Says

There have been a variety of research reports which suggest that institutionalization in early childhood can result in significant retardation of a child's language development (45). Other studies (76) seem to indicate that a critical period for oral language growth exists, which, if passed by without the proper emotional and linguistic nurturing, may result in permanent retardation in language development. (Jamie's case was an illustration of this.)

It seems obvious, though, that orphanages, in themselves, are not to be blamed. Often the most consistent difference between the environment of an institutionalized child and a noninstitutionalized one is the relative opportunity for the noninstitutionalized child to receive plenty of attention and affection (62). The orphanage child is competing with dozens of other children for the attention of a few harried adults who may develop little or no emotional attachment for any of the youngsters.

Few teachers have to be concerned with a previously institutionalized child, but, of course, that is not the point. The point is that before children come to school for the first time, they have experienced a wide range of adult contacts. The range of emotional-linguistic contacts with adults varies all the way from an overprotected only child to an orphan. Children who have lived with their parents from birth, but who have not received sufficient emotional and linguistic nurturing, may enter school retarded in language development (77). To expect all children in the third grade to be similar in oral language skills is, of course, naïve.

Birth Order and Number of Siblings

Sandy, An Only Child

Sandy is an only child living with two upper-middle-class parents. During both meals the conversations are fairly lively, and Sandy does at least her share of the talking—probably more. At bedtime her father reads her a story, and her mother has a brief chat with her before turning out the light. Her room contains a desk, well stocked with pencils and paper, and a bookcase spilling over with her own books and books borrowed from the library. Her parents are both avid readers and frequently engage in conversation about mutually read material. Sandy has consistently topped every reading and language test she has taken. Her participation in classroom discussions is enthusiastic, and she frequently volunteers to give reports or to discuss an experience she has had. Her teachers like her very much!

Sandy has all the cards stacked in her favor—as far as language maturity is concerned. She is an "only child" and gets a great deal of adult attention. Just being an only child may give her a better chance for oral language growth than her friends with siblings.

What the Research Says

Studies done on birth order and number of children in the family suggest that "only children" tend to be more mature in oral language than children with siblings, at least during the early childhood years (2, 32, 83). In her study of "share and tell," Higgenbotham (32) found that singletons (only children) gave longer talks, used longer sentences, spoke more slowly, were more easily heard, and had more correct articulation than children with siblings. (The fact that they speak more slowly may be readily understandable when you consider that only children don't have such competition for "air-wave" control as do children with siblings.)

Other research indicates that birth order may have its effect not only on language development but also on general intellectual development as well (69, 83). Zajonc and Markus (83) compared results on intelligence testing from large-scale studies done in the United States, Scotland, France, and the Netherlands. They found that in all four countries, first-born children and children from small families did better on intelligence tests than later-born children and children from large families, regardless of class, race, or income. These findings agree with Aserlind's (2) in a study examining the verbal skills of children in families of very low socio-economic status. Despite the consistently low status of the families, she was able to differentiate the children on the basis of language development. Those children whose language skills were relatively mature *tended* (on the average) to have fewer siblings.

A child who is third out of five may grow up in a home environment heavily influenced by four other "immature" minds. This third child is competing with four others for adult attention. By contrast, the first-born child may grow up in a home environment heavily influenced by two "mature" minds—the parents or guardians. Zajonc and Markus (83) point out, however, that if children are sufficiently spaced, giving the older ones time to develop greater intellectual ability, the younger ones may not suffer in intellectual development.

Twins have also been found to be inferior in oral language maturity to singletons during the early childhood years (45, 83). Zajonc and Markus (83) found that twins usually score lower than do singletons on IQ tests and that when a twin is stillborn or dies within a month of birth, the test scores of the surviving twin reach nearly normal levels.

From the results of the studies above, you might expect triplets to be even more inferior in oral language maturity and in intelligence test scores than either singletons or twins. This is exactly what has been found (83).

From this research, you may have generalized that the *quantity* of adult contacts is a major factor in oral language development. Numerous studies (62, 74, 77), however, have shown that quantity alone is not enough and that *quality* of adult contacts is another important factor in children's oral language development. Milner (48), for example, found that the first graders she studied who attained high scores on the language part of an intelligence test had breakfast with their families; had active conversation with adults at breakfast, before school, and at supper; and also received more affection from the adults. In contrast, families of low scorers did not eat breakfast together, and the children in those families had no conversations with adults during breakfast, before school, or at supper. Furthermore, they seldom talked to siblings at breakfast or before school.

The Importance of Quality Adult Contacts

Bruce, Another Only Child

Bruce began to stutter at the age of six, at least that is when his parents decided he was a "stutterer." He'd been perceived as a nervous child by his mother and father for several years, and they had tried various ways of "calming him down." Sometimes they spanked him, sometimes they scolded, but usually they relied upon threats. Bruce tended to be negligent about almost everything that adults consider important—such as getting to bed on time, washing his hands before dinner, and keeping out of the mud. Both parents attempted to "straighten him out" by nagging him and keeping a close eye on him. Sometimes an "evil eye" was enough to keep Bruce in line.

After the parents decided that Bruce had a stuttering problem, they began to work on it. When Bruce was trying to say something his mother would often supply a word for him, whereas the father insisted that he stop and start over, but "think before you speak!" Bruce is now in college and still stutters. He feels that "my parents have never understood me."

This story about Bruce should demonstrate that *quantity* of adult contacts is not enough. Even though Bruce was the only child in a home environment that had two adult parents, his language development was certainly not typical of those singletons of the previously mentioned studies.

What the Research Says

Research on stuttering demonstrates that the hypothetical story of Bruce is illustrative of many stutterers. Many studies have found that parents' attitudes and behavior contribute to the onset of stuttering. It has been found (again, on the average) that parents of stutterers often disagree on disciplinary matters; that mothers of stutterers tend to use harsh disciplinary measures, such as corporal punishment, threats, or humiliation; that the parents are often inconsistent in their eating and sleeping requirements, and that they tend to scold and call attention to their children for stuttering (50). It has also been found that mothers of stuttering boys tend to reject their sons more often than do mothers of non-stuttering boys (38) and that mothers of stutterers maintain higher standards and are more critical of their children's behavior (49).

In Duncan's study (21) of college-age stutterers, it was found that stutterers often felt their parents didn't understand them; they felt lack of affection in their home environment; they perceived their parents as being disappointed in them; and they tended to view one or more of their parents as very nervous. A study by Wood (80) may confirm the reader's growing suspicion that the parents in these cases may be as "nervous" as the children, if not more so. He discovered that the mothers of fifty articulatory defectives tended to score higher on neuroticism and lower on self-adjustment than women in the norm group for the test. The fathers as a group did not differ significantly from the norm group on neuroticism, but they did score lower on self-adjustment. The mothers of stutterers also tended to have higher social standards than women in the norm groups. Wood found, moreover, that 96 percent of the children with articulation problems had one or both parents who ranked below the forty-fifth percentile on the self-adjustment scale.

A study of adult stutterers (10) showed that they are usually *not* severely maladjusted socially. However, they do tend to be more anxious, less self-confident, and more socially withdrawn than adult nonstutterers. In a study by Woods (81) that compared fluent boys with stuttering boys, the stuttering boys both expected to be rated and *were* rated significantly poorer as speakers than were the normally fluent boys. However, in the same study, no significant differences were found between the two groups of boys on social position measures, suggesting that whether or not an elementary boy stutters may be of minor importance in determining his social status among his peers.

It is reasonably evident, then, that stuttering and other speech defects, when not physiologically caused, are often related to a somewhat mentally unhealthy home environment. Children free of such defects tend to come from homes in which parents have positive feelings toward themselves, accept their children and display affection toward them, maintain consistent but mild discipline, avoid setting impossible standards for children, and provide ample opportunities for them to speak without being under tension. *It is likely that these criteria for a mentally healthy home environment also apply to the school environment.*

Home–School Language Differences

Carmen

Carmen lives with her parents, three older brothers, and two younger sisters. Since her parents are seasonal farm workers and move to follow the crops, Carmen changes schools about three times a year. At home and in her small community she feels very comfortable and speaks Spanish most of the time. Since her parents know little English, the only practice Carmen gets with English outside of school is when she goes to the local grocery store which is run by an "anglo" couple. Sometimes she fools around with her brothers and sisters and uses English expressions picked up from her peers at school.

At school, however, Carmen is not allowed to speak Spanish at all. This is the philosophy of the faculty: "if we allow children to use Spanish, they will never learn the proper English they need to get along in our society."

At age twelve, Carmen is only in the third grade and is considered very shy and retiring. Her teacher says, "Carmen just sits there; she doesn't ask any questions, and she never hands in any work."

Although the name is fictitious, the story of Carmen is true. And, there *are* schools and faculties who believe in the "English only" philosophy. It may not be an openly admitted philosophy, but underneath the advertised "tolerance" and behind closed classroom doors it becomes evident to those whose home language is Spanish. In fact, it even can become evident when the classroom doors are opened and the children are allowed to frequent the playground. In Carmen's school, for example, a student teacher who spoke Spanish (the only Spanish-speaking teacher in the school) was sometimes given playground duty for the express purpose of "catching kids who swear in Spanish."

It is probable that Carmen is shy and retiring in school (unlike her behavior at home) because she doesn't know enough English to understand the assignments or even to ask in the "proper" language for help. What happens to children whose oral language patterns learned in the home are looked down upon at school? Surely, their sense of self-respect must be damaged. Little research, however, has been done on the effects of this type of discrimination. Let's turn our attention now to what the research does have to say about children who are expected to function with two different languages—a home language and a school language.

WHAT THE RESEARCH SAYS

One out of every six people in the United States does not use English as his first language. (Spanish is the next most common language.) A third of the native Americans in our country speak their own language as their first language (73). One out of every five *new* citizens of our country is an immigrant (8). In the state of Illinois, for example, 141 different languages have been identified (36). One out of nine Americans is black. Most blacks in our country speak one of the variants of the black dialect, either as a first or second language.

One out of every six people in the United States does not use English as his first language.

LOS ANGELES TIMES PHOTO

Several investigations (17, 78) have shown that children whose home language is different from that of the school environment demonstrate lower verbal abilities than those children whose home and school languages are the same. Hickey (31) argues for the popular explanation: that it is the testing procedures, testing instruments, and other evaluative techniques that cause such results. There is considerable merit in this argument, since most methods of evaluation are biased and nongeneralizable to all ethnic groups. However, is the issue one of how best to evaluate childen's verbal skills, or is it rather one of how to teach children whose home and school language differ? The latter issue seems to be the more practical one. Whether we test children or not, they're still going to be waiting for someone to respect them and teach them. If they speak a language or dialect that differs from the teacher's or that differs from what the teacher perceives should be taught, then something has to be done *in that classroom*. Changes in testing procedures alone will not handle the problem.

One way of handling the problem of home-school language differences has been to "teach English as a second language." This method has the virtue of not labeling a child's language or dialect as "incorrect," seeking instead to teach Standard English as a dialect or language that is necessary for all citizens to know in order to become "successful," both socially and financially.

However, there is a tendency of those who advocate this method to look at those who do not speak English or the standard dialect of English, as handicapped. They further propose that Standard English be taught as soon as possible so that the so-called handicapped students can function properly in a regular classroom (20). With this approach, we almost drown out the children's earlier means of communicating by saturating them with Standard English. Instead of building upon the preschool language learnings of these children, we tend to ignore those learnings and proceed to "start all over again." The child enters and is encompassed by a strange new world of *school* language (24). Is it any wonder that children whose home language is not Standard English often do poorly on tests of language skills?

Bilingual classroom environments—those which incorporate both the home language and Standard English into the educational program—have sometimes shown more positive results. For example, in one study (39) of children in a school that utilized English and Chinese simultaneously to teach reading and writing skills, the incidence of reading disabilities at the end of grade three was much lower than the reported national average. Furthermore, the children in this school consistently had the highest scholastic average in the Vancouver, B.C., public school system. Similar results (53, 75) have been reported for classroom environments which incorporated both English and Spanish. Ching (14), however, cites three studies in which the bilingual approach was compared with the traditional Standard English approach. In only one of these studies did they find that the bilingual approach was superior, and in that one both schools and the teachers' training were superior to begin with.

It is most likely that the bilingual approach *will* require a school setting in which teachers have extra training and motivation. So far, however, we have no assurances based on experimental research. Most of the arguments for the bilingual approach at the present time are based on logic, politics, subjective observations, and humanistic concern. Yet a concerted effort to assist minority children must be made, and the bilingual approach seems to be the most promising one at this point. Studies cited earlier seem to discredit arguments that speaking two languages (or two dialects) will confuse children and create serious learning problems.

Although short-term confusion may occur (which is quite usual in many learning situations), the long-term benefits may be worth it. Studies by Peal and Lambert (55) and by Landry (40), for example, suggest that individuals who learn two languages develop more creative flexibility in their thinking. This is probably because they have learned two labeling and patterning systems and are led to pay attention to more aspects of their environment.

Even if greater creativity were not found to be a consistent result of the bilingual approach, a higher sense of self-respect *might* be. This greater sense of self-respect could have a significant impact on children's willingness to pick up Standard English along with improvements in their own dialect or language. The bilingual approach is probably the most difficult one of all for a profession whose bilinguists number very few. But, in the long run (and we need much more research to help us determine this), it may prove to be the only way that works.

Effects of Cultural Conditions and Expectations

Dennis

Dennis is a twelve-year old boy who lives in a large Eastern city with museums, playhouses, art centers, libraries, and inexpensive public transportation. Dennis has never been to a museum, playhouse, art center, or public library; in fact, he has never been more than twenty-five blocks from his home. His home consists of a two-room apartment shared by nine people. Their bathroom is shared by many more. You would look in vain for a book in this apartment; not even a pencil or pen can be found.

Dennis has mixed feelings about school. He enjoys getting out of the apartment and "horsing around" with the boys on the playground and in the halls. But schoolwork is frustrating and boring. Dennis can read at about the first grade level, but he hates reading because the reading books "always talk about those rich white kids." His major participation in discussion is to giggle when another boy "pops off." He writes his name with pleasure but avoids writing whenever he can.

Because of their income and location, the parents of Dennis have lower-class status. Because of their skin color their opportunity for climbing the status ladder is lower than it is for whites. Because of his particular style of verbal performance, Dennis would be labeled by the white middle-class culture as "illiterate."

Dennis is similar to many children in this city who have been labeled "culturally deprived" or "disadvantaged" (19). Fortunately, these labels are going out of style, as they imply that one culture is superior to another. What we're really talking about are children, who because of the particular economic condition and life style experienced in the home, do not fit easily into the typical white, middle-class school.

These children, of course, need more than "Sesame Street" or "The Electric Company," as valuable as these programs are. They need a special kind of assistance from teachers—not because they are inferior, which they're not— but because society owes it to them. As long as we insist that all children in our country go to essentially the same kind of school with essentially the same curriculum, it becomes the obligation of the schools to provide compensatory types of education for those who don't fit in as well as others.

WHAT THE RESEARCH SAYS

Studies of the forties, fifties, and sixties (17) consistently seemed to demonstrate that children from low SES (socio-economic status) families had lower levels of cognitive (intellectual) abilities. However, more recent studies, along with a decreased class and racial bias among investigators, have revealed far less "cognitive deficiency" among low SES families than was formerly suspected. For example, Golden, Bridger, and Montare (27) studied a group of two-year-old white children from different SES groups. The children were presented with identical learning tasks under verbal and nonverbal conditions. Under the nonverbal conditions, there were no differences in learning abilities that could be attributed to socio-economic class. However, under the *verbal* conditions, the high SES subjects improved their performance and were superior to the low SES subjects.

In most studies comparing low SES families with high SES families (20, 27, 37, 42, 70), the children from low SES families demonstrate lower levels of oral language proficiency. Some people feel that these differences between low and high SES subjects are merely the result of the biased testing procedures— using test stimuli that are highly oriented toward middle-class experiences, using test directions with middle-class dialect, and using interviewing techniques which turn on middle-class children and turn off lower-class children. Such biased testing procedures definitely exist and undoubtedly explain some of the differences between low SES and high SES scores on oral language tests.

On the other hand, several researchers have found significant differences in the manner in which low SES and high SES families regulate their children's behavior. The study by Schubert and Cropley (64), for instance, compared the ways in which the behavior of Native American children of the same tribe but of different socio-economic classes was regulated. The behavior of low SES rural children was *verbally* regulated far less than the behavior of the high SES urban children. Bernstein (7) has provided additional evidence that the difference in the way children use verbal information to learn and to regulate their behavior may be due to SES differences in their language experiences. These studies seem to suggest that in contrast to low SES adults, high SES adults tend to use more specific terminology and rely more on language to transmit information and to regulate their children's behavior.

In fact, that is what Hess and Shipman (30) and Schoggen (63) showed in their studies. They found that middle-class mothers press more for verbal description and clarification than do lower-class mothers. Children from poverty homes are less stimulated to verbalize actions, objects, and intentions and are less stimulated to relate present action to future events. Blank and Solomon's study (9) also supports this. They found that many low SES children use language to direct their problem solving only when asked. The children do not spontaneously use language without external requirements. It is not absence of words that handicaps poverty children, the researchers felt, but rather their reluctance to use them without specific demands. Jensen (35) reported a similar picture. He found that the difference between lower SES and upper SES children was not in their ability to name things but, rather, in the low SES children's inability to do so spontaneously; they had to be instructed to do so.

In another study (33), though, it was found that the abbreviated speech of low SES children occurred only in a formal and constrained situation where they interacted with persons they perceived as authority figures. In contrast, the language they used naturally with friends and family was characterized by greater ease and fluency. This same observation was reported by Stewart (68).

The research makes it abundantly clear that the home environment, with its cultural background, behavioral expectations, methods of teaching and interacting, and socio-economic status, affects the language development of children. In a study analyzing the ways that Anglo-American, Mexican-American, and Chinese-American mothers teach their sons, Steward and Steward (67) found that the best predictor of how a boy will respond to his mother's teaching was ethnicity. Each ethnic group of mothers had its own expectations and style of teaching and interacting.

Children from different cultural back grounds bring different types of language skills and different expectations about language into the classroom.

The children in your classroom have all experienced different learning environments in their homes, including different cultural conditions and expectations. This results in different language skills and different expectations about language brought by them into your classroom.

Birth Weight, Sex, and TV as Factors in Language Development

Birth Weight

Research indicates that three other factors affect children's oral language development: birth weight, sex, and TV. Studies (18, 57) have shown that at the start of school, the premature children studied were significantly inferior in language comprehension, number of words used, sentence elaboration, and definitions. (Note that all of these tests are indicative of linguistic maturation.) Minimal brain damage is presumed to be the cause of language deficiencies as well as other deficiencies of low birth weight children. In turn, poor maternal nutrition, and inadequate prenatal care are viewed as causation of both low birth weight and of the minimal brain damage (13).

Sex

A second factor is gender. It seems that, typically, upon entering school, girls (as a group) show themselves to be superior to boys (as a group) in oral language development. When IQ, SES, and stimulus are held constant, the differences in language growth are consistently in favor of the girls. Researchers (11, 34, 47, 70, 72) have found differences favoring girls on such variables as length of response, number of different words, and structural complexity of sentences. These findings seem to be consistent with the general observation that girls mature about two years earlier than boys. Jarvis (34) and Brimer (11), however, have found that boys are superior to girls in listening comprehension, and this seems consistent with a study done by Dunsdon and Roberts (22) who found that in four orally administered vocabulary tests, boys at every age level from five to fourteen did better than girls.

With respect to speech defects, the difference between the sexes is highly significant. Many more boys than girls are victims of stuttering and articulatory disorders in our society. Yedinack (82), for example , found that 75 percent of those suffering from nonorganic articulatory defects were boys. Her population consisted of second graders selected from forty-three schools in ten cities. In Moncur's investigation of stuttering (50), 83 percent of the stutterers were boys. In explaining such research findings, McCarthy (47) suggests that a boy receives much less satisfaction from imitating the speech habits of his mother (or female baby sitter), who is around much more than the father; consequently, he imitates less than girls. Also, noisy, energetic boys are sent out to play more often and, thus, are given less linguistic practice with an adult. Furthermore, she says, boys tend to receive more rejection. It should also be pointed out, moreover, that certain aspects of this antilinguistic reinforcement are repeated in the classroom.

It seems that girls have the advantage over boys in language development (except in listening comprehension). However, as Tyler (72) points out, the differences in oral language abilities *within* a group of girls or boys is far greater than the differences in oral language abilities *between* the two sexes. In other words, on a language test you are more likely to find large differences between Johnny and Tommy than you are between the average score of the girls and the average score of the boys.

Television

A third factor to be considered is the modern child's third parent, namely, the television set. What influence does this "parent" have on oral language growth? Numerous studies have shown that children watch TV as many hours as they spend in school. Witty (79) found that viewing time varied considerably among children and between grade levels. Sixth graders tended to stare at the box more than second graders; and high school students, less than elementary school students. However, he found no evidence that television viewing, per se, either hindered or enhanced school achievement. In a random sample of about 2,500 seventh and eighth grade students in California, Ridder (58) found no significant relationship between academic achievement and the amount of television viewing.

"Sesame Street" has shown that television *can* teach children specific cognitive skills. An evaluation of the program done by Ball and Bogatz for The Educational Testing Service (3) revealed that, in terms of the Workshop's own goals, "Sesame Street" had been highly effective. Children who viewed "Sesame Street" achieved many of the stated goals in learning letters, numbers, and geometric forms, and they gained appreciably in their skill in sorting and classifying.

The ETS study also reported that frequent viewers of "Sesame Street" surpassed infrequent viewers; that children at home in "disadvantaged" communities watching "Sesame Street" gained, in some goal areas, more than children from the same communities who attended preschool. The study also found that children who viewed the program in their own homes were at no disadvantage to those who watched in peer-group environments, supervised by a teacher. And finally, ETS found that children who watched and learned more came from homes where "Sesame Street" was watched by both mother and child and where the mother talked with the child about the show. It looks as though TV does and can play a significant part in a child's cognitive development. This, in turn, should be greatly beneficial to language development.

Although no significant relationship has been found between academic achievement and the amount of television viewing, this may be mostly a result of inadequate measurements. The standardized achievement tests used in schools to measure scholastic growth are notoriously unrelated to a host of specific factors in the home and the school. Educators often tear at their hair because a training program they have tried (and have spent so many hours preparing) seems to have no effect on standardized achievement scores. Possibly it doesn't occur to them that the yardstick they're using is at fault rather than the program.

The evaluation team for "Sesame Street" *found* significant results because they invented measuring instruments which were specific and appropriate to what they wanted to measure. Because of the age of the subjects, the evaluation team didn't rely on the much more generalized standard testing approach.

Very little has been done to develop measuring instruments (if, indeed it can be done at all) which show the actual effects of television on children. Many studies have been done to determine whether television makes children more violent, but apparently none have been done to determine whether television makes children more superficially sophisticated, more cynical, and more bored with school.

Perhaps the most important idea to be gained from this module is that there is no "typical" child. You cannot say that because Sandy is a boy, watches twenty-eight hours per week of TV, and is an only child, he will be at a particular level in his oral language development. What I've been trying to say, and what research has demonstrated, is that there are many factors which go into making up each individual child's oral language patterns. As teachers, we need to have some feeling and understanding as to how and why we get the varying stages of language development that occur in classrooms. We need to keep these factors in mind when we make our long-range outcomes and performance objectives for our classroom. Furthermore, an understanding and awareness of the many different factors in home environment that affect our students' oral language development will make us better able to communicate with parents.

The effects of oral language development that we've talked about so far are beyond our control. What about the school environment; does it have any effect? The next part of this module deals with answers to this question.

Effects of School Environment

A major thesis of this book is that the school can have an influence on the development of language skills. (Specific suggestions will come in the modules to follow.) As we have seen, many aspects of oral language are, to a large extent, habitual by the time a child enters kindergarten or first grade. Templin (70) found that there was little change after the age of three in the parts of speech used. She also found that the greatest growth in articulation took place between the ages of three and four. However, research done by Chomsky (15) on children from five to ten shows that the process of learning to construct sentences does continue actively during the early school years. Thus, through specific instruction, we may have a direct impact on this aspect of language development.

Effects of Teacher Behavior

The effect of teachers' daily speaking habits on children's speech is difficult to determine because there is so little research on this. Although young children do tend to imitate a teacher's *mannerisms,* it seems doubtful that children learn basic oral language patterns merely from casual listening to the teacher talking. This is particularly true if the teacher does most of the talking during the day. In a study (6) of fifteen high school classes in "Problems of a Democracy," it was found that the teacher spoke an average of 72 percent of the words. (The actual range of speaking for the teachers was from 60 percent to 93 percent!) Such a verbal barrage hardly gives students much time to practice oral language skills, especially if the remaining 28 percent is divided among twenty-eight pupils.

Although the characteristics of a teacher's speech are only mildly influential, the leadership patterns of teachers may have a much greater impact on oral language growth. Lippitt and White (41), in their classic boys' club study, found that a democratic leadership pattern used by the teacher encouraged friendly discussion of personal matters, joking, asking opinions of each other, and making suggestions on group policy. The authoritarian pattern of leadership, however, resulted in either apathetic withdrawal (which would hinder oral language practice) or aggressive resistance (which would channel oral language into narrow destructive uses). Similarly, Ryans (61) found that teachers who were understanding and friendly, yet organized and stimulating (similar to Lippitt and White's "democratic" pattern of leadership), encouraged productive and confident participation.

Other studies (25) demonstrate the positive effects of supportive teachers on the self-confidence of students and on their willingness to participate. In fact, researchers (51, 54) have found that the percent of teacher statements that make use of ideas and opinions previously expressed by pupils is directly related to test scores for language skills, social study skills, and science skills. Christensen (16) discovered that vocabulary growth was significantly greater under teachers whose pupils rated them high on a "warmth scale." It is apparent, then, that certain types of leadership patterns on the part of teachers encourage more practice in oral communication. It is likely that with this greater amount of practice, the students would gain in oral language skills.

A study by Rosenthal and Jacobson (60) indicated that teachers may influence children's language behavior by the kinds of expectations they have about each student. This effect has been labeled the "Pygmalion Effect," based on Shaw's character in *My Fair Lady.* Rosenthal and Jacobson report that teachers' expectations serve as self-fulfilling prophecies; if a teacher expects a child to attain a high level of language skills (or any other set of skills), that child will make greater effort to attain a high level of language skills. Although the methodology used in Rosenthal's study has been questioned (66, 71), similar results have been attained by others (12, 66), indicating that teachers' expectations may influence children's achievement.

Effects of Administrative Organization

The effects of administrative organization on student growth are generally difficult to ascertain because many nonorganizational elements in a study are not controlled. Nevertheless, some studies have been made on administrative organizations, such as ability grouping, multi-age grouping, nongrading, open classroom, and team teaching. The results are inconclusive and inconsistent and can be interpreted only by discovering exactly what different teachers did under the different administrative arrangements. If one group of teachers, for example, spends more time on language development under the administrative organization called "team teaching" than another group of teachers in self-contained classrooms, the resulting superiority of the "team students" should not be attributed to team teaching as such.

Most studies on team teaching, for example, demonstrate that scores on standardized achievement tests are about the same under team teaching as they are under self-contained classroom teaching (29). On the other hand, Gamsky (26) found that a team teaching approach could have a positive impact on students' attitudes toward their teachers, on their interest in subject matter, on their sense of personal freedom, and on their feelings of self-reliance.

There is an understandable absence of research concerning the "open classroom." Research about the effectiveness of open classrooms would be difficult to conduct, to say the least, since there is little agreement on the nature of the open classroom. Some proponents of the open classroom believe that it means fewer physical walls, with everything centering around a main hub (usually the resource center of the school). Other proponents feel that a single teacher in a physically enclosed, four-walled room may run a very successful "open" classroom. Openness, they say, is a frame of mind in which teachers and children work together toward objectives held by both, Obviously trying to compare open classrooms with traditional classrooms would be nearly impossible.

Will the administrative structure of the school influence the language development of students? This unanswerable question is often asked in reference to various academic areas or to specific skills. It is almost as useless as asking, "Will the seating arrangement at a banquet affect the guests' digestion?" The number of uncontrolled variables related to either question approaches infinity.

Effects of Instructional Program

While it is conceivable that the administrative organization of a school may have some influence on the opportunities which children have for oral language development, research indicates that the provision for highly specific instruction is the main agent of change. In writing of the accomplishments of "Sesame Street," Polsky (56, p. 104) reaffirms this when he says, "It showed educators the value of careful planning, clearly defined objectives, and summative evaluation."

What Studies Say About Specific Instruction

Research points out the relationship between specific instruction and specific results. As just one example, Emerick (23) randomly assigned forty-seven children to morning and afternoon kindergarten sessions. The average age, the parental occupations, and the articulation (consonant pronunciation) test scores were similar for the two groups. On the basis of a coin toss, the afternoon group was selected to receive twenty-six speech improvement lessons, each lasting between ten and fifteen minutes and given twice weekly for thirteen weeks. The results showed the average articulation errors of the afternoon group changed from thirty-six to sixteen, while the average articulation errors of the morning group changed only from thirty-three to twenty-nine.

A comparison of two types of specific instruction with fourth, sixth, and eighth grade groups was made by Moyer (52). Some of the groups used written drill on "grammatical usage," while the other groups used oral drill with a tape recorder. Improvements in written and oral usage were greater for the groups using the oral approach.

These are just two examples of the principle: If you want specific improvements in children's language abilities, you need to provide very specific instruction and practice.

SUMMARY

In working on a child's language, we are working on a significant aspect of that child's self-concept. If teachers are to be effective in language instruction, they must understand the types of environmental experiences which influence oral language development. In this module, we have looked at research reports which lend support to the general observation that the home and school are forces of vital importance in the development of oral language.

In the home, such factors as the extent of adult contacts, the degree and kinds of pressure from parents, the cultural customs, and the socio-economic position can influence the level of oral language maturity which children attain. In the school, the oral language proficiency of children can be enhanced by instructional programs which offer specific practice in articulation, grammatical usage, and other elements of oral expression.

It has been suggested here that teachers can have an influence on the language development of children. Later modules will provide suggestions on how to make that influence a positive and significant one.

REFERENCES AND BIBLIOGRAPHY

1. Anderson, Robert H. "Organizational Character of Education: Staff Utilization and Development." *Review of Educational Research* 34 (Oct. 1964): 456–58.

2. Aserlind, LeRoy, Jr. "An Investigation of Maternal Factors Related to the Acquisition of Verbal Skills of Infants in a Culturally Disadvantaged Population." Ph.D. dissertation: University of Wisconsin, 1963.

3. Ball, Samuel, and Bogatz, Gerry Ann. *The First Year of Sesame Street: An Evaluation.* Princeton, N.J.: Educational Testing Service, 1970.

4. Baratz, J. *Language and Cognitive Assessment of Negro Children: Assumptions and Research Needs.* Rockville, Md.: American Speech and Hearing Association, March 1969.

5. Barth, Ronald S. "Starting Open Classrooms: Some Assumptions." *National Elementary Principal* 52 (Nov. 1973): 68–69.

6. Bellack, Arno A., and Davitz, Joel R. *The Language of the Classroom.* New York: Cooperative Research Project No. 1497, Institute of Psychological Research, Teachers College, Columbia University, 1963.

7. Bernstein, B. "Social Structure, Language and Learning." In *The Psychology of Language, Thought, and Instruction,* edited by J. Dececco. New York: Holt, Rinehart, and Winston, 1967.

8. Bethell, Thomas. "Becoming an American." *Newsweek* (May 26, 1975): 13.

9. Blank, M., and Solomon, F. "A Tutorial Program to Develop Abstract Thinking in Socially Disadvantaged Pre-School Children." *Child Development* 39 (1968): 379–89.

10. Block, E.L., and Goodstein, L.D. "Functional Speech Disorders and Personality: A Decade of Research." *Journal of Speech and Hearing Disorders* 36 (1971): 295–314.

11. Brimer, M.A. "Sex Differences in Listening Comprehension." *Journal of Research and Development in Education* 3 (1970): 72–76.

12. Brophy, Jere E., and Good, Thomas L. "Teachers' Communication of Differential Expectations for Children's Classroom Performance:

Some Behavioral Data." *Journal of Educational Psychology* 61 (Oct. 1970): 365–74.

13. Caputo, Daniel V., and Mandell, Wallace. "Consequences of Low Birth Weight." *Developmental Psychology* 3 (1970): 363–83.

14. Ching, Doris. *Reading and the Bilingual Child.* Newark, Del.: International Reading Association, 1976.

15. Chomsky, Carol. *The Acquisition of Syntax in Children from 5–10.* Cambridge, Mass.: Massachusetts Institute of Technology, 1969.

16. Christensen, C.M. "Relationships Between Pupil Achievement, Pupil Affect-Need, Teacher Warmth, and Teacher Permissiveness." *Journal of Educational Psychology* 51 (June 1960): 169–74.

17. Coleman, J.S. *Equality of Educational Opportunity.* Monograph produced under a grant from the U.S. Office of Education, U.S. Government Printing Office, 1966.

18. De Hirsch, K.; Jansky, J.; and Langford, W.S. "Comparisons Between Prematurely and Maturely Born Children at Three Age Levels." *American Journal of Orthopsychiatry* 36 (1966): 616–28.

19. Deutsch, Martin. "The Disadvantaged Child and the Learning Process." In *Education in Depressed Areas,* edited by A. Harry Passow. New York: Bureau of Publications, Teachers College, Columbia University, 1963.

20. Donoghue, Mildred P. *The Child and the English Language Arts.* Dubuque, Ia.: Wm. C. Brown Co., Publishers, 1971.

21. Duncan, Melba H. "Home Adjustment of Stutterers versus Non-Stutterers." *Journal of Speech and Hearing Disorders* 14 (Sept. 1949): 255–59.

22. Dunsdon, and Fraser-Roberts. "A Study of the Performance of 2,000 Children in Four Vocabulary Tests." *British Journal of Psychology* 10 (1957): 1–16.

23. Emerick, Lonnie. "Speech Improvement in the Kindergarten." *Education* 84 (May 1964): 565–68.

24. Feeley, Joan. "Teaching Non-English Speaking First Graders to Read." *Elementary English* (Feb. 1970): 199–208.

25. Flanders, Ned A. "Personal-Social Anxiety as a Factor in Experimental Learning Situations." *Journal of Educational Research* 45 (1951): 100–10.

26. Gamsky, Neal R. "Team Teaching, Student Achievement and Attitudes." *The Journal of Experimental Education* 39 (Fall 1970): 42–45.

27. Golden, Mark; Bridger, Wagner H.; and Montare, Albert. "Social Class Differences in the Ability of Young Children to Use Verbal Information to Facilitate Learning." *American Journal of Orthopsychiatry* 44 (Jan. 1974): 86–91.

28. Hapgood, Marilyn. "The Open Classroom: Protect It From Its Friends." *National Elementary Principal* 52 (Nov. 1973): 43–48.

29. Heathers, Glen. "Research on Implementing and Evaluating Cooperative Teaching." *National Elementary Principal* 44 (Jan. 1965): 27–33.

30. Hess, R., and Shipman, V. "Early Experience and the Socialization of Cognitive Modes in Children." *Child Development* 39 (1965): 869–86.

31. Hickey, Tom. "Bilingualism and the Measurement of Intelligence and Verbal Learning Ability." *Exceptional Children* 39 (Sept. 1972): 24–28.

32. Higgenbotham, Dorothy C. "A Study of the Speech of Kindergarten, First, and Second Grade Children in Audience Situations with Particular Attention to Maturation and Learning as Evidenced in Content, Form, and Delivery." Ph.D. dissertation, Northwestern University, 1961.

33. Houston, S. "A Reexamination of Some Assumptions About the Language of the Disadvantaged Child." *Child Development* 41 (1970): 947–63.

34. Jarvis, Oscar T. "Boy-Girl Ability Differences in Elementary School Language Arts." *Childhood Education* 42 (Mar. 1966): 198–200.

35. Jensen, A. "The Role of Verbal Mediation in Mental Development." *Journal of Genetic Psychology* 118 (Jan. 1971): 39–70.

36. Johnson, Laura. "Bilingual Bicultural Education: A Two-Way Street." *Reading Teacher* 29 (Dec. 1975): 231–39.

37. Jones, Pauline A., and McMillan, William B. "Speech Characteristics as a Function of Social Class and Situational Factors." *Child Development* 44 (Feb. 1973): 117–21.

38. Kinstler, Donald B. "Covert and Overt Maternal Rejection in Stuttering." *Journal of Speech and Hearing Disorders* 26 (May 1961): 145–55.

39. Kline, Carl L., and Lee, Norma. "A Transcultural Study of Dyslexia: Analysis of Language Disabilities in 227 Chinese Children Simultaneously Learning to Read and Write in English and in Chinese." *The Journal of Special Education* 6 (Spring 1972): 9–26.

40. Landry, Richard G. "The Relationship of Second Language Learning and Verbal Creativity." *Modern Language Journal* 57 (Mar. 1973): 110–13.

41. Lippitt, Ronald, and White, Ralph K. "An Experimental Study of Leadership and Group Life." In *Readings in Social Psychology*, edited by Eleanor E. Maccoby et al. New York: Holt, Rinehart & Winston, 1958.

42. Loban, Walter D. *The Language of Elementary School Children*. Research Report No. 1. Champaign, Illinois: National Council of Teachers of English, 1963.

43. Manolakes, Theodore. "Introduction: The Open Eudcation Movement." *National Elementary Principal* 52 (Nov. 1973): 10–15.

44. May, Frank B. *Teaching Language as Communication to Children*. Columbus, Ohio: Charles E. Merrill, 1967.

45. McCarthy, Dorothea. "Language Development in Children." In *A Manual of Child Psychology*, edited by Leonard Carmichael, pp. 492–630. New York: John Wiley & Sons, 1954.

46. ———. "Language Disorder and Parent-Child Relationships." *Journal of Speech and Hearing Disorders* 19 (Dec. 1954): 514–23.

47. ———. "Some Possible Explanations of Sex Differences in Language Development and Disorders." *Journal of Psychology* 35 (Jan. 1953): 155–60.

48. Milner, Esther. "A Study of the Relationship Between Reading Readiness in Grade One School Children and Patterns of Parent-Child Interaction." *Child Development* 22 (June 1951): 95–112.

49. Moll, Kenneth L., and Darley, Frederic L. "Attitudes of Mothers of Articulatory-Impaired and Speech-Retarded Children." *Journal of Speech and Hearing Disorders* 25 (Nov. 1960): 377–84.

50. Moncur, John P. "Environmental Factors Differentiating Stuttering Children from Non-Stuttering Children." *Speech Monographs* 18 (Nov. 1951): 312–25.

51. Morrison, B.M. "The Reactions of Children to Patterns of Teaching Behavior." Ph.D. dissertation: University of Michigan, 1966.

52. Moyer, Haverly O. "Can Ear-Training Improve English Usage?" *Elementary English* 33 (Apr. 1956): 216–19.

53. Nedler, S., and Sebera, P. "Intervention Strategies for Spanish-Speaking Preschool Children." *Child Development* 42 (1971): 259–67.

54. Nelson, Lois Ney. "The Effect of Classroom Interaction on Pupil Linguistic Performance." *Dissertation Abstracts* 25 (1964): 789.

55. Peal, E., and Lambert, W. "The Relation of Bilingualism to Intelligence." *Psychological Monographs* 76 (1962): 127–34.

56. Polsky, Richard M. *Getting to Sesame Street: Origins of the Children's Television Workshop.* New York: Praeger Publishers, 1974.

57. Rabinovitch, M.S.; Bibace, R.; and Caplan, H. "Consequences of Prematurity: Psychological Test Findings." *Canadian Medical Association Journal* 84 (1961): 822–24.

58. Ridder, Joyce M. "Pupil Opinions and the Relationship of Television Viewing to Academic Achievement." *Journal of Educational Research* 57 (Dec. 1963): 204–6.

59. Riesman, Frank. *The Culturally Deprived Child.* New York: Harper & Row, Publishers, 1962.

60. Rosenthal, Robert, and Jacobson, Lenore. *Pygmalion in the Classroom.* New York: Holt, Rinehart and Winston, 1968.

61. Ryans, David G. "Some Relationships Between Pupil Behavior and Certain Teacher Characteristics." *Journal of Educational Psychology* 52 (Apr. 1961): 82–90.

62. Saltz, Rosalyn. "Effects of Part-time 'Mothering' on IQ and SQ of Young Institutionalized Children." *Child Development* 44 (1973): 166–70.

63. Schoggen, M. "The Imprint of Low Income Homes on Young Children." In *Research Change and Social Responsibility: An Illustrative Model From Early Education,* edited by S. Gray and J. Miller. Nashville: George Peabody Teachers College, 1967.

64. Schubert, J., and Cropley, A. "Verbal Regulations of Behavior and IQ in Canadian Indian and White Children." *Developmental Psychology* 7 (1972): 295–301.

65. _____. "Measurement of Vocabulary of Young Bilingual Children in Both of the Language Used." *Journal of Genetic Psychology* 74 (June 1949): 305–10.

66. Snow, Richard E. "Unfinished Pygmalion." *Contemporary Psychology* 14 (Apr. 1969): 197–99.

67. Steward, Margaret, and Steward, David. "The Observation of Anglo-, Mexican-, and Chinese-American Mothers Teaching Their Young Sons." *Child Development* 44 (1973): 329–37.

68. Stewart, William A. "On the Use of Negro Dialect in the Teaching of Reading." In *Teaching Black Children to Read,* edited by Joan Baratz and Roger Shuy, pp. 156–219. Washington, D.C.: Center for Applied Linguistics, 1969.

69. Sutton-Smith, and Rosenberg, B.G. "The Sibling." New York: Holt, Rinehart & Winston, 1970.

70. Templin, Mildred C. *Certain Language Skills in Children: Their Development and Interrelationships.* Minneapolis: University of Minnesota Press, 1957.

71. Thorndike, Robert L. "Review of Pygmalion in the Classroom." *American Educational Research Journal* 5 (Nov. 1968): 708–11.

72. Tyler, Leona E. *The Psychology of Human Differences.* New York: Appleton-Century-Crofts, 1965.

73. U.S. Commission on Civil Rights. *A Better Chance to Learn: Bilingual-Bicultural Education.* Clearing House Publication #51, May 1975.

74. Watts, Jean Carew; Halfargood, Christine; and Chan, Itty. "Environment, Experience and Intellectual Development of Young Children in Home Care." *American Journal of Orthopsychiatry* 44 (Oct. 1974): 773–81.

75. Weffer, R.C. "Effects of First Language Instruction in Academic and Psychological Development of Bilingual Children." Ph.D. dissertation, Illinois Institute of Technology, 1972.

76. Weiner, Paul S. "A Language-Delayed Child at Adolescence." *Journal of Speech and Hearing Disorders* 39 (May 1974): 202–12.

77. Whitehurst, Grover J.; Novak, Gary; and Zorn, Glen A. "Delayed Speech Studied in the Home." *Developmental Psychology* 7 (1972): 169–77.

78. Williams, Evelyn, and Adams, Jane. "Learning by the Discovery and Verbal Reception Methods in Bilingual and Unilingual Children." *Journal of Educational Research* 69 (Dec. 1975): 142–45.

79. Witty, Paul. "Some Results of Twelve Yearly Studies of Televiewing." *Science Education* 46 (Apr. 1962): 222–29.

80. Wood, Kenneth S. "Parental Maladjustment and Functional Articulatory Defects in Children." *Journal of Speech and Hearing Disorders* 11 (Dec. 1946): 255–75.

81. Woods, C. Lee. "Social Position and Speaking Competence of Stuttering and Normally Fluent Boys." *Journal of Speech and Hearing Research* 17 (Dec. 1974): 740–47.

82. Yedinack, Jeanette G. "A Study of Linguistic Functioning of Children with Articulation and Reading Difficulties." *Journal of Genetic Psychology* 74 (Mar. 1949): 23–59.

83. Zajonc, R.B., and Markus, Gregory B. "Birth Order and Intellectual Development." *Psychological Review* 82 (Jan. 1975): 74–88.

Using Learning Principles to Make Instruction Effective

. . . vether it's worth while goin' through so much to learn
so little . . . is a matter o' taste.
                        Mr. Weller (Charles Dickens)

We have discussed the importance of planning language arts instruction in terms of long-range outcomes and performance objectives. We have discussed the importance of understanding and appreciating children's previous language experiences if teachers are to develop a communicative instructional environment, one which enables children to improve their basic skills of communication by using what they've already learned. This module is concerned with a third dimension of language arts instruction: the teacher's use of learning principles. There are three factors related to helping children learn that often stand in the way of a teacher's making progress with those children. By unscrambling the italicized words in the next three sentences you can determine what those three factors are:

1. The teacher has to help provide the children with the *otmiavtion* to learn.
2. The teacher has to teach them in such a way that *tenertion* takes place, i.e., "the learning goes in and sticks."
3. The teacher has to handle their *simebahivor,* especially on sunny days when they would rather be outside playing.

Whether you were able to unscramble the three words is not terribly significant at this point. What *is* important is the fact that you're reading this page with at least a slight sense of involvement, perhaps a degree of tension, and maybe even some irritation (depending on how well you did on the scrambled words).

Assuming you *are* slightly involved at this point, what principle of *motivation* was used to get you involved? Was there enough meaning in the unscrambling exercise to aid your *retention* of the three factors? Was the tension just enough to get you ready for learning? Or was the tension so much that *misbehavior,* such as shutting the book or drawing doodles, was the result?

In any case, most college students, whether undergraduate or graduate, are painfully aware of the fact that an instructor may have learned a great deal about a subject but be completely incapable of helping a student learn about that subject. Teachers who know a lot but cannot *transmit* what they know are like giant computers that have become unplugged.

The problem of transmission, of course, can afflict language arts teachers as well as professors of geology or linguistics. Just knowing standard spelling, etc. is not enough. Before this information can be transmitted, the teacher needs to be able to handle three very practical problems:

1. How to motivate children to learn from instruction and learning experiences related to the language arts.
2. How to teach speaking, listening, reading, and writing skills in such a way that children learn them well—and hang on to what they learn.
3. How to manage the child who misbehaves instead of becoming involved in the learning experience.

Your ability to handle these three problems, as well as the problem of communicating with your colleagues about them, is the focus of this module.

Special Prerequisites for Module 3

There are no special prerequisites for this module, other than those communication and thinking abilities assumed to be present among undergraduate and graduate students who are teachers-in-training.

Long-range Outcomes Related to Module 3

This module should help you as a teacher to do the following:

1. Communicate with other professional educators about the use of learning principles in the teaching of the language arts.
2. Motivate a child to learn from instruction and from learning experiences related to the language arts.
3. Teach communication skills in such a way that retention takes place.
4. Manage a child who misbehaves during language arts instruction.

Study Guide and Performance Objectives for Knowledge Level

To give yourself an overview of what is expected of you in this module, you should first scan the objectives and performance standards at all three levels—knowledge, simulation, and teaching. Then use the performance objectives for the knowledge level as a study guide during your reading of the module. *As you find information related to each performance objective write it down in the available space or on a separate sheet of paper.* Then review this information shortly before your knowledge level examination.

1.1 On a closed-book examination you will be given two lists—one list containing some terms related to learning principles and the other list containing some examples of learner or teacher behavior which illustrate those terms. The following are the terms you will need to understand. To help you prepare for the examination, write a definition and/or a brief example next to each. Try to do this from memory as much as possible.

1. positive reinforcement

2. negative reinforcement

3. extinction

4. reinforcement theory

5. feedback

6. mastery

7. positive transfer

8. negative transfer

1.2 On the same examination, you will be presented with samples of teacher behavior in which the teacher is using principles related to *motivating* a child to learn from language arts instruction. After each sample of teacher behavior you will be asked to *recall and write* the principle that the teacher is using. To help you prepare for this part of the examination, try writing the four principles of motivation from memory.

1.

2.

3.

4.

1.3 On the same examination, you will be presented with samples of teacher behavior in which the teacher is using principles related to *teaching language arts skills that stick*. After each sample of teacher behavior, you will be asked to *recall and write* the principle that the teacher is using. To help you prepare for this part of the examination, try writing the four principles of retention from memory.

1.

2.

3.

4.

1.4 On the same examination, you will be presented with samples of teacher behavior in which the teacher is using principles related to *managing a child who misbehaves during language arts instruction.* After each sample of teacher behavior you will be asked to *recall and write* the principle that the teacher is using. To help you prepare for this part of the examination, try writing the five principles of management from memory.

1.

2.

3.

4.

5.

1.5 On the same closed-book examination, you will be presented with samples of teacher behavior in which the teacher is *not* using principles of learning. After each sample of teacher behavior you will be asked to *recall* and *write* the learning principle that is being *violated.*

Performance Standards for Knowledge Level

A. Twenty-five minute time limit on 1.1 through 1.5 combined.

B. Completion deadline: instructor will notify.

C. Recommended grading standards, if grades are used: 96% = A; 92% = A—; 88% = B; 84% = B—; 80% = C; below 80% = incomplete; should be completed at 80% or better before you go on to performance objectives for simulation level. (The instructor may wish to permit a grade of A or B only the first time the test is given in order to encourage more intensive study.)

Performance Objectives for Simulation Level

2.1 On a closed-book examination, you will be given a sample (about ten to fifteen minutes) of a teacher providing language arts instruction. The teacher behavior will either be dramatized or presented on film, video-tape, or audio-tape. (The instructor will select the sample, ask a committee of students to select it, or ask the committee to dramatize a sample of teacher behavior.) You will be asked to write a critique in which you tell what learning principles were utilized and what ones were violated, citing an example in each case.

2.2 (Alternative objective for teachers-in-training *not* on independent study.) With a team of your peers, one acting as the teacher and the rest as the elementary school children, dramatize a *very brief* language arts lesson, taught twice—the first time violating a learning principle and the second time making use of it. The audience should then guess what principle was illustrated. (The instructor may wish to assure that each team illustrates a different principle.)

Performance Standards for Simulation Level

A. For Objective 2.1 (Critique)
   1. The teacher-in-training observes the learning principles which were utilized in the teaching episode and selects appropriate examples from the episode to illustrate those principles.
   2. The teacher-in-training observes the learning principles which were violated in the teaching episode and selects appropriate examples from the episode to illustrate these principles.
   3. Suggested grading standard, if grades are used: should be completed at C level or better before going on to the next module. (Grade is based on judgment of instructor and/or peers.)

B. For Objective 2.2 (Dramatization)
   1. The team dramatizes the learning principle in such a way that the audience has little difficulty deciding what principle was illustrated.
   2. The team demonstrates a clear understanding of the learning principle and does not confuse the audience on the nature of the principle.
   3. Suggested grading standard, if grades are used: should be completed at C level or better before going on to the next module. (A team grade is based on judgment of instructor and/or peers.)

Performance Objectives for Teaching Level

In your micro-teaching, observation, student teaching, intern or supervised teaching situations for later modules, use the principles of learning discussed in this module. The teaching level performance standards for most of the subsequent modules will include "the appropriate use of principles of learning." Therefore, no specific objectives at the teaching level are necessary for the present module. The performance standards which will be used for *subsequent* modules are as follows.

Performance Standards for Teaching Level

A. Uses principles of learning related to motivating children to learn from language arts instruction; does not violate any principles.

B. Uses principles of learning related to teaching language arts skills that "stick"; does not violate any principles.

C. Uses principles of learning related to managing any children who misbehave during the language arts instruction; does not violate any principles.

Terms Often Used
When Discussing Principles of Learning

You are probably already familiar with most of the terms which will be discussed in this section. At this point, you will receive a brief reminder of them. In the following sections they will be used in the context of teaching the language arts.

Positive reinforcement—anything which the learner perceives as a pleasant consequence of his behavior. The positive reinforcer might be in the form of praise, a high score, a good grade (or other symbol), just knowing that he got the correct answer, the vicarious pleasure that comes from reading a good book, or any other kind of pleasurable consequence.

Negative reinforcement—anything which the learner perceives as an unpleasant consequence of her behavior. The negative reinforcer might take the form of a punishment, a frown, a low score, a bad grade (or other symbol), knowing that she got the wrong answer, the frustration that results from reading a book that is too difficult, or any other kind of unpleasant consequence.

Extinction—the elimination or reduction of behavior that receives little or no reinforcement. When a type of behavior is ignored or seems unrewarding, it usually becomes extinct. The classroom humorist who never gets a response, pleasant or unpleasant, eventually seeks another method of getting attention. The humorist behavior is extinguished.

Reinforcement theory—a theory of behavior modification that has been verified by experimental evidence. Reinforcement theory includes these four principles:

1. Positive reinforcement, when applied immediately after a response, makes that response more probable in the future. For example, when the butter is passed immediately after Billy says, "Please pass the butter," he is more likely to say the same thing the next time he wants the butter.

2. Negative reinforcement, when applied immediately after a response, makes that response less probable in the future. It also makes the response which *takes away* the negative reinforcement *more* probable. For example, when Billy receives a dirty look for saying, "Please pass the dratted butter," he is less likely to say that again. He is more likely to try something that takes away the frown, such as asking sweetly, "Please pass the butter," or such as reaching far across the table for the butter when the frowner isn't looking.

3. Extinction of a response occurs when little or no reinforcement, positive or negative, follows the response. For instance, Billy asks for the butter nicely seven times without getting any response. His "asking nicely" behavior is becoming extinct.

4. Behavior is strengthened and extinction avoided by *scheduling* the positive reinforcement. In general, the reinforcement must be applied very frequently at first and then gradually diminished. For example, a good way to make Billy's "asking nicely" behavior strong and resistant to extinction is first to praise him every time he does it, then approximately every other time, then every fifth or sixth time, and so on (making sure, of course, that he gets the butter when he asks for it.)

Feedback—information given to the learner about whether she's right or wrong, or how well she is doing, or what she's doing right, or what she's doing wrong. Such information generally becomes either a positive reinforcer or a negative reinforcer. Feedback may take the form of a nod or shake of the head, a yes or no, a specific comment, a score, a grade, a passing of the butter, or any other response which informs the learner about the desirability of his behavior.

Mastery—a level of skill or understanding that is high enough to meet specified criteria or standards of accomplishment. Learning for mastery is essentially what you're doing with this module. You are striving to master the material in this module well enough to meet the standards specified for the module's performance objectives. (Mastery does not necessarily mean 100 percent, as the specified standard for mastery might be only 80 or 90 percent.)

Positive transfer—the effect that previous learning has in *helping* one learn something new. When Billy has success in getting the butter by asking for it nicely, positive transfer will likely occur when he tries to get the salt. Asking for the salt and asking for the butter are similar learning tasks; learning one of them will help Billy learn the other much more easily.

Negative transfer—the effect that previous learning has in *hindering* one who is trying to learn something new. When Billy eats lunch in a poorly supervised school cafeteria, he may find that he misses out on the butter for a day or two. His asking for it nicely doesn't seem to work; in fact, it interferes with his new learning task—getting the butter in a "not-nice" place.

How to Motivate Children to Learn from Language Arts Instruction

Four principles of motivation are discussed in this section. Neither these four principles nor the nine principles described in later sections are meant to be all-inclusive. They are presented, rather, as minimal tools for effective teaching of the language arts and are based on research done by educators and behavioral scientists.

Like other principles, they have their exceptions and will not always work exactly as teachers would desire them to. When they don't work, however, it's often because teachers haven't observed carefully enough the many variables that interact in a crowded classroom. With practice, along with critical evaluation of your practice, you will probably find these principles working more and more frequently. If you feel the need at the end of this module for greater understanding of these learning principles, you are urged to examine the programmed booklets written by Hunter (5, 6, 7, 8, 9).

Principle 1: Help Satisfy Basic Needs

According to Maslow's well-known theory of motivation (12), human beings have six basic types of needs: the physiological need; the need for physical and psychological safety; the need for belonging and love; the need for esteem from self and others; the need for self-actualization; and the need for knowledge, understanding, and beauty. The physiological needs for food, warmth, sleep, and so on are generally dominant until they are at least partially satisfied. Once satisfied, however, they give way to the need for safety (security, stability, structure). Having satisfied the physiological need and the safety need, human beings are then usually dominated by the need for belonging (love, companionship, friendship, affection).

As each set of needs is satisfied, the next set in the hierarchy takes over—after love, the need for esteem (importance, success, self-respect, recognition); after esteem, the need for self-actualization (self-fulfillment, satisfying one's potential, meeting one's self-ideal, doing what one is fitted for); and, finally, after self-actualization, the need that relates most to schooling (knowledge, understanding, and beauty). This hierarchy of needs is shown graphically in Figure 3.1.

Generally speaking, then, the "lower" needs—physiological, safety, love, and esteem—must be at least partially met before the "higher" needs of self-actualization and intellectual understanding will emerge. What this means, in a practical sense, is that the teacher who ignores Bobby's lower needs will find it difficult to motivate him to learn something just to satisfy his intellectual curiosity or his desire to become a more skilled person. These so-called lower needs must be dealt with during the entire school day, of course, but even during a brief lesson a teacher who is conscious of them can be more successful than one who ignores them.[1]

---

[1] The word *lesson* is a convenient term for designating a structured learning experience. A lesson may be carried on with or without the presence of a teacher, e.g., with an individual worksheet or programmed booklet.

FIGURE 3.1   The Ladder of Human Needs

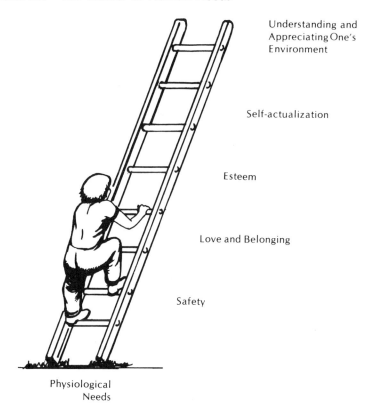

Understanding and
Appreciating One's
Environment

Self-actualization

Esteem

Love and Belonging

Safety

Physiological
Needs

Let's take, for example, the physiological needs of oxygen and exercise. Teachers may easily fall short of motivating children simply because they have failed to make sure that everyone has enough oxygen. Without a sufficient supply of oxygen, the brain becomes sluggish, curiosity dies, and boredom is the response to your frantic efforts to teach. Making sure there is plenty of fresh air in your classroom is a help, of course, but it's often not enough. What some teachers have discovered is that some type of invigorating activity at periodic intervals is essential to most children throughout the day. Such activity, rather than interfering with learning, actually seems to enhance it.

This doesn't mean that your classroom must be conducted like a three-ring circus, of course. It does mean, though, that large-muscle movement should be frequently encouraged. Even if you do no more than ask them to touch their toes before they sit down for a reading lesson, you will stand a better chance of getting their intellectual attention. And during the lesson, you can get them up to the board occasionally or have them pantomime a word or sentence. (Some teachers behave as though their students were bodiless minds: lavatory use is strictly scheduled, getting out of seats without permission is forbidden, and one intellectual activity follows another without any break for a physical activity.)

Which of these times would be best for having a session of dancing, rhythms, or dramatic play?

1. Just before recess so they can take their noise and excitement outside afterwards.

2. Between two quiet intellectual sessions so they get the exercise they need.
3. Right after recess because they'll be calmer then.

Hopefully you decided to use the dancing, rhythms, or dramatic play as an opportunity for plenty of movement—a chance for a physical break between two intellectual activities.

Now let's talk about the need for safety or security. This need can be met during language arts instruction in a number of ways: by providing each child with success, by accepting mistakes as natural allies of learning, and by assuring that the instruction is carried on under reasonably orderly conditions. Obviously, children are not going to feel secure if a lesson confronts them with a series of failures. To be motivated to engage in an intellectual exercise, they must experience success during that exercise. Nor are children going to feel secure if they perceive an intolerant attitude toward their mistakes. Nor will they feel secure if other children are continually misbehaving and things seem out of control to them.

In a spelling lesson, you ask Jimmy to circle a VCE word and he circles a VC word.[2] Which of these would be your best response?

1. Boys and girls, did Jimmy circle the right kind of word?
2. No, Jimmy, you weren't listening. You'd better sit down.
3. Not quite, Jimmy. You've circled a VC word. See if you can circle a VCE word.

You might argue that Response 1 would be the best response because it would keep the rest of the kids alert. That's true, it would. They'd be all ready to pounce as soon as one of their friends went up to the board. But think of the harmful side effects that might be incurred: a loss of security, a loss of a sense of belonging, and a loss of esteem, all in one blow. Response 2 would certainly not give the child a feeling of success; it would more than likely have a negative effect on his sense of security. Only in the case where the teacher feels the need to use negative reinforcement with a nonlistener would this type of response be a useful one. (See section on misbehavior.)

Response 3 does provide the child with an opportunity for success without destroying his sense of security. Thus, it would probably motivate him to continue learning.

Sarah is a second grader with a minor articulation problem. Her teacher feels that Sarah is a "needy" child. Sarah's need for love (affection, warmth, friendliness, and sense of belonging), like the need for security and the physiological needs, has to be considered throughout the school day. But even during a single lesson it can be partially met by letting her know that you and her peers are on her side in her efforts to improve her communication skills. In order to meet both the need for security and the need for a sense of belong-

---

[2]A VC word is a one-syllable word like *cat* or *sip,* with the end of the word spelled with a vowel letter (V) and a consonant letter (C). A VCE word is a one-syllable word like *cape* or *pipe,* in which the final e is silent and the vowel sound is long.

ing, children should be vigorously discouraged from making fun of those who make mistakes. This effort is made considerably easier, of course, when the teacher refrains from careless smiles and sarcastic remarks.

Instead of reading "I see three cookies on the table," Sarah reads it, "I see free cookies on the table." What would be the best response for the teacher to make? (The answer should be obvious.)

1. Sarah, let me help you make the *th* sound. Watch my mouth.
2. Sarah, I've told you many times—the *th* digraph is not pronounced like *f*.
3. Free! I didn't know the cookies were free. Did you, boys and girls?

The need for esteem can be met during a lesson by making Jimmy and Sarah feel important to you and their peers. A child who is rarely called upon, for example, is not going to feel very important. And yet, this can easily happen when teachers hurry to cover the material or call on only the brightest students in order to avoid the effort of teaching the slower ones. (This tends to happen especially when teachers are tired.)

Ms. Ronalds has decided to use a bit of team competition on a spelling game. Which would be the best way for her to select the teams?

1. Let two captains choose up the sides. This is the way they're used to doing it on the playground.
2. Ms. Ronalds should choose the teams, carefully balancing them with strong and weak players.
3. Let each child draw blindly from a set of cards labeled Team A and Team B, because this is fairest.

If Ms. Ronalds lets captains choose the teams, how important will the last two people chosen feel? Perhaps the playground approach should be reserved for the playground. Ms. Ronalds should be more concerned with human needs than with proper form. If she is skillful enough, she might be able to choose the teams herself without harming anyone's sense of importance. Sometimes, though, the chance approach works best, especially if you firmly discourage the children from cheering the good guys. (Some teachers feel that team competition on academic games is not worth the negative side effects and use individual or cooperative-type games instead.)

When teachers are aware of a child's physiological needs and his needs for security, belonging, and importance, they are much more likely to motivate the child toward self-actualization and intellectual understanding. The need for self-actualization, for most children, includes the desire to communicate better. *Most* children seem to perceive communication as "adult" and something they would like to be able to do as skillfully as adults do. Children who seem not to *want* to learn how to communicate better ("disadvantaged" children from all ethnic groups and economic strata) are frequently those who have been unable to meet their "lower" needs. Attempts to motivate such children without taking their needs into account will often be unsuccessful.

Principle 2: Teach at the Appropriate Level of Difficulty

Perhaps this principle is violated more than any other principle of motivation. Most teachers learn quickly from experience that a learning task which is too easy for children will be boring and one that is too hard will cause them to withdraw. This is easy enough to see, but what can be done about it? How can you select a learning task that will be just the right level of difficulty for each child?

Probably you can't. But to successfully motivate children, you have to make the attempt to come as close as possible to a task that will challenge them but not overly frustrate them. As an illustration of this point, let's take Coach Cassidy, a track coach, working with a high jumper named Phil. Coach Cassidy puts the cross bar down fairly low the first time, so that Phil can clear it easily. Then he raises it slightly so that a little more effort has to be expended by Phil the next time. Then the coach raises it again, not so high that Phil misses and becomes frustrated, but just high enough to make him put a little more effort into the jump than he did the time before. This same gradual increase is continued, making the task hard enough to be challenging but easy enough to be positively reinforcing: high enough to spur on the jumper to greater achievement, low enough to assure success. *Success and difficulty go hand in hand to motivate the learner.*

For the language arts teacher, the task of finding the right level of difficulty is not as easy. A major step in the right direction, however, is to teach

Success and difficulty go hand in hand to motivate the learner.

diagnostically. This means finding out, through observation and informal testing procedures, the specific communication difficulties each child has. (Making an observation check list based on the long-range outcomes listed in Module 1 is a good way to begin this diagnostic process.)

Having assessed the levels and problems of each pupil, you will often be able either to (1) teach them individually, (2) form small groups of pupils who are experiencing the same difficulties, or (3) form groups of those who are on approximately the same developmental level. But suppose you're still not sure whether the lesson you're about to use with a group of children is really at their level of difficulty? One approach is to present your follow-up worksheet at the *beginning* of the lesson. Those who feel they can do the worksheet without your help are then excused from the group lesson. Those who cannot are often motivated to learn from the lesson so that they, too, can complete the worksheet. This works pretty well for children in the upper grades, but for children in the first two or three grades it can be too frustrating an experience, particularly if the lesson is developmental rather than review. For children in the early grades, it may be better to abbreviate your lesson, if most of the group do seem to be grasping it, and to spend the extra time working with the few who do not, while the rest move on to a follow-up worksheet.

In very few cases, however, is it advisable to ignore the difficulties that some children may be having, thinking "they'll get it when they're older." There is nothing more dampening to motivation than to have one concept after another go by you and to fall farther and farther behind. (More about this will be discussed under Principle 5.) Nor is it advisable in your planning to overlook the prerequisites for the lesson. By carefully listing in your mind (or on paper) the concepts which the children need before they can understand the lesson and by teaching those prerequisite concepts first, you can avoid a serious motivation problem.

In some instances, of course, the teacher can handle this type of motivation problem by using a highly individualized program which allows a great deal of self-pacing, such as IPI (Individually Prescribed Instruction) or IGE (Individually Guided Education). Some teachers would argue, however, that it is often more efficient and conducive to learning to use *some* type of flexible grouping; i.e., those children experiencing similar difficulties should be grouped temporarily and given help at the same time.

Halfway through a lesson on finding the root in words having an *ed* suffix, you notice that Ronny understands it well and is looking quite bored. Which of these might be best to do?

1. Challenge him to find the root in some nonsense words like *ruckled* or some hard words like *investigated*.

2. Do nothing special for him, as extra practice never hurt anyone.

3. Tell him that since he thinks he knows so much perhaps he'd like to take over the lesson.

Hopefully, you decided to challenge him with difficult or nonsense words. That extra practice excuse, which teachers sometimes use to cover an inability to assess students' levels and disabilities, may be just the thing that makes Ronny decide that spelling is no fun. The implied criticism in Alternative 3 may cause Ronny to please you by erasing his look of boredom, but it won't eliminate his real frustration at being forced to learn something he already knows.

During a lesson on the VCE pattern, you discover that only two of the children have mastered the long and short sounds of the vowel letters. What should you do?

1. Postpone your lesson on the VCE pattern and teach all of the long and short sounds of the vowel letters.
2. Have the two children do something else while you teach the rest of the group the long and short sounds of the vowel letters.
3. Continue the lesson the best you can; otherwise, you may never cover what you're expected to cover in a year's time.

If you selected Alternative 3, you deserve a "brownie point" for dogged determination in the face of conflicting evidence, but it is doubtful that you'll win a prize for the year's most successful teacher. Is it really true that "they" expect you to cover certain material, or is the real expectation (or hope) that you'll truly improve your pupils' abilities to communicate?

If you selected Alternative 1, you have shown your awareness of the need for prerequisite learning to take place before a new concept is taught. However, since two of the children already have the prerequisite learning, wouldn't it be best to have them do something else while you work with the rest?

Principle 3: Provide Frequent and Specific Feedback

In brief, the procedure for following Principle 3 is to present a small amount of information (probably the more inexperienced the students, the smaller the amount) and to follow it with a request for some type of response from the students: answering a question, circling something on the board, completing a worksheet, pantomiming what has been described, etc. Feedback is then provided to the students in the form of a nod of approval, the correct answer to compare with their own answer, a score, a token, or whatever will inform them about the adequacy of their understanding. (You may have noticed that this module follows this principle.)

If you have been skillful in presenting information, the feedback you give will usually be positive reinforcement, and the students will want to continue learning. With elementary school children, it is generally best to expose them to information for only a very brief period of time (often only a few seconds) before having them respond in some way and giving them feedback related to their responses.

You are planning to show an information film to your fourth grade class in order to prepare them for some social studies drama they will be doing. Which of these procedures would be best?

1. Show the film without stopping and give a test at the end of it.
2. Stop the film every few minutes, ask a question, have them write a brief answer, discuss the answer briefly before proceeding.
3. Show the film without stopping, ask the children if they enjoyed it, tell them that maybe you'll show another film next week.

If you selected Procedure 3, you should be paid for baby-sitting. If you selected Procedure 1, you are at least thinking about feedback—providing you go over the test with them immediately after the film. On the other hand, wouldn't they have higher motivation during the film and also learn more from it if you were to stop the film every few minutes, ask a question, have them write a brief answer (to make sure everyone is involved), and then give them immediate feedback by discussing the answer? (This procedure, of course, is *not* recommended when your major aim in showing the film is to provide an emotional experience for the children.)

In addition to motivating your pupils with *frequent* feedback, you should also make the feedback as *specific* as possible. Which type of *oral* feedback for a worksheet would probably be the most motivating?

1. Your grade on this was C—, John. You must try harder on the next one.

2. You missed five out of twenty on this, John. Not bad . . . Not bad . . . Could be better, but not bad.

3. You have a good understanding of the VCE pattern, John. You missed only one of the questions on that. Since you missed four of the words with a VC pattern, perhaps I should help you a bit more on that. Now, do you see this word here? It has . . . .

If you picked the last alternative you probably already have a good understanding of the importance of specific feedback to both motivation and improved learning. Naturally by *specific* it is not meant that the teacher should employ only negative criticism; a good measure of specific *praise* is also necessary. But if the praise is simply "Good work, John," or "Keep up the good work," John is not going to know what particular things he did well. Consequently, most of the positive reinforcement goes down the drain, and John has to guess what it

Motivation is enhanced by frequent and specific feedback.

was that you liked so much. Of course, there are times when it is perfectly obvious what you're praising him for, but when it's not so obvious, it pays to be specific.

Principle 4: Add Novelty to Learning Experiences

This principle is perhaps so simple it needn't be discussed. But what about the children who daily suffer the tedium of teaching procedures and workbook formats which never vary? The novelty principle may be simple and obvious, but how often we teachers ignore it, although it's easy to understand why a tired, harrassed elementary school teacher might prefer the comfort of familiarity.

Following the novelty principle needn't be as time-consuming and energy consuming for the teacher as it sounds. Something as simple as having the children occasionally write on butcher paper with a felt pen instead of the usual chalkboard routine often is enough to cause a sharp rise in motivation. Or sitting on the floor instead of on chairs. Or writing in the afternoon instead of morning. Or using sign language for part of the lesson. Or using a game for part of the lesson. Or giving a different piece of colored chalk to each child to use on the board. All these are little things that take a bit of imagination but not much extra energy on the teacher's part.

Which of these presentations of a follow-up assignment might be the most motivating?

1. All right, boys and girls, please get out your workbooks and turn to page 186.
2. Well, as usual, boys and girls, the person who gets his worksheet all right will get a gold star on his paper.
3. Here's your airplane, I mean, your worksheet. Just unfold it, and we'll look at the directions together.

It's true that the teacher who makes the worksheets into airplanes will have to spend a few extra minutes of preparation time. And naturally it would lose its novelty effect if it were done very often. But it will raise the motivational level a notch, especially if the children know you'll let them fly the airplanes during recess (as soon as you've given them feedback on their work).

How to Teach Communication Skills That Stick

Let's assume that by concerning yourself with their basic needs and by using the principles related to novelty, feedback, and difficulty, you have now sufficiently motivated your students; they are *ready* to learn certain concepts necessary for skilled communication. How should these be taught? Is there a way for children to experience them so that they understand them quickly and well—so well they don't forget them in a few weeks? To answer this question, we must consider four additional principles of learning.

Principle 5: Teach for Mastery

In a nutshell, this principle means to teach with thoroughness and meaningfulness. It means to avoid covering material for the sake of covering. It means to teach toward the accomplishment of specific objectives. And, it means that what is taught should be clear and make sense to the learner.

Three of the following practices would be helpful in encouraging learning for mastery. Which practice would *not* encourage mastery?

1. Planning lessons in terms of performance objectives.
2. Dividing the reading text by the number of school days and assigning that many pages each day.
3. Basing the content of a lesson on the children's previous experiences.
4. Comparing and contrasting the concept you're teaching with other concepts.

The use of performance objectives, of course, implies that you *are* teaching for mastery. A performance objective requires very specific accomplishments for a lesson and helps the teacher think about what level of mastery is sufficient. It almost forces you to teach for mastery. Procedure 2, believe it or not, is the procedure used by some teachers—understandably, too, if their goal is coverage rather than mastery.

Procedure 3 is one which adds meaning to the lesson, encourages positive transfer from previous learning to new learning, and, therefore, aids in the goal of mastery. Procedure 3 is one of the best means of adding depth of meaning to a concept, thus making it easier to master.

But why teach for mastery? Who cares whether children master what you teach them? Isn't it enough to simply introduce them to something and let them master it later if they want to? These are very appealing questions, ones which often arise when the teacher is tired and discouraged, and ready to give up on Betty or Tommy. And, undoubtedly there *are* some things which should only be introduced rather than mastered—things that lie in the realm of appreciations, such as listening to symphonic music or having an enjoyable craft experience.

But what about basic communication skills that people are expected to have and use throughout their lives; skills which, if not acquired, will often cause people to think of themselves as failures. Here it seems that we're talking about things that should be learned very well indeed. What happens, for example, to Shauna when she doesn't master what is taught in one lesson, and another, and still another? Her accumulated failures being to interfere with future learning (a case of negative transfer). Furthermore, she gradually develops a habit of *not* learning and forms a picture of herself as a person who is incapable of learning. Teaching for mastery can help avoid such negative self-concepts.

To make the concept of mastery more meaningful to you, imagine yourself taking a foreign language course. During the first week, you are expected to learn thirty words, but you only learn twenty of them. During the second week, you are expected to learn thirty more words, but you only learn fifteen of them.

Already your first week's failure has probably made it more difficult for you to learn the words for the second week. During the third week, you are expected to learn thirty more; and, of course, all along you have been expected to use the words in spoken sentences and understand them when used by others. By the end of the third week, what attitude are you *not* likely to have?

1. I'm really a dummy when it comes to learning a foreign language.
2. This instructor is sure a lousy teacher.
3. Hey, this is fun. I think I can get it!

Suppose that you have decided that Janice, a seven year old, needs to learn to spell sixteen spelling demons. You provide her with a set of flashcards with the words printed on them and ask her to practice writing the words. How should she practice them each day so that mastery is obtained?

1. Eight words the first day, eight more the second day, and all sixteen on the third day.
2. Four words the first day, the same four plus four more the second day, the same eight plus four more the third day, the same twelve plus four more the fourth day, all sixteen the fifth day, all sixteen three or four days later, only those she's still having trouble with the next day, all sixteen the next day, all sixteen two weeks later.
3. All sixteen every day until she gets them all right.

This time the answer was perhaps not quite as obvious. Only one approach avoids covering too much at one time, thus eliminating the problem of accumulated failures interfering with new learning. Which one is that? (The same one that provides a review of words already learned.)

   In brief, mastery is best obtained by not covering too much new information at once.

Principle 6: Provide Massed Practice Followed by Distributed Practice

One might think that this principle means simply to give lots of practice and to review often. But it's not as simple as that. If Janice has learned to spell a word that has quite a bit of meaning, such as *mother* or her own name, she'll remember it with little or no practice. But for less meaningful words like *their, right,* and *already,* it is likely that she'll need massed practice at first followed by distributed practice later. The example of Janice learning to spell sixteen spelling demons, discussed under Principle 5, demonstrates this type of practice. Frequent, closely spaced practice of only a few new words is provided at first, making sure that the child is spelling the words correctly. This is followed by practice that is distributed over several days or weeks, with the space between practice periods getting longer and longer.

There is no magic formula for this distribution. It will depend on how meaningful the material is, how motivated the child is, and what problems the child is having in learning the material. The main things to remember in developing a practice schedule are (1) the student may need considerable guidance in the introductory session; (2) the practice sessions which immediately follow the introductory session should be brief, frequent, and closely spaced; and (3) the remaining practice sessions should be farther and farther apart.

Which of these do you think is the best schedule of practice for learning to punctuate dialogue?

1. During a twenty minute lesson, with a ten minute worksheet right after the lesson, for three minutes before going home, three minutes twice the next day, three minutes once the following day, three minutes once during the following week, and just occasionally for the rest of the year.

2. During a forty minute lesson, a twenty minute worksheet, and a five minute review once a week for the rest of the year.

3. During a ten minute lesson, a ten minute worksheet, and a five minute review once a week for the rest of the year.

If you decided that the first schedule would provide the children with massed practice at first and distributed practice thereafter, you were right. Schedule 2 is not as uncommon as it should be, although frequently the review period is omitted.

Mr. Skippy, for example, often uses this schedule, *not* because he is striving for mastery but rather because he is striving for greater coverage. That is, he wants to cover as many concepts as possible in a single lesson. For instance, Mr. Skippy might try to teach a single lesson on spelling words with a VV pattern, such as *boat, bait,* and *beat,* without first having three separate lessons: (1) long *o* in a VV pattern (*boat, soap, toad*), (2) long *a* in a VV pattern (*bait, paid, chain*), and (3) long *e* in a VV pattern (*beat, seal, leaf*). Except for a review lesson, trying to teach all of this in one lesson would be too much, not only because of the overload of information but because of the fatigue factor.

Schedule 3 has the virtue of brevity but probably doesn't allow for enough guided practice at first. Nor does it follow reinforcement theory, in that positive reinforcement (praise and/or correct answers) which is given so regularly is not as effective in strengthening a response as positive reinforcement that is gradually diminished in frequency. In other words, a five minute review once a week (with positive reinforcement for correct answers) would probably not be as effective as the distributed schedule suggested in Schedule 1.

Principle 7: Get Everyone Involved in Each Step

If you want maximum learning to take place, make an attempt to get *each* child involved in *each* problem you pose, *each* question you ask, *each* step along the way. (Naturally, this is a goal rather than something you can continuously accomplish.)

Which of these approaches would get the most students involved in Mr. Sanchez's class?

1. John, would you please go to the board and circle a word with the VCE pattern? (Mr. Sanchez watches John.)
2. Now I'd like someone to go to the board and circle a word with the VCE pattern. (Mr. Sanchez looks from one child to the next.)
3. Whose turn is it to go to the board? Mary? Ok, you go to the board and circle a word with the VCE pattern. (Mr. Sanchez watches Mary.)
4. Now, boys and girls, please watch while I circle the words that have a VCE pattern.

Approach 4 requires the responsibility of no one but the teacher, although he might *hope* that all the children will actually watch and think about what they're watching. Unfortunately, this is often a vain hope. Very little tension or challenge has been developed; all that the children have to do is tilt their heads in the direction of the board, thus fooling Mr. Sanchez into thinking that learning is taking place.

Approach 1 and Approach 3 require the responsibility of one child, but the others are free to dream and scheme. The only approach which is likely to get them *all* involved is 2, since none of the children is sure who's going to be called upon next. (Naturally this approach can't be used *all* of the time.)

Now let's try another situation. Which of these would encourage the most involvement?

1. Present a little bit of information, give them a problem or question, present a little more information, give them a problem or question, present a little more information.
2. Present all your information at once and then ask if there are any questions. Then say, "Well if there are no questions, I assume you understand it perfectly."
3. Present a problem or question, give them a little bit of information, present another problem or question, give them a little more information, present another problem or question.

Did you recognize Method 2 as a familiar approach? It is used frequently by some teachers; however, this method does not get students actively involved.

Either Method 1 or 3 would work much better, with Method 3 usually having a slight edge. For example, children would probably get more involved in a listening exercise on auditory discrimination if you began with a problem, e.g., "Who can tell me a word that has the same beginning sound as the word *pet*?" rather than beginning the lesson with information, e.g., "The three words on the board all begin with the /p/ sound."

Why does active involvement seem to increase learning and retention? For one thing, by getting a student personally involved, you've increased the amount of emotional impact that the instruction has; learning that takes place "with feeling" generally is retained longer. In addition, the personal in-volvement results in the student's receiving a greater amount of feedback and reinforcement, usually of a positive nature if you've done a good job of teach-ing. Positive reinforcement strengthens the desire to learn; feedback provides the learner with a check on how well she is doing.

Active involvement increases learning and retention.

Which of these activities will probably produce the greatest amount of learning? One of them is not a good activity for active involvement, and it's a tossup between the other two. As a bit of novelty, you'll receive *no* feedback on this problem.

1. All of you close your eyes and put your finger on your chin when-ever you hear a word with the sound of long *a* in it.

2. Jackie, will you help the girls and boys by putting up your hand whenever you hear a word with the sound of long *a* in it.

3. All right, see if you can catch me. I'm going to say ten words after you close your eyes. The words which have a long *a* sound in them I'll say louder than the rest, *but* I might make a mistake. You put your fingers on your chin when you think I've made a mistake.

Principle 8: Help Positive Transfer Occur

Positive transfer, you may remember, is the effect that previous learning has in helping a person learn something new. Teachers and researchers have discov-ered, however, that positive transfer often does not take place automatically. Rather, it takes place only when the learner *perceives the similarity* between one learning situation and a later learning situation. And frequently, the similarity has to be drawn to the learner's attention by the teacher. In which of the following situations would positive transfer most likely take place?

1. Learning to write *cat,* followed soon by learning to write *mouse.*
2. A lesson on writing the letter *b,* followed soon by a lesson on writing the letter *d.*
3. Learning to write *cat,* followed soon by learning to write *cats.*
4. A lesson on spelling the long *a* sound in a VCE pattern (e.g., *bake*), followed soon by a lesson in spelling the long *i* sound in a VCE pattern (e.g., *bike*).

Very little positive transfer can take place in Alternative 1 since it would be difficult for the learner to perceive any similarity between the writing of *cat* and *mouse.* In Alternative 2, the learner might perceive the similarity between the two learning situations, all right; but that's just the problem. Rather than positive transfer taking place, you are more likely to have negative transfer. In fact, children often get *b* and *d* confused, especially if one is introduced before the other one is learned quite well. (Once the two have become confused, all you can do is bring them together in the same lesson and show the learner how the two of them *differ.*)

In Alternative 3, the learning of the word *cat* will probably help the child learn the word *cats,* particularly if she learns the word *cat* quite well before the word *cats* is introduced and particularly if the teacher helps the child to see what it is that makes the two words similar and different. Alternative 4 is also conducive to positive transfer, providing again that the long *a* in a VCE pattern is first mastered and providing the teacher helps the child to see the essential similarity between the two situations.

Of course there's an obvious type of transfer which the language arts teacher wants to take place: to have children spell words that they need in "letters to Grandma" just the way they learn to spell them in a spelling lesson. This is why many teachers try to provide practice in *context* during the course of a lesson. By having children write a word in the context of a meaningful sentence, the teachers make the practice during instruction very similar to the long-range skill they're trying to develop. Thus, positive transfer is more likely to occur.

How to Manage a Child Who Misbehaves during Language Arts Instruction

Having learned about the principles related to mastery, involvement, transfer, and practice, you may be determined to use them when you teach communication skills. But what if a child misbehaves so much while you're trying to teach, you find yourself too busy with a discipline problem to do much in the way of instruction?

There are at least three approaches to this type of problem, and in some cases, all three need to be tried. First, you might ask yourself whether you are violating any of the principles related to motivation. Is Ned restless, for example, because you've given him little chance to use his large muscles? Does he feel a loss of status because of the way you called him to the instructional group? Is the lesson too easy or hard for him?

Secondly, you might ask yourself whether you are violating any of the principles related to retention. Are you going so fast that he can't master one step before moving on to the next? Are you getting him involved with each problem or question?

Thirdly, you may decide to use the behavior modification approach, based on reinforcement theory. This approach involves the following five principles.

Principle 9: Help the Child Understand Exactly What Behavior You Expect

Let's say, for example, that Cleo continually talks to her neighbor instead of following your carefully structured review lesson on spelling with the VV pattern, a lesson which she seems to need very much, judging from her poor performance on her last spelling test. Her neighbor listens to Cleo and giggles but doesn't say anything. Which of these might be the best thing to do with Cleo first?

1. Send her out into the hall so she won't bother the others who really want to learn.
2. Tell her to stop talking. This makes it clear to everyone that talking bothers you.
3. Tell her—directly or indirectly—that talking now, instead of listening, will keep her from learning what she needs to know.

The answer should be fairly clear-cut. By sending Cleo into the hall, she won't learn what you want her to learn. By telling her to stop talking, you've only told her what *not* to do. By letting her know that her behavior is interfering with her chance to learn something she needs, you have helped her realize what behavior you want.

With some children, of course, you have to be pretty obvious, e.g., "What do you think you should do, Cleo, to help you learn what I'm going to teach you?" With others you can go about this more indirectly, e.g., "I like the way most of you are listening carefully. Since all of you had trouble with this on that test I gave last week, I hope you'll all listen hard so you won't have any more trouble with it." If neither approach gets you anywhere, you may have to resort to using negative reinforcement (see Principle 12).

Principle 10: Use Positive Reinforcement for the Behavior You Desire

Since Cleo missed out on the praise given for good listening, let's suppose that she eagerly answers a question you ask concerning the spelling of a VV word. What should you do?

1. Ask her to please raise her hand and wait to be called on when she has anything to say.
2. Praise her for listening so well to your question.
3. Praise her for "really knowing about the VV pattern."

Perhaps this answer was not quite so obvious as the last one. It's true that she didn't raise her hand, and by accepting her answer you might be reinforcing another type of behavior you don't like. (The plot thickens—as it so often does in the act of teaching.) However, since your major concern at this moment is that of helping Cleo learn something she needs to know in order to spell better, probably it would be best to ignore temporarily the other behavior that bothers you. (If Cleo begins to "hog the show" by answering all the questions, you'll have to modify *that* behavior, of course.)

What about praising her for "really knowing about the VV pattern"? This is a bit premature. After only one response from her, you don't have enough evidence. Besides, the behavior you're trying to change at the moment

Positive behavior is reinforced by positive reinforcement.

is her talking. So, the best way to reward her is to praise her for the behavior you temporarily desire—that of paying attention to your instruction.

Is praise the only reinforcement possible in this situation? No, not if her answer is correct. Just by answering your question correctly she is being rewarded for listening. Whether you use praise as an additional reinforcement should depend on the child and how well that child responds to praise. What if Cleo just sits there quietly, without answering any questions? Well, if you want behavior to recur, remember, it has to be reinforced. Which of these would you do?

1. I wouldn't rock the boat. Since she's listening so well, she'll be reinforced by getting her worksheet correct after the lesson.

2. Praise her for listening so well and call on her shortly after that to answer a question.

3. Call on her to answer a question and praise her for listening so well if she gets the answer right.

Alternative 1 is a bit risky. How do you know she's listening? How do you know she'll do well on the worksheet? Alternative 3 won't work too well if she gets the answer wrong. You'll increase your chances of having her answer one correctly if you praise her for listening shortly *before* you ask her a question.

Principle 11: If Possible, Ignore Misbehavior That Is New to a Child

Suppose that talking to her neighbor during a reading lesson is a new type of behavior for Cleo, or one that occurs very infrequently. What would be the best thing to do about it when you see it occur?

1. Pretend that you don't even notice it, while, at the same time, you praise others for listening so well.

2. Nip it in the bud. Let her know immediately that she is misbehaving. That way, the habit will never get started.

3. After she sees you looking at her, ignore her completely.

It might be tempting to select Alternative 2 and nip it in the bud. By using negative reinforcement of this sort you might be able to suppress her behavior temporarily, but you won't extinguish it. In fact, for some children, the attention you give them by scolding is a form of *positive* reinforcement. By scolding, you put them in the spotlight and perhaps even give them a bit of prestige.

If you chose 3 you may be in for trouble, for essentially you're saying that even though you saw her misbehaving, it doesn't really matter to you. Alternative 1 is probably the best response—*providing the behavior is new or very infrequent.* By ignoring the behavior, you may provide the opportunity for the behavior to go unrewarded (depending on how much reinforcement she gets from her neighbor) and, thus, to become extinct.

Principle 12: Use Negative Reinforcement When Positive Reinforcement Fails to Get the Desired Response (Be Aware of Possible Side Effects)

Let's say that Cleo doesn't care whether you praise others for listening, that she gives you no opportunity for rewarding her in any way, and that your ignoring her seems to encourage her to talk louder and louder and to generally disrupt your instruction. What should you do?

1. Send her to the principal who is trained to handle problems like this.
2. Tell her that since she's missed part of the lesson by talking, she'll have to stay in for part of the recess to learn what she missed.
3. Warn her to stop talking or she'll be in trouble.

Procedure 1 is a way of telling the child that she's too much for you to handle. Sometimes one has to admit defeat like this, but obviously it's not solving your problem very well, particularly since Cleo is missing a spelling lesson that she needs. Procedure 3 may suppress the undesired behavior, but the warning is so vague it may have an undesirable side effect. Instead of paying attention to the rest of your lesson, she may spend several minutes wondering just what kind of trouble she might be in if she talks to her neighbor again.

Procedure 2, or something like it, would clearly indicate not only what behavior you *don't* want but also what behavior you *do* want. In addition, it signals to her that the more she misses of the lesson, the more she'll miss a chance to talk to her friends during recess. Of course, it may also have the undesirable side effect of making her think of you as an "old meanie," the type of side effect which often occurs with the use of negative reinforcement. However, during the first few minutes of recess, you can cancel out some of this by briefly and kindly explaining to her what behavior is important during a lesson, by asking her to listen carefully while you briefly check her comprehension of the previous lesson, by praising her for correctly answering your questions, and by sending her out for the rest of recess *immediately* after reviewing the lesson—don't spoil the effect by scolding her once more before dismissing her.

The approach advocated for Cleo is not the approach to use with all children who interrupt a lesson by talking to their neighbors. It is merely one illustration of how negative reinforcement can be used, if necessary. The *principle* of negative reinforcement is the important thing to grasp, of course, rather than the exact language used by the teacher in the hypothetical situation just discussed.

Principle 13: Schedule the Positive Reinforcement Motivating Them to Learn

Unfortunately, permanent behavior modification seldom occurs during the course of a single lesson or other type of interaction between child and teacher.

It takes time and scheduled reinforcement. To help Cleo's behavior become more permanent, which should you do?

1. Praise her every time she pays attention in all future lessons.
2. Keep praise to a minimum and keep her in for recess whenever she talks to her neighbor.
3. Praise her frequently at first but gradually diminish your praise.

Continual praise (Alternative 1) is too much of a good thing and may make the child dependent on you. What you want, eventually, is to have the learning of communication skills become its own reward or at least to have Cleo learning without constantly needing your emotional support. Alternative 2 (minimum reward and maximum punishment) will convince her you're an "old meanie" and may destroy her desire to relate to you and learn from you.

Alternative 3 (praise that is frequent at first but gradually diminished) is more likely to succeed in the long run. By giving frequent praise at first, you will help to "set" the behavior you desire. (In using the word *praise,* of course, we are not referring to the syrupy drivel which turns off as many children as it excites. Often, a smile, a friendly nod, or a quiet "Good thinking, Cleo" are sufficient.) By gradually diminishing your praise, you will probably strengthen her desire for praise, her urge to learn from you in order to receive it, and eventually her chance to be rewarded just by learning itself.

A Review of the Learning Principles

The thirteen principles of learning discussed in this module will now be presented to you in a different order so that a mnemonic device can be used. This mnemonic device will help you to remember the learning princples as you are engaged in teaching.

Motivating Them to Learn

When you think about motivating children, think of this sentence: NOVELTY NEEDS LEVEL FEEDBACK. This will remind you that you should:

1. Add NOVELTY to their learning experiences.
2. Help them satisfy their basic NEEDS.
3. Teach them at the appropriate LEVEL of difficulty.
4. Provide frequent and specific FEEDBACK.

Getting Learning to Stick

When you want to get greater retention, think of this sentence: INVOLVED MASTERS PRACTICE TRANSFER. This will remind you that you should:

5. Get everyone INVOLVED at all times.
6. Teach for MASTERY rather than coverage.
7. Provide massed PRACTICE followed by distributed practice.
8. Help positive TRANSFER occur (and watch out for negative transfer.

Managing Misbehavior

If the principles of motivation and retention don't seem to be working, and you decide to use a more direct behavior approach, think of this urgent telegram:

UNDERSTAND POSITIVE SCHEDULE.
IGNORE NEGATIVE.

This will remind you that you should:

9. Help the child UNDERSTAND exactly what behavior you want (not just what you *don't* want).
10. Use POSITIVE reinforcement for behavior you desire.
11. SCHEDULE the positive reinforcement.
12. If possible, IGNORE misbehavior that is new to the child.
13. Use NEGATIVE reinforcement when positive reinforcement fails to get the desired response, but be aware of possible side effects.

REFERENCES AND BIBLIOGRAPHY

1. Cronbach, Lee J. *Educational Psychology*. New York: Harcourt Brace Jovanovich, 1977. See particularly the chapter dealing with purposes and aspirations.

2. Fargo, George A.; Behrns, Charlene; and Nolen, Patricia; eds. *Behavior Modification in the Classroom*. Belmont, Calif.: Wadsworth, 1970. See particularly pages 112–47 on using behavior modification techniques in the "normal" elementary classroom.

3. Glaser, Robert. "Learning." In *Encyclopedia of Educational Research,* 4th ed., edited by Robert L. Ebel, pp. 706–33. New York: Macmillan, 1969.

4. Honig, Werner K., ed. *Handbook of Operant Behavior*. New York: Appleton-Century-Crofts, 1977.

5. Hunter, Madeline. *Motivation Theory for Teachers*. TIP Publications (P.O. Box 514, El Segundo, Calif. 90245), 1967, programmed booklet.

6. _____. *Reinforcement Theory for Teachers*. TIP Publications, 1967, programmed booklet.

7. _____. *Retention Theory for Teachers*. TIP Publications, 1967, programmed booklet.

8. _____. *Teach More—Faster!* TIP Publications, 1969, programmed booklet.

9. _____. *Teach for Transfer*. TIP Publications, 1971, programmed booklet.

10. Klausmeier, Herbert J., and Davis, J. Kent. "Transfer of Learning." In *Encyclopedia of Educational Research,* edited by Robert L. Ebel, pp. 1483–93. New York: Macmillan, 1969.

11. Klausmeier, Herbert J., and Goodwin, William. *Learning and Human Abilities, Education Psychology*. New York: Harper & Row, 1975. See chapter on "Motivation" and on "Retention and Transfer."

12. Maslow, Abraham H. *Motivation and Personality*. New York: Harper and Row, 1970.

13. Pitts, Carl E., ed. *Operant Conditioning in the Classroom, Introductory Readings in Education Psychology*. New York: Crowell, 1971. See particularly the article by B.F. Skinner, "The Technology of Teaching," pp. 34–53. This article provides specific examples of the effectiveness of the behavior modification approach.

14. White, William F., *Psychosocial Principles Applied to Classroom Teaching*. New York: McGraw-Hill, 1969. See especially Chapter 1 on "Attention and Motivation."

2

THE ELEMENTS OF LANGUAGE ARTS INSTRUCTION

module

4

Encouraging Fluent Speech and Writing

There once was a man from Blighter's Peak
Who didn't know how to write or speak.
His grammar was loose.
His words were obtuse.
And he became meeker than meek.

Nearly everyone would like to speak or write with greater fluency. Speech or writing that flows easily, readily, and smoothly is often associated with admiration, success, and self-esteem. Fluent speech is the goal of the one year old, struggling desperately to get that "giant" taking care of him to understand what he wants. Fluent speaking and writing are the goals of most school-age children, trying to win friends and influence powerful adults. And, they're the goals of the adult, attempting to sell goods, services, ideas, and self to customers, students, employees, employers, and members of the opposite sex.

But what does it require to be fluent? It requires, first of all, a feeling that you're okay. And this is where fluency gets lost for some people, for without sufficient self-esteem the words just tend to get in each other's way. It requires the desire to communicate with someone, of course. But it also requires an intuitive sense of grammar—that large body of devices which each language has for signaling meaning. Such a sense of grammar requires a reservoir of sentence patterns and methods of rearranging and expanding them, as well as a collection of methods for signaling meaning through pitch changes, pauses, and dialects.

Fluency also requires a vocabulary, not only of words and phrases but also of prefixes, suffixes, word pronunciations, and phoneme articulations. And the vocabulary cannot be limited to words with single meanings, for most words have more than one meaning. Communication can be difficult if not impossible when the would-be communicators are unaware of the various meanings a word can have. This module should provide you with ideas for helping children develop self-confidence, increase their vocabulary, and expand their awareness of grammatical signals.[1]

[1] Although fluent writing also requires a good spelling vocabulary and readily produced legible handwriting, as well as a knowledge of punctuation, these topics will be reserved for Module 5. In Module 6, various means of encouraging the creative processes related to writing will be discussed.

Special Prerequisites for Module 4

It is recommended that you complete Modules 1–3 for background information before beginning this module. There are no other special prerequisites.

Long-range Outcomes Related to Module 4

This module should help you as a teacher to do the following:

1. Communicate with other professional educators about methods of encouraging fluent speaking and writing.
2. Expand children's reservoir of grammatical sentence patterns alterations, and expansions.
3. Enlarge children's vocabularies.
4. Plan a bilingual approach.
5. Improve children's articulation, enunciation, and pronunciation.
6. Foster self-confidence and fluency through creative drama.

Performance Objectives for Knowledge Level

To give yourself an overview of what is expected of you in this module, you should first scan the objectives and performance standards at all three levels— knowledge, simulation, and teaching. Then use the study guide during your reading of the module. As you find information related to the study guide, write it down in the available blanks or on separate paper. Then review this information shortly before your knowledge level examination.

1.1 On a closed-book examination you should be able to match terms with definitions, terms with illustrations, sentence patterns with sample sentences illustrating those patterns, and common pattern alterations or expansions with illustrations of those alterations or expansions. The terms, sentence patterns, and common pattern alterations or expansions are described in the Study Guide.

1.2 On the same examination, you will be asked to write in missing teaching steps related to the encouragement of fluency. Space is available in the Study Guide for review.

1.3 On the same examination, you will be asked to write in the missing layers of Dale's Cone of Experience. In the Study Guide you will find space available for reviewing these steps.

1.4 On the same examination, you should be able to tell whether a dialect difference is related to a black dialect, Spanish dialect, neither, or both.

Study Guide for Knowledge Level Examination

1. Next to each term write a sentence illustrating that term. Also underline the word that illustrates the term. The first one has been done for you.

   determiner   <u>That</u> person was just here.

   direct object

   indirect object

   transitive verb

   intransitive verb

   linking verb

2. Below each basic sentence pattern write a sentence illustrating that pattern. The first one has been done for you.

   (D) + Noun + Be verb + Adverb

       The coyote was there.

   (D) + Noun + Intransitive verb + (Adverb)

   (D) + Noun + Linking verb + Adjective

   (D) + Noun + Linking verb + Noun

(D) + Noun + Transitive verb + (D) + Noun

(D) + Noun + Verb + (D) + Noun + (D) + Noun

3. Alter and expand one of these two sentences in the same way as shown in Table 4.2, page 120. *My brother lost my money* or *The flebonk rizzled her tadwack.*

present tense:

future:

present perfect:

past perfect:

future perfect:

progressive:

infinitive:

did, does, do:

plural subject:

passive voice:

pronoun:

did? does? do?

negative:

what? who? whom?

when? where? why? how?

there:

sequence:

adjective expansion:

prepositional phrase:

adverb:

compound subject:

compound predicate:

relative clause:

compound sentence:

dependent clause:

4. List the four steps for direct instruction on sentence patterns, alterations, and expansions. This type of instruction is sometimes called creative grammar. (List the steps from memory if possible.)

5. Write in the missing layers of Dale's Cone of Experience.

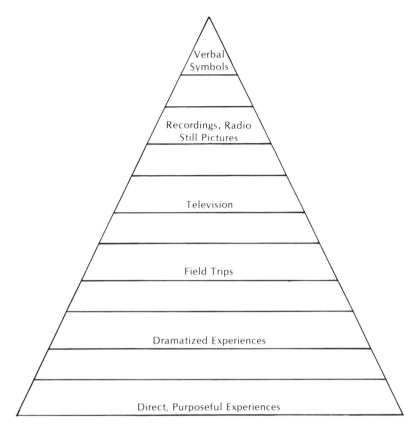

6. List the three ways that dialects differ.

7. Next to each example of dialect difference, write *black, Spanish, neither,* or *both.* One of them has been done for you.

She is doctor.

He look at the picture.

"Es-top!" he cried.

Yesterday he give I two book.   neither (Cantonese)

I got many pencil.

I have fife ropes that I wear.

Give me Bill pencil.

That's a berry bad man.

They lets us do it.

That pleaseman will put you in jail.

I tole him he was a baa man.

Doze are deh ones.

Yesterday I ring the bell.

They be readin'.

I ain't got no candy.

The beard covered his shin.

It's his fought for hepping dem foe losers.

I keeked the teen can.

8. Next to each term write either a definition or an illustration to help you remember its meaning.

   articulation

   enunciation

   pronunciation

9. Write in the missing steps suggested in Module 4 for teaching creative drama.

a. Total group movement to music.

b.

c. Total group pantomime.

d.

e. Total group dialogue and characterization.

f.

g. Role playing.

h.

PerformaNce StaNdARds for KNowLEdGE LEvEl

A. Twenty-five minute time limit on 1.1 through 1.4.
B. Completion deadline: instructor will notify.
C. Recommended grading standards if grades are used: 96% = A; 92% = A—; 88% = B; 84% = B—; 80% = C; below 80% = incomplete; should be completed at 80% or better before you go on to performance objectives for simulation level. (The instructor may wish to permit a grade of A or B only the first time the test is given in order to encourage more intensive study.)

Performance Objectives for Simulation Level

2.1 As a take-home examination, observe in an elementary class-room for approximately two hours. Record the specific ways in which children's vocabulary is enriched or enlarged through the conscious or subconscious methods of the teacher. Also indicate ways in which opportunities for vocabulary growth were overlooked by the teacher. Write a report on your findings.

2.2 (Alternative Objective) As a take-home exam, develop a lesson plan which will serve as a basis for "teaching" two or more of your peers any speaking skill you wish. The lesson plan is for your own use only and is *not* to be handed in, unless the instructor requests it. Hand in a tape recording of your lesson. (If you and your instructor decide on Alternative 2.2, you may wish to discuss the possibility of using peer evaluations in addition to or instead of instructor evaluation.)

2.3 (Alternative Objective) Direct your classmates in a creative drama experience, using one of the first five steps recommended in this module. Be sure to establish definite rules before you begin. (You may wish to do this as a team project; the first person uses Steps 1 and 2; second person uses Step 3; third person, Step 4; fourth person, Step 5.)

Performance Standards for Simulation Level

A. For Objective 2.1 (Observation in Classroom)
  1. Shows knowledge of Dale's Cone of Experience.
  2. Demonstrates awareness of need for both nonverbal and verbal experiences.
  3. Report is legible and free of spelling and punctuation errors.
  4. Describes a sufficient quantity of methods to indicate close observation as well as imagination.

B. For Objective 2.2 (Peer Teaching Tape)
  1. The teacher-in-training shows by her efforts to evaluate the progress of the "students" during the lesson that she has clear-cut performance objectives in mind.
  2. Shows a clear understanding of the speaking skill he is teaching.
  3. Uses learning principles effectively and does not violate any of those discussed in Module 1.
  4. Uses appropriately one or more of the methods described in this module.

C. For Objective 2.3 (Directing Creative Drama Activity)
  1. Establishes definite rules with "students."
  2. Keeps activity focused on drama experience rather than on individuals.

3. Encourages self-confidence through example and discussion.
4. Chooses activity that encourages either self-confidence, fluency, or both.

D. For Objectives 2.1–2.3: Should be completed at C level or better before going on to Teaching level.

Performance Objectives for Teaching Level

3.1 In a micro-teaching, observation, student teaching, intern, or supervised teaching situation, carry on a *"creative grammar"* experience with two or more children. Lesson plan, worksheet, and self-critique are required. Your lesson plan should include the following:

a. Approximate age level for which this activity might be appropriate, e.g., 5–7, 6–8, 11–13, etc.
b. Size of group for which this activity might be appropriate: entire class, small group, or individual.
c. Long-range outcome.
d. Performance objectives.
e. Prerequisite skills children might need.
f. Learning activity and procedural steps.
g. Necessary materials.

Include the following in your self-critique after you finish the lesson:

a. To what extent your performance objectives were met.
b. What might be done to help children who did *not* meet your performance standards.
c. What problems you had, if any.
d. What might have been done to implement your desired long-range outcome more effectively.
e. What type of follow-up activity might provide useful practice for these students at a later date.

Your cooperating teacher, supervisor, or instructor will probably want to see your critique after you teach and your lesson plan before you teach.

3.2 (Alternative Objective) In the same setting described in 3.1, teach any one of the speaking skills discussed in this module.

Performance Standards for Teaching Level

A. Standards A.1–A.2 and B.1–B.4 for the simulation level may be appropriate.

B. Uses learning principles effectively and does not violate any of those discussed in Module 3.

C. Additional standards or modified standards may have to be developed by the cooperating teacher, instructor, supervisor, or teachers-in-training. It is best, of course, to state these standards in advance of the required performance.

Fluency with Sentences

Mr. Campbell wants to help his third graders become more fluent in their speech and writing. He decides to try "creative grammar" (13), an approach that worked with his students the previous year. He writes this sentence on the board and reads it to them: *The barko nopped the filker.* Mr. Campbell asks the children what the barko did.

"He nopped the filker," Sylvia says, shyly.

"Well, who did the nopping, then?" he asks.

"The barko did," they all say, grinning.

"Well, who did he nop?"

"The filker," they shout.

"Well, let me ask you this, then. Is that barko nopping the filker right now, or did that mean old barko already do the nopping?"

"He already done the noppin," yells Tyrone, very pleased with himself for being the one to discover such an important fact.

"Yeah," says Glynnis. "He already did it."

Mr. Campbell is tempted to ask how she knows for sure but remembers just in time not to kill their enthusiasm with an analytic discussion.

"Okay," he says, "the barko already did the nopping. But who—" Mr. Campbell pauses with raised finger and looks around the room, building up suspense and giving them a chance to anticipate his next question. "Who did the barko nop?"

"The filker!" the children shout.

"You are so alert," says Mr. Campbell, rushing to another part of the chalkboard. There he writes this:

The _____ _____ the _____.

"What word goes in this blank?" he says, pointing to the first blank and pretending impatience. "Hurry, hurry, hurry."

"Barko!" yells Tommy.

"Right," says Mr. Campbell as he writes the word in the blank.

"Jimmy, what goes in the third blank over here?"

"Filker," Jimmy says, after checking to make sure.

"Good," says Mr. Campbell as he fills in the third blank. "And what should we put in this second blank?"

Tyrone is all ready for the question: "Nopped/ Write n-o-p-p-e-d."

"Fantastic," says Mr. Campbell, as he follows Tyrone's orders.

"Okay, now," continues Mr. Campbell, still in a slightly rushed mood. "We have to hurry now, because I want you all to get in the Barko Club."

"Barko Club?" says Carmen. "What's that?"

"It's a secret club. To get in the club you have to figure out the secret."

The children are giggling and wisecracking in anticipation as Mr. Campbell returns to the board and writes this again under the first one:

The _____ _____ the _____.

Then he writes several more just like it underneath.

"Okay, now," he says, "I know the secret, so I can get in the Barko Club easily." In the first space, he writes the word *barko*. In the second space, he writes the word *broke*. In the third space, he writes the word *doll*. "The barko broke the doll."

"Aw," says James. "Is that all it means?"

"Oh no," Mr. Campbell quickly assures him. "It means hundreds and thousands of things." Quickly he fills in the next set of blanks with *barko, killed* and *dragon*. "See," he says, "it also means the barko killed the dragon."

"I don't get it," says Melissa.

"You will very soon. To get in the Barko Club all you have to do is give me a sentence like my sentences."

"That's easy," says Tyrone. "The barko killed the lion."

"Right," says Mr. Campbell. "You're in the club, Tyrone."

Tyrone looks around to gloat at all the nonmembers.

"Oh, I get it," says Ralph. "The barko killed the tiger. Am I in the club?"

"You're in, Ralph. Who else wants to try?"•

James waves his hand, and Mr. Campbell calls on him. "The barko killed the gorilla." James grins because he's sure he's now in the club.

"You almost got in the club, James."

James says, "Almost?"

"Almost. You see, two other people already used the word *killed*, so to get in the club you have to use another word.

"James looks puzzled for a moment, but then he waves his hand again.

"Yes?"

"The barko ate the gorilla."

Mr. Campbell grins and tells James he's in the club. Alice gives her sentence: "The barko ate my lunch."

Tyrone doesn't like this because she used the word *my* instead of *the*, but Mr. Campbell insists that she's still in the club. "You can use *my* or *the* or *this* or *that* or anything that fits," he says.

Glynnis says, "That mean old barko stole my money."

"Great!" says Mr. Campbell. "You're really in the club, Glynnis."

"That mean old barko is stealing my pencil," shouts Georgine.

"Oh, you almost made it in the club," says Mr. Campbell. "You listen some more and try again in a few minutes, okay."

Georgine looks puzzled and scratches her head.

"That barko took my bagga marbles," says Albert.

"You're in the club," says Mr. Campbell.

Georgine tries again: "That mean old barko took my pencil."

"I knew you'd get in the club, Georgine," Mr. Campbell says.

Georgine beams a smile at him, and Mr. Campbell continues, urging the nonmembers to keep trying. In a few more minutes, everyone is in the club, and the game is over.

Using the Learning Principles

Mr. Campbell has demonstrated for us some excellent techniques for encouraging fluency, as well as reviewing some of the principles of learning:

1. He kept the thinking pace rapid and light without being threatening. (He showed concern for their *need* for security and provided the appropriate *level* of difficulty. The light but rapid pace kept most of them actively *involved*.)

2. He promoted feelings of belonging and self-esteem. (He was concerned about their psychological *needs*.)

3. He avoided the analytical approach in favor of a creative, intuitive approach to sentence construction. (Mr. Campbell knew that *transfer* to creative writing and other types of writing would best be encouraged through *practice* that was similar to what would be required for such writing.)

4. He avoided making an issue of dialect differences, e.g., Tyrone used *done* in the past tense instead of *did*. (He sensed that Tyrone's *need* at this point was for belonging and not for a grammar lesson. He knew he would be able to show the difference between *did* and *done* better in a separate pattern lesson. For example, the first part of the lesson might be like this:

   The boy did the washing.
   The girl did the cooking.
   The barko did the blinching.

The second part of the lesson might be like this:

   The boy has done the washing.
   The girl has done the cooking.
   The barko has done the blinching.

5. He gently forced the children to follow unstated grammatical rules, i.e., the verb had to be in the past tense and the sentence pattern had to be Noun—Transitive Verb—Noun. (Mr. Campbell seemed to understand that *mastery* of rules requires not only active *involvement* in the learning process but *practice* in context as well.)

Thus, Mr. Campbell was teaching them in the "natural way"—the way they had been learning unstated language rules since they were babies. Like other children, these children have grown up listening to a small set of basic sentence patterns and to a great variety of ways of altering or expanding those patterns. The most common patterns are shown in Table 4.1.

TABLE 4.1   Basic Sentence Patterns

1. (Determiner) + Noun + Be verb + Adverb	The doctor was here.
2. (D) + Noun + Intransitive verb + (Adverb)	The doctor came quickly.
3. (D) + Noun + Linking verb + Adjective	The woman looked sad.
4. (D) + Noun + Linking verb + (D) + Noun	The boy was his friend.
5. (D) + Noun + Transitive verb + (D) + Noun	The hunter shot the wolf.
6. (D) + Noun + Transitive verb + (D) + Noun + (D) + Noun	The man gave his wife the car.

Note: the parenthesized word forms do not have to appear in order to make the pattern complete. If the word form is *not* in parentheses, however, this does not mean that *any* member of the word form will work. In Pattern 1, for example, an "ly adverb" like *quickly* would not work.

Many children have already learned intuitively these six patterns before they start school. Some children, however, may find some of the patterns unfamiliar and confusing when then hear them or meet them in print. Both minority and majority children may come from homes where verbal facility is not encouraged. Minimal verbal experience makes it very difficult for some children to develop fluent speech. It also makes it difficult for them to understand people who speak with unfamiliar patterns. This, in turn, makes it difficult for them to translate printed sentences into oral patterns they can recognize as they attempt to read.

Just hearing the patterns uttered on TV often isn't enough. To make the patterns part of their speaking and listening tools, many children need to hear *themselves* utter the patterns and be reinforced by significant others, such as their parents. In a home in which verbal fluency is considered highly desirable, this type of reinforcement continually takes place. The child says, for example, "Daddy shoe," and the mother spontaneously replies, "Yes, those are Daddy's shoes."

Before we go on to how you can help children expand their reservoir of sentence arrangements, we need to do three things: (1) review a few terms necessary for an understanding of this subject, (2) see how well you understand the six basic sentence patterns, and (3) introduce some of the common pattern alterations and expansions.

Terminology

Determiner—In the following two sentences, the determiners are in italics: *The* house is mine. *This* green house is mine. A determiner is a type of word used to signal a noun or a descriptive adjective followed by a noun. The determiner class includes *a, an, the, my, their, this, that, these, those, his, her,* and *your.*

Direct object—In the following two sentences, the direct objects are in italics: The lady beat the *rug*. The boy kissed the *girl*. A direct object represents the person or thing receiving the action.

Indirect object—In the following two sentences, the indirect objects are in italics: The policeman gave my *father* a ticket. The lady gave the *door* a kick. In the first sentence, the direct object is *ticket,* and the indirect object is *father.* In the second sentence, the direct object is *kick,* and the indirect object is *door.* As you can see, the indirect object represents the person or thing receiving the direct object.

Transitive verb—In the following sentence, the transitive verb is in italics: The boy *ate* the pie. The direct object of *ate* is *pie.* A transitive verb is a verb that is accompanied by a direct object (and can be changed to a passive form: the pie was eaten by the boy.)

Intransitive verb—In the following two sentences, the intransitive verbs are in italics: The mail *came*. He *jumped* off the chair. Neither *came* nor *jumped* have a direct object in these sentences. (The word *came* is almost always an intransitive verb, but *jumped* could be either a transitive or intransitive verb, depending on the sentence. If it had a direct object, as in "The horse jumped the creek," then it would be a transitive verb.) An intransitive verb, then, is one which is *not* accompanied by a direct object (and cannot be changed to a passive form).

Linking verb—In the following sentences, the linking verbs are in italics: The child *is* happy. The child *seems* happy. The child *is* a boy. A boy *becomes* a man. In slightly oversimplified terms, a linking verb is a special type of verb that serves as a connection between the subject and a word that describes or complements the subject. A "Be Verb" (*is, was,* etc.) is often a linking verb but not always, e.g., in "He was killing time," *was* is not a linking verb.

PRACTICE EXERCISE 1

1. Underline the determiner: Your umbrella is poking me.
2. Underline the direct object: The fox ate the rabbit.
3. Circle the indirect object: We gave our mother a present.
4. Circle the transitive verb: She threw the water on the fire.
5. Underline the intransitive verb: George Washington slept here.
6. Underline the linking verb: The food tasted rotten.
7. Write *a* if the word in italics is a transitive verb; *b* if it is an intransitive verb; *c,* linking verb; *d,* direct object; *e,* indirect object; and *f,* determiner. Use each letter only once.

   _____ You *seem* distressed.
   _____ Please give *Bill* the money.
   _____ The doctor *came* yesterday.
   _____ *That* food stinks.

_____ We *love* animals.

_____ I hate his *assignments.*

Answers to Practice Exercise 1

1. Your   5. slept
2. rabbit   6. tasted
3. mother   7. c, e, b, f, a, d
4. threw

Understanding the Basic Sentence Patterns

In order for you to help children increase their comprehension of sentence patterns, of course, you need to make sure you understand them yourself. The following illustrations can be used both for your own understanding and for sample sentences to use with your students: Here are some more examples of Pattern 1. After reading them, *out loud if possible,* see if you can think of a few more.

Pattern 1

(D) + Noun + Be verb + Adverb
The girl was here.
My friend was outside.
The bear was in the zoo.
The doctor was in.
The doctor was in the hospital.
His doctor was out.
A nurse was here.
The flebonk was in the malps.

Now you make up two or three. Check them later with one of your colleagues. Note that a prepositional phrase can act as an adverb.

Here are more examples of Pattern 2. (Read them out loud, if possible.)

Pattern 2

(D) + Noun + Intransitive verb + (Adverb)
The boy walked slowly.
The boy walked.
That girl played here.
This girl played in the park.
My mother worked in the morning.
The giant spoke grumpily.

That flebonk ate whappily.
My flebonk lived in the malps.

Now it's your turn again. Make one of them a nonsense sentence if you can.

The following are more examples of Pattern 3.

Pattern 3

(D) + Noun + Linking verb + Adjective
The candy seemed sweet.
That candy was sweet.
His shorts looked dirty.
Your dress was pretty.
The monkey seemed clever.
That child could be cruel.
Alice appeared snobbish.
The flebonk was masty.
That flebonk smelled yucky.
My flebonk tasted delicious.

Here are more examples of Pattern 4.

Pattern 4

(D) + Noun + Linking verb + (D) + Noun
The dog was his friend.
The dog became his friend.
The dog remained his friend.
Bob was a snob.
That girl became my sweetheart.
Her brother remained a fink.
Your costume was a scream.
My flebonk became a skiddle.
His skiddle remained a murgle.

The following are more examples of Pattern 5.

Pattern 5

(D) + Noun + Transitive verb + (D) + Noun
The monkey climbed the ladder.
My father drove a car.
This motor ran the pulley.
Jim owned this place.
The train jumped the track.
Your sister liked my brother.
Her flebonk zagged his delbur.
His delbur zagged a flurptop.

And here are more examples of Pattern 6.

Pattern 6

(D) + Noun + Transitive verb + (D) + Noun + (D) + Noun
The woman gave her dog a bone.
The woman fed her son a steak.
My father spared the beggar a dime.
The king granted Columbus an audience.
The club awarded Felix a prize.
A man offered Mother a hand.
My uncle left my sister a fortune.
This flebonk passed my delbur a flurptop.
That profnick gave my flebonk a pickle.

Pattern Alterations and Expansions

Now that you understand the basic sentence patterns, we can move on briefly to some of the common pattern alterations and expansions. First study Table 4.2. Then check your understanding by altering and expanding one of the two sentences below in the same way. You may wish to think them out rather than write them. However, if you write them out, you can compare them with a colleague later. The sentences to alter and expand are below. (For each one, go through as

TABLE 4.2   Common Pattern Alterations and Expansions

Pattern Alterations

1. present	The boy eats the apple.
2. future	The boy will (would, etc.) eat the apple.
3. present perfect	The boy has eaten the apple.
4. past perfect	The boy had eaten the apple.
5. future perfect	The boy will (would, etc.) have eaten the apple.
6. progressive	The boy was eating the apple.
7. infinitive	The boy had to eat the apple.
8. did	The boy did eat the apple.
9. plural subject	The boys eat the apple.
10. passive	The apple was eaten by the boy.
11. pronoun	He ate it.
12. did?	Did the boy eat the apple?
13. negative	The boy did not eat the apple.
14. what? who? whom?	What did the boy eat?
15. when? where? why? how?	When did the boy eat the apple?
16. there	An apple is here. There is an apple here.
17. sequence	The boy came quickly. Quickly the boy came.

Pattern Expansions

1. adjective	The hungry boy ate the apple.
2. prepositional phrase	The boy with the hat ate the apple from the tree.
3. adverb	The boy ate the apple quickly.
4. compound subject	The boy and girl ate the apple.
5. compound predicate	The boy picked and ate the apple.
6. relative clause	The boy who wore a hat ate the apple.
7. compound sentence	The apple was here, and the boy came quickly
8. dependent clause	Because the apple was there, the boy ate the apple.

many alterations and expansions shown in Table 4.2 as you can. Space is provided in the Study Guide on page 104, if you wish.)

> My brother lost my money.
> The flebonk rizzled her tadwack.

Please alter the two sentences above before proceeding.

For further practice and to help you prepare for the knowledge examination, see if you can match the basic sentence patterns with the sample sentences which illustrate those patterns.

PRACTICE EXERCISE 2

_____ 1. The boy ate my apple.

a. (D) + Noun + Be verb + Adverb

_____ 2. The lady was in the taxi.

b. (D) + Noun + Intransitive verb + (Adverb)

_____ 3. The boy gave the mother the key.

c. (D) + Noun + Linking verb + Adjective

_____ 4. The dog barked.

d. (D) + Noun + Linking verb + (D) + Noun

_____ 5. The girl was a princess.

e. (D) + Noun + Transitive verb + (D) + Noun

_____ 6. This thing looks terrible.

f. (D) + Noun + Transitive verb + (D) + Noun + (D) + Noun

_____ 7. Bill jumped.

Answers to Practice Exercise 2

1. e	5. d
2. a	6. c
3. f	7. b
4. b	

Teaching Procedures for Encouraging Sentence Fluency

In an earlier section, you saw how Mr. Campbell used the creative grammar approach in encouraging fluency. Creative grammar has been used with, and seems to be suitable for, any grade level, including kindergarten, providing the teacher uses very simple sentences and requires little, if any, writing with very inexperienced writers. The basic steps to follow in using the creative grammar approach are as follows:

1. Introduce the children (preferably a small group) to a set of "model sentences," in print, if possible, but orally if the children are unable to do any reading. For Pattern 2, for instance, you might use the set you have already seen:

    The boy walked slowly.
    That girl played here.
    This girl played in the park.
    My mother worked in the morning.
    The giant spoke grumpily.
    That flebonk ate whappily.
    My flebonk lived in the malps.

2. Have them make up sentences which are like these. This should be done *orally* at this point. Some written sentences can be required at the end of the lesson, if you wish to evaluate how well each child comprehends the pattern, and if the children are ca-

pable of writing them. If a child states a sentence which doesn't fit the pattern, simply say something like, "You're almost in the Pattern Club, but not quite. Listen some more and try again later."

3. After they are all in the Pattern Club, have them first alter the pattern orally and then expand it orally. You may wish to accept any alteration or expansion at this point. However, if you think they need practice on particular types of modification, show them how to modify two or three of the model sentences and start a new Pattern Club. For example, suppose you wish to concentrate on the plural alteration. First you would have them change the previous sentences to the present tense: The boy walks slowly, That girl plays here, etc. Then you would have them make a second alteration, this time the plural one: Boys walk slowly, Those girls play here, and so on. You may wish to move on then to some expansions, such as: Tired boys walk slowly, Those frisky girls play here, etc.

4. Provide massed and distributed practice. If they are capable of writing, have them complete a worksheet at the end of the lesson. For part of the distributed practice, have them find examples of the pattern in their reading books, or have them write one as a "password," or see how many they can create together in one minute.

In summary, the four steps recommended for direct instruction on sentence patterns, alterations, and expansions are as follows:

1. Introduce them to a set of model sentences (all illustrating the pattern you wish them to understand.

2. Have them create sentences like the model ones (orally at first, later in writing).

3. Have them create alterations and expansions of the model sentences (as well as some of the other sentences they have created in Step 2).

4. Provided massed and distributed practice.

One of the secrets to successful use of creative grammar is to *avoid analyzing* the sentences. Numerous studies (20) have demonstrated that most young children are not capable of gaining much from an analytical approach toward grammar. Practical experience shows that the analytical approach quickly produces a glazed look usually reserved for college students in a lecture hall.

Another secret to success is to keep the lessons quite short, about ten to fifteen minutes or even less. Pattern lessons are excellent for that five minute lull before breaking for lunch or music. Short, lighthearted, and speedy— this is the way to encourage fluency when using the creative grammar approach. The whole idea is to get them to enjoy hearing and speaking a variety of patterns, alterations, and expansions.

Along with creative grammar, another way of encouraging sentence fluency is to read to the students daily. In this way, they will hear a greater variety of sentence arrangements than you, the teacher, can present to them in your own speech. (The purpose here is not to have them listen for sentence arrangements, of course. Rather, it is to help them internalize these sentence arrangements and get the "feel" of fluent language.) Some of the authors of children's books have even recorded their own stories so that the children can hear the actual voice of the author.

Don't forget to let them create their own stories and poems. They need to hear a variety of sentence arrangements, but they also need to invent their own sentences. Give them a chance to dictate stories to you or to a tape recorder, even if they can write. Read their stories back to the class or play the tape recording of their stories. Let them hear themselves speak and gain confidence in themselves as fluent speakers. (Many more ideas on creative speaking and writing will be found in Module 6.)

Integrating the Basics Through Creative Grammar

Perhaps you noticed while reading the section on creative grammar that all four of the language arts—reading, writing, listening, and speaking—are often brought together in order to intensify the learning experience and to make the learning of basic skills more meaningful. In teaching creative grammar, for instance, we have children *listen* to sentences, *read* them, and produce their own through *speaking* and *writing*. In this way, the language arts are not taught as isolated entities with isolated work sheets serving as the only medium for learning.

As you read the next section on vocabulary development, carefully observe the many ways that basic skills can be taught through the interaction between and among the four language arts. Notice, for instance, how Michael and Tricia learn the word *ocean* and how David and others learn the words *rozaga hunt*.

Fluency with Words: Developing Children's Vocabularies

How often have you found yourself in a situation in which the right word just wouldn't come to mind? Often, the reason is just plain nervousness in that particular situation. But sometimes it's because the word you wanted wasn't really "yours." It was one you'd heard a few times or read several times but not one you were used to using in your everyday speech.

Our speaking vocabulary is often our smallest vocabulary, if we're adults. For young children, of course, the smallest vocabulary is either the writing vocabulary or the reading vocabulary. And for any age, the listening vocabulary is generally the largest. (Although for avid readers the reading vocabulary may be even larger.) We understand many words that we never use in our speech. Although the enrichment of these vocabularies in a school setting requires a slightly different approach for each one, there is a basic approach common to all four.

For a word to truly belong to Michael's vocabulary, he has to have had two types of experiences related to that word: nonverbal and verbal. Take the word *ocean,* for instance. Michael understands the word *ocean* very well. In his ten years of life, he's been to the ocean approximately two hundred times. This is because he and his family live very near the ocean and enjoy going to the beach for picnics. Michael has swum in a glassy smooth ocean, body surfed in a wave-ruffled ocean, and gagged on its salty liquid. He has listened to the words hundreds of times: "Wanna go to the ocean, Mikey?" and "Get ready to go to the ocean, Michael." He has spoken the word hundreds of times: "I want to go to the ocean," and "When are we going to the ocean," and "Why can't we go to the ocean?" He has read the word hundreds of times: "Ocean Fresh Shrimp for Sale" and "Ocean Shores Motel" and "Gems O' The Ocean Shop." The word *ocean* is truly part of Michael's vocabulary.

Tricia has never been to the ocean in all of her ten years of life. Very seldom does she hear the word spoken or read it or speak it herself. Tricia lives in Kansas about a thousand miles from the nearest ocean and several hundred miles from the Great Lakes. She has seen the ocean in pictures and movies and has heard people talk about it, but it means very little to her. She learned how to spell it for a spelling test and now recognizes the word when she sees it in books. So you might say it's part of Tricia's vocabulary too, although in a very different way from the way it's part of Michael's vocabulary.

Both Tricia and Michael have had nonverbal and verbal experiences with the word *ocean.* But Michael's nonverbal experiences have been personal and direct; while Tricia's have been impersonal and vicarious, limited to the indirect experiences of seeing the ocean in pictures and movies.

Richard, a ten-year-old neighbor of Tricia's has never seen a picture of an ocean or seen it in the movies. He's heard the word a few times but doesn't know how to spell it or recognize it in print. His only experiences with the word have been verbal rather than experiential. In a writing or speaking situation requiring the word *ocean,* it is unlikely that the word would come to him.

To understand a word, children need both verbal and non-verbal experiences.

Using Dale's Cone of Experience

Edgar Dale (6) has developed a useful model for teachers to use when planning ways to help children improve their vocabularies. This model is called the Cone of Experience and is shown in Figure 4.1. To oversimplify Dale's theory, children learn at the deepest and most intense level through direct, purposeful experiences, the base of Dale's cone. They learn at the shallowest and least intense level through sheer verbal experiences, the tip of the cone. In between the base and the tip of the cone are vicarious (indirect) experiences which provide different depths and intensities of learning. Next to a direct experience of driving a car, for instance, the deepest and most intense experience would be that of a contrived experience with a "mock-up" car, one that simulates a road and a crash, etc.

FIGURE 4.1   Dale's Cone of Experience

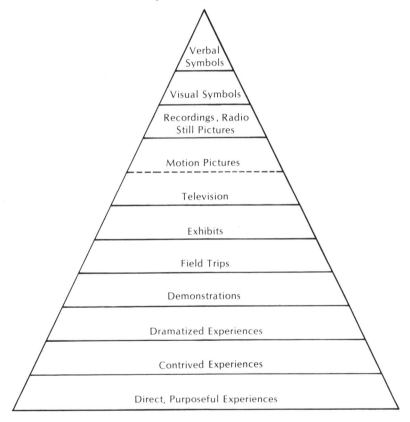

Verbal
Symbols

Visual Symbols

Recordings, Radio
Still Pictures

Motion Pictures

Television

Exhibits

Field Trips

Demonstrations

Dramatized Experiences

Contrived Experiences

Direct, Purposeful Experiences

From *Audiovisual Methods in Teaching*, 3d ed., by Edgar Dale. Copyright © 1946, 1954, 1969 by Holt, Rinehart and Winston, Inc. Reprinted by permission of Holt, Rinehart, and Winston, Inc.

In theory at least, the information we receive at the verbal level (including new words) often goes in one ear and out the other, sticking inside just long enough to use it for passing a test. Information we receive at the direct level of experience (such as the word *hot* the moment we touch a hot stove) tends to stay with us longer and to become a part of our readily available source of words or concepts.

Let's take the words *rozaga hunt* for an example. The best way to teach David about a rozaga hunt would be to take him on one. Let him get up with you in the middle of the night, carry one of the four-celled flashlights in one hand and the sharpened spear in the other, and stumble through the woods toward the swamp. Let him listen to the hurrumping of the bull frogs, the hooting of the owls, and that eerie low whistle of the rozaga. Let him shiver with fright as he unexpectedly comes face to face with one, its fangs and yellow eyes highlighting the swan-like neck covered with dark leathery scales, its snake-like tongue darting in and out of its mouth only three feet away from David's right arm. Let him hear your shout of warning and feel his tight-muscled arm jab the spear through the vital spot, right through the neck. Do you have any doubt that David will ever forget the word *rozaga?* (The reader should be assured that there are no rozogas lurking about. The rozaga is a creature of your author's imagination.)

Assuming for a moment that the rozaga is a real animal, let us suppose you are teaching a social studies unit on the rozaga hunters of North Borneo. You are trying to show how these people have adapted to their environment, and since rozaga hunting is their chief means of survival, it is important that your students understand the words *rozaga hunt.* Since you plan to discuss these people on and off for the next few weeks you want your students to make the words *rozaga hunt* part of their vocabulary. What should you do?

Obviously, you can't provide them with the direct experience of rozaga hunting. So, looking at Dale's Cone of Experience, what would be your next best learning experience? A contrived experience would probably be out because of the time and expense. (Although taking apart and putting together a plaster model of a rozaga would be one type of contrived experience.)

What about a dramatized experience of a rozaga hunt? This would be excellent *after* they have developed some simpler ideas of what a rozaga is and how a rozaga hunt is carried out. In fact, telling the students that they will eventually get to enact a rozaga hunt will spur most of them on to finding out more about a rozaga hunt.

The next layers of the Cone of Experience suggest the use of demonstrations, field trips, and exhibits. Having someone (such as the teacher) who has seen a movie of a rozaga hunt provide a demonstration of the hunt would help the children get a deeper understanding of the concept. A field trip, in this case, would be impractical, unless you were able to take them to a museum showing exhibits related to the rozaga hunt. At an exhibit, they would be able to see the weapon and perhaps a stuffed rozaga close at hand.

A movie or a televised documentary, although not providing the close-at-hand experience of the exhibit, would provide the emotional impact that has so-far been missing in your attempts to get them to understand a rozaga hunt. But if nothing else is available, perhaps you'll at least have some still pictures showing the rozaga and the hunters and perhaps a recording of someone describing an actual rozaga hunt.

As you can see, we've reached the top of the Cone of Experience with nothing left but visual symbols (such as diagrams or maps) and verbal symbols (words and definitions). You *could* simply write the word *rozaga* on the board and say, "A rozaga is an amphibian with dark leathery scales and a swan-like neck living in the swamps of North Borneo." That would take a lot less time than all the vicarious experiences we've been talking about. And there are plenty of times when that's all a word deserves. But if you truly want the children to make a word part of their vocabularies, you've got to back up the verbal experience with one or more nonverbal ones.

Using the Cone of Experience to Provide Vocabulary Enrichment

You probably noticed that a speaking vocabulary is gained not just by speaking words but also by listening to them, reading them, and writing them. Whenever possible, the language arts should be taught together, each one enhancing the other in a multi-sensory, communicative way.

Let's now look at each level of the Cone of Experience for more examples of what it might offer to the teacher in the way of ideas for enriching children's vocabulary.

Direct, Purposeful Experiences

1. Have them create a map of their school or their classroom so that words such as *symbol, key, north,* and *scale* become "real" to them.

2. Have them saw logs with a loggers' two-man bucksaw to see more clearly what words such as *bucksaw, saw,* and *logger* mean.

3. Have them dig their own clay, prepare it, shape it, fire it and glaze it—picking up such words as *clay, kiln, fire,* and *glaze* while they're at it.

4. Have children *pass out* paper, *give* each child a pencil, *take back* the scissors, and so on. Do you see how much we teach vocabulary through direct experiences?

5. Make cookies together. Make an "experience chart" together after making the cookies. (An experience chart is made by having children dictate sentences to the teacher describing their experience.) Before the experience chart is made, put some of the words on the board that the children were using while they made the cookies: *cup, one-fourth, measure, stir, beat,* etc.

Contrived Experiences

1. Get plastic models of the human body, the eye, the ear, etc. Have them discuss the words they pick up from the experience. Make a list of the words related to each model.

2. Set up a store in your classroom, using real objects, such as donated comic books, homemade cookies, and so on. Use simulated money such as bottle caps. Help them learn economic terms such as *supply, demand, currency, barter,* and so on.

3. Have the children develop advertisements for objects in the store.

DRAMATIZED EXPERIENCES

1. Have the children dramatize a story from their basal reader, showing what some of the hard words mean by their actions.

2. Have the children dramatize events and conditions described in their social studies books. List on the board some of the terms that need to be explained through the drama before the drama begins.

3. Have children dramatize words that you put on the board and pronounce for them, such as *lift, stretch, climb, angry,* and *sad.* (Use no audience in this situation; everyone dramatizes the words at the same time.)

4. Take multi-meaning words, such as *cut, run,* and *jump* and have the children pantomime some of the different meanings.

DEMONSTRATIONS

1. Let the children demonstrate science terms such as *pitch* (with a sound instrument) or *fulcrum* (with a simple machines experiment).

2. Have children demonstrate different ways to walk: The man *marched* across the room. In place of *marched,* also use *pranced, rushed, skipped, swaggered, paraded, stumbled, shuffled, toddled, waddled,* and *tiptoed.*

3. When a word is unfamiliar to most of the class, have someone pantomime the action represented by the word.

Field Trips

1. Take field trips around the school yard looking for words. See how many words they can come back with (*grass, swings, children, igneous rocks*).

2. Before taking the traditional spring field trip, have the children prepare booklets describing their plans and what they hope to see. Include a list of words related to things they will see. When they return, have them write short definitions or prepare illustrations related to the words. Encourage them to show the booklets to their parents.

3. Before a unit on pioneers or some other group of people, take the children to a museum to see an exhibit related to those people. Organize the trip around words that they learn rather than letting them drift aimlessly from one exhibit to another. Each child should be responsible for bringing back a five-by-eight card with five words and related definitions or illustrations.

4. Prepare experience charts related to the field trips.

Exhibits

1. Prepare children for a new social studies unit by bringing in artifacts related to another culture or to a particular occupation. Arrange these artifacts in an exhibit with labels and questions next to each artifact; e.g., This is an adz. What do you think it is used for?

2. See 3 under *Field Trips* (the museum trip).

3. Have children bring in examples of their hobby and exhibit them. (It's usually best to have no more than five or six exhibiting at a time.) Have the children prepare labels and explanations for their exhibits.

4. For a new story in the children's reading book, bring in an object that was important in the story. Have them discuss it before the children read the story. Ask them to imagine why this object might be important in the story.

Television and Motion Pictures

1. Discuss three or four words that will be important in the film or television show. Afterward, check to see whether they now understand the words.

2. Show a film related to a culture they are studying in social studies or in their reading program. Show it first without the sound and ask them to provide narration. Then show it with the sound turned on. Compare the two interpretations.

3. Have the children watch a particular television show and bring back two new words they picked up while watching the show. Give them a three-by-five card before they go home so they can write the words on the card. (They don't have to write the definitions; just have them jot down the words so they'll remember them.)

Recordings, Radio, and Still Pictures

1. Have children listen to Pete Seeger's *American Game and Activity Songs for Children* (Folkway Records, 1962) and follow along. Encourage them to say things with Pete.

2. Occasionally have them listen to the radio or a record and learn a popular song together. (You may wish to put the words on an experience chart.

3. Have them produce on tape their own radio program of songs they have learned; also poems, stories, and news.

4. Show the class a picture and ask them to think of as many words as they can that the picture makes them think of. You may wish to record the words on the chalkboard.

5. Before reading a unit in a social studies textbook, have them look at the pictures with you first. Ask them to tell you what they think might be happening in the pictures. Have them also make a list of words that the picutres make them think of.

Visual Symbols

1. Make a list of terms on maps that are unfamiliar. Have them create a map of their own house or school to make the terms seem real to them.

2. Have them create their own bar graphs from information gathered from an almanac or from information gathered by classroom reporters about birthdays, pets, etc. Do this project together so that you can discuss unfamiliar terms with them as you proceed.

3. Place drawings of a circle, square, triangle, and rectangle up on the board and discuss their differences. Then have the children find those shapes in the room environment, on the playground, etc.

4. Use a flannelboard and felt cutouts to tell a familiar story. Then let the children try it, having each one tell a small part of the story while manipulating the felt pieces.

5. Let the children use the flannelboard to help them depict story problems in mathematics.

Verbal Symbols

1. Have the children each prepare three vocabulary cards per week based on their free reading in library books. The cards should have a sentence from the book with the unfamiliar word underlined. Underneath should be a brief dictionary definition *which fits the sentence.* Once a week have them play a card game with a partner. First they swap cards and ask each other to define words. When a child can't define a word, he has to hand over his card to the other child. Whoever has the most cards when time is called is the winner. (Children should put their initials on their cards so they can get them back at the end of the game.)

2. Same as 1 but have them prepare three vocabulary cards per week based on their television viewing.

3. Have them make up context sentences such as this: The man popped the raw oyster into his mouth and let it slide down his *esophagus.* They are then to read their sentence to the class and ask them to guess the meaning of the underlined word. Show them how to prepare sentences that provide enough context clues.

Fluency with Standard English (Pros and Cons)

In which language or dialect should children be fluent? Should they be expected to become fluent in Standard English? in black English? in Spanish? in one of the native American dialects? What is our role as teachers in this respect?

Answers to these questions cannot be found through examination of research reports. Furthermore, it is doubtful that educators will agree on the answers for some time to come. Let me prepare the two extreme sides on this issue so that you can decide where you stand at this time.

Dialect Defined

Before we begin the debate, we need to define the term *dialect*. What is a dialect? To the person who speaks it, of course, it's the "mother tongue."

A dialect is a variation of a language. One dialect differs from another in three ways. First of all, it differs *phonologically*. That is, it differs in the way people produce phonemes or in the particular phonemes that are used. For example, in some parts of the deep South, native speakers say "fee-ish" for *fish,* adding a long e should before the short i sound. People in Northern parts, who use only the short i sound find that addition quite amusing (although some linguists say that the Southern dialect comes closer to the English of the British Isles in colonial days).

Secondly, it differs *grammatically*. That is, it might differ in the way verb tense, negation, number, and other structural changes are signaled. For instance, someone speaking black English might say "From now on, I don't

In which language or dialect should children be fluent?

be playing"; whereas, someone speaking Standard English (or Anglo English) would say "From now on, I'm not going to play."

Thirdly, it differs *semantically*. That is, actual words or vocabulary used may differ. Someone speaking black English might say, "Please carry me home," while someone speaking Anglo English would say, "Please take me home." Someone in certain parts of New England would call a toilet a "flush." Others would call it a "water closet" or a "toilet."

Dialect differences are not indications of sloppy speech, as some teachers are prone to claim. They are systematic variations of a common language. If you listen to two people speaking black English, for instance, the differences between black and Anglo dialects are consistent.

Let us look now at some fairly systematic differences between black English and Standard English:[2]

1. Omission of the /s/ phoneme at the end of the third person singular, present tense verb, e.g., He look at the picture.

2. Omission of /s/ on plural noun preceded by quantitative modifier, e.g., I got thirteen pencil. I got several pencil. I got many pencil.

3. Omission of /s/ in possessive case, e.g., Give me Bill pencil.

4. Addition of /s/ to first person or third person plural forms of verbs, e.g., I sees it. They lets us do it.

5. Omission of the /d/ phoneme at the end of words, e.g., "tole" for *told*, "ba" for *bad*.

6. Substitution of the /d/ phoneme for voiced /th/ at the beginning of words, e.g., "deh" for *the*, "dat" for *that*.

7. Use of present tense form for past tense verbs, e.g., He ring the bell yesterday. Yesterday I jump rope.

8. Variations on forms of "to be," e.g., They is readin'. They be readin'. They readin'.

9. Double negative for emphasis, e.g., I ain't got no candy.

10. Omission of /r/ at the end of words and syllables, e.g., "foe" for *four*, "Pass" for *Paris*, "cat" for *carrot*.

11. Omission of /l/ at the end of words or near the end of words, e.g., "foo" for *fool*, "fought" for *fault*, "hep" for *help*.

Now let us look at some differences between Spanish and English:[3]

1. The /th/ heard in *thanks* may be pronounced as /t/, making thanks sound like *tanks*. In some dialects the voiced /th/ may be pronounced /d/, making *those* sound like *doze*.

---

[2] It should be noted that just as there are subdialects within Standard English, there are also subdialects within black English. Such subdialects have been ignored here.

[3] The subdialects of Spanish have not been differentiated here. For more detail on dialect differences, see Ching (4).

2. The /ch/ sound and the /sh/ sound may be interchanged, e.g., *chin* may be pronounced *shin* after the child has learned the /sh/ sound.

3. The short /i/ sound may be pronounced like long /e/, e.g., *tin* becomes *teen*.

4. The voiced /s/ heard in *rise* and the unvoiced /s/ heard in *rice* may be interchanged, e.g., *rise* becomes *rice* or *police* becomes *please*.

5. The /v/ sound heard in *very* may be pronounced more like /b/, making *very* sound like *berry*. Also the /b/ may become /v/ in medial positions, e.g., *havit* for *habit*.

6. In words that have a voiced consonant sound at the end (the sound made by vibrating the vocal chords while the mouth is in a consonant position), the voiced sound may be omitted, e.g., *robe* becomes *rope*, *five* becomes *fife*, *dead* becomes *debt*, and *tug* becomes *tuck*.

7. The /s/ sound at the beginning of a word may be preceded by a vowel sound if the /s/ sound is blended with a consonant, e.g., *stop* becomes *es-top*.

8. Noun determiners are sometimes omitted, e.g., She is doctor.

A Debate: Standard vs. Nonstandard English

STANDARD: *Children should be taught Standard English no matter what their background. What makes this country great is the melting pot concept: People coming here from all over the world, learning our language and customs and becoming one great nation.*

NONSTANDARD: *Not a bad idea if it worked. But it hasn't worked and it never will. One out of every six people in this country does not use English as his first language. A third of the native Americans speak their own language as their first language (24).*

STANDARD: *Sure, I know a few people don't speak much English, but they ought to learn it if they want to be Americans.*

NONSTANDARD: *Did you say a few? I said one out of six. And do you realize how many different languages are spoken in this country? In Illinois, just to take one of the states, 141 different languages have been identified (11). And that doesn't count all the dialects of those languages. Furthermore, one of every five new citizens of our country is an immigrant (2). And don't forget, one out of nine Americans is black. Most black in our country speak one of the variants of the black dialect, either as a first or second language. So maybe you'd better face facts: America is not a melting pot. The melting pot idea is a myth. This is a pluralistic society with people trying to maintain their identity—even if it means going against the wishes of the majority culture.*

STANDARD: *I don't care how many languages there are in the United States or how many dialects. The language that counts is Standard English. It's the language of successful people. It's the language you need if you want to get the top jobs. And, since America is a land of opportunity, everyone has the right to learn it so they can be successful and get the good jobs.*

NONSTANDARD: *I agree that Standard English is still the language of power. But that's changing. More and more, people are being hired for positions not because of the color of their skin or the particular way they speak English but because of their competence.*

STANDARD: *You're a dreamer. People have always looked down their noses at those who speak differently from them. Right now the people who have power and prestige—most of them, anyway—speak Standard English. Therefore, to get power and prestige you have to learn Standard English.*

NONSTANDARD: *You haven't been watching television lately. You're just as likely to hear TV stars speak non-standard English as you are to hear them speak Standard English. Archie Bunker wouldn't even be funny if he spoke Standard English.*

STANDARD: *Just my point. One of the reasons we laugh at Archie is because he doesn't speak Standard English. And everyone knows that behind stage when the stars are trying to impress people instead of making them laugh, they're speaking mostly Standard English.*

NONSTANDARD: *You're out-of-date. People don't care anymore how other people speak anymore than they care how they dress. Intelligent people know that one dialect communicates as well as another one. If I say, "I brung you your coat," that communicates just as well as "I brought you your coat." If I say, "He be here," that communicates just as well as "He is here." The person I'm talking to knows exactly what I mean.*

STANDARD: *I may know exactly what you mean, but you can't stop me from feeling that you're ignorant.*

NONSTANDARD: *Go ahead and feel that way. Puff yourself up with your own superiority. The ignorant person is the one who doesn't realize the irrational nature of his own prejudices.*

STANDARD: *I admit that it's irrational, but the world is quite full of irrational people like me, ready to pounce on someone whose clothes or speech are not in fashion. And that's exactly why Standard English should be taught in the schools. Everyone should have the opportunity to avoid such irrational prejudice if they choose.*

NONSTANDARD: *Standard English is doomed. You can't get two people to agree on what it is. A friend of mine (13) sent a questionnaire to a bunch of English professors, high school English teachers, authors, editors, and other people who use the English language a lot in their work. He asked them to look at nineteen sentences and tell him whether they would be acceptable in educated circles. Do you know how many sentences they could agree on? Only two out of the nineteen.*

STANDARD: *I know which questionnaire you're referring to. Those nineteen sentences were concerned with trivial differences, such as whether you should split an infinitive or not. I agree that no one cares about that anymore. But they do care about whether you use* brung *or* brought. *If you take two people with the same job qualifications, the one who says* brought *will get the job.*

NONSTANDARD: *You're out-of-date.*

STANDARD: *We'll see.*

Teaching Standard English

If you do decide to help children speak Standard English more fluently, here is a suggestion: *Appreciate* the vernacular (language or dialect) and culture of your student. Teachers often treat foreign exchange students with respect, offering them extra help and asking them to share their culture with the rest of the class. Those same teachers are sometimes ready to pounce on a student who speaks with a Spanish dialect, black dialect, or Appalachian dialect. Imagine the psychological damage that is done to children who are told, in essence, that they and their parents must be stupid.

The point is that teachers should not so much "help" children learn Standard English as they should share on an *equal* basis their different languages or dialects and their different cultures. The attitude needed by teachers is one of being a student as well as a teacher. Not so you can trick the children into learning Standard English but so that you can establish an honest environment of learning together.

This problem of teacher attitude occurs all over the world. Children on the border between Brazil and Uruguay, for example, speak a dialect that is quite dissimilar from the dialect used in the schools. Eloisa (8), the chief of the mental retardation section at the Inter-American Children's Institute in Montevideo, Uruguay, says that these border children are typically way behind the other children in the schools. The problem, she says, is the teachers. Many of them refuse to treat the border dialect as a valid language with long roots in history and one through which its users "can express their full personalities."

One way to appreciate a minority child's culture and vernacular is to use her language or dialect as a temporary teaching medium. This is called the bilingual approach and simply means that the children learn how to read and write in their native language or dialect while at the same time becoming more fluent in Standard English. This approach often requires special teachers or aides who understand the dialect or language better than the regular teacher. It has been used with some success in various parts of the country.

Because of the problem of finding sufficient materials for reading instruction, the bilingual approach usually requires the use of the language experience approach. In essence, this approach requires a bilingual teacher or aide to take dictation from the children in their language or dialect. The transcribed dictation then becomes the source of reading materials. Naturally, such practice in dictating experiences and ideas to a sympathetic adult is highly appropriate for increasing children's fluency in speech. As the children learn more and more Standard English, the experience charts reflect the changes in their speech, from monolingual to bilingual (from using only their mother tongue to using both mother tongue and Standard English).

Using Creative Grammar

The use of creative grammar is very appropriate in a bilingual approach. The bilingual teacher or aide can begin the creative grammar experiences by using the sentence patterns common to the children's particular dialect or language. As the children acquire more facility with Standard English, the patterns can be gradually altered to reflect this greater facility. Once children are becoming comfortable with the idea of speaking two dialects or languages, they can be taught by the creative grammar approach to refine the elements of Standard English that they need help with.

For instance, if you're trying to get them to use the standard *isn't* as well as the nonstandard *ain't,* you could begin with the pattern: "He ain't in the house, He ain't by the barn, He ain't down the road, etc." After they all get in this particular pattern club, you give them a new pattern: "He isn't in the house, He isn't by the barn, He isn't down the road, etc." The goal is not to make them ashamed of their particular dialect of language or to feel that one is correct and one isn't. The goal is to make the children bilingual or bidialectal.

Fluency with Phonological and Grammatical Symbols

So far, we've talked about fluency with sentences, words, and Standard English. A fluent speaker also needs to be skillful with such things as articulation, enunciation, pronunciation, pitch changes, volume changes, rate changes, morpheme stress, pauses, and gestures. Let's look at some of these briefly.

Articulation

By the time a child reaches kindergarten age, she can normally articulate all of the phonemes except for the following:

/l/ as in *lump* or *belly* (The child might say "wump")
/r/ as in *running* or *carrot* ("wunning")
/s/ as in *six* or *bus* ("buth")
/v/ as in *valentine* or *love* ("balentine")
/z/ as in *zoo* or *does* ("soo")
/th/ as in *this* or *that* ("dis")
/th/ as in *think* or *bath* ("baf")
/zh/ as in *measure* or *television* ("meajure")
/sh/ as in *sugar* or *rash* ("rass")

Normally, children learn to articulate all of these phonemes by the time they reach their eighth birthday. Some teachers prefer to "let nature take its course," and ignore misarticulations until the child reaches the age of eight. This practice might be all right except for the problem of teasing peers and nervous parents. Some parents are so worried about their children's misarticulations they begin to "jump" on their child at every instance, thus making the child overly conscious of his speech. This type of overconcern could lead to worse problems such as stuttering (12).

Our recommendation is that teachers in the early grades very casually work with their students on articulation, using articulation games, songs, and records such as those described in *Talking Time* (20). If some of the children continue to misarticulate, then they should be referred to a speech therapist. In any event, it is *not* advisable to wait past the middle of first grade to make such a referral. Waiting longer than this could lead to psychological damage caused by teasing from peers and pressure from anxious adults.

Enunciation

Children may know how to articulate each of the phonemes associated with letters but not always enunciate those sounds. Poor enunciation leads to frustrated listeners and poor communication. Sometimes weak enunciation is simply related to a dialect difference. For example, a child speaking black English will often omit the /s/, /d/, /r/, and /l/ phonemes at the end of words, saying He *look* instead of He *looks,* or *baa* for *bad.* Sometimes weak enunciation is caused by shyness and a related fear that one's words will be rejected. There seems to be an unconscious hope that by not enunciating the words clearly, the rejection will be less severe (similar to the child who doesn't know how to spell a word and, therefore, writes it as sloppily as possible).

Whatever the cause, one of the best ways of helping children see the value of better enunciation is through the use of creative drama, choral reading, choral reciting, and choral singing. With choral reading, for example, a poem is selected *that the children really like.* Some parts are read by the entire group, some by two people as a duet, and some by soloists. If the poem is easy enough, the children can recite it by heart. A similar kind of arrangement can be made with songs. After you have several selections ready, invite another group of children to hear your renditions.

Choral arrangements provide the children with an incentive for careful enunciation so that the audience will hear each word clearly. In preparation for the audience, children in your group should take turns sitting in the back and listening for words that are not clear. (Using a tape recorder also provides very useful feedback.)

Pronunciation

Why does Kathy say "nú-que-lar" rather than "nú-cle-ar" for the word, *nuclear?* Why does Robin say "chimbley" instead of *chimney?* Mispronunciations such as these are caused either by hearing other people mispronounce the words or by misperceiving the word. One of the best ways of correcting mispronunciations, surprisingly enough, is through weekly spelling tests. In preparation for the spelling tests, you can work with the children on the correct pronunciation, showing them how the correct pronunciation will often help them in spelling a word correctly.

Sometimes the terms *articulation, enunciation,* and *pronunciation* are confused. The following are definitions of the three words and examples of each:

> *articulation*—forming phonemes correctly with the tongue, teeth, lips, and other parts of the mouth. Example: He's running vs. He's wunning.
>
> *enunciation*—clear, precise speaking of beginnings and endings of words, giving each syllable and word its full value. Example: What are you doing? vs. Whacha doin?
>
> *pronunciation*—saying a word in a way that is acceptable in "educated circles." Example: I tacked the pick-cher to the wall, instead of I tacked the pit-cher to the wall.

Pitch, Stress, and Juncture

Three things which communicate meaning to a listener and also make the speaker more interesting are the speaker's pitch variations, stress signals, and pauses—the expressiveness of the person's speech. Since expressiveness can best be introduced through reading and writing exercises, we will discuss instructional strategies for this under "Encouraging Better Punctuation" in Module 5.

Fluency and Self-confidence Through Creative Drama

"The play's the thing wherein I'll catch the imagination . . ." (Shakespeare, *Hamlet*). The play *is* the thing. Children are natural actors and actresses. From the age of two on, they spend a great deal of their time imagining they are someone else. (Some of us never get out of the habit.) Creative, spontaneous drama is almost as natural as breathing to preschoolers. It is unfortunate that such spontaneity and fluency in speech is discouraged as they grow older.

It takes a skillful teacher to take children back to that natural state, but it can be done, and it's well worth the effort. Primary grade teachers in Great Britain have been using creative drama for decades as a basic medium for developing poise, self-confidence, and fluency in speech. In the schools of the United States, it seems to move into the curriculum as a fad every so often and then disappear as another fad takes its place.

I have watched the shyest of children become confident and fluent during period after period of creative drama, with their newfound self-assurance creeping into their daily communication. It won't work for all children, of course, but for many, it's the surest way I know of breaking the emotional block that keeps them from expressing themselves with ease.

A creative drama program is best incorporated into an ongoing language arts program that is creative in spirit. Ways of developing this spirit are discussed in Module 6. This module will concentrate on specific procedures for engaging children in creative drama experiences. The most common mistake made by teachers is to place children in audience situations too soon. Children are asked to do something in front of the rest of the group. Some of them are born hams and enjoy it immensely. Others feel like fools and vow never to engage in creative drama again.

The actor-audience ratio should be a crucial concern of the teacher involved in helping children express themselves through creative drama. Beginning experiences in drama should almost always have something like a thirty to zero ratio—in other words, thirty actors and no audience. Only very gradually should you work up to a one to thirty ratio.

The following is one recommended sequence of creative drama experiences for children:

1. Total group movement to music (no audience).
2. Total group movement—no music (no audience).
3. Total group pantomime (each child following the teacher's directions).
4. Total group dialogue and characterization in pairs (each child has audience of one).
5. Total group dialogue and characterization in clusters (audience of three or four).
6. Small group skits (three or more actors; rest of group as audience).
7. Role playing (two or three actors; rest of group as audience).
8. Monologue (one actor; rest of group as audience).

Let's look at each of these steps briefly to illustrate how they might be carried out in a regular classroom situation.

Total Group Movement to Music

In this initial step, you will probably need to be very firm in establishing and maintaining rules. Discourage anyone from watching anyone else. Have them pretend they are all by themselves in an empty room with nothing to hear but the music. Have them spread out so that they do not touch each other. Discourage any touching at this point. If possible have them get on their knees at first and move to the music without using their feet. Try not to let anyone talk or break the mood of the music in any way. Have them close their eyes if it helps them move more freely.

Then have them open their eyes and get up slowly to the music without looking at anyone else. This requires a great deal of discipline for some children, so you may have to quietly remind them several times. Use slow music the first few times in order to maintain a calm atmosphere. Encourage them to move every part of their bodies. Once the music is playing, though, do not call attention to anyone, either with encouragement or disapproval. Sometimes it helps to tell them to move as if they were part of a slow-motion movie.

Total Group Movement—No Music

This step should be combined with Step 1 at first. Simply stop the music every now and then and have them move as if the music were still playing. Again, discourage them from looking at each other. The object is to get them completely wrapped up in the movements they are making. Tell them to think of themselves not as people but just as something that moves.

Total Group Pantomime

This step is a natural outgrowth of the first two steps. Sometime during the course of their movement to music and their movement without music, you can direct them to be something. "Be a chicken pecking its way out of the egg. Be a bird with only one wing. Be a drummer marching in a parade."

Later you can try more complicated pantomimes in which they have to listen to a series of steps. For example, describe to them in detail how you got up in the morning while they pantomime everything you say: "And then I unscrewed the cap from the toothpaste, squeezed some paste on my brush, brushed my lower teeth, and then my upper teeth, etc. Meanwhile, they are all pantomiming the same thing and pretending that no one else is in the room.

Total Group Dialogue and Characterization in Pairs

For this step, you will need to find a partner for each child. (You may have to be one of the partners.) Have them sit or stand close to their partners and carry on a nonviolent argument. For instance, you could have them imagine they are watching television and arguing about which program they're going to watch, why one is better than the other and why they simply have to watch a particular one rather than the one the partner wants to watch. Or have them argue about who's the best movie star or best music group or which sport is the best. In any case, there should be no audience. Every pair is talking at the same time. This keeps them from getting self-conscious and allowing their flow of speech to stop.

After they have done this with several different partners and with several different arguments, you are ready to develop characterization. Instead of having them speak for themselves, have them imagine they are someone else. At first you'll want to assign a character to them: "One of you be an old, tired farmer who's just finished a day of harvesting wheat. The other person should be a young city person who has just finished a day at the office. Argue with each other about who has to work the hardest.

After several of these experiences, you can increase the level of the characterization by describing the characters they are to play in much greater detail and by presenting a more detailed conflict; e.g., "One of you will be an old, tired shopkeeper about to close up your toy shop. You want to get home soon because your granddaughter is sick and you want to fix supper for the two of you. The toy shop has been losing money lately, and you think you'll have to close it up. But you don't know how you'll earn enough money to take care of yourself and your ten-year-old granddaughter. Your stomach's been acting up lately, and you wonder if you shouldn't see a doctor.

The other person is a young person with a good job and plenty of money. Just as the stores are closing, you realize that you forgot to get your ten-year-old daughter a birthday present. Your mind is on all the money you plan to make during the next year. You just want to get a toy quickly and get on home to a good meal. But here's the *conflict:* You manage to get into the store even though the shopkeeper is turning out the lights. But he doesn't want to sell you anything. He has closed up his cash drawer and wants to go home. You simply *have* to get a toy for your daughter or she will be very disappointed."

Total Group Dialogue and Characterization in Clusters

This is similar to Step 4, but instead you set up situations that make it possible for people to eavesdrop on other people's conversations. For instance, half the class can be selling their goods at an open-air market. Let each person decide what he is selling. The other half of the class walks around and stops individually to find out what an individual seller is selling. At any one point, then, you might have every seller busy selling to a buyer; but more likely, you'll have some sellers busy selling, some buyers busy buying, and the rest of the sellers and buyers just listening to the dialogues. Thus, you have introduced a real audience.

Small Group Skits

By this time, the children are used to acting in front of others (even though they weren't supposed to be watching each other). You can now move with little trouble into small group performances in front of an audience (as long as this audience is composed of the children who have been participating all along in the other activities.) Steps 4 and 5 can now be modified so that three or more people are interacting. For instance, three people can be arguing over which television program to watch. A third person can come into that toy shop and act as a referee.

Once these skits have been well developed without an audience (everyone carrying on their skits at the same time), you can ask one small group to repeat its skit for the rest of the large group. Then another small group can show how it handled the situation in a different way, and so on. Eventually,

Creative drama can be an excellent medium for encouraging fluency and self-confidence.

you'll be able to get to the point where you can state the situation, the characters, and the conflict and let one small group at a time try its hand at dramatizing the scene while the rest of the large group watch.

Using Small Group Skits to Enrich the Curriculum

Ideas that are presented to children through their reading of social studies texts, basal readers, or library books can often be made more meaningful through creative dramatizations. The following is a description of one teacher's approach toward the use of creative drama in his fifth-grade social studies program.

Mr. Novick and his pupils were studying European exploration of the Americas. The class was divided into five groups, one which chose to study Coronado, one to study Columbus, and so on. Each group was given help in finding information from library sources and the textbook. Each group then planned a skit that would present the major ideas about the explorer. The plans were presented by each small group to Mr. Novick. Mr. Novick praised them for their work but asked questions to show them where they still needed to do more research. After further research, the groups modified their plans for their skits and again presented their ideas to Mr. Novick. If Mr. Novick approved their plans, they were free to rehearse their skits in earnest.

Once all five groups had their skits ready, they presented them in a theater-in-the-round fashion (skit in the middle of the room—audience in a circle). After each skit was over, the audience provided praise and specific suggestions for improvement. Further rehearsals prepared the groups for their presentation of the skits to another class.

Mr. Novick's approach was very well-structured and certainly made the social studies concepts and terms more real to the children. However, not all drama experiences related to the curriculum need to be this elaborate. Once the children have become used to giving spontaneous skits, they can be invited at any time to dramatize something they've been reading about. After one small group has tried it, another group can be asked to give an interpretation. Inviting another class into the room (or another group in a team-teaching situation) can be reserved for very special occasions when the children have decided with you to polish a skit for a larger audience.

Role Playing

Role playing is a sophisticated form of creative drama and is generally not recommended before the students have been engaged in the earlier steps. In a role-playing situation, two or more people are usually asked to confront each other. Both people have their roles defined for them, but this role definition is kept secret from each other. For example, one person is asked to play the part of a parent who suspects that her child has been taking money out of the family cash drawer. That person is secretly told how to behave—sometimes by way of written instructions, sometimes by word of mouth. The other person is asked to play the part of the child who actually has been taking money but wishes to deny it. No solution is proposed to the two actors. The solution arises out of the interaction of the two role players. After one pair solves the problem, usually another pair carries on the role playing again, solving it in another way.

A simpler form of role playing is one in which the teacher takes one of the roles and the children confront the teacher one at a time. For instance, the teacher can play the role of a stern gatekeeper who won't let the children past the gate into Magic Land unless they have a very good excuse. Here is an example of one such role-playing situation.

GATEKEEPER: *Who are you and what is your problem?*
MAXINE: *I'm a little baby and I'm not growing up fast enough.*
GATEKEEPER: *Why do you want to grow up faster?*
MAXINE: *(Thinks hard) Because . . . my brothers and sisters all know how to walk and run, and they get to go places. I have to lie on my back all the time, and I get very bored.*
GATEKEEPER: *Everyone gets bored sometimes. That's not a very good reason for wanting to grow up faster.*
MAXINE: *(Thinks again) Well, I want to grow up faster because I heard that gatekeepers don't live forever.*
GATEKEEPER: *That's true, but what does that have to do with it?*
MAXINE: *Well, I want to be a gatekeeper, and since you look*

so old, you probably won't live much longer, and so I've got to grow up and take your place real soon.

GATEKEEPER: *(Laughing) That's a very good reason. You may pass. (Looking sternly at the next person in line) Who are you and what is your problem?*

Monologue

The monologue step, of course, is the most sophisticated step of all. It is not often reached by a group of children. In this step we find children standing up in front of a group (small at first, then large), talking to no one but themselves. In other words, they are to have a conversation with themselves. Topics used for this purpose are often the I wonder if or I wonder why variety: "I wonder what would happen if I didn't go to school today? I'll just get off the bus where they change and keep walking right down to that store I've always wanted to go to. and when I get there I'll say, 'I'd like a hot fudge sundae, please.' And he'll say, 'What's a little girl like you doing buying a hot fudge sundae when she should be going to school.' And I'll say to him. . . ."

Another format is simply that of telling a story of something that really happened, using dialogue whenever appropriate and sometimes demonstrating the action that took place. In either case, the students are encouraged to talk as actors—putting themselves across as a character in a play—using gestures, action, and facial expressions.

Integrating the Basics Through Creative Drama

You have probably noticed that creative drama can be an excellent medium for developing many of the basic skills. Either in acting or audience situations, children have to listen carefully to follow a sequence of events or ideas, predict events which should logically follow, distinguish between literal and figurative expressions, respond creatively to problems, and apply critical evaluations to performances. As speaking actors, they have to quickly select from their own personal reservoir those words, sentence arrangements, dialects, and elements of style that will not only communicate to other actors but interest the audience as well. They have to enunciate clearly and articulate accurately, as well as select the appropriate volume, rate, pitch changes, stress, pauses, and gestures.

As creators of plays, particularly those which relate to social studies and other areas of the curriculum, they are often involved in reading and writing activities. Their reading activities require them to practice their decoding skills, develop associations and images from their reading, follow a sequence of events and ideas, recognize significant details and main ideas, determine accuracy of printed information, and respond creatively to what is read. Their writing activities demand good spelling, handwriting, and punctuation—all necessary for communicating to the actors—note-taking abilities, and interest-attracting techniques of communication.

SUMMARY

In this module, the desire and need for greater fluency that most children experience is discussed. It is suggested that fluency requires self-confidence, a need to communicate, and reservoirs of words, sentence arrangements, and grammatical signals. Learning activities for increasing those reservoirs and procedures for calling them into use through creative grammar exercises and creative drama are illustrated. Fluency in speech and writing is the goal of all those who wish to communicate better. Teachers can provide the verbal and nonverbal experiences necessary for helping children reach that goal.

REFERENCES AND BIBLIOGRAPHY

1. Barnfield, Gabriel. *Creative Drama in Schools*. New York: Hart, 1968.

2. Bethell, Thomas. "Becoming an American." *Newsweek* (May 26, 1975): 13.

3. Bordan, Sylvia D. *Plays as Teaching Tools in the Elementary School*. Englewood Cliffs, N.J.: Parker, 1970.

4. Brown, Margaret. "A Practical Approach to Analyzing Children's Talk in the Classroom." *Language Arts* 54 (May, 1977): 506–10.

5. Ching, Doris C. *Reading and the Bilingual Child*. Newark, Del.: International Reading Association, 1976.

6. Dale, Edgar. *Audiovisual Methods in Teaching*. New York: Holt, Rinehart and Winston, 1969.

7. Edelsky, Carole. "Teaching Oral Language." *Language Arts* 55 (March 1978): 291–96.

8. Eloisa, Maria Garcia De Lorenzo. "Frontier Dialect: A Challenge to Education." *Reading Teacher* 28 (April 1975): 653–58.

9. Gillies, Emily. *Creative Dramatics for All Children*. Washington, D.C.: Association for Childhood Education International, 1973.

10. Goodridge, Janet. *Creative Drama and Improvised Movement for Children*. Boston: Plays, 1971.

11. Johnson, Laura. "Bilingual Bicultural Education: A Two-Way Street." *Reading Teacher* 29 (Dec. 1975): 231–39.

12. Johnson, Wendell. *Stuttering and What You Can Do About It*. Danville, Ill.: Interstate, 1966.

13. Lewis, Norman. "How Correct Must Correct English Be?" *Harpers* 198 (March 1949): 68–74.

14. Marcoux, J.P. "Helping Emotionally Disturbed Children Through Creative Dramatics." *Community Education* 25 (March 1976): 174–77.

15. May, Frank B., and Odegaard, Joanne. "Creative Grammar and the Writing of Third Graders." *Elementary School Journal* 72 (Dec. 1972): 433–38.

16. Mazor, Rickey. "Drama as Experience." *Language Arts* 55 (March 1978): 328–33.

17. McCaslin, Nellie. *Creative Dramatics in the Classroom*. New York: David McKay, 1968.

18. Ross, E.P., and Roe, B.D. "Creative Drama Builds Proficiency in Reading." *Reading Teacher* 30 (Jan. 1977): 383–87.

19. Sanders, Sandra. *Creating Plays with Children*. New York: Citation Press, 1970.

20. Scott, Louise B., and Thompson, Jesse J. *Talking Time*. New York: McGraw-Hill, 1966.

21. Siks, Geraldine Brain. *Drama with Children*. New York: Harper & Row, 1977.

22. Stewig, John W. *Spantaneous Drama: A Language Art*. Columbus, O.: Charles E. Merrill, 1973.

23. Strom, Ingrid M. "Research in Grammar and Usage and Its Implications for Teaching Writing." *Bulletin of the School of Education, Indiana University* 36 (Sept. 1960).

24. U.S. Commission on Human Rights. *A Better Chance to Learn: Bilingual-Bicultural Education*. Washington, D.C.: Clearing House Publication #51, May 1975.

25. Way, Brian. *Development Through Drama*. New York: Humanities Press, 1967.

Teaching the Basic Skills of Handwriting, Spelling, and Punctuation

Methods are the masters of masters.
Alexander A. Talleyrande-Perigord

Custom is the universal sovereign.
Pindar

Most of the requirements for fluent speech are also requirements for fluent writing. Both speaking and writing require self-confidence, a large vocabulary, a reservoir of sentence arrangements and grammatical signals, and an awareness of the dialect required for a particular social situation.

But writing requires more. In order to write fluently, children must also master the intricate motions required for producing the written representation of the words they speak. They must gain intuitively the phonological and morphological principles which enable them to predict the spelling of many words they don't know how to spell. They must memorize a large number of words whose letters do not correspond to their sounds. And they must learn how to signal pitch, stress, and juncture with written symbols.

In this module, the nature of spelling, punctuation, and legible handwriting will be discussed. Techniques for teaching these three skills will be suggested, along with ideas for incorporating them in the total language arts program.

Special Prerequisites for Module 5

It is recommended that you complete Modules 1–4 before beginning this module. There are no other special prerequisites.

Long-range Outcomes Related to Module 5

This module should help you as a teacher to do the following:

1. Communicate with other professional educators about methods of teaching spelling, punctuation, and handwriting.

2. Instruct children in the mechanics of legible manuscript and cursive writing.
3. Use effective teaching steps in introducing children to new letter formations.
4. Help children evaluate their own handwriting.
5. Provide special help to left-handed children.
6. Select appropriate words to emphasize in a spelling program.
7. Use learning principles to motivate children to improve their spelling.
8. Use learning principles to aid children's retention of a spelling vocabulary.
9. Utilize all of the language arts to teach punctuation, spelling, and handwriting.

Performance Objectives for Knowledge Level

To give yourself an overview of what is expected of you in this module, you should first scan the objectives and performance standards at all three levels— knowledge, simulation, and teaching. Then use the study guide during your reading of the module. As you find information related to the study guide, write it down in the available blanks or on a separate piece of paper. Then review this information shortly before your knowledge level examination.

1.1 On a closed-book examination, you should be able to select the best alternative for each multiple-choice question and circle the letter of your choice. The multiple-choice questions (given in the study guide without the alternatives) will be selected from those shown in the study guide. Next to each one write the alternative that you predict will be the correct one on the examination.

1.2 On the same examination, you will be expected to provide information in short, concise sentences either by producing a list, completing a list, or by writing principles of learning. The information called for is described in the study guide.

1.3 On the same examination, you will be presented with samples of teacher behavior in which the teacher is using principles of *motivation* to encourage an increase in spelling vocabulary. After each sample, you will be asked to write the learning principle which the teacher is using the most. To help you prepare for this part of the examination, you may want to write the four principles of motivation from memory in the space given in the study guide.

1.4 On the same examination, you will be presented with samples of teacher behavior in which the teacher is using principles of learning to encourage *retention* of a spelling vocabulary. To help you prepare for this part of the examination, you may want to write the four principles of retention from memory in the space given in the study guide.

1.5 On the same examination, you will be asked to match types of spelling errors with samples of those errors. The types of spelling errors are listed in the study guide.

Study Guide for Knowledge Level Examination

1. Because of poor handwriting, how many letters end up in the "dead letter" pile each year in U.S. Post Offices?

2. What is the major goal of handwriting instruction today?

3. List the five major causes of illegible handwriting.

4. In providing readiness experiences for handwriting, it is traditional to have children draw their lines from top to bottom and their circles counterclockwise starting at the two o'clock position. What is one possible disadvantage of this procedure?

5. What is the major advantage of the continuous-stroke method of teaching manuscript over the circle-line method?

6. When is the transfer from manuscript to cursive usually made?

7. Write in the missing steps for teaching manuscript or cursive letters.

   a. Meaningful word
   b.

   c. Analysis of strokes
   d. Imitation of word

   e.
   f.

   g. Independent production of word

8. Hooked writing is not very amenable to correction after what grade?

9. Five suggestions for helping left-handers were given. Summarize those suggestions here.

10. What should be done about most children with mixed preference?

11. What method of having children evaluate their own handwriting is probably the most effective?

12. There are about forty-five different phonemes in the English language. About how many graphemes are there?

13. What determines the placement of a spelling word in a commercial program?

14. How was the "Basic Sight Vocabulary of 96 Irregular Words" obtained?

15. On the examination, you will be given samples of teacher behavior in which the teacher is using principles of motivation as these relate to the spelling program. To prepare for this part of the exam, try writing the principles from memory.

      Motivation (Novelty Needs Level Feedback)

16. On the examination, you will be expected to match types of spelling errors with samples of those errors. The types are listed below. Next to each one, write a sample to help you remember the type. The first one has been done for you.
    a. Pronunciation: chimley for chimney
    b. Suffixes:
    c. Prefixes:
    d. Transposals:
         reversals:
         inversions:

   e. Homophones:
   f. Regularized
      spelling:
   g. Phonic
      elements:
   h. Vowel patterns:
   i. Handwriting:

17. How is the Baf Test useful for teaching spelling?

18. The four-day plan for proofreading was suggested as a way of keeping form and substance separated. With as few words as possible, describe what happens on each of the four days.

Day one: Write with little regard for spelling or punctuation.

Day two:

Day three:

Day four:

19. In the Mini-Test Spelling Program, what happens on each day; summarize with as few words as possible.

Pretest on first set; correction & study;
Monday: post test, correction

Tuesday:

Wednesday:

Thursday:

Friday:

20. Horn recommends six study steps for learning to spell new words. Write in the missing steps.

   a. Look at the word and say it to yourself.
   b.
   c. Check to see if you were right. (If not, repeat steps a–c.)
   d.
   e. Check to see if you were right. (If not, repeat steps d and e.)
   f.

21. Special steps for dyslexic children are recommended. Write in the missing steps.

    a. Have each child write each word on the board, saying each letter out loud as he writes it.

    b.

    c. Then have them close their eyes and trace it while spelling it out loud.

    d.

    e. Have them check to see if they are right. If not, they should repeat steps 4 and 5—or if necessary, repeat steps 1–5.

    f.

22. Try writing from memory the principles of retention.

    Principles of Retention (Involved Masters Practice Transfer)

23. List three ways of encouraging better punctuation.

Performance Standards for Knowledge Level

A. Twenty-five minute time limit on 1.1 through 1.5 combined.

B. Completion deadline: instructor will notify.

C. Recommended grading standards—if grades are used: 96% = A; 92% = A—; 88% = B; 84% = C; below 80% = incomplete; should be completed at 80% or better before you go on to performance objectives for simulation level. (The instructor may wish to permit a grade of A or B only the first time the test is given in order to encourage more intensive study.)

Performance Objectives for Simulation Level

2.1 On a closed-book examination, you will be given the written compositions of two children, one demonstrating three or more types of handwriting problems and the other demonstrating three or more types of spelling errors.

2.2 For the one designated "Handwriting," diagnose the child's handwriting problems. List, in order of their severity, the three types of problems that are most severe. After each type of problem, indicate briefly how you would help the child remedy his problem.

2.3 For the one designated "Spelling," diagnose the child's spelling errors. List, in order of their severity, the three types of errors that are most severe. After each type of error, indicate how you would help the child remedy his error.

Performance Standards for Simulation Level

A. Forty minute time limit.

B. Completion deadline: instructor will notify.

C. About 80 percent agreement with instructor on problems and errors listed, order of listing, and specific remedies.

D. Should be completed at C level or better before moving on to teaching level.

Performance Objectives for Teaching Level

3.1 In a micro-teaching, observation, student teaching, intern, or supervised situation, diagnose the spelling and handwriting problems of two or more children and provide specific remedial instruction whenever appropriate. Write up a brief report of what you found and what you did.

3.2 (Alternative Objective) In the same type of setting described in 3.1, teach one or more lessons on handwriting, spelling, or punctuation. Lesson plan, worksheet, and critique are required. (See Module 4 for a review of what should be included.)

Performance Standards for Teaching Level

A. For objective 3.1 (diagnosis of spelling and handwriting problems)
   1. Report is clear and concise; free of spelling and punctuation errors.
   2. Shows understanding of handwriting problems and spelling errors.
   3. Attempted to apply appropriate remediation procedures.
   4. Uses learning principles effectively; does not violate any of those discussed in Module 3.

B. For objective 3.2 (lesson on spelling, handwriting, or punctuation)
   1. Performance objectives clearly state behavior desired, the conditions under which the behavior is to be performed, and those performance standards which will indicate sufficient mastery of the desired behavior.
   2. Performance objectives relate directly to the long-range outcome; the learning activities relate both to the performance objectives and the long-range outcome.
   3. Shows clear understanding of the skill or concept being taught.
   4. Uses learning principles effectively; does not violate any of those discussed in Module 3.

The Importance of Good Handwriting

Because of poor handwriting, nearly a million letters a year end up in the "dead letter" pile in U.S. Post Offices. Nearly a half-million income tax refunds are delayed each year because the Internal Revenue Service can't read the illegible returns. In fact, illegible handwriting causes U.S. businesses to lose over $1 million a *week* because of scrambled orders, lost time, missent deliveries, and other clerical mistakes (13).

Some say the answer to this type of problem is to make people use a typewriter. The typewriter, however, is not as portable as a pen or pencil. Thus, the pen or pencil is the preferred writing device: it is handier, less expensive, easier to carry, and much quieter.

Some say the answer is to have people use the telephone or dictaphone. This is certainly one good solution, providing everyone enunciates perfectly, uses the same dialect, and listens with 100 percent concentration—conditions which are obviously impossible. And what if the person at the other end of the line has to take a message?

Handwriting is still in common use today and probably will remain so for many years to come. Surveys (13) show that the most common uses for handwriting are the following:

1. Making out checks
2. Filling out forms (such as job applications)
3. Writing letters to friends
4. Keeping records (business and personal)
5. Jotting down reminder notes
6. Preparing shopping lists

This list doesn't even include the numerous moments that students must use a pencil or pen—to take notes, to take an examination, to "head" their papers, and to fill in worksheets.

Before continuing, produce a sample of your own handwriting. Either in the space below or on a separate sheet of paper *that you keep until you have completed Module 5,* write the following sentence *three* times, as *fast* as you can: I pledge allegiance to the flag of the United States of America and to the republic for which it stands.

Now write the sentence only once but write it slowly with *your very best hand-writing.*

The Goals of Handwriting Instruction

Assuming, then, that good handwriting is still important in today's world, what do you think the major goal of handwriting instruction should be? At one time, a major goal was beauty—the more flourishes and curlicues one's handwriting had, the better. Thus, you would get writing that might look like Figure 5.1.

The problem with this type of writing was that everyone tried to outdo the other person. Writing became an art form with each person trying to be more artistic than everyone else. Naturally, with all that individuality and all those curlicues, writing was sometimes very illegible. It was lovely to look at

FIGURE 5.1

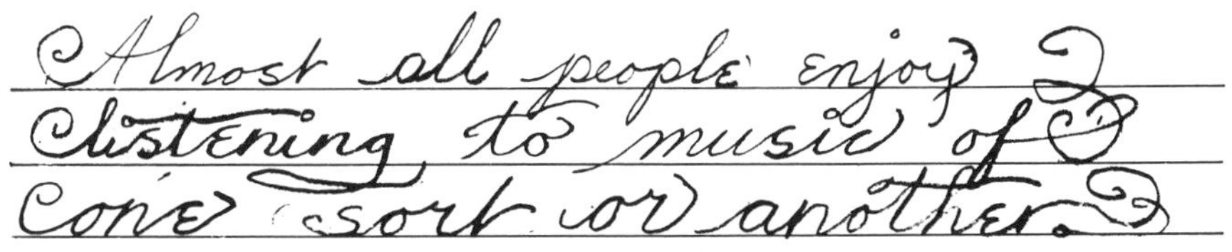

and next to impossible to read. In fact, in spite of the complaints from employers and parents today that handwriting "ain't what it used to be," it was no more legible in the early 1900's than it is today (4).

The next movement in handwriting instruction was one of standardization. Make everyone write in the very same way, then we'll all be able to read each other's writing. And while you're at it, get rid of the curlicues and other fancy squiggles. Make it legible but still pretty—and above all, make it the same for everybody.

But that goal didn't work either. The problem was who should determine the standard way to write. Publishing houses which produced handwriting programs for teachers and students disagreed on such matters. And teachers didn't always follow the handwriting programs they were supposed to follow. Mrs. Kintzle, for instance, didn't like the way she was supposed to teach the children to make the capital P. It wasn't the way she had learned to make it, and her way was better.

To make things even more complicated, the children didn't go along with the standardization idea. Some children wanted to express their own personalities through their handwriting. For example, one might have wanted to put a curlicue in her S even though Mrs. Kintzle didn't like it. Another might have wanted to make a nice simple F instead of the funny one Mrs. Kintzle wanted him to make. The battle line was drawn: Mrs. Kintzle, wielding her terrible red pencil, smote down the students whenever they dared to hand in a paper with their own S and F. The students, waging that ever-popular form of rebellion called psychological warfare, slipped in their own S and F at every opportunity.

The standardization goal might have worked in a more authoritarian society, perhaps with a dictator deciding once and for all which shape was the standard shape for letters. But it failed in our society.

Today, our goal in handwriting instruction is simply *legibility*—writing that is not necessarily beautiful, not necessarily like that of everyone else, but easily produced and easily read.

The Nature of Legible Writing

To determine the nature of legible writing, we need to look at it from a negative standpoint: What makes writing illegible? There are five main causes of illegibility. Let's look at them one at a time. What is the major cause of illegibility in Figure 5.2?

FIGURE 5.2 Cause of Illegibility #1

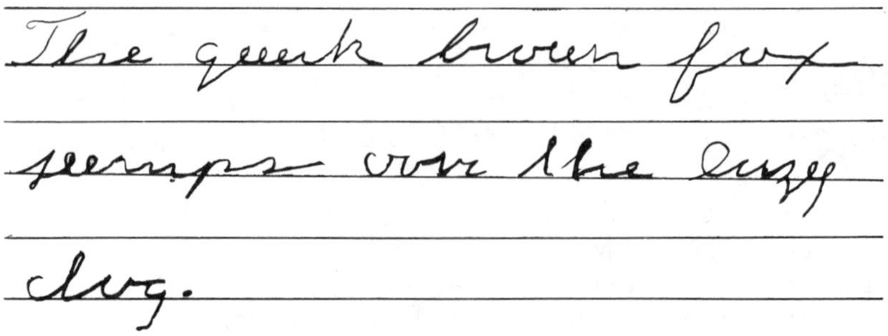

In Figure 5.2, we see that a major cause of illegibility and perhaps the most important one, is the *shape* of the letters. The shape or form of many letters is not clear: the *h* in *The* looks like *l-r*; the *u* in *quick* looks like *e-e*; the *b* in *brown* looks like *l*; the *o* in *fox* looks like *u*; the *m* in *jumps* looks like *r-n*; the *e* in *over* looks like *i*; the *t* in *the* looks like *l*; the *l* in *lazy* looks like *e*; and the *d* in *dog* looks like *c-l*. Thus, the simple sentence, The quick brown fox jumps over the lazy dog, looks like this: Tlre qeeeik lrueen fux jeernps uvir llre euzee club. This type of handwriting obviously does not communicate.

What is the major cause of illegibility in Figure 5.3? In Figure 5.3, we find that another cause of illegibility is the lack of *alignment* of the letters and words. One tends to get a bit seasick as one tries to follow the wavy flow of words. Although poor alignment is not as serious a problem as poorly defined shapes of letters, it is, nevertheless, a distracting factor for the reader, who must expend extra energy in deciphering the message.

FIGURE 5.3 Cause of Illegibility #2

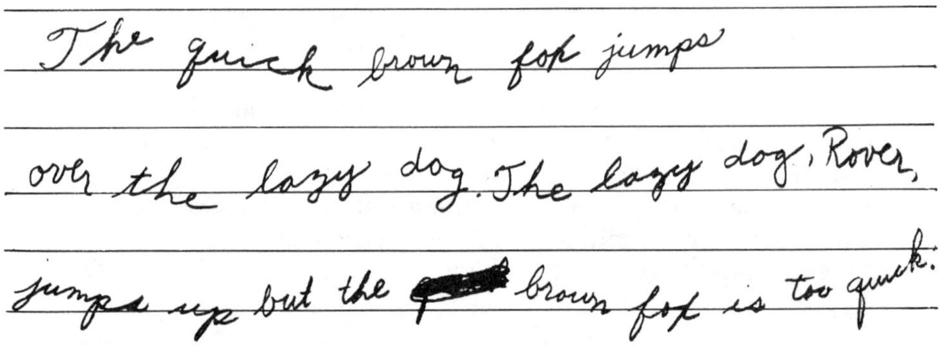

What is the major cause of illegibility in Figure 5.4? Figure 5.4 shows a third cause of illegibility, the inconsistent *slant* of the writer. For purposes of legibility, it doesn't really matter which way the letters are slanted, as long as they are all slanted the same way. When the letters are inconsistently slanted, however, it tends to make the writing less legible.

What is the major cause of illegibility in Figure 5.5? The fourth cause of illegibility, as shown in Figure 5.5, is inconsistency of *size*. As long as

FIGURE 5.4 Cause of Illegibility #3

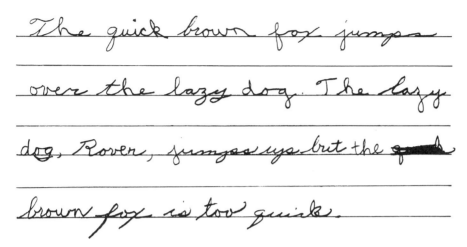

the size of the letters is consistent, legibility tends to be good (assuming other factors are held constant). Writing that is large is not necessarily easier to read than writing that is small (except for people who are extremely farsighted). It is the consistency of size rather than the size itself that influences legibility.

FIGURE 5.5 Cause of Illegibility #4

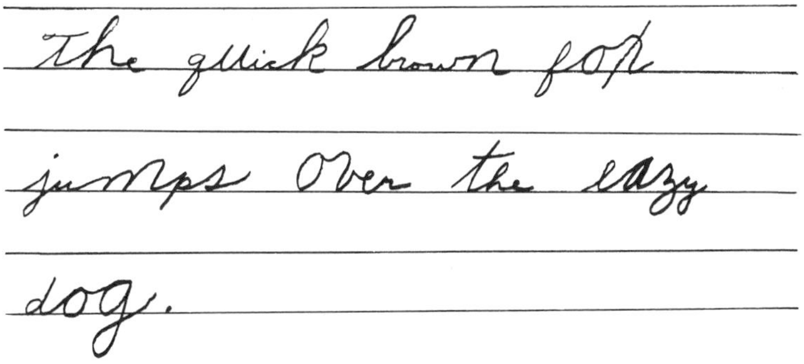

What is the major cause of illegibility in Figure 5.6? The fifth cause of illegibility, as shown in Figure 5.6, is inconsistency of *spacing*. If the distance between letters is not approximately the same throughout the written passage, legibility tends to suffer. This is also true of the distance between the words.

There are five factors, then, that are related to illegibility: shape, alignment, slant, size, and spacing. As a memory device, you might think of the word *sass,* spelled with three *s*'s at the end: S . . . A . . . S . . . S . . . S.

Now that you're aware of the five factors of illegibility, diagnose the two major problems shown in Figure 5.7 that Roland, a second grader, is having with his writing.

BE SURE TO DIAGNOSE ROLAND'S HANDWRITING PROBLEMS BEFORE READING ANY FURTHER. . . . Now that you have examined Roland's

FIGURE 5.6 Cause of Illegibility #5

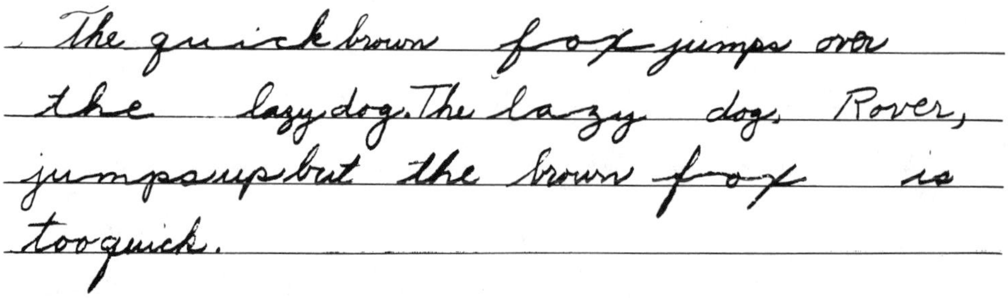

> *The quick brown fox jumps over the lazy dog. The lazy dog, Rover, jumps up but the brown fox is too quick.*

FIGURE 5.7 A Sample of Roland's Handwriting

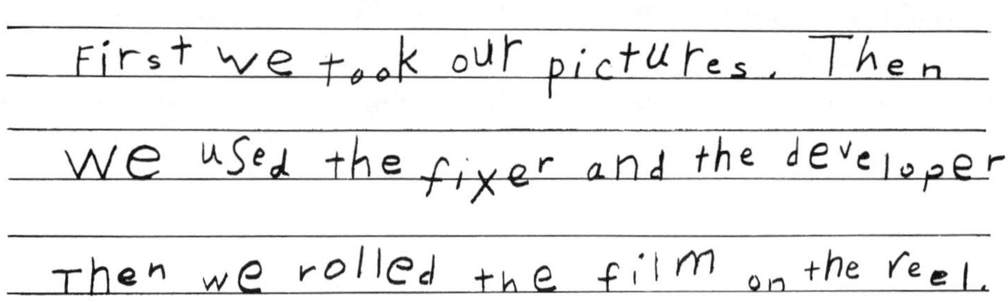

> First we took our pictures. Then we used the fixer and the developer. Then we rolled the film on the reel.

writing in Figure 5.7, you probably know that he needs help on two skills related to legible writing. First, he needs to develop the skill of keeping his letters properly aligned. Second, he needs to develop the habit of producing his letters with a consistent size.

Now look at a sample of Brenda's writing in Figure 5.8. What two major problems does Brenda need help with?

FIGURE 5.8 A Sample of Brenda's Handwriting

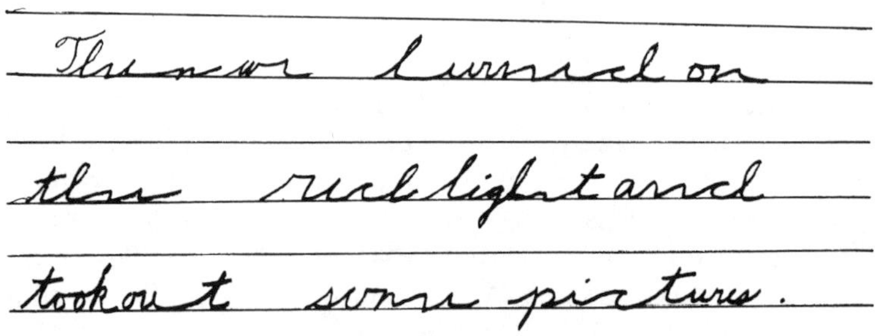

> *Then we turned on the red light and took out some pictures.*

In case you couldn't make out what Brenda was saying, she was trying to say this: Then we turned on the red light and took out some pictures. Brenda has severe problems with spacing and with the accurate formation (shape) of the letters. In preparation for the simulation examination, you should now turn to Appendix A at the end of the book, where you will be given more opportunities to diagnose children's handwriting problems.

Readiness Experiences Before Handwriting Instruction

In kindergarten, children are often provided with readiness experiences for hand-writing rather than formal handwriting lessons. Since the psychomotor skills involved in handwriting relate mainly to hand-eye coordination and hand-arm agility, coordination and agility exercises are incorporated into many of the ordinary kindergarten experiences. Throwing and catching bean bags, putting puzzles together, drawing, coloring, painting, cutting, and pasting all contribute to better coordination and agility.

Having the children draw circles and vertical lines provides more specific readiness experience. It is traditional to have the children draw their lines from top to bottom and their circles counterclockwise starting at the two o'clock position. This is a good idea if they are to be taught manuscript in first grade through the circle-line method. However, if they are to be taught manuscript through the continuous-stroke method, this type of readiness experience may lead to negative transfer later on. (The two methods of teaching manuscript will be discussed in the next section.)

Teaching Manuscript

In the first and second grades, children are usually taught to write with the style called manuscript (10). Manuscript seems to be easier for most young children to learn than the more elaborate flowing script called cursive. Furthermore, manuscript is much closer in form to the print that young children are expected to read. Therefore, when manuscript rather than cursive is taught, it is likely that there is more positive transfer between writing and reading experiences. (Reading experiences are enhanced by what has been learned through writing experiences; writing experiences are enhanced by what has been learned through reading experiences.) Samples of manuscript and cursive writing are shown in Figure 5.9.

Two different methods for teaching manuscript are used in the schools. Until recently, the most common method was the circle-line method, a method of creating most of the letters from a simple circle and one or more straight lines. The letters *a, b, d, l, p,* and *q,* for instance, can be made with nothing more than a circle and a vertical straight line:

FIGURE 5.9 Samples of Manuscript and Cursive Writing

Manuscript Writing

I saw the bear.

Cursive Writing

I saw the bear.

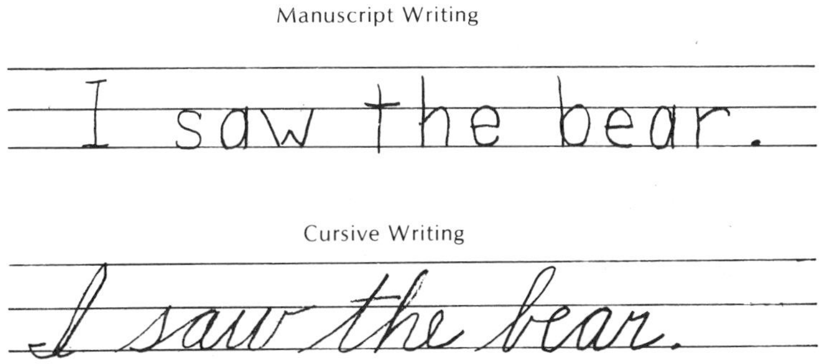

a b d p q

Other letters can be made simply by using a part of a circle (arc) and short straight lines at various angles:

c g h v z m

This method has the advantage of providing children with a minimal set of forms to learn—the circle, line, and arc—that are put together to make up the letters. It has the disadvantage of causing children to draw the letters rather than write them in one continuous stroke, which is what they will be expected to do later.

Because of this disadvantage, the continuous-stroke method is now being used in many schools. One of the continuous-stroke programs is called the D'Nealian Method and looks something like the illustration in Figure 5.10.[1]

FIGURE 5.10 The D'Nealian Handwriting Method

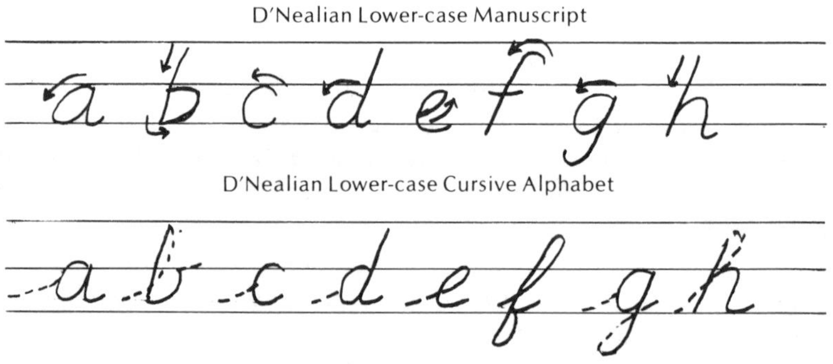

D'Nealian Lower-case Manuscript

a b c d e f g h

D'Nealian Lower-case Cursive Alphabet

a b c d e f g h

The advantages of the continuous-stroke method for teaching manuscript are the following:

1. *Most letters are made with one continuous stroke.* Thus, there is a strong similarity between manuscript writing and cursive writing, making the transfer to cursive an easy one. The use of a continuous stroke also makes it easier for children suffering from specific language disability (sometimes referred to as dyslexia). These children often get confused when they have to lift their pencil to make separate lines or circles.

2. *The letters are slanted rather than perpendicular.* Thus, there is again a strong similarity between manuscript and cursive writing, making the transfer to cursive easier.

[1] The D'Nealian Program is published by Scott, Foresman, 1978.

3. *The actual shapes of the letters are similar in manuscript and cursive.* The transfer from manuscript to cursive is made mostly with simple joining strokes.

Teaching Techniques for Manuscript and Cursive

The transfer from manuscript to cursive is usually made at the beginning of third grade or the end of the second grade. As just indicated, the transfer is quite simple when a continuous-stroke method has been used to teach manuscript. If the circle-line method has been used, however, the transfer will not be quite as easy. In fact, there will probably be some negative transfer to overcome. For instance, with the circle-line method, children are taught to hold their paper straight up and down. When they switch to cursive they must hold their paper at an angle to their body (which is the way they are taught with methods similar to the D'Nealian method).

With cursive writing (as with the continuous-stroke manuscript method), the children are taught to slant their papers according to whether they are left- or right-handed. Right-handers slant their paper with the top right-hand corner higher than the left; left-handers slant theirs with the top left-hand corner higher than the right. The exact angle is truly up to individual comfort, as there is no recommended angle based on experimental research (23).

When either manuscript or cursive is first being taught, teachers usually spend fifteen to twenty minutes a day in formal instruction (8). Most of them use some type of commercial program which provides each child with a writing booklet. However, additional worksheets are often prepared when children are having difficulty with certain letters.

With either cursive or manuscript instruction, it is probably wise to add more meaning to the lessons by using whole words whenever possible, rather than single letters. For instance, the fairly simple letters, *l, e, t,* and *i* can be taught through the words *let, it, tell, lie,* and *tie.* The exact order of difficulty of letters has not been established, although commercial handwriting programs each use their own definite sequence. When commercial programs are not available, it is probably advisable to use as meaningful a sequence as possible. Many capital letters, for example, can be learned through children's names. A word like *dad* has a considerable degree of meaning and would be good for introducing the letters *d* and *a.* A word like *mom* also has a considerable degree of meaning and would be appropriate for introducing the letters *m* and *o* in a manuscript lesson. For a cursive lesson, however, the word *mom* would be very inappropriate for an introduction to *m* and *o* since the first *m* and the last *m* in *mom* will not be formed in the same way (*mom*).

In general, these steps may be used for teaching either manuscript or cursive letters:

1. On a lined chalkboard (or lined newsprint), write a meaningful word which incorporates the letters you wish to teach. (You may wish to draw your lines by using the device used by music teachers to draw a staff.)

2. Have the children watch you write it two or three times without your analysis of the movements. In other words, you are giving them a quick overview of the final product.

3. Write the word again, this time analyzing each stroke as you make it.

4. Have the children write the word as you write it—stroke by stroke.

5. Have them write each letter in the word three or four times with you—stroke by stroke.

6. Ask the children to write the whole word with you again—stroke by stroke.

7. Have them write the word on their own several times while you walk around and help individuals.

Here is a summary of the seven steps:

1. Meaningful word
2. Overview of word
3. Analysis of strokes
4. Imitation of word
5. Imitation of letters
6. Imitation of word again
7. Independent production of word

According to research (7, 23) the size of the paper, the distance between the horizontal lines, and the size of the pencil are details which teachers have worried about in vain. They seem to make little difference. Adult lined paper and adult pencils work just as well for most children as special primary paper and extra large pencils. In fact, children tend to prefer the "real thing." Children in the early grades have been taught quite satisfactorily with regular college ruled paper, using two spaces for the tall letters and skipping one space between each line of words.

Having small groups of children take turns working at the board instead of their seats is a good idea. In this way, you can spot their difficulties early and quickly. Also, they can make use of their larger, more developed muscles to produce the letters. Although the research evidence is inconclusive, there is a strong possibility that this type of kinesthetic approach toward writing helps some children remember the letter formations better. This may be particularly true of children suffering from dyslexia (specific language disability).

Special Help for Left–Handed Children

In every group of thirty youngsters, you are likely to find two or three who are left-handed. These children need to be given special help if they are not to develop habits which will inhibit the natural flow of their writing. Perhaps all of us have run across a person who uses "hooked" writing. Hooked writing is a form of writing used by some left-handers who learned to write by trying to imitate right-handers. Hooked writing is done with the hand upside down and the wrist bent in a manner which looks very uncomfortable. Hooked writing and other distortions usually come about because of improper instruction during the first year of handwriting instruction. It is not amenable to correction after the third or fourth grade (13).

Since most teachers are right-handed, it is important for the teacher to understand the special difficulties which a left-handed child can have. To aid this understanding, let's try a simple exercise. Draw a circle with your right hand and then with your left hand. Then draw a straight horizontal line with your right hand and then with your left hand. What differences in your arm movements do you notice?

Please do this before reading any further.

There is a tendency for some people to make their circles clockwise with one hand and counterclockwise with the other. There is also a ten-

By writing at the chalkboard, children can make use of their larger, more developed muscles to produce the letters.

dency to make a horizontal line from left to right with one hand and from right to left with the other. Before they're taught otherwise, left-handers tend to draw circles in a clockwise direction and horizontal lines from right to left; the opposite is true for right-handers. In other words, left-handers do tend to make their pencil movements differently from right-handers. Therefore, if you attempt to teach left-handers at the same time you're teaching right-handers, the left-handers often get confused. This is particularly true with the initial instruction in manuscript or the initial instruction in cursive.

The following are suggestions for providing special help to left-handed writers:

1. Teach them separately from right-handers as much as possible.
2. Teach them at the chalkboard as often as possible.
3. Make sure they position their papers *at least* 90 degrees to the right of the position for right handers. (To avoid hooked writing, as much as 120 degrees may be required by some left-handers.)

Usual Left-Handed Position   Usual Right-Handed Position

4. Have them hold their pencil or pen about 1½ inches from the tip. Place a rubber band there to help them remember. Holding it this far from the tip makes it easier for them to see what they're writing. (Left-handers are moving *into* their writing rather than away from their writing as right-handers are. This wouldn't happen if we allowed left-handers to write from right to left, but, of course, this would cause all kinds of communication problems.)
5. Allow them to slant their letters any way they wish as long as the slant is a consistent one.

Children with Mixed Preference

Some children are left-handed and right-eyed or right-handed and left-eyed. Some educators who have been working with children suffering from specific language disability have found that helping a child switch handedness to match the dominance of the eye often leads to improvement in the child's language performance. So far, researchers have not been sure whether the switch in handedness causes the improvement or whether the extra attention is the cause. Research on large groups of "normal" children indicates that children with mixed preference (mixed dominance) are no more likely to have language problems than children with single dominance (6). Other research indicates, however, that among children who have been singled out as children with specific language disabilities, there is a high proportion with mixed dominance (19).

It is not recommended that classroom teachers determine that a child has mixed preference and, therefore, should "write with the other hand." This type of decision should probably be left up to a specialist in consultation with the parents.

Evaluation of Handwriting

To motivate children to improve their own handwriting, it is useful to have them evaluate the legibility of their own writing. One of the best ways of doing this is to maintain a folder for each child in which you keep a series of dated and numbered samples of his handwriting. By passing out the folders every few weeks, you can provide feedback to the children that is highly personal and meaningful.

Having them compare their own writing to a model prepared by an adult is somewhat risky. There is always the possibility that a child will be so discouraged by this comparison, she will be less motivated than she was before to make improvements. On the other hand, as you pass out their own folders of handwriting samples, most of the children will naturally compare their own writing to that of their peers. This is a fairer comparison and will probably have a more positive influence on the children's motivation.

After the children have become somewhat skilled in the movements required for making manuscript or cursive letters, you may wish to teach them the five causes of illegibility. In this way, they may evaluate their folders more specifically and work toward more specific improvement. This type of improvement is also aided by using an overhead projector to show papers anonymously of children *not* in the class. The children are asked to suggest "ways the writing of this person could be improved."

Once you have completed your formal instruction in handwriting, you might want to reinforce good handwriting by using some sort of extrinsic rewards such as praise, bulletin board displays, and some type of marking system. For instance, Mr. Ray gives his fifth graders a handwriting "grade" on their final spelling test for the week. If Billy's handwriting is excellent (for Billy), Mr. Ray writes H: + on his paper. If his handwriting is satisfactory, Mr. Ray writes

H:S; if it's below par, he writes H: — . Mr. Ray has found this simple device to be highly motivating for his particular group of children. Other children may need a different form of reinforcement.

Mrs. Sampson uses a more intrinsic form of motivation. When children have written a particularly good story or poem, she invites them to put it in the class notebook, a book that is placed in the library corner for children and visitors to read. However, before they can put it in the notebook, they have to rewrite it with their very best handwriting.

At this time, look at the sample you produced of your own handwriting. If you have not already evaluated your own handwriting, you may wish to do so now.

Nature of English Spelling

The battle has only begun when children do learn to produce the letters of the alphabet in a legible fashion. A next step is spelling—the translation of speech sounds called phonemes into the customary graphemes. The sound heard at the beginning of the word *car,* for instance, has to be translated into the letter *c.* If the word a child is thinking of happens to be *kitty,* though, he'll have to translate the sound into the letter *k.* In a word like *school,* he'll have to use the digraph *ch*; and if he's thinking of *tack,* the digraph *ck.*

At first glance, it would appear that asking children to learn to spell is asking the impossible. There are about 380 graphemes for only about 45 phonemes. (As you may recall, a grapheme is one or more letters used to represent a single speech sound called a phoneme; there are three phonemes in the word *thick* and three related graphemes—*th, i,* and *ck.*) The first phoneme heard in the word *eat,* for example, has 16 different graphemes. In other words, the long *e* sound can be spelled 16 different ways: *Caesar, equal, team, see, e'en, deceive, receipt, people, demesne, key, machine, field, debris, amoeba, quay, pity.*

Here are a few other phonemes and the number of related graphemes.[2]

long *a* as in *cape*—25
short *e* as in *bed*—15
f as in *fan*—5
long *i* as in *ice*—13
j as in *jet*—10
k as in *kitty*—16
long *o* as in *go*—19
y as in *you*—3
long *u* as in *use*—11

[2] For the exact graphemes see the "Table of Common English Spellings" in the unabridged edition of *The Random House Dictionary of the English Language* (New York: Random House, 1973). Similar tables can be found in other unabridged dictionaries.

Spelling of the English language would be a great deal easier, of course, if there were exactly forty-five graphemes to match forty-five phonemes, i.e., if each phoneme had one and only one way of spelling it. Unfortunately for the speller, the spelling of a language doesn't change as rapidly as its pronunciation. The word *knight,* for instance, once long ago, represented five phonemes instead of three: /k/ + /n/ + /i/ + /h/ + /t/.

Once a particular spelling becomes fashionable among the "educated" people, it tends to become very resistant to change. No educated person spells *knight* the way it probably should be spelled—n-i-t-e—for fear of being considered ignorant. (The *Chicago Daily News* tried it for a while but received too many complaints.) But fashion is not the only enemy of spelling reform. For centuries, the English-speaking people have been borrowing words from other countries without bothering to make sufficient changes in the spelling of those words—words such as *chandelier* and *chartreuse,* for example, which were borrowed directly from the French. In fact, over half of today's "English" words do not have their origin in the original Anglo-Saxon culture of the British Isles (14).

It is not uncommon for educators to point to the irrationality of English spelling as a reason for despair when it comes to the *teaching* of spelling. (It's also a handy excuse for students when handing in papers with spelling errors.) They point with dismay at words like *done, gone, none* and *one,* which "ought to be spelled" *dun, gawn, nun,* and *wun.* Meanwhile, they ignore the consistency of words like *bone, clone, cone, drone, hone, phone, pone, shone, stone, tone,* and *zone.* For these fifteen *o-n-e* words, eleven have a regular spelling—a batting average of .733 or 73 percent. And, if you move away from the commonly quoted troublemakers, you will often find even more consistency. Take the *ill* family, for instance: *bill, chill, dill, drill, fill, frill, gill, grill, hill, ill, Jill, kill, mill, pill, quill, rill, sill, spill, still, till, trill, thrill,* and *will.*

Computer analysis by Hanna and others (8) has demonstrated that the English language can still be called a "phonetic language," in spite of its multitude of interesting variations and its abundance of traps for the unwary. In Table 5.1 we may observe some of the most common graphemes for the various phonemes.

Which Words to Emphasize

With something like 500,000 words to choose from, it is obvious that some selection has to be made in the words which children are expected to master as part of their writing vocabulary. Most commercial spelling programs are limited to between 3000 and 4000 words from grades one through six. These words have traditionally been those which have the highest frequency in the writing of adults and children.

More recently, however, particularly since the Stanford computer studies (8), many of the words are selected in order to demonstrate a phonics pattern or spelling "rule." Words such as *boat, coat, float,* and *goat,* for instance, are placed in the same spelling lesson to illustrate the vowel-vowel (VV) pattern (as well as the *o-a-t* phonogram).

TABLE 5.1   Phonemes and Graphemes Used in American English

Written Representations of Phonemes	Common Graphemes	Sample Words
/ă/	a	fat
/ā/	ai, a, ay	laid, name, pay
/â/	ai(r), a(r)	hair, fare
/ä/	a(l), a(r)	calm, car
/b/	b, bb	tub, rubber
/ch/	ch, tch	peach, witch
/d/	d, dd	food, ladder
/ĕ/	e	net
/ē/	e, ea, ee, y	equal, beat, feet, happy
/ê/	ea(r), ee(r)	hear, cheer
/f/	f, ff, ph	fish, puff, phone
/g/	g, gg	big, beggar
/h/	h	hack
/hw/	wh	what
/ĭ/	i	in
/ī/	i	lice
/j/	j, dg	jar, fudge
/k/	k, ck	take, tack
/l/	l, ll	left, bellow
/m/	m, mm	him, summer
/n/	n, nn	won, winner
/n̂g/	ng	thing
/ŏ/	o	box
/ō/	o, oa	hope, coat
/ô/	a(ll), aw	ball, awful
/ōo/	oo	food
/ŏo/	oo	look
/p/	p, pp	nip, shopper
/r/	r, rr	red, furry
/s/	s, ss	sit, mess
/sh/	sh, t(i)	bush, nation
/t/	t, tt	bat, butter
/th/	th	bath
/t͟h/	th	smooth
/ŭ/	u, o	supper, love
/û/	u(r), i(r)	burn, girl
/v/	v	liver
/w/	w	win
/y/	y	yet
/z/	z, s	zip, hose
/zh/	s(i), g(e)	decision, mirage
/ə/	a, e, i, o, u	about, system, pencil scallop, circus

Adapted from May and Eliot, *To Help Children Read*, 2d ed. Copyright © 1978 by Charles E. Merrill Publishing Co.

Note: Other phonemes not listed include different degrees of stress and pitch and different types of pauses. Such phonemes are just as important as "letter sounds" but are too complicated to deal with here; see Module 7 for further discussion.

Commercial spelling programs today usually emphasize most or all of the following spelling rules and patterns:

1. The c rule. When c comes just before *a, o* or *u*, it usually has the *hard* sound heard in *cat, cot,* and *cut.* Otherwise, it usually has the soft sound heard in *cent, city,* and *bicycle.*

2. The g rule. (Similar to the c rule). When g comes at the end of words or just before *a, o,* or *u,* it usually has the *hard* sound heard in *tag, game, go,* and *gush.* Otherwise, it usually has the soft sound heard in *gem, giant,* and *gym.* (Some important exceptions are *get, give, begin,* and *girl.*)

3. The VC pattern. This pattern is seen in words such as *an, can, candy,* and *dinner.* As a verbal generalization, it might be stated as follows: In either a word or a syllable, a single vowel letter followed by a consonant letter, digraph, or blend usually represents a short vowel sound. (Most teachers find it easier for children to remember the pattern rather than the rule. Note that C stands for either a consonant letter, consonant digraph, or consonant blend, e.g., *bat, bath, bask.*)

4. The VV (vowel digraph) pattern. This pattern is seen in words such as *eat, beater, peach, see, feed, bait, float,* and *play.* As a verbal generalization, it might be stated like this: In a word or syllable containing a vowel digraph, the first letter in the digraph usually represents the long vowel sound and the second letter is usually silent. ("When two vowel letters go walking, the first one does the talking.") According to Clymer (quoted in 13), this generalization is quite reliable for *ee, oa,* and *ay (fee, coat, tray)* and works about two-thirds of the time for *ea* and *ai (seat, bait)* but is not reliable for other vowel digraphs such as *ei, ie,* or *oo (eight, chief, boot).* And, of course, it is not valid for diphthongs represented by *oi, oy, ou,* and *ow (oil, boy, out, cow).*

5. The VCE (final e) pattern. This pattern is seen in words such as *ice, nice, ate, plate, paste, flute, vote,* and *clothe.* As a generalization, it might be stated this way: In one-syllable words containing two vowel letters, one of which is a final e, the first vowel letter usually represents a long vowel sound, and the final e is silent.

6. The CV pattern. This pattern is seen in words or syllables such as *he, she, go, my, cry, hotel, going,* and *flying.* As a generalization, it could be stated like this: When there is only one vowel letter in a word or syllable and it comes at the end of the word or syllable, it usually represents the long vowel sound.

7. The r rule. This rule applies to words like *far, fare, fair, girl, fur, her,* and *here.* As a generalization, it might be stated as follows: The letter r usually modifies the short or long sound of the preceding vowel letter. For instance, the word *car* does not illustrate the VC pattern seen in the word *cat;* nor does *fir* represent the VC pattern seen in *fit.* The word *care* usually doesn't illustrate the VCE pattern seen in the word *cape* (although in some

dialects it does). Likewise, the word *fair* usually doesn't illustrate the VV pattern seen in *wait*.

It has been shown that selecting more than 4000 words for a commercial spelling program has diminishing returns. While it is true that there may be a half-million words in the dictionary, most people use a very small proportion of them in their daily writing.

The exact set of 3000 to 4000 words varies from publisher to publisher, but only a little. Since most of the words *are* high frequency words, they have a habit of appearing on list after list. Naturally, no one is advocating that only these words be learned, but these are the words that serve as a "security set" for schools that wish their students to gain basic adequacy in spelling.

Within those 4000 words are two sets of words which should receive special attention. One set is shown in Table 5.2 and comprises those words which occur quite frequently in writing and speech and are also irregular in their spelling. Because the graphemes in these words cannot be easily predicted from the phonemes, these words will have to be learned through visual memory techniques. While words like *bone, cone,* and *stone* can be learned as an example of a vowel-consonant-final-e (VCE) phonics pattern, a word like *done* has to be learned through visual memory. Through memory, a child has to learn to spell it *d-o-n-e* instead of *d-u-n*.

Table 5.2 was developed by selecting only the irregular words that showed up on at least two of the eight lists of high frequency "basic" sight words shown in Table 5.3 (17).

TABLE 5.2   A Basic Sight Vocabulary of 96 Irregular Words: Spelling Demons—Set A

a	do	give	many	people	the	want
again	does	goes	might	put	their	wanted
almost	dog	gone	money	right	there	was
always	done	great	mother		there's	water
another	don't	group	Mr.	said	they	were
any	door		Mrs.	says	they're	what
anything	enough	have	night	school	thought	where
are	father	head	nothing	should	through	who
been	four	heard	of	some	to	work
because	friend	house	off*	something	today	would
both	from*	knew	on*	sometimes	together	year
brother	full	know	once		two	you
brought		light	one		very	your
buy		live	only			
city		long*	other			
come			our			
could			own			

*Words considered regular or irregular depending upon one's dialect.

TABLE 5.3 Lists of High Frequency Basic Sight Words Used for Development of Table 5.2

Compilers	Sources
Barnard and DeGracie (1)	Kindergarten and first grade basal readers from eight different series (found 103 words common to all eight series).
Dolch (3)	The "basic sight words" based on compilations done in the 1920's.
Hillerich (11)	School texts in grades three through nine, creative writing of children in grades one through eight, adult printed material, primary grade library books, the Dolch lists.
Johns (16)	School texts in grades three through nine, primary grade library books, adult printed material, speech of kindergarten and first grade children.
Johns (17)	The forty-six nouns common to the high frequency words in three out of four of the compilations examined in Johns' 1974 study.
Johnson (18)	Adult printed material and the speech of kindergarten and first grade children.
Moe and Hopkins (22)	Speech of kindergarten, first, and second grade children living in middle-class neighborhoods.
Sherk (25)	Speech of four-, five-, and six-year-old children living in lower-class neighborhoods.

The second set of words which should receive special attention are those words often referred to as "spelling demons." These are simply those words which teachers have found that children frequently miss. Not only do a great many children miss them but also they tend to miss them again and again. Numerous lists of spelling demons have been made. Table 5.4 is a list made up from several other lists and from the author's own experiences in working with children. (Those words already listed in Table 5.2 have been omitted from this list.)

Both lists of spelling demons—the list of irregular, high frequency words and the list of other spelling demons—should probably be learned partly through visual memory techniques. These techniques will be explained in a later section on how to teach for retention. The first set—Set A—should, in most cases, be mastered by the end of grade three, since these words are so important for success in reading. An attempt to have the children master Set B by the end of grade five or six should be made, since these words are used so often by children in their writing.

Using Learning Principles to Motivate Children Toward Better Spelling

In Module 3, you were given a mnemonic device—NOVELTY NEEDS LEVEL FEEDBACK—for remembering the four principles of motivation:

1. Add NOVELTY to their learning experiences.
2. Help satisfy their basic NEEDS.
3. Teach them at the appropriate LEVEL of difficulty.
4. Provide frequent and specific FEEDBACK.

Let's take each of these principles and see how it applies to the teaching of spelling:

Add Novelty to Learning Experiences

One of the best ways of adding novelty to the spelling program is through the use of games and activities. Games can never take the place of systematic instruction, but they can make learning to spell more fun. The games and activities need not be elaborate; in fact, they need not always pertain exactly to the particular spelling goals toward which you are working. Sometimes, spelling games may be used merely as a reward for industrious study or for unusual performance. (In some of the games it is advisable to have the children write the words rather than spell them orally; oral spelling is seldom required in real-life situations.) The following are illustrations of the type of games and activities that make "spelling time" a pleasurable experience.

Spelling Games and Activities

1. To play "Spelling Sense," two teams are formed. Teams alternate sending a person to the teacher's desk where there are a number of objects hidden from sight in a box. The teacher has the child touch, listen to, look at, smell, or taste the object, depending on what it is. If the child guesses correctly, she gets one point for her team. If she can write the correct spelling of the object on the chalkboard, she gets an additional point for her team.
2. To play "Spelling Duel," partners are formed (or two people can play this in a learning center). Each partner has ten cards with a spelling demon written on each. Partner A pronounces his words one at a time to Partner B who must spell each one correctly *in writing* on a sheet of paper. After each one is pronounced and spelled, the spelling of Partner B is checked against the correct spelling held by Partner A. If Partner B misses a word, he must place the card in his "debt pile." After five words have been pronounced, the partners change roles. Whoever has the fewest cards at the end of a previously designated time is the winner.
3. "Baseball Spelling" requires two teams and a pitcher (a person pronouncing the words). The batter writes the word on the board and moves to first base if it is correct. Previous batters advance to second and third base or home. Each person arriving home

TABLE 5.4   Spelling Demons: Set B—Other
Words Often Misspelled

about	getting	quit
above	going	quite
address	good	quiet
afraid	good-bye	queen
afternoon	guess	question
all right	guest	receive
along	Halloween	received
always	handkerchief	release
answer	has	remember
anyway	haven't	Santa Claus
April	having	Saturday
arithmetic	hear	saw
aunt	hello	sent
awhile	here	sincerely
baby	his	snowing
balloon	hospital	snowman
basketball	how	soon
before	hundred	stationary
birthday	I'll	studying
bought	I'm	teacher
boys	isn't	Thanksgiving
can't	it's	that's
children	I've	then
Christmas	January	think
close	just	tomorrow
clothes	lesson	tonight
coming	letter	too
couldn't	little	toys
cousin	love	truly
December	loving	until
didn't	maybe	useless
different	Miss	vacation
doing	Ms.	weather
down	much	when
Easter	nice	whether
every	none	with
everybody	November	won't
everyone	o'clock	write
February	October	writing
first	out	young
football	outside	zero
found	party	zoo
four	plays	
Friday	played	
front	please	
	pretty	

scores a point for the team. After three outs (misspelled words), the other team gets to bat.

4. "Ringtoss Spelling" is played with four bottles with a tall neck, four teams, four sets of rubber jar rings—one for each player, a list of spelling words, and a word caller. The word caller (usually the teacher) pronounces a word for one team. The person in the front of the line gets to throw a ring at his team's bottle if he spells the word correctly on the chalkboard. The next word, or the misspelled word, is then pronounced for the second team, and so on. The team with the most rings around the bottle neck wins. (Some players may get two rings if the teams are uneven.)

5. In "Spellgo," a ditto sheet with twenty-five squares is passed out to each child. The teacher then has the children write *free* in the middle square and dictates twenty-four other words. The children write the words in the squares in random fashion. The teacher then reads one word at a time in a different order and the children place paper markers (or sugar-coated cereal) on the squares of the words that are called. The first one to get five in a row calls "Spellgo" and then reads the words in the row, spelling each word after reading it. If she spells them all correctly, she wins; otherwise, the game continues.

6. In "Cootie Spelling," a child designated as the leader, draws several blank spaces on the board—one for each letter of the spelling word she has in mind. Children then guess the letters one at a time. If someone guesses correctly, the leader writes that letter in the correct space. If someone guesses incorrectly, the leader writes the incorrect letter somewhere else on the board and makes a part of the cootie. If the cootie is completed before the word, the leader has another turn. The cootie can be drawn on the board or a plastic model can be used; count one miss for the body, one for the head, one for the antennae, one for the eyes, one for the legs, and one for the tail.

7. With "Category Spelling Race," the teacher gives the children a category such as animals, television stars' last names, fruits and vegetables, or cities. In three minutes, they are to write as many words as they can which fit that category. The winner is the one who has the most correctly spelled words that fit the category. A run-off race may have to be held if several people tie.

Other Ways to Add Novelty

The use of games and activities is one way to increase the degree of novelty in your spelling program. Another way is to make minor changes, such as the following, in your teaching procedures.

1. After a spelling test, instead of always writing the words on the board, send five children at a time up to the board to write the words. But don't let them sit down until the class agrees that they have their words correct.

2. Instead of circling a misspelled word in a child's composition, just place a check mark in the margin so that he has to search for the misspelled word. (Use two checks for two misspelled words in the same line.)

3. Pass out colored paper instead of white occasionally.

4. Change the time of day for spelling occasionally.

5. Use a spelling bee as a reward for industrious study. Each child is given three tickets. One ticket is relinquished each time a word is misspelled. When all these tickets are gone, *then* the child has to sit down.

6. Let them proofread their papers with proofreader's pencils (red or blue).

7. Let them spell their words in "Pig Latin" or use the Zoom Code.

8. Have them scramble the spelling words for each other and invite their classmates to unscramble them.

Help Children Satisfy Basic Needs

A spelling program can help children meet some of their basic needs in a number of ways. The need for importance and belonging can be met by using games of chance as well as games of skill. In "Spellgo," an average speller has a better chance of winning than he usually does because of the chance factor introduced in the game. Team games are also good for the average or poor speller, who can feel success through a team victory.

Having total-class goals is another way of helping all the children feel they are important and belong. Each week, for instance, you can set a class goal of so many correct words on the final test. Other means of increasing the sense of belonging and importance are as follows:

1. Have superior spellers help poor spellers during study time.

2. Have children write the words on the board after a test. (This meets their physical need for activity as well.)

3. Don't dirty up a child's paper with red circles around misspelled words. Write the words lightly with pencil in the margins or at the bottom of the page. Or just put light check marks in the margins and let them find their own errors.

4. Invite children to put their compositions in the "Class Book" for other children and visitors to read; help them with their spelling so that the copy which goes in the book is error free.

Use Appropriate Level of Difficulty

Finding the appropriate level of difficulty for each child is not easy to do. Children who are failing their spelling tests week after week should not be continued in the same program as the other children. Either the number of words they are expected to learn should be cut in half or they should be given a much easier list of words. Children who are making 100 percent time after time should be challenged to learn a few hard words each time. These hard words can be selected from the social studies text or science text or from the children's library books. These words should not be counted against their total score on a spelling test, but if they get them right, they should be allowed to count them against any errors they might have made on the regular words.

A multi-sensory approach to the teaching of spelling will also help you keep the instruction at the proper level of difficulty for the various individuals you are teaching. Some children learn better from a visual approach toward spelling; some, from an auditory approach; and possibly some, from a kinesthetic approach in which the large muscles and the sense of touch are used. Since it has not been found useful to work with visual learners separately from auditory learners (21), it is probably best to use a multi-sensory approach to spelling instruction. This simply means incorporating in your instruction the three modes of learning: Have children sometimes spell words out loud as they write them; listen to you spell them out loud as you write them; and use the chalkboard often so that more use of the large muscles and the sense of touch can be made. With some children who are having a great deal of difficulty, you may wish to have them trace the word on the chalkboard, in sand, on fine sandpaper, or on other materials. (Steps to help the child experiencing specific language disability will be mentioned in the next section.)

Commercial spelling programs are usually based on the words common to the use and difficulties particular to each grade level. These programs are based on "average" children, of course, which means that many children will not fit the program and will need special help or stimulation from the teacher.

When it comes to spelling errors in compositions, there *are* no average children. With some children, you will learn to expect 100 percent perfection; with others, you will learn to be happy when they spell 60 percent of the words correctly instead of the 40 percent record they usually have had. An expectation of 100 percent from everyone is unrealistic. An expectation of improvement from everyone is not.

Provide Frequent and Specific Feedback

In the teaching of spelling, feedback of a specific and frequent nature is not only essential but also quite easy to provide. Tests can be corrected, *with each child correcting his own paper,* immediately after the test has been completed. Specific feedback can be provided by writing each word on the board and spelling it orally at the same time (or children can write the correct spelling on the board and be asked to spell it orally before returning to their seats). The teacher can walk around the room and double check the children's spelling to make sure they have not overlooked an error. (Some teachers prefer to check the final test of the week themselves.)

Further feedback can be provided by having each child keep a graph of her weekly progress. The graph used is usually a line graph which shows the child at a glance whether she is improving, slipping, or maintaining her level from week to week. This type of graph is shown in Figure 5.11.

If you check the final test of the week yourself and if you check children's compositions for spelling errors, you can provide other types of highly

FIGURE 5.11 Line Graph for Weekly Spelling Tests

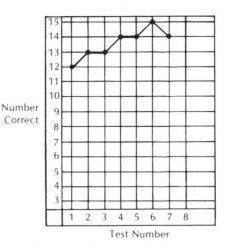

specific feedback as well as specific remediation. In order to do this, however, you need to know the types of spelling errors children make and how to provide specific instruction which will remedy those errors. In Table 5.5, you will find a list of error types, with examples and specific remediation.

TABLE 5.5 Types of Spelling Errors and Specific Remediation

1. Pronunciation	*chimley* for *chimney* *nuquelar* for *nuclear* *dis* for *this*	Use auditory discrimination exercises (see Module 8); use auditory memory exercises (see Module 7); teach exact pronunciation; use tape recorded "flashcards."*
2. Suffixes	*stoped* for *stopped* *haveing* for *having* *happyly* for *happily*	Teach lesson on dropping e before adding *ing, er, ed, est*; teach lesson on doubling consonant to maintain VC pattern (see Module 8); teach lesson on changing y to i. Remind child if lessons have already been taught.
3. Prefixes	*mispelling* for *misspelling* *rentry* for *reentry* *uneedy* for *unneedy* *imediately* for *immediately*	Teach specific lesson on maintaining full spelling of prefixes. Remind child if lesson has been taught.
4. Transposals, reversals, inversions	*saw* for *was* (*gril* for *girl*) *dack* for *back* *pnu* for *bun*	Could be a dyslexic (see next section on retention); also see *To Help Children Read* (21). Could be just writing too fast, if error is occasional. Encourage child to proofread.

TABLE 5.5 (cont)

5. Homophones	*night* for *knight* *do* for *due* *hole* for *whole*	Teach lessons on homophones unless covered by commercial spelling program. Have children go for a "homophone hunt" to see who can gather the most homophones. Remind child if lessons have been taught.
6. Regularized spelling	*clime* for *climb* *nite* for *night* *dun* for *done*	Use visual memory techniques to teach irregular words (see next section on retention); when teaching phonics lessons, don't sweep exceptions under the rug—emphasize their uniqueness.
7. Phonic elements	*bed* for *bad* *klapped* for *clapped* *stap* for *strap*	In some cases, may be pronunciation problem; otherwise, child may not have mastered phonic elements—use regular phonics lessons in reading and spelling programs; for review use the "Baf Test" (see Table 5.6) as a teaching device (also see Module 8).
8. Vowel patterns	*cape* for *cap* *hop* for *hope* *boan* for *bone* *cote* for *coat* *bot* for *boat*	Use regular phonics lessons in reading and spelling programs; for review use Lessons F & G of the "Baf Test" (see Table 5.6) as a teaching device (also see Module 8). Help children see difference between VCE pattern as in *note* and VV pattern as in *boat*. Use visual memory techniques when problem is presistent (see next section on retention).
9. Handwriting	*stors* for *stars* *cloes* for *does* *sone* for *some*	Provide specific worksheets or assignments on letters which are improperly formed. Be sure the child must use the letters in words and not just in isolation.

*Child looks at flashcard, pronounces word, runs card through machine and listens to correct pronunciation: *The Language Master* (Bell & Howell) or the *Magnetic Card Reader* (Teaching Technology Corp.) or the *e f i Audio Flashcard System* (Educational Futures).

For error types 7 and 8 (phonic elements and vowel patterns), you may wish to provide specific review by using the "Baf Test" (21) as a device for teaching the regular spelling of eighty-one different phonetic sounds. This test is normally used for determining which phonic elements a child is having trouble decoding, but it can also be used as a set of short spelling tests. Eleven of the consonant letters, for instance, can serve as one lesson comprising a pretest, correction, discussion, and posttest. A suggested organization for the review lessons is shown in Table 5.6.

TABLE 5.6 Using the Baf Test as Review Lessons on the Regular Spelling of Phonic Elements

---

Format for Lessons: Pretest—Correction—Discussion—Posttest

Lesson A: Consonant Letters—baf, caf, daf, faf, gaf, haf, jaf, kaf, laf, maf, naf (all pronounced with short a)

Lesson B: Other Consonant Letters—paf, raf, saf, taf, vaf, waf, yaf, bax

Lesson C: Consonant Digraphs—chaf, phaf, (starts like phone), shaf, thaf, whaf, fack, fang, fank

Lesson D: Consonant Blends—blaf, braf, claf, craf, draf, dwaf, flaf, fraf, glaf, graf, fand, plaf, praf, quaf, scaf (or skaf)

Lesson E: More Consonant Blends—scraf, slaf, smaf, snaf, spaf, splaf, spraf, squaf, staf, straf, swaf, thraf, traf, twaf

Lesson F: Vowel Patterns—baf, (bafe, baif),* bef (befe, beaf),* (burf, birf, berf)* barf, (bawf, bauf)*

Lesson G: More Vowel Patterns—bof, borf, (bofe, boaf,)* boif, boof,† bufe,†bif, bife, buf, (bouf, bowf)*

---

*When more than one spelling is required, say, "Spell it two ways," or "Spell it three ways."

†For these two words, say, "This word is pronounced two ways," and then provide the two pronunciations. With *boof* pronounce the vowel as in *good* and as in *food*. With *bufe* pronounce the vowel as in *tooth* and as in *mule*.

Encouraging Retention of Spelling Vocabulary

This section applies the four principles of retention to spelling. Don't forget to use the mnemonic device—INVOLVED MASTERS PRACTICE TRANSFER—to help you remember the four principles:

1. Get everyone INVOLVED.
2. Teach for MASTERY rather than coverage.
3. Provide massed PRACTICE followed by distributed practice.
4. Help positive TRANSFER occur.

Get Everyone Involved

One of the best ways of involving people is to "put them to the test." Actually, it isn't as simple as that. The test must provide sufficient tension to make people alert but not cause so much tension that emotional blocking occurs (21). Spelling tests, *when used as learning experiences,* can produce just about the right amount of involvement. In fact, it was found in one study that spelling tests that were corrected immediately accounted for most of the learning that took place (14).

Another way of increasing involvement is to make children *responsible* for the spelling program and for spelling improvement. Children can be held responsible, for example, for keeping their own records of spelling improvement on their individual graphs. They can be held responsible for accurately correcting their own tests, for helping each other study, and for helping the class obtain a good spelling record for the week. Most of all, they can be held responsible for proofreading their own compositions.

Involvement Through Proofreading

Proofreading is a skill that has to be taught. It is also an attitude, however. To get children to actively proofread, it is usually necessary to develop a sense of pride in their papers through positive reinforcement and occasional negative reinforcement. If teachers encourage the attitude that "anything goes," they'll simply encourage children to think that spelling isn't important. This is probably not fair to children since spelling *is* important in our society. The actual *statistical* correlations between spelling and intelligence are generally positive but quite low. In other words, many intelligent people can't spell very well. However, the *psychological* correlation between spelling and intelligence that people often make can be a very devastating one: "He couldn't be very bright. Look at his atrocious spelling."

This is not to say that everything children write should be done with near-perfect spelling. There are times when children should be encouraged to write creatively and personally without regard for spelling. Often these papers are just read out loud by the child and are not given to anyone else to read. Consequently, spelling is not important in these situations. But when it *is* important to communication, it should be emphasized. Children generally have the ability to tell the difference between those times that spelling is important and those times when it's not. Usually all that is required by the teacher is a reminder as to whether the writing they're engaged in requires good spelling.

Sometimes it is a good idea to help children separate two difficult tasks: (1) communicating through form (correct spelling, punctuation, etc.) and (2) communicating through substance (saying something worth saying). To encourage this separation, a four-day plan can be used:

Day One: Let them write their composition with little regard for spelling and punctuation. The emphasis should be on getting down the ideas as quickly as possible while they're "hot." Have them hand in their papers for safekeeping.

Day Two: Hand back their papers without having looked at them. Pass out proofreading pencils (pencils of another color) and have them change their papers as much as they want—spelling, punctuation, ideas, words, and sentence structure. Walk around the room offering praise and suggestions. Write common words on the board that children ask you to spell. (This stage will require some training by using the overhead projector with other children's papers and showing them how to make important changes; be sure to get them involved in suggesting the changes.) Have them hand in their papers for safekeeping.

Day Three: Pass out the papers again. Have them now rewrite them, using their best handwriting, spelling, and punctuation. Walk around the room giving praise and suggestions. Have them pass in *both* copies of their papers.

Day Four: Pass back their papers with numerous positive comments and no more than a few negative remarks. (see Module 6 for a discussion of this). This can be done either during an individual conference or to all the children at the same time. The individual conference should be used sometimes in order to provide each child with individual praise and suggestions. In either case, make a decision with the children as to what is to be done with the papers. Are they to be taken home for a parent's signature? Are they to be put in a class book? Are they to be shared with others in any way? Are they suitable for a bulletin board display? Should they be kept in their individual writing folders as samples of their writing?

This four-step plan has been used with children in the lower grades as well as the upper grades very effectively. However, it is not advisable to use this approach for more than one paper per week. It is a rigorous program and if used too much could lead to a negative attitude toward writing. The important thing is to treat the four-step program as an opportunity to make children feel proud of their writing.

Teach for Mastery

One way of increasing mastery is to break down a task into "bite-sized chunks" and have the children thoroughly digest (master) each chunk before going on to the next one. Spelling lends itself to the mastery approach very well. Research (21) has shown that, instead of giving the children fifteen to twenty words to learn all at once, you should expect them to learn only a few words at a time. Table 5.7 shows a spelling program designed to encourage a high degree of mastery—and thus retention—of the correct spelling for words.

Another way of increasing mastery is to teach children to use efficient study steps. The study method suggested by Horn (13) seems to be an effective one for most children. Here, in modified form, is Horn's method:

1. Look at the word and say it to yourself.
2. Close your eyes and imagine yourself writing the word.
3. Check to see if you were right. (If not, repeat Steps 1–3.)
4. Cover the word and write it.
5. Check to see if you were right. (If not, repeat Steps 4 and 5.)
6. Repeat Steps 4 and 5 twice more.

For dyslexic children (children suffering from specific language disability) and for other children having extreme difficulty with spelling, you may wish to use an approach which permits a more vivid and multi-sensory impression of each word:

1. Have each child write the word on the board, saying each letter out loud as he writes it.
2. After the children have written the word, they should then trace it at the board while they spell it out loud again.

3. Then have them *close their eyes* and trace it while spelling it out loud.
4. Next, have them cover up the correct spelling and write it again on the chalkboard.
5. Have them check to see if they are right. If not, they should repeat Steps 4 and 5 or if necessary, repeat Steps 1–5.
6. Have them sit down and write the word from memory on paper.

TABLE 5.7　　A Mini-Test Spelling Program Emphasizing Mastery

Monday:	A. Pretest on first set of new words (5–7 words)	3	minutes
	B. Correction and study time	5	"
	C. Posttest on first set	3	"
	D. Correction	2	"
Tuesday:	A. Pretest on second set of new words	3	"
	B. Correction and study time (new words plus words missed on yesterday's posttest)	5	"
	C. Posttest on second set	3	"
	D. Correction	2	"
Wednesday:	A. Pretest on remaining words in week's list	3	"
	B. Correction and study time (new words plus words missed on last two posttests)	6	"
	C. Posttest on third set	3	"
	D. Correction	2	"
Thursday:	A. Games related to all three sets plus this week's "demons"—those missed on posttests by several people plus "demons" from former weeks. (See section on motivation for specific games.)	15	"
	1. "Spelling Baseball"		
	2. "Spellgo" (a game of "Bingo")		
	3. "Ringtoss Spelling"		
	4. "Spelling Duel"		
	5. Others that lend themselves to using a particular set of words rather than those words which randomly come to mind.		
	6. "Spelling Sense," "Cootie Spelling," "Category Spelling Race," etc. (if children do not need extra practice on particular words)		
Friday:	A. Study of former demons plus this week's demons (with a partner)	6	"
	B. Test on demons (use same number each week so that progress graph may be used)	5	"
	C. Correction	3	"
	D. Recording of score on progress graph	2	"
	Total Weekly Time	71	minutes

Two other ways of increasing mastery are through writing and reading. A spelling program which includes only weekly tests is never enough. Opportunities for using their spelling vocabulary in compositions and other types of writing should be provided, along with opportunities for proofreading and correcting their mistakes. Opportunities for reading also reinforce what has been learned through spelling instruction. Although reading and spelling do not require the same skills, they seem to be mutually reinforcing. Naturally, reading alone will not assure mastery of a spelling vocabulary (14).

Provide Massed and Distributed Practice

Tests probably give the best practice, providing the test is checked by the child immediately after it has been completed. The mini-test approach described earlier provides distributed practice as well as massed practice, which seems to be more effective according to research (14). The mini-test approach distributes the practice of a week's spelling demons over the week. It also permits the distribution of practice on persistent demons throughout the school year.

Another kind of practice, of course, is through the compositions and other forms of practical and personal writing which children are expected to do throughout the year. The following is a list of practical situations calling for writing:

1. Thank-you letters to speakers and other guests
2. Greeting cards
3. Registration cards and other forms
4. Math problems for classmates
5. Advertisements for a class play
6. Other advertisements for class sales
7. Contributions to school or class paper
8. Riddles and puzzles for classmates
9. Original skits and plays
10. Original poems and compositions

11. Plans for a field trip
12. Proposals to the teacher or principal for special projects
13. Handwriting practice
14. Spelling tests
15. Other tests requiring writing
16. Information reports
17. Invitations to parents and other guests of the school
18. Bulletin boards
19. Displays needing identification
20. Supplies needing labels

21. Class diaries
22. Pen pal letters
23. Minutes for club meetings
24. Notes while listening to a record, film, or speaker
25. Recipes for parents and friends

26. Bibliographies
27. Names of children in class
28. Checks and receipts for a play store
29. Worksheets and workbooks
30. Science notebooks

Help Positive Transfer Occur

To encourage positive transfer, a teacher first has to decide what should transfer from what. If you want mastery of spelling words through a testing program to transfer to regular writing, then you'll have to provide many opportunities for that transfer to take place. You'll also have to make the effort to correct children's spelling in their compositions and other forms of writing or to help them find their own errors through proofreading.

If you want them to transfer spelling rules or generalizations from one word to the next, you'll have to decide which rules or generalizations are worthy of teaching and teach them specifically. (It's true that some children will discover them on their own, but many will not.) Some of the vowel patterns are worthy of teaching both in the reading and spelling components of your language arts program. These are discussed in detail in this module on pages 173 to 174. Very few spelling rules are easy enough for children to learn, have few exceptions, have wide application to many words, and seem to increase children's ability to learn more words. According to Horn (14) the only rules which meet those criteria are the following:

1. The rules for adding suffixes (changing *y* to *i,* dropping final *e,* doubling the final consonant).
2. The letter *q* is followed by *u* in common English words.
3. English words rarely end in *v*.
4. Proper nouns and most adjectives formed from proper nouns begin with capital letters.
5. A period is used in most abbreviations.
6. The rules for the correct use of the apostrophe in contractions and to show possession.

If you want the children to transfer the spelling of root words (base words) to derived forms of those root words, you will have to provide most children with specific lessons on derivations (unless these are provided in your commercial spelling program). Children usually enjoy "derivative hunts"—providing them with a base word and having them think of as many derivatives as they can. What derivatives might they think of, for example, for the word *happy*? (*happier, happiest, happily, unhappier, unhappiest, unhappily*) What derivatives might they think of for *atom* (*atomic, atomize, atomizer, subatomic*) What about *help*?

If you want to avoid *negative* transfer, you will probably want to avoid discussing the "hard spots" in words—a teaching technique which used to be prevalent. Discussing hard spots merely teaches children to make the mistakes that they wouldn't have made if you hadn't pointed out the hard spots. Research (14) shows that this practice does more harm than good. For example, suppose you point out what you think is the hard spot in the word *truly*. You might say, "Some people want to put an *e* in there because they expect an *e* to be there. The way it is now you're not sure whether that's a short *u* or a long *u*. An *e* would make it a long *u,* but you don't want to put an *e* in there." You can see why some children who never put an *e* there before might be tempted to put one there the next time.

Teaching Punctuation as Expression

Suppose someone says these words: He—is—driving—Tom. What do these words mean? Take your pick:

1. *He* is driving, Tom. No one else is going to drive.
2. He is driving *Tom,* and no one else.
3. He is *driving,* Tom. He's not flying.
4. He *is* driving, Tom, no matter what you say.
5. *He* is driving Tom. No one else is going to drive Tom there.
6. *He* is driving, Tom? You're going to let that guy drive?
7. He *is* driving, Tom? I thought he wasn't.
8. He is *driving,* Tom? I thought he was flying.
9. He is driving *Tom?* I thought he was driving Bob.

Which of those meanings was correct? It depends on which words were stressed (accented), which words were spoken with a higher pitch than others, and where the speaker paused (juncture). And it depends on whether the speaker put enough "expression" into her speaking to communicate the proper meaning.

Children who do not know how to punctuate properly often do not understand the purpose of punctuation. To develop this understanding, it is advisable to use all four of the language arts in harmony. The use of the language experience chart provides one good example of this. As children dictate their story of an experience they have shared, the teacher writes down their words on a large chart (often a piece of newsprint or butcher paper). As children *speak,* the other children are encouraged to *listen* in order to help the teacher (or another child) indicate pauses, pitch changes, and stress by *writing* commas, periods, exclamation points, question marks, quotation marks, and underlining. After the experience chart has been written, the children are asked to *read* it, using the correct expression called for by the punctuation marks.

As you take the children's dictation for an experience chart, you can show them how to use commas to show pauses; how to use periods, question marks, and exclamation marks to show pitch changes at the ends of sentences; and how to underline or use capital letters to show stress (accent). As they learn how to do this, you can ask *them* to indicate stress, pitch changes, and pauses: "Is there a word you'd like to underline in that sentence to show

how you said it? Your voice went up at the end of that sentence. Do you want me to use a period, a question mark, or an exclamation mark?"

Often when teachers spend more time helping children *read* punctuation with understanding, they find the children using punctuation in their writing with greater understanding. As they understand punctuation in their reading, they tend to read with greater expression. This in turn seems to increase their reading comprehension (since the child is now doing a better job of translating the written symbols into speech).

Teaching Punctuation and Expression Through Reading Lessons

The teacher has three tasks involved in teaching punctuation and expression through reading lessons. These tasks are described below.

Task 1: Showing Them Why Expression Is Important

This can be handled in a manner similar to the way this text tried to show *you* why it is important. For instance, suppose you and the pupils come across this passage in a story from a basal reader:

> Bill watched Jim throw the ball.
> Bill called, "Hey! Show me how to throw, Jim."

By reading the second sentence out loud to the children in a variety of ways, you can help them see the relationships between punctuation and expression and between expression and comprehension. Some of the ways this sentence can be read are as follows:

1. Bill called, "Hey! Show me how to <u>throw</u>, Jim."
2. Bill called, "Hey, Show <u>me</u> how to throw, Jim."
3. "Bill!" called Hey. "Show me how to throw <u>Jim</u>."
4. Bill called, "Hey! Show me how to throw <u>Jim</u>?"
5. Bill called, "Hey! Show me how to throw <u>Jim</u>!"
6. Bill called, "Hey! Show me how to throw <u>Jim</u>."

Just by reading this sentence in a variety of ways—and letting the children try their hand at it—you can help them discover intuitively why pauses, pitch changes, and stress variations are important. The subtle differences between interpretations 1 and 3 show clearly the importance of pausing in the proper place. The difference between 1 and 2 shows the importance of stressing one word rather than another. And the difference between 4, 5, and 6 demonstrates the significance of pitch variations, particularly at the end of sentences.

Task 2: Showing Them What Symbols Are Used in Print to Indicate Expression

The need for printed symbols for stress, pitch, and pauses becomes evident to children during an experience like the one just described. The importance of commas seems obvious to them when they realize that without them, *Jim* is thrown instead of the ball and Bill is called by Hey instead of calling "Hey!" himself. They also can see that a period, a question mark, and an exclamation point are not just simple stops like commas but indicators of pitch changes.

With older children, you can have fun approximating these pitch changes with numbers. By dividing pitch into four ranges and calling the highest pitch 4, the lowest pitch 1, and so on, you can show what different types of sentences "look like";

> 2   2 2 2 3 1
> She married a *banker*.   (Statement)
> 2   2 2 2 3 3
> She married a *banker*?   (Question)
> 2   2 2 2 4 1
> She married a *banker*!   (Exclamation)

Try saying those sentences to yourself, and you'll see the effects of pitch changes on meaning (even though the *stressed* word remains constant).

Task 3: Showing Them How to Determine the Proper Pitch, Stress, and Pauses

While children can be taught to look for punctuation signals of pitch and pauses, they must be taught to look for other types of signals for stress. Sometimes, of course, stress is indicated by letters in italics or upper-case, e.g., "I want *you* to eat it. I've had ENOUGH!" But often, a reader is expected to provide his own italics, as in the case of the following passage:

> Bill watched Jim teaching Harry how to throw.
> Bill called, "Hey! Show me how to throw, Jim."

In a case such as this, the child must learn to rely on context for a clue as to which word to stress. Since Bill has been watching Jim teach Harry how to throw, it is likely (but not certain) that Bill would say, "Hey! Show *me* how to throw, Jim."

In addition to the types of experiences with stress, pauses, and pitch that have already been described, the teacher can provide the children with dittoed stories that are completely lacking in punctuation. The children are then asked to insert capital letters, periods, commas, question marks, and exclamation marks *and* to underline the word in each sentence which should be given the most stress.

Excellent practice in reading with expression can be gained by having the children read plays to each other, or stories which have a lot of dialogue. Whatever practice materials are used, however, positive reinforcement should be given for *meaningful* expression and not just for interesting variations in pitch or stress. Some children can appear to be reading with magnificent expression, yet show through their answers to questions that they had very little idea of what they were reading. (If you don't believe this can be done, try it sometime. Concentrate *just* on your intonation, and you'll find that your comprehension may be very slight indeed.)

The Effects of Reading with Expression on Other Language Skills

We teach children to read with expression *not* primarily to enable them to entertain, although this certainly has some social value, but to help them translate print into meaningful speech; in short, to read with comprehension. Variations in pitch and stress, along with proper pauses, are often just as important in reading comprehension as the words one is decoding.

We also teach children to read with expression to help them develop a rationale for *speaking* with expression and to provide them with practice in speaking with expression during oral reading situations. Reading out loud to each other is an excellent way of encouraging such expression. Of course, when children read out loud to each other the other children should generally have no books to refer to. In other words, the situation should be an audience situation requiring good oral reading and good listening.

We teach children to "read with expression" in order to enhance their listening abilities. As children learn the importance of stress, pitch changes, and juncture (pauses), they are more likely to pay attention to such signals as they listen to others speak. This, in turn, should lead to better communication as they listen to the whole message instead of just the words.

Last, but not least, we teach children to read with expression in order to improve their ability to communicate through writing. Only when they grasp the significance of punctuation will they strive to punctuate well as they write. As mentioned earlier, the experience chart is a natural medium for helping children see the connections between speaking, listening, writing, and reading—and the connections between punctuation, expression, and meaning.

Incorporating Spelling, Handwriting, and Punctuation into the Total Language Arts Program

Mrs. Sanchez gives her third graders special lessons on handwriting, spelling, and punctuation, but she also has her students apply these three skills in a variety of ways. Each Friday afternoon, for example, they prepare a "Report to Parents," telling of the most significant events that occurred during the week. This report is dictated by the children to Mrs. Sanchez, who asks children for advice on spelling and punctuation as she writes it on the chalkboard. Then, one of the children, a new one each week, has the responsibility of copying the report on a ditto master and signing his or her name. The ditto master is then used to make enough copies for each child to be able to take one home for the weekend.

At least one letter per week is written by the students: a letter of invitation to their parents to see a class play; an invitation to a fireman to visit their room; a request for information about a company's posters; a sympathy note to a sick classmate; a thank-you note to Mr. Roberts for getting them a Christmas tree for their classroom.

Home-made greeting cards are made for many of the holidays; charts and bulletin boards are the responsibility of the children as well as the teacher; worksheets are corrected not only for content but for spelling and handwriting as well; children are constantly encouraged to produce riddles, jokes, stories, and poems for others to read; materials and supplies are labeled by the children.

Experience charts are used frequently to share and record common experiences. Children draw pictures to illustrate their "books" about their private experiences. Lessons on creative grammar (see Module 4) often end with children writing their own special sentences. Science lessons often require recording of observations. Children sometimes write their own math problems for each other. Field trips usually lead to large single-copy books describing their plans and their adventures and including photographs and drawings produced by the children.

Children write evaluations of their own progress every few months. After proofreading them and getting help from the teacher on their spelling, punctuation, and handwriting, the children take the evaluation reports home for signatures from their parents. Evaluations of their classroom behavior or their performance in a developing class play are often produced in small groups with one child acting as recorder as others dictate their ideas.

The opportunities for children to practice better spelling, handwriting, and punctuation are endless in Mrs. Sanchez's room. Writing, in her classroom, is often a natural outgrowth of planning, experiencing, and evaluating. The basic skills are very important to Mrs. Sanchez. "I want to do everything I possibly can," she says, "to move these children toward the high level of literacy that they deserve. I give them all kinds of drill on spelling, phonics, handwriting, punctuation—things like that. But I also try to make it all meaningful to them by providing practice situations that make sense to them."

REFERENCES AND BIBLIOGRAPHY

1. Barnard, Douglas P., and DeGracie, James. "Vocabulary Analysis of New Primary Reading Series." *Reading Teacher* 30 (November 1976): 177–80.

2. Cholden, Harriett B. "Wastebasket Writing Is Garbage," *Language Arts* 54 (March 1977): 308–9.

3. Dolch, Edward W. "A Basic Sight Vocabulary." *Elementary School Journal* 36 (February 1936): 456–60.

4. Erlebacher, Adrienne, and Herrick, Virgil E. "Quality of Handwriting Today and Yesterday." *Elementary School Journal* 62 (1961): 89–93.

5. Gould, Sandra M. "Spelling Isn't Reading Backwards." *Journal of Reading* 20 (December 1976): 220–25.

6. Gray, William S. "Reading." In *Encyclopedia of Educational Research,* edited by Chester W. Harris. New York: Macmillan, 1960.

7. Halpin, G., and Halpin, G. "Special Paper for Beginning Handwriting: An Unjustified Practice?" *Journal of Educational Research* 69 (March 1976): 267–69.

8. Hanna, Paul R. et al. *Phoneme-Grapheme Correspondences as Clues to Spelling Improvement.* Washington, D.C.: U.S. Office of Education Cooperative Research Project No. 1991. Government Printing Office, 1966.

9. Harris, Theodore L. "Handwriting." In *Encyclopedia of Educational Research,* edited by Chester W. Harris. New York: Macmillan, 1960.

10. Herrick, Virgil E., and Okada, Nora. "The Present Scene: Practices in the Teaching of Handwriting in the U.S. — 1960." In *New Horizons for Research in Handwriting,* edited by Virgil E. Herrick. Madison, Wis.: University of Wisconsin Press, 1963.

11. Hillerich, Robert L. "Word Lists—Getting It All Together." *Reading Teacher* 27 (January 1974): 353–60.

12. _____. "Let's Teach Spelling—Not Phonetic Misspelling." *Language Arts* 54 (March 1977): 301–7.

13. Horn, Ernest. "Spelling." In *Encyclopedia of Educational Research,* edited by Chester W. Harris. New York: Macmillan, 1960.

14. Horn, Thomas D. "Spelling." In *Encyclopedia of Educational Research,* edited by Robert L. Ebel. New York: Macmillan, 1969.

15. Hunter, Diana Lee. "Spoken and Written Word Lists: A Comparison." *Reading Teacher* 29 (December 1975): 250–53.

16. Johns, Jerry L. "Updating the Dolch Basic Sight Vocabulary for the Schools of the 1970's." Paper presented at the annual convention of the International Reading Association, New Orleans, May 1974.

17. _____. "Dolch List of Common Nouns—A Comparison." *Reading Teacher* 28 (March 1975): 538–40.

18. Johnson, Dale D. "A Basic Vocabulary for Beginning Reading." *Elementary School Journal* 72 (October 1971): 29–34.

19. Klasen, Edith. *The Syndrome of Specific Dyslexia.* Boston: University Park Press, 1972.

20. May, Frank B., and Eliot, Susan B. "A Basic List of 96 Irregular Words for Linguistic Programs." *Reading Teacher* 31 (April 1978): 794–97.

21. _____. *To Help Children Read,* 2d ed. Columbus, Ohio: Charles E. Merrill, 1978.

22. Moe, Alden J., And Hopkins, Carol J. "The Speaking Vocabularies of Kindergarten, First-grade, and Second-grade Children." *Research in Education,* March 1975. ERIC ED 105 465. Arlington, Virginia, ERIC Document Reproduction Service.

23. Otto, Wayne, and Andersen, Dan W. "Handwriting." In *Encyclopedia of Educational Research,* edited by Robert L. Ebel. New York: Macmillan, 1969.

24. Schofer, Gill. "Teachers Should be Dictators." *Language Arts* 54 (April 1977): 401–2.

25. Sherk, John K., Jr. *A Word Count of Spoken English of Culturally Disadvantaged Preschool and Elementary Pupils.* Kansas City: University of Missouri, 1973.

module

6

Encouraging Creative Processes That Lead to Interesting Speech and Writing

Where we cannot invent, we may at least improve; we may give somewhat of novelty to that which was old, condensation to that which was diffuse, perspicuity to that which was obscure, and currency to that which was recondite.

Caleb C. Colton

In Module 1, basic skills were defined as "those skills necessary for finding and maintaining a job, making friends, raising children, and exhibiting functional and self-actualizing behaviors." Module 4 discussed the basic skills related to fluent writing and speaking. Module 5 described the basic skills required for writing that communicates within the bounds of custom and legibility. Now Module 6 discusses abilities which are less obviously related to our definition of basic skills.

Although it is obvious that a person who speaks with fluency and spells with exactness has advantages in finding a job, influencing people, and making friends, it may be less obvious that a person with *interesting* speech and writing has similar advantages. And yet, it is the people who can interest others in their ideas, qualifications, and personalities who are often most successful in exhibiting functional and self-actualizing behaviors. It is often these people who get the best jobs and make the most friends.

But what makes Gary interesting to talk to? Is it all the places he's been to? Or is it also the way he uses words to make you feel that you are there? What makes Nancy such a fun person to be with? Is it just her cheerfulness, or is it also the naturalness of her conversation—making you smile at the way she makes bland small talk turn into a flavorful discussion. Why do you enjoy Aunt Marie's letters so much? Because of all the gossip or also because of her keen insights into human nature? And what about Uncle Al? Why do all the adults crowd around when he's telling stories to the kids? Is it just his infectious enthusiasm for the story, or is it also because he weaves the tale with clarity, conciseness, and inventiveness? The listeners know who's who and what's happening. Only enough is told to keep you on the edge of your chair, and every character is as unusual and interesting as Uncle Al himself.

In short, the quality which makes some people more interesting than others is their creative and natural use of language. Not all of us can be an Uncle Al or Aunt Marie. But all of us can learn to have more fun with language and, consequently, to become more interesting people in the process. In a school setting, Ronny is going to have difficulty meeting his needs for belonging and self-esteem if he is unable to interest others through verbal expression. Even the very young student who can express himself in an interesting way usually gets the attention and affection of others (including the teacher). The child whose expression is drab or confusing has much more difficulty attracting friends and followers.

The purpose of this module is to help you learn how to help children use language more creatively. To accomplish this in the classroom, a teacher must establish a creative atmosphere, become keenly aware of the characteristics of interesting writing and speech, and encourage the various processes of creative thinking.

Special Prerequisites for Module 6

It is recommended that you complete at least Modules 1–3 before beginning this module. There are no other special prerequisites.

Long-range Outcomes Related to Module 6

This module should help you as a teacher to do the following:

1. Communicate with other professional educators about ways of fostering interesting and creative speaking and writing.
2. Provide children with specific positive feedback and learning activities designed to reinforce characteristics of interesting speaking and writing.
3. Recognize and reinforce those personality characteristics in all children which are generally considered characteristics of highly creative people.
4. Provide encouragement and activities related to the four stages of creative thinking.
5. Use speaking and writing exercises conducive to the development of those mental abilities related to creative thinking.
6. Use specific stimuli for motivating children's compositions.

Study Guide and Performance Objectives for Knowledge Level Examination

To give yourself an overview of what is expected of you in this module, you should first scan the objectives and performance standards at all three levels—knowledge, simulation, and teaching. Then use the performance objectives for the knowledge level as a study guide during your reading of the module. As you find information related to each performance objective, write it down in the available blanks or on a separate sheet of paper. Then review this information shortly before your knowledge level examination.

1.1 On a closed-book examination, you should be able to list three reasons (given at the beginning of Module 6) for helping children learn to speak and write in a more interesting fashion.

1.

2.

3.

1.2 On the same examination, you will be expected to list the two conditions that are necessary for a creative atmosphere in the classroom.

1.

2.

1.3 On the same examination, you will be asked to list five personality characteristics usually associated with creative people.

1.

2.

3.

4.

5.

1.4 On the same examination, you should be able to match the four stages of creative thinking with a set of language arts experiences designed to encourage each stage. The four stages are listed below. After each one write down a language arts experience (discussed in the module) which will remind you of a way of encouraging that stage.

Preparing

Focusing

Executing

Communicating

1.5 On the same examination, you will be asked to match a set of mental abilities related to creative thinking with a set of classroom exercises designed to strengthen those abilities. The six mental abilities are listed below. After each one, write down a classroom exercise (discussed in the module) which will remind you of a way of strengthening that ability.

Word fluency

Ideational fluency

Associational fluency

Redefinition

Sensitivity to problems

Originality

1.6 On a closed-book examination, you will be given a children's composition with each sentence numbered. You will then be given multiple-choice questions similar to the following: "Sentence 7 is a good example of which one of the eight characteristics of interesting writing and speaking discussed in Module 6?" For each multiple-choice question, you should be able to select the characteristic that is best demonstrated by the designated sentence. In preparation for this part of the examination be sure to do the practice exercises in the section "Teaching the Characteristics of Interesting Speaking and Writing." As further preparation, see if you can define each of the eight characteristics below:

Imagery

Naturalness

Inventiveness

Insight

Sincerity

Flexible Style

Conciseness

Clarity

1.7 On the same examination, you will be asked to list the three creative processes referred to in Module 6.

   1.

2.

3.

Performance Standards for Knowledge Level

A. Twenty-five minute time limit on 1.1 through 1.7 combined.
B. Completion deadline: instructor will notify.
C. Recommended grading standards if grades are used: 96% = A; 92% = A—; 88% = B; 84% = B—; 80% = C; below 80% = incomplete; should be completed at 80% or better before you go on to performance objectives for simulation level. (The instructor may wish to permit a grade of A or B only the first time the test is given in order to encourage more intensive study.)

Performance Objectives for Simulation Level

2.1 On a closed-book examination, you will be given a child's composition to read and critique. In the margins of the composition, write *positive* comments which show your understanding of the characteristics of interesting speech and writing discussed in Module 6 and your ability to reinforce them. (Not all eight characteristics may show up in this composition.)

2.2 (Alternative objective) same as 2.1, only a take-home examination would be given instead of a closed-book one.

2.3 (Alternative objective) In a school setting, you will be asked to observe an elementary school child who the teacher feels is highly creative. You will be expected to write down behavioral samples related to autonomy, goal-directness, and other characteristics attributed to highly creative people. You should be able to write up a report on this child, including suggestions for encouraging his or her creativity. One copy of this report should be made for your instructor and one for the child's teacher.

2.4 (Alternative objective) As a take-home exam, develop a lesson plan which will serve as a basis for helping children understand one of the characteristics of interesting speaking and writing.

Performance Standards for Simulation Level

A. For Objectives 2.1 and 2.2 (Critique of Child's Composition)
1. The comments are positive and specifically related to the characteristics being reinforced.
2. All of the characteristics displayed in the composition are observed and reinforced.
3. The comments are written in words that most children would understand and consider reinforcing.

B. For Objective 2.3 (School Observations)
1. Shows understanding of the nature of the personality characteristics attributed to highly creative people.
2. Identifies at least three of the six characteristics.
3. Suggestions for encouraging child's creativity relate appropriately to each of the characteristics.
4. Report is very legible and shows no mistakes in standard spelling, punctuation, or grammar.
5. Shows that sufficient observations were made.

C. For Objective 2.4 (Lesson Plan)
1. The performance objectives clearly state the behavior desired, the conditions under which the behavior is to be performed, and those performance standards which will indicate sufficient mastery of the desired behavior.
2. The performance objectives relate directly to the long-range outcome; the learning activities relate to both the performance objectives and the long-range outcome.
3. The teacher-in-training shows a clear understanding of the characteristic she decides to encourage through the lesson.
4. The following are included in the lesson plan:
   a. Approximate age level for which this learning experience might be appropriate, e.g., 5–7, 6–8, 11–13, etc.
   b. Size of group for which this activity might be appropriate: entire class, small group, or individual.
   c. Long-range outcome desired.
   d. Performance objectives related to long-range outcome.
   e. Prerequisite skills children might need.
   f. Learning activities created or selected—list briefly the procedural steps.
   g. Materials that might be needed.

D. For Objectives 2.1–2.4
1. Suggested grading standard if grades are used; should be completed at C level or better before going on to performance objectives for the teaching level. (Grades based on judgment of instructor and/or peers.)
2. Time limit and completion deadline: instructor will notify.

3. Additional standards or modified standards may be developed by the instructor and/or teachers-in-training. It is best, however, to state these standards *in advance* of the required performance.

Performance Objectives for Teaching Level

3.1 In a micro-teaching, observation, student teaching, intern or supervised teaching situation, write positive comments in the margins of at least three children's compositions. These comments should reinforce the characteristics of interesting writing and speaking discussed in Module 6. Then have a brief conference with each child about his or her composition.

No lesson plan is necessary, but a brief report should be written after the conference; in this report explain your procedures and your general results. Your cooperating teacher, supervisor, or instructor will want to see your report and the compositions with your comments on them.

3.2 (Alternative Objective) In the same type of setting described in 3.1, work with two or more children to help them understand one of the characteristics of interesting speaking and writing. Lesson plan, worksheet, and critique are required.

Your critique should indicate (1) to what extent your performance objectives were met, (2) what might be done to help children who did not meet your performance standards, (3) what problems you had, if any, (4) what might have been done to implement your desired long-range outcome more effectively, and (5) what type of follow-up activity might provide useful practice for these students at a later date. Your cooperating teacher, supervisor, or instructor will probably want to see your critique.

Performance Standards for Teaching Level

A. For Objective 3.1 (Children's Compositions)
   1. Standards A-1–A-3 for the simulation experience may be appropriate.
   2. Report shows awareness of children's verbal reactions and feelings about the comments.
   3. Report is legible, with no spelling, punctuation, or grammatical errors.

B. For Objective 3.2 (Lesson)
   1. Standards C-1–C-4 for the simulation experience may be appropriate.

2. Uses learning principles effectively; does not violate any of those discussed in Module 3.
3. Additional standards or modified standards may be developed by the cooperating teacher, instructor, supervisor, and/or teacher-in-training—*in advance* of the required performance.

Foundation Stones for Encouraging Creative Communication

TEACHER: *Fred, why aren't you writing a story?*
FRED: *Aw, I don't know how to write.*
TEACHER: *Why sure you do, Fred. All you have to do is think of something to write about.*
FRED: *I can't think of anything.*
TEACHER: *Surely you can think of something to write about.*
FRED: *Nope. Can't think of a thing.*
TEACHER: *How about writing about your pet.*
FRED: *Ain't got one.*
TEACHER: *Well then, write about your hobby.*
FRED: *Ain't got one of them neither.*
TEACHER: *Well, write about something you like to do more than anything else.*
FRED: *I don't like to do nothing that much.*
TEACHER: *Then write about something you hate to do more than anything else.*
FRED: *Can't.*
TEACHER: *Why not?*
FRED: *I hate writing the most.*

Depending on the personality of the particular teacher involved, a boy like Fred is capable of inducing feelings ranging all the way from depression to hate. The middle range of feeling might be classified as frustration. In general, there have been two methods which teachers have used to combat this frustration. One method is to deny that creative expression is very important: "so why teach it, anyway." The other method is to search continually and frantically for motivating gimmicks such as mood music, curtain pullers (stories half-read), and stimulating titles: "The Fun I Had Minding Baby Sister" or "The Case of the Missing Pencil Sharpener."

Examination of the *Education Index* reveals that the mass of articles on creative communication is heavily loaded with gimmicks for inducing children to write. Most of the gimmicks are probably useful. Yet, research (41) shows that they are weak foundation stones for a creative writing-creative speaking program. Instead, the program should rest on two pillars: the classroom atmosphere which fosters creativity and the thinking processes involved in writing and speaking creatively (see Figure 6.1).

CREATIVE ATMOSPHERE

A creative atmosphere must pervade the total school program, and it must prevail during the entire school year. Without this pervasive atmosphere, the attempt to teach children to speak and write creatively will probably be no more successful than flying a kite in a vacuum.

But how does a classroom teacher develop a creative atmosphere? A creative atmosphere in the classroom requires at least two conditions. The first condition is a teacher who desires to be personally creative. A study by Torrance (41) demonstrates the importance of creative motivations on the part of the teacher. Several groups of intermediate grade children were given specific training in creative writing for a period of three months. All of the groups carried on approximately the same activities. Before the training began, the teachers of the groups were given a Personal-Social Motivations Inventory designed to measure creative motivation. The inventory requires true and false responses to such items as the following: "I enjoy work in which I must keep trying out new approaches." The pupils of teachers with strong creative motivations showed gains that were significantly higher than those pupils whose teachers had weak creative motivations. The latter group of pupils showed almost no gain despite the fact that the training time was the same for all groups.

The second condition of a creative atmosphere in the classroom is a teacher who reacts positively toward personality characteristics of creative people. Psychologists have long emphasized the importance of reinforcement in causing behavior to become habitual. Teachers who do not reward, or at least tolerate, the characteristics usually exhibited by creative people cannot expect to have a creative atmosphere in the classroom.

What are the typical personality characteristics of highly creative people? Research (1, 10, 15, 21, 41) has shown that a highly creative individual can usually be described with the following adjectives:

1. *Autonomous*—Makes judgments without relying very much on the opinions of others; has a high degree of self-confidence; goes against the crowd in the interest of seeking truth.

2. *Visionary*—Has a sense of personal destiny; desires change and perceives change as possible.

3. *Goal Oriented*—Has many ideas for keeping occupied; applies considerable effort to projects which interest him or her.

4. *Flexible*—Shows a high degree of adaptability in problem situations; has a keen sense of humor.

5. *Open*—Demonstrates abundant curiosity; shows reluctance to apply judgment too quickly; seldom uses mechanisms of suppression and repression; tolerates and seeks new ideas.

6. *Adventurous*—Takes risks; likes to try something new; prefers complexity.

Unfortunately, some teachers might perceive those six characteristics as follows:

1. *Autonomous*—stubborn; brash; conceited; can't follow directions.

FIGURE 6.1

Creative Writing and Speaking Program Based on Gimmicks

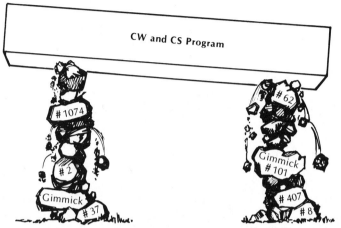

Creative Writing and Speaking Program Based on Creative
Atmosphere and Creative Thinking Processes

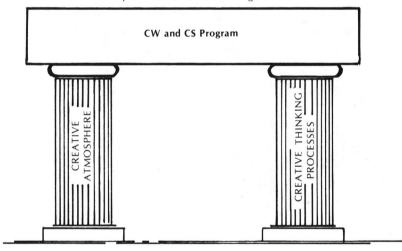

2. *Visionary*—rabble rouser; daydreamer.

3. *Goal Oriented*—can't apply himself to school work.

4. *Flexible*—unprincipled; annoying sense of humor.

5. *Open*—always asking silly questions; too introverted.

6. *Adventurous*—troublemaker; poor judgment.

It is unlikely that a teacher with those perceptions would be capable of developing a creative atmosphere in the classroom.

Some studies demonstrate that not all teachers find it easy to reinforce the characteristic behavior of creative students. Getzels and Jackson (14) found that most of the high school teachers involved in their study preferred the high-IQ students to the high-creative students. Torrance (40) found that the elementary school teachers involved in his studies also preferred the high-IQ children to the high-creative children. Furthermore, the teachers admitted that they "knew" the high-IQ pupils better than the high-creative pupils. These studies do not indicate that most teachers are incapable of reinforcing creative behavior. They do indicate, however, that some teachers may have to change their perceptions of what constitutes a "good" student before they can achieve greater success in motivating creative writing and speaking.

To repeat an important idea, two conditions of a creative atmosphere in the classroom are a creatively motivated teacher and a teacher who reinforces those behavior patterns that we usually associate with creative individuals. Can teachers become creatively motivated? A study by Meadow and Parnes (21) shows that they probably can. Is it possible for teachers to change their reinforcement patterns? Again, this change can occur only when teachers change their perceptions of what constitutes a "good" student. It is encouraging to find that teachers have changed their perceptions once they were taught to recognize the characteristics of creative individuals (40).

A creative classroom atmosphere is encouraged by a creatively motivated teacher who reinforces creative personality characteristics.

CREATIVE PROCESSES

In addition to establishing a creative atmosphere in the classroom, the teacher should instruct children in the specific thinking processes related to creative writing and speaking. The teaching of creative expression has one thing in common with the teaching of any other skill: if there are specific abilities which one wants to see developed, then one had better teach them in a specific way and not hope for them in a general way.

Some educators argue that the best procedure for encouraging creativity is to get out of the child's way. This argument probably has merit if one is referring to the actual act of creating. But prior to the act of creating, children need help in learning to use the tools, media, and thinking processes of the creative act. Like painters who need knowledge of their media as well as a sensitivity to their own creative urges, writers or speakers must understand their media of words and the thinking processes which lead to a creative product. There are at least three thinking processes which can be taught to children:

1. The stages of creative thinking.
2. The mental abilities involved in creative thinking.
3. The characteristics of interesting communication which one must think about in preparing a creative speech or composition.

Process 1: Stages in Creative Thinking

One framework is that of the stages which are often experienced in creative thinking. Wallas (45) describes the stages as preparation, incubation, illumination, and verification. Foshay (13) describes them as openness, focus, discipline, and closure. Sessions (35) calls them inspiration, conception, and execution. For purposes of teaching creative writing and speaking, however, it is recommended that the teacher keep in mind the following stages of creative thinking: preparing, focusing, executing, and communicating.

Preparing. This stage often involves careful, open-minded observation of a person, an event, an object, or any other subject of one's investigation. A mind which is relatively free of bias and one which is willing to be surprised is more capable of insightful description than a mind which habitually classifies its environment too soon or screens out unusual, disturbing phenomena. Sometimes this stage involves the sensing of problems, gaps in knowledge, or other deficiencies in one's environment. The "soul cries out" for something better—something more just, or more elegant, or more truthful.

This is the stage during which a writer sees the need for a new organization of society, a new concept of human nature, or a new form of poetic expression. At times, this stage involves the act of seeking inspiration—through music, through beautiful poetry or prose, through nature, through the memory of past glories, through daydreaming. And at times, this stage involves the more mundane operation of gathering facts through reading, interviewing, or observing.

Focusing. This stage involves the act of perceiving a solution to a problem, a procedure to follow, or an end product. "Oh, I've got it!" "Say, how about doing it this way!" "Now I know how to say it!" Sometimes the perception or insight comes during the process of conscious reasoning. Frequently, however, the insight comes after a period of incubation, during which time the mind has been seemingly concentrating on problems which are unrelated to the creative task (32). Some people have their greatest insights while taking a shower, or riding on a bus, or playing cards. Some people induce insight by leaving their creative task for a period and returning to it later. All methods of inducing insight, however, involve the necessity of listening to oneself, and this is one point, among many, at which the preparing and focusing stage merge. (None of the stages is discrete.)

Focusing also involves commitment on the part of the creator to a particular form, procedure, or product. Sometimes this is very difficult because alternative ideas may plead for attention. At times, the alternatives may be so forceful in the would-be creator's mind that he cannot make a decision, and the next stage of creativity is never entered upon.

Executing.   This stage requires hard work! It might be called the "sweat and tears stage," and many embryonic creators haven't the perseverance to last through it. This is the stage at which the sins of procrastination are most tempting—time to sharpen all of one's pencils, clean one's desk, or chat with a friend. A tremendous amount of resolution is often needed to prevent premature closure; the temptation to rush it through, to get it in its "final" form, to cut it off too soon, is stronger than many can withstand.

On the other hand, there are some writers who would fuss until doomsday on every little word if some kind teacher or editor didn't snatch the product from their hands and push them on to the next stage. Knowing when to stop, then, is also part of the executing stage.

Communicating.   Although some people may create with no desire to share their product, such a mode of operation is hardly typical. Most of us can hardly wait to share our marvelous ideas with others. Not that this stage is always pleasurable. On the contrary, it may be quite painful and even traumatic. It's a rare public speaker who feels no pain in the delivery room. How few the writers must be who can toss their products to the wolves without fear and trembling. Yet, despite such agonies, the desire to communicate to a sympathetic audience remains.

Encouraging the Four Stages.   How can a teacher encourage those four stages as they apply to creative writing and speaking? Here are some ways of aiding the preparing stage:

1. Encourage children to observe with as little bias as possible; to avoid immediate structuring of perceptions; to accept all of the data though some of it might be threatening. Possible types of experiences for children:
   a. Examine a familiar object as if you are seeing it for the first time. Discuss or write about your observations.
   b. Discuss things that frighten you.
   c. Discuss a person that you dislike but describe only his good points.
   d. After viewing a skit or film with moral overtones, describe what happened without making any judgment or using emotional words.
   e. Describe a landscape without using any value words such as *beautiful* or *glorious.*

2. Encourage children to use the "deferred judgment" techniques (29). Parnes and Meadow (30) have found that this technique is conducive to original and useful ideas. The essence of the technique is simply to accept, for a period of time, any ideas which come to mind. Possible types of experiences for children:
   a. Before deciding upon a writing topic, list as many ideas for topics as you can; defer judgment of your ideas until you have created a long list. Then select one topic to write on.

  b. Use the deferred judgment principle to develop a list of names of the characters in your story.

  c. Use the deferred judgment principle to develop a list of sources that might be used to get more information on your topic.

3. Encourage children to use all of their senses whenever possible during observation. Possible types of experiences for children:

  a. Look at an object in the room; describe it orally or on paper. Then, touch the object, shake it, and listen to the noise it makes. Smell it and even taste it, if the situation is sufficiently sanitary. Describe the object again. Discuss the differences in the two descriptions.

  b. Describe another object in the room after some children have only looked at it, some have only felt it (eyes shut), some have only listened to it while the teacher shakes it, and some have only tasted it. (The class will have to be divided into small groups in different parts of the room.) Discuss the differences in the descriptions.

4. Encourage children to be sensitive to deficiencies in their environment. Possible types of experiences for children:

  a. List as many ways as you can of improving the chalkboard in this classroom. Discuss the ideas in a complimentary rather than critical way.

  b. Write about (or describe orally) an "ideal" school—one which you would like to go to. Share your ideas.

  c. Describe (or write about) a means of transporting people which would be better than the way done in your town. Discuss your ideas; send some to the mayor or city manager.

5. Encourage children to develop imaginative foresight. Possible types of experiences for children:

  a. What would happen if people stopped drinking milk because they thought it was poisonous? List as many things that might happen as you can. Discuss.

  b. What if all boys had to prove they were men by cutting off the little finger on their left hand?

  c. What if we had a severe shortage of sugar—so severe that only 100 pounds were available for the next six months?

  d. Have the children make up their own "What if" questions.

Here are some ways of aiding the focusing stage:

1. After the preparing stage has occurred, encourage children to decide on their own way of making sense out of their observations. Possible types of experiences for children:

  a. Plan a story, poem, or play (or give a talk) based on the previous observations during the preparing stage.

  b. Plan an essay expounding a theory based on the previous observations.

2. Encourage children to utilize the process of incubation. Possible types of experiences for children:
   a. After deciding on the means of focusing, concentrate for several minutes on the anticipated project; then take time off for recess or some other easy task; return to the creative task.
   b. Make an "idea" notebook for your school desk and also one for home. Write down ideas as soon as possible after they occur. Expand these ideas during your spare time and during the time set aside by the teacher for this purpose.
3. Encourage them to commit themselves in the presence of others to a definite product (after adequate time has been given for the preparing stage).

Here are some ways of aiding the executing stage:

1. Provide a period each day for uninterrupted work, perhaps during the end of the school day so that children might carry on a project at home while their pens are hot.
2. Provide adequate materials so that children are not tempted to quit because of lack of resources (paper, pencils, tape recorder for the child who wants to think out loud, "stenographers" for children who have difficulty writing, time).
3. Reward persistence through individual praise.

Here are some ways of aiding the communicating stage:

1. Permit children to choose among several alternate ways of sharing their work with others, e.g., classmates guess student author after teacher reads aloud; student places her creative writing product in an anonymous author file or a teacher only file; student gives a spontaneous talk or reads her paper.
2. Develop a classroom newspaper, magazine, or book to share with parents, children in the same school, children in another school, children in another city, or children in another country.
3. Refer to children frequently with terms such as *authors, writers, poets,* and *reporters.*
4. Invite poets and other writers into the classroom.

Process 2:
Mental Abilities Involved in Creative Thinking

A second process to be taught is the process of using the specific mental abilities involved in creative thinking. Guilford and his associates (18) have defined creative thinking, by means of tests and factor analyses, as a composite of several abilities. These abilities include fluency, spontaneous flexibility, adaptive flexibility, redefinition, sensitivity to problems, and originality.

According to Guilford et al. (19), there are four types of fluency. These will now be defined; also related activities for teaching creative writing and speaking will be described.

Word Fluency. Word fluency is the ability to think rapidly of words which have particular structural characteristics. This ability is helpful, for example, in writing poetry which requires a definite rhythm or rhyme.

Sample activities:

1. In two minutes, think of several words which end with the syllable *ate,* e.g., *refrigerate.*
2. In one minute, think of several words which rhyme with *rusty.*
3. In two minutes, think of several phrases which have the same beat or rhythm as "down the dusty road," and "over the breaking waves."

Ideational Fluency. Ideational fluency is the ability to think rapidly of ideas which are appropriate to a given situation.

Sample activities:

1. In three minutes, think of several titles for the following plot: A perfume peddler ran out of gasoline on a deserted road. He poured several bottles of perfume in the gasoline tank and managed to drive to the nearest town. Example: "An Odorous Solution."
2. In three minutes, think of several titles for this cartoon (selected by teacher).
3. In three minutes, think of as many uses as you can for a broom.
4. In three minutes, think of as many interesting titles as you can for the story you just read. (Before you do this one, it's a good idea to talk about the story: How did the characters change? What events may have caused the changes? What events were happy? Sad? Strange? What mistakes were made?)

Associational Fluency. Associational fluency refers to the ability to think rapidly of words which have a specified relationship to a given word. This ability is useful, for example, when repeating an idea in a variety of ways or in expressing vivid images.

Sample activities:

1. In two minutes, think of several words which mean the same as *nervous* (See thesaurus for other words with many synonyms).
2. In two minutes, think of several similes for this sentence: He ran down the hall like a _____.
3. In two minutes, think of several words which mean the opposite of *pleasant.*

Expressional Fluency. Expressional fluency is the ability to think rapidly of phrases or sentences which have a restricted structure. This ability is necessary, for example, in producing newspaper headlines or a rhythmic line.

Sample activities:
1. In three minutes, make several five-word sentences. Each word must begin with the given letter. No word may be used twice.
   Example:

   M_____ g_____ a_____ r_____ f_____.
     Margorie's   granny   ate   rotten   figs

2. In three minutes, describe the following situation with several three-word headlines: Mrs. Smith left her purse on a bus. She later caught a bus which she assumed was the one on which she had left her purse. Mrs. Smith found her purse, but another woman named Mrs. Hammer, was holding it. Mrs. Hammer insisted it was hers, whereupon, Mrs. Smith slapped Mrs. Hammer and retrieved the purse.

   Example: Smith Beats Hammer

Redefinition. Spontaneous flexibility, adaptive flexibility, and redefinition are defined as separate creative-thinking abilities by Guilford et al. (10). However, because those three abilities have overlapping characteristics, they will be considered here as a composite ability called redefinition. Redefinition will be considered as the ability to restructure a problem situation in order to produce a variety of solutions. In creative writing and speaking, redefinition is most noticeable when a person produces a humorous remark by using words which have several meanings. In each of the following activities, the child must consider more than one meaning of a key word.

Sample activities: (Use words with multiple meanings.)
1. In three minutes, think of several short sentences in which the word *hand* is used in different ways.
   Responses which show a lack of redefinition:
   a. I hurt my hand.
   b. I cut my hand.
   c. Your hand is cold.
   d. His hand is small.
   Responses which show that redefinition has taken place:
   a. I hurt my hand.
   b. Hand me that book.
   c. He was a hired hand.
   d. The audience gave her a hand.

2. Make up a funny remark for each of the following:
   Example: Why didn't you catch the train? I forgot my butterfly net.
   a. Does your father smoke?
   b. Did the bull charge?
   c. Do you have a rubber band?

3. Make up a riddle with each of the following words (words with multiple meanings):

Example: *runs* What is made of cloth and runs all by itself?
Answer: nylon stocking.
a. change
b. spring
c. light

4. Make up some "Tom Swifties."
Examples:
"There's a ghost town," he said, spiritedly.
"I'm looking out the window," he said, painfully.
"This coat is definitely not made of lamb's wool," she said with a sheepish grin.

Sensitivity. Sensitivity to problems is the ability to perceive deficiencies, gaps, or weaknesses (10). Without such an ability, an inventor would have no impetus to invent; nor an author to improve his writing. With respect to creative writing and speaking, there are probably several components of the ability called sensitivity to problems. Sensitivity to gaps in descriptions could be considered one such component.

Sample activities:
1. Sensitivity to gaps in descriptions: After the description, list several questions which, if answered, would help you to understand the situation better.
   a. The mountain lion sniffed the air. The branch of the tree began to crack. The sound of a shot was heard.
   Sample question: Who heard the shot?
2. Sensitivity to weak imagery: For each sentence think of two words that would sound more interesting than the italicized word.
   a. The snake *gave* a loud warning as we came near.
   The child who has learned to be sensitive to weak imagery might substitute two onomatopoetic words, such as *hissed* and *rattled.*
   b. The stars *moved* across the sky.
   The child who has learned to be sensitive to weak imagery might substitute metaphors such as *slid* and *rolled.*

Originality. Originality is the ability to respond to a situation in an unusual, remote, or clever manner (13). The originality of a response can be most easily determined by the relative frequency of its occurrence within a particular population, such as a classroom group or all sixth grade students in one school. A response which occurred only once or twice in a class of thirty youngsters would be considered original. A response which occurred several times would not be considered original.

Sample activities:
1. Time *goes* on and on. The teacher should have the students substitute more interesting words for the italicized word. After determining the most common responses, such as *marches* or *travels,* give the students the exercise again at a later date. This time direct them to use interesting words other than *marches,*

travels, or whatever words are common for the group of children.

2. Invent a new ending for "Goldilocks and the Three Bears." Try to create an ending which you think no one else in the class will think of.

3. Invent similes of this sentence: After working all day, he felt as weak as a _____. After determining the most common responses, such as *kitten* or *newborn babe,* the teacher should give the exercise at a later date. This time direct the children to invent similes other than *kitten, newborn babe,* or whatever similes are common for the group of children.

Process 3:
Characteristics of Interesting Speaking and Writing

A third process is the process of using those speaking and writing characteristics that are considered interesting by others. Let us look, then, at those traits which seem to characterize interesting speaking and writing. The following list was prepared on the basis of three referents: 1) research reports and opinions of famous authors and speakers (16, 9, 12, 20, 22, 28, 38, 39), 2) years of intensive reading and listening, and 3) personal prejudices.

1. *Imagery*—Describing a situation or subject in vivid, colorful, concrete language.

2. *Naturalness*—Using informal language (except on those rare occasions when formality is expected); maintaining personal contact with listeners or readers; expressing one's individuality.

3. *Inventiveness*—Inventing fresh analogies, characters, settings, plots, or words; playing with homonyms, alliteration, and other humorous devices.

4. *Insight*—Portraying human strengths and weaknesses by means of satire, humorous incongruity, philosophical generalization, realistic description, and other devices.

5. *Sincerity*—Demonstrating keen interest or feeling regarding one's subject, story, or characters.

6. *Flexible Style*—Avoiding monotony by altering sentence length, clause position, sentence type, and other elements of style.

7. *Conciseness*—Expressing the essence of an idea or situation; avoiding words and details which distract from the main ideas or impressions to be conveyed.

8. *Clarity*—Avoiding pronouns with hazy referents, dangling participles, slang or jargon, mystic phrases, and other habits of speech which are likely to confuse listeners or readers.

It is doubtful that these criteria are met by all speakers and writers considered to be "good." It would be impossible, furthermore, for us to agree on the most important criteria. However, we can probably agree that anyone who consistently violates these eight criteria will find it difficult to attract listeners or readers. Thus, it is important for teachers to encourage children who do not violate these criteria and to provide special help for those who do. This role, of course, requires a teacher who recognizes effective and ineffective verbal expression.

Teaching the Characteristics of Interesting Speaking and Writing

At least two ways of teaching these characteristics may be used: the exercise approach and the reinforcement approach.

Exercise Approach

With the *exercise approach,* the teacher provides a series of practice exercises related to the specific characteristics of interesting speech and writing that she is trying to encourage. The following are examples.

Imagery—Describing a situation or person in vivid, colorful, concrete language.

Sample activities:
1. Compare these two verses. Which one creates the most interesting picture in your mind? Why?
   a. Once there was a teddy bear
      Poor little thing had no hair
      Yes, had no hair I did declare
      But actually, he didn't care.
   b. Teddy is bald from head to toe.
      His skin is smooth as a leather purse.
      But he's not feeling sad and low,
      For after all it won't get worse.
2. Describe how a relative or friend of yours looks when he is angry. Invent some metaphors and similes to make your description interesting. (It is assumed that the teacher will first teach the children how to use metaphors and similes.)

Naturalness—Using informal language; maintaining personal contact with the listeners or readers; expressing one's individuality.

Sample activities:
1. Compare these two stories. Which one is most interesting? Why?
   a. Once there was a rabbit by the name of Herman. This rabbit was a very happy rabbit. Also, he wasn't very bright. Now

most of you would think a rabbit would live in woods and eat green things, but not Herman. Herman lived at the South Pole, of all places, and ate fish all the time! Herman had a mother, a father, and a sister whose name was Kadiddily. One day, Herman had to take Kadiddily for a walk. This he hated very much. He didn't want to be a sissy! . . .

b. Herman was a rabbit who lived at the South Pole. His daily diet consisted of fish. Although Herman was very happy, he was a rather ignorant rabbit. He lived with his mother, father, and sister, Kadiddily. Each day he took his sister for a walk. Herman did not care for this job. . . .

2. Try writing a short story as if you were writing a letter to a good friend who knows how you feel about things.

3. Give a five minute talk on any topic you choose. Talk to the class as if you were telling your story to your best friend.

Inventiveness—Inventing fresh analogies, characters, settings, plots, or words; playing with homonyms, alliteration, and other humorous devices.

Sample activities:

1. Compare these two descriptions. Which one seems more fresh and interesting? Why?
   a. Bill fought like a tiger. As quick as a wink he threw Jim to the ground. Jim's glasses broke on the sidewalk. This made him so mad he started kicking like a steer. Bill was kept busy as a bee dodging Jim's thrashing feet.
   b. Bill fought like a robin having a tug of war with a worm. With one swift tug he threw Jim to the ground, shattering Jim's glasses on the sidewalk. Jim swelled up with anger and began kicking his feet as if he were running upside down after Bill. Bill dodged Jim's feet by inventing a new dance.

2. Make up a story about an animal which is different from any animal you have ever heard of. Have him do things which no other animal would do. Make up a name for the animal.

3. Make up an alliterative phrase for each description:
   a. large wads of dirty grease—great gobs of grimy grease
   b. little bright shoes—
   c. a half dozen sick Navy men—

4. Think of "unlikely spots" for:
   a. a man to have a sneezing attack
      Example:
      when swearing in on the witness stand

   b. a woman to put on lipstick:

    c. children to play baseball:

    d. a teacher to jump rope:

5. Rewrite or retell a familiar story, such as "The Three Bears"; keep the same characters and setting, but make several important changes in the plot.

6. Rewrite or retell a familiar story; keep the same plot and characters but make several important changes in the setting.

7. Rewrite or retell a familiar story; keep the same plot and setting but make several important changes in the characters. For example, instead of Goldilocks, have Charlie Brown find the three bears' house. Change the three bears to three favorite cartoon characters. Then change the dialogue to fit the new characters in the story. (This is a good project to do together with the teacher and a tape recorder.)

Insight—Portraying human strengths and weaknesses by means of satire, humorous incongruity, philosophical generalization, realistic description, and other devices.

Sample activities:

1. Which of the following situations would probably make the funniest story? Why? After you decide, then tell your story or write it down.
    a. A monkey who was caught by a zoo keeper, or a man who was caught by a dog catcher
    b. A child who gets spanked by his father or a father who gets spanked by his child

2. Describe a person getting out of bed in the morning. Try to make us understand how many people feel about it.

3. Same as 2 using other situations which would make it possible to depict human nature, e.g., spilling milk on the tablecloth, practicing the piano, helping a younger person learn how to do something, saving another person from being hurt.

4. You have probably noticed that children often argue a great deal while they play baseball. You can write a humorous satire of this situation by exaggerating such arguments. For instance, in your satire you might have the game begin by having one boy hit the ball down the third base line; then the entire recess is spent arguing about whether the ball was foul or fair. In what other ways could you satirize this activity?

5. Write a humorous satire about other situations, e.g., older children and the clothes they wear, fathers getting ready for a fishing trip, mothers shopping for a pair of shoes.

6. Make a list of "Things I've Learned about People," e.g., Some mothers like to _____. When a person gets excited he's likely to _____. (After a list has been made, have the children write a short story about one of their statements.)

Sincerity—Demonstrating keen interest or feeling regarding one's subject, story or characters.

Sample activities:

1. Listen to a tape recording (made by the teacher) of a story or talk—given once with enthusiasm and feeling and a second time in a drab and lifeless manner. Discuss the difference. Why is the first way of speaking more interesting than the second?

2. Before giving a talk or reading a story in front of the class, practice it with the tape recorder. See how much feeling you can get into your presentation.

3. Give a talk or write a chapter for a class book about an animal in which you are particularly interested. Be sure to find some facts about this animal which you have never known before and which probably no one in the class knows. For instance, did you know that lions are good swimmers?

Flexible Style—Avoiding monotony by altering sentence length, clause position, sentence type, and other elements of style.

Sample activities:

1. Which of these is the most interesting description? Why?
   a. Mr. Simpson flew down the hall. He grabbed Jerry by the back of the collar. He pushed Jerry against the wall. Mr. Simpson commanded Jerry to tell why he had done it. Jerry was feeling very much ashamed! He didn't want to tell Mr. Simpson the real reason.
   b. Mr. Simpson flew down the hall. He grabbed Jerry by the back of his collar and pushed him against the wall. Shaking his finger in Jerry's face, Mr. Simpson demanded to know why he had done it. Jerry felt so ashamed! He didn't want to tell Mr. Simpson the real reason.

2. Rewrite this sentence several times without changing the main idea. Verb forms may be changed and words such as *while* and *as* added. Phil ran quickly down the street, leaving a trail of gumdrops behind him.
   Example: Quickly, Phil ran down the street, leaving a trail of gumdrops behind him.

3. After writing a story or tape recording a talk, count the number of times you used the same sentence pattern. Did you overuse any pattern?

Conciseness—Expressing the essence of an idea or situation; avoiding words and details which distract from the main ideas or impressions to be conveyed.

Sample activities:
1. Which set of directions is more interesting and easier to understand? Why?
   a. So as to understand something about magnetism, one might perform an experiment. Get some paper clips from your teacher or your parents. Or, purchase some from an office supply store. Place the paper clips on a table or desk. Ask a science teacher to loan you a magnet. Some magnets are called horseshoe magnets, because they are in the shape of a horseshoe. Some magnets are bent to form a U-shaped magnet. Any type of magnet will work in this experiment. Place the end or ends of your magnet on the paper clips. Now try to pick up other materials, such as paper, glass, or wood with your magnet.
   b. What kinds of material will a magnet pick up? Try as many materials as you can.

2. Rewrite the following passage in twelve words or less.
   I think that it might be necessary to find a way of covering the hole in this boat so as to keep the boat from becoming so full of water that it will sink.

Clarity—Avoiding pronouns with hazy referents, dangling participles, mystic phrases, and other habits of speech which are likely to confuse listeners or readers.

Sample activities:
1. Which of these sentences is easier to understand? Why?
   a. Having finished his sketch, we began to ask the artist questions.
   b. After the artist finished his sketch, we asked him questions.

2. Rewrite these sentences to make them easier to understand.
   a. Being painted in a color he did not like, Mr. Snow did not wish to buy the car.
   b. Running after him as fast as we could, the dog got away.

3. Find a way to make this paragraph easier to understand.
   Joan took her sister over to Aunt Mary's house. She was dirty and her clothes were torn, but she didn't mind. She had a good time, and she was glad she had brought her.

4. What's wrong with these sentences? Can you find any mystical phrases?
   a. He knew that somewhere in the great unknown he would find the mystery of the mysterious and the wonder of the wonderful.

b. And if we do this we can be sure of continual progress toward the fulfillment of life's dreams and the revelation of better days ahead.

5. Underline the words and phrases which are hard to understand. Then rewrite the paragraph so that it is both interesting and clear.

The thingamabob on this steering gismo doesn't work. I tried to make with the music down the street when a man-child ran out in front of me, but the music was dead, man, dead. If the brakes weren't so nifty-keeno, the man-child would have been dead too.

Reinforcement Approach

With the *reinforcement approach,* the teacher praises the children (or arranges for the children to be praised by their peers) whenever one or more of the characteristics show up in their speech or writing. Burrows (4) describes a procedure for accomplishing this type of reinforcement in an informal, but fairly systematic, manner. As the school year begins, the teacher reads every day a composition or two written by children from a previous year. The compositions are praised for specific characteristics by the teacher and the children. *No criticism of the compositions is permitted.* Only positive comments are allowed in order to set the stage for the children to want to have the teacher read their future compositions.

Every time the teacher reads a composition, the children are invited to write their own—either at home, at school during a study period, or right away if there is something for the nonwriters to do. With Burrows' approach, a child is never forced to write. In her study (4) of children in grades one through six, she and her colleagues found that all the children eventually wanted to write when they were exposed to this type of encouragement.

Once the children are writing and handing in their compositions for the teacher to read out loud, they can be reinforced by the teacher and their peers for displaying the desired characteristics. The teacher also reinforces those characteristics through brief conferences with the children about their compositions. During these conferences, only praise is used unless the child specifically asks for criticism concerning a particular point in his writing. It has been found by your author and in the Burrows study that negative comments about children's writing is a sure way of cutting off the flow of creative expression for *some* children.

Negative vs. Positive Criticism

A considerable amount of debate has occurred among educators as to whether one should apply negative criticism to children's writing and speaking. The Commission on Composition for the National Council of Teachers of English took the position that pupils "should not be discouraged by negative correction and proscription" (25). Groff (17), on the other hand, pointed out that most of the research indicates that negative criticism of mechanical skills such as

Treating children as real authors stimulates further writing.

punctuation and spelling actually improves the overall quality of children's writing.

Unfortunately, research reports usually hide an important characteristic of children, namely, their individuality. Research conclusions are based on average scores and average results and hide the fact, for example, that Sue responded one way to criticism and Sandy responded a very different way. In a debate such as this, we will have to opt for our own observations as well as research results as a basis for decision. My observations have shown that some children do respond well to negative criticism—in fact, they ask for it! Other children are absolutely crushed by the slightest hint that you disapprove of their efforts.

My advice on this matter is this: When in doubt do *not* use negative reinforcement for children's *creative* efforts. Save your negative criticism for work that is much less personal, such as a spelling paper or a hall poster. Or better yet, let the purpose for the particular writing or speaking task determine the degree of negative criticism. If, for example, Karen is writing creatively and intends to submit her product to the class magazine, she will have a purpose for correcting her spelling or strengthening her imagery before completing her *final* draft. On the other hand, if she is giving a spontaneous talk or is writing a story which she may or may not read to the class, the teacher certainly should not hover over her with a red pen or use her as a living grammar lesson.

The same type of positive reinforcement used for interesting writing should also be used, of course, for interesting speech. When children are giving reports or participating in show and tell or just conversing with the teacher, an occasional word of praise for a specific characteristic is advisable: "Hey, Jim that was a very clear way of putting that. I really understand how to do that now." Or "Sally, that was a beautiful way of describing the rabbit you saw. I could really picture the way it was moving through the grass."

Practice in Using the Reinforcement Approach

The reinforcement approach requires that you understand the characteristics of interesting speaking and writing. It also requires the ability to find those characteristics in children's speech or writing and to praise them when they occur. We will now look at several compositions written by third and sixth grade children. Once you have learned to detect the characteristics in children's writing, you should be able to transfer this ability, without too much trouble, to children's speech.

In a study by May and Tabachnick (23), compositions by 300 third graders and 300 sixth graders were judged "creative" or "not creative" by twelve judges. Six of the judges were graduate students in English, and the other six were graduate students in education. Since each composition was read by all twelve judges, the score for a composition could range from 0 to 12. A score of 5, for example, would indicate that five out of twelve judges considered the story creative. The compositions which we will consider were written in response to a sketch that included a person, a hill, a tree, and a flying bird. First, we will examine three sixth grade compositions. The first is a story which nearly all of the judges considered creative.

Grade 6—Story 1: Score 11

"Jack, wake up," called his mother. Jack dove under his blankets. But after a few moments of darkness he raised his head from beneath the blankets. To his horror it was 20 to nine. He sprang out of bed and into his clothes and hustled downstairs. Jack grabbed the piece of toast his mother had set out for him and hurried on to school. On the way it seemed strange and quiet. Then the terrible truth struck him. He had forgotten to set the clock back one hour for daylight saving time. Now he was one hour early for school with nothing to do.

Jack kicked a can as hard as he could. To his amazement the can said "Ouch!" He had nothing to do so he investigated further. He slowly lifted up the can and out jumped a leprechaun. Jack had heard of leprechauns in Ireland, but surely not here! The leprechaun whose name was Peter told Jack that he was on a goodwill mission here and wanted to help people. "Could you help me?" said Jack. He told Peter the predicament that he was in. At once the leprechaun sent Jack back through time. Jack found himself back in bed. "Jack, wake up." Jack looked up at the clock to find it only 20 to eight. Down at breakfast he looked out the window to see a tin can with a dent in it. He winked at the tin can and it winked back.

This story appears to meet all eight criteria. The author, an eleven-year-old boy, uses abundant imagery, e.g., "dove under his blankets," "sprang out of bed." There is a naturalness to his expression which some of us adults can never hope to attain, e.g., "Jack had heard of leprechauns in Ireland, but surely not here." His inventiveness is evidenced by his ability to breathe life and gaiety into the simple event of turning back the clock. He demonstrated at least a modicum of insight into human behavior by portraying a boy who is reluctant to get out of bed, bored with "nothing to do" for a whole hour, and imaginative enough to wink at a tin can. His composition demonstrates sincerity, conciseness, clarity, and a reasonably flexible style, although his repertoire of sentence types is naturally limited at this age. In addition to meeting the eight criteria, he also shows an ability to introduce a bit of suspense or mystery in a story, e.g., "He slowly lifted up the can . . ." "On the way it seemed strange and quiet."

In contrast to the creative story, here is one which all of the judges rated as not-creative. Although this composition demonstrates a tiny spark of talent, it lacks the imagery, naturalness, and inventiveness of the creative composition.

Grade 6—Story 6: Score 0

This is a story about a boy who, at the end of the year, got his report card. This boy was very happy because he got five A's and the rest B's.

When the boy got home he told his mother the good news. When his father got home he told him. His father said that for having improved so much he could stay up until 8:30 p.m.

The next morning, as he was going out to play, the phone rang. His mother answered the phone. On the phone was the boy's teacher. His teacher said that the boy's report card got mixed up, that the boy had the wrong card. So the boy's mother, Mrs. Jones, brought out the boy's report card. The boy's teacher gave Mrs. Jones his report card.

When the father came home they told him. Then they opened up the pamphlet and read his grades. They were A's and B's. That night he got 50 ¢ for every A and 25 ¢ for every B.

The average score for the sixth grade compositions was approximately 4. The following is a story which might be considered average. Imagery and inventiveness are used more often in this story than in the one rated 0, although not as skillfully as in the story rated 11. While the first story, rated 11, demonstrated all eight of the characteristics, this one is reasonably strong on clarity, conciseness, flexible style, and inventiveness.

Grade 6—Story 10: Score 4

Jimmy Jackson lived in Maine along the ocean with his grandparents. Jimmy was nine and very curious with a mind of his own.

The day was sunny. He walked along the high banks overlooking the ocean. Ahead he saw his destination, Pine Mountain. Pine Mountain was hollowed out with many caves and caverns. He walked and walked until he stepped into a large hole. He looked into the hole and there saw a large, monstrous dragon with six eyes and ten legs and two feet on each leg. The dragon had a large arm on the top of its head and pulled Jimmy down into the hole. He ran around dodging the twenty feet. Soon he found a door. He opened up the door and ran down a long hallway. On the sides of the hallway were cages. In the cages were little purple men with pink feet. Soon he got outside and ran home. A seagull cawed loudly overhead.

Having examined sixth graders' compositions at three levels of creativity, let us now look at three stories written by third graders in response to the same stimulus that was given to the sixth graders. The first one was considered creative by nearly all of the judges. This story seems to meet especially the criteria of naturalness and inventiveness. Although there seems to be less imagery in stories written by third graders than in those written by sixth graders, this is probably due to the relatively limited vocabulary which third graders generally have in comparison to sixth graders.

Grade 3 — Story 1: Score 10

One day there was a little boy named Johnny Ring. He lived in a village by the meadow. His mother and daddy were very cruel to him. One morning he crept out of his bed. He had a window in his bedroom, so he crept out of it. When he got outside he ran and ran. When Johnny got to a big oak tree he stopped. Something was strange about the tree. It had golden leaves on it. He saw a little man painting with golden paint. He said "Hi" to the little man. The little man heard it and jumped out of his pants because he thought Johnny was a giant. After that they made friends. He was a magic elf man. He turned Johnny down to his size. They played and played together, and Johnny was so happy he lived happily ever after. His mother and father never saw him again.

Grade 3 — Story 5: Score 0

Once upon a time there was a boy named Tom.

One day he ran up to a tree and climbed up it and got a red apple from the tree. He went down the tree and ran into the house and got a drink of water, and ran outside and played with his friends Bill and Jack, and went to his mother and asked if he could go to Bill's house.

Mother said, "Yes, you can go to Bill's house but be back by seven o'clock."

Bill asked if he could have Tom and Jack here until seven o'clock.

His mother said, "Yes, you can have Tom and Jack here until seven o'clock."

Bill said, "Jack and Tom here."

And then it started to rain and Jack and Bill and Tom ran to Bill's house and Jack called his mother. And his mother came to Bill's house. And Tom called his mother and she was not home. So he went to Jack's house. He called his mother and she was home. She came to get him. And she called the doctor and he came and he said he had gotten a cold in the nose. He was sick for nineteen days.

The average score for the third grade compositions was approximately 3. The following is a story which might be considered average.

Grade 3 — Story 9: Score 3

> *One day a boy was running up the street. When he got by the big tree he saw a big bird coming after him. The boy ran, ran, ran, ran, ran, and ran. He wasn't getting any place. The bird had the boy in his claws. The bird flew away with the boy. On top of the tree the bird stabbed the boy and the boy's soul went up to heaven, and the bird went down to hell. The boy was happy in heaven, but the bird was not happy down in hell.*
> *AND THE BOY LIVED HAPPY IN HEAVEN.*

Now it is time to try your hand at providing *specific* praise for characteristics of interesting writing. For each of the compositions which follows, write specific comments to indicate your positive reinforcement of the eight characteristics of interesting writing and speaking. For example, if lines 2 and 3 contain good imagery, write a comment like this: "Good picture word," or "I can picture this clearly," or "Good choice of words." Use the margins or a separate sheet of paper.

Two of the stories were rated high by the judges and two were rated low. The two rated low will provide you with a realistic challenge to find at least *one* characteristic to praise. Remember, no negative comments this time; only positive. Your role is to keep the spark of creativity burning.

Story A

1.　　　　*This was an important day in the life of John Walters.*
2. *He sensed it somewhere deep inside him. The impatient voice of his*
3. *mother, the smell of pancakes for breakfast, all these were in the*
4. *normal span of his day; yet, somehow, they held an undercurrent of*
5. *excitement.*
6.　　　　*"Something's gonna happen today," he announced at*
7. *breakfast. "Yes, dear, be sure to drink your orange juice." That was his*
8. *mother's voice. Sometimes it seemed to John that she had no imagi-*
9. *nation.*
10.　　　　*Along the well-traveled road to school he kept think-*
11. *ing, "There's something special going on today." Would it be at*
12. *school? Yes, John was sure of that. But his Iowa Tests were finished*
13. *and, surely, what could be more important?*
14.　　　　*As he fumbled in his pocket for a piece of candy, he*
15. *felt a grimey, wrinkled sheet of paper. His permission slip for Scout*
16. *Camp! Quickly he ran home, taking the few blocks as fast as he could.*
17. *After having his father sign it, he sped again away to school. John was*
18. *sure then that this "Something" had to do with running. Not the short*
19. *kind, but a long, grueling trek that was a matter of life and death.*

20.   *The morning at school passed endlessly. He was terribly*
21. *absent-minded, and could not for the life of him think of the product*
22. *of 6 x 9.*
23.   *Then, as Mr. Herwing, the physical education instruc-*
24. *tor, appeared at the classroom door, he felt his muscles tighten. This*
25. *something was about to happen, but, as he trooped outside with the*
26. *others, a sense of foreboding took hold of him as he saw the colored*
27. *pennants at each end of the playgound.*
28.   *He was about to burst with curiosity, fear, and excite-*
29. *ment, but the voice of Mr. Herwing interrupted his thoughts . . .*
30. *"Ready all, for the 600 yard walk-run!"*

Story B

1.   *One day a boy was walking in the woods. He had a*
2. *picnic basket under his arm. It wasn't noon so he thought he would*
3. *sit around and watch the birds and other animals. Soon it was time to*
4. *eat so he sat by the creek and opened his picnic basket. When he was*
5. *eating his chicken he heard a noise in the bushes. He looked around*
6. *but he couldn't see anything. The next time the noise grew louder.*
7. *Suddenly a big grizzly bear came charging out of the bushes.*
8.   *Right away the boy knew the bear was after his lunch.*
9. *He quickly ran and climbed a tree while the bear ate his lunch.*

Story C

1.   *This story is going to be one I think you will like. One*
2. *day there was a boy who liked to run a very long time. Once he was*
3. *running in the field when he came to a place he never saw before.*
4. *It was not like other places he saw.*
5.   *Then he saw something, it was flying creature that was*
6. *very ugly. It started after him. He got very scared and started to run.*
7. *All of a sudden a very strange tree grew arms and tried to catch him.*
8. *Luckily he could run fast, but the tree started after him too. Then he*
9. *got even more scared. The sand beneath his feet got hotter.*
10.   *The boy thought he might be finished. The sun was*
11. *getting hotter and hotter. He was slowing down, but a cool wave was*
12. *coming from a cave. He ran into the cave and found some unknown*
13. *animals.*
14.   *He said, "Where am I?" The animals all said together,*
15. *"The lost desert." The boy asked still another question. "Where does*

16. *this cave lead to?"*
17. *"It leads to a beautiful place where flowers grow and a*
18. *nice pink house." The boy said, "That's my house!" He followed the*
19. *tunnel, and sure enough it was his house.*

Story D

1. *Once upon a time there was a little boy. His name was*
2. *Pete. Pete liked to run. He always ran to school and he ran back.*
3. *One day when he was in school his teacher asked him what he was*
4. *going to be when he was big. He said, "I'm going to be a runner. I like*
5. *to run a lot." When he got home, he started to run in the field. He saw*
6. *the green grass and trees. He said to himself, "I want to be a farmer*
7. *like dad." And a great farmer he was. He still could run very fast.*

Stimulating Written and Oral Compositions

In a previous section, it was suggested that a successful creative writing-creative speaking program cannot be based on gimmicks. A successful program requires a teacher who knows how to develop a creative atmosphere in the classroom and one who understands the processes of creative thinking. Three processes and related activities for encouraging them were suggested. Most of those activities, however, were designed for purposes of specific training in the processes of creative thinking. Another aspect of the creative language program should be that of providing children with ample opportunities to prepare oral and written compositions, in which they can apply the training they have been given.

What, then, should the teacher use to stimulate such compositions? Burrows and her colleagues (4) found that the only stimulation needed was that of reading the children's compositions out loud. Yet hundreds of articles and books have been written on the subject of specific stimuli for stimulating creative expression, demonstrating that the Burrows approach is not necessarily the most popular. The number of different stimuli dreamed up by teachers, writers, and researchers approaches infinity.

Witty and Martin (46) found that a symbolic film without narration motivated children to write stories of high quality. Carlson (5) found that four stimuli—interesting toys, pictures, unusual experiences, and daydreams—encouraged more original stories than a choice of topics did. In Sofell's study (36), it was found that *chosen* topics as compared with *assigned* topics resulted in children's compositions that were rated better on writing mechanics, organization, and literary quality.

Edmunds (11) discovered that children's stories based on vicarious experiences included more words and a greater number of descriptive words than stories based on direct experiences. Furthermore, the vicarious experiences (movies, TV, daydreaming) resulted in more "creative" stories according to a panel of judges. Ujlaki and Macdonald (44) found that free choice of topics was more effective than abstract music.

Cramer and Cramer (8) motivated children to write better by having them imitate professional writers. This requires the teacher to read several poems or stories written by one author and then have the children write something of their own. It was found that the children could imitate highly patterned poems and stories quite well. Tway (43) studied methods used in British primary schools and found that many teachers there use a method called "team writing." With this method, teams of children write, illustrate, and bind their own books as a cooperative venture. The children seem less self-conscious about their writing and more willing to try new ideas. Tway also found (in the United States setting) that encouraging children to talk together in pairs about their compositions before writing them increased the "maturity" of their work.

None of the research just discussed has been concerned with the specific characteristics which distinguish one stimulus from another. Yet research indicates that creative people may be attracted to particular types of stimuli. MacKinnon's study (21) of creative writers, architects, and engineers suggests that creative people are challenged by complex, unfinished, and unorganized stimuli. Barron's study (1) of air force captains demonstrated that creative people tend to like and construct things which are not simply ordered. Drews (10), however, found that highly creative adolescents are fond of making original interpretations of simple, organized, and common stimuli.

Research indicates, then, that although creativity may be stimulated by an organized stimulus, it can also be stimulated by an unorganized stimulus. Research does not indicate, however, the relative effectiveness of the two types of stimuli in promoting creative writing and speaking. With this problem in mind, May and Tabachnick (23) compared the results of three different stimuli on the written compositions of 600 third and sixth graders. These children had been randomly assigned to one of three groups. Each group, consisting of one-third of the population, received a different stimulus—organized, unorganized, or a choice between the organized and unorganized. The organized stimulus was a sketch which included a person, a hill, a tree, and a flying bird. The unorganized stimulus was simply a set of lines and shapes created by cutting up the organized sketch and rearranging the pieces in a meaningless order.

For the third grade students, there were no significant differences in average creativity ratings among the three stimulus situations. For the sixth grade students, however, the girls performed considerably better than the boys in the organized and choice situations, while the boys performed much better than the girls in the unorganized situation. The *combination* of choice and unorganized stimulus resulted in higher creativity ratings than any one of the stimuli by itself.

This study indicates that the stimuli used to motivate creative speaking and writing should include opportunities to respond not only to organized stimuli but also to unorganized stimuli. An experimental approach by the teacher would be that of mixing the stimuli—using an organized stimulus on one occasion, an unorganized stimulus on another occasion, and a choice on another.

For teachers who are not used to using unorganized stimuli to motivate creative compositions, here are several suggestions:

1. Abstract paintings (reprints or slides) such as Mondrian's "Horizontal Tree" or Kandinsky's "Black Lines."

2. Modern music such as Bloch's "Schelomo" or Prokofiev's "Symphony No. 5."

3. Abstract drawings or paintings produced by the children.

4. Scrambled words—the teacher reads a list of five or six unrelated words or writes the words on the board. (The children should not be told that they have to use the words in their composition; the words are used only to get them started.)

5. Scrambled objects—unrelated objects are hung up or placed on a table in front of the room, e.g., fly swatter, hat, knife, book.

6. Scrambled odors—children walk up to a table four at a time and smell the contents, concealed by cheesecloth, of four cans. (Discussion should be discouraged at this point.) The cans should contain very unusual spices, etc.

7. Mysterious objects—children walk up to a table four at a time and feel the contents of four boxes without looking into the opening of the boxes. (Discussion should be discouraged at this point.) The boxes should contain very unusual objects, such as an irregular piece of smooth wood or a ball of wet paper. Objects should be selected which will not leave telltale marks on the hand.

8. Abstract sculpture produced by the children or by local artists.

A Final Statement on Goals

Creative writing and creative speaking are not goals in themselves. Our function as teachers is not to discover the John Steinbeck, Dale Carnegie, Dorothy Sayers, and Helen Van Slyke of the future. Our function is to teach those skills which will enable children to make friends, feel better about themselves, and move toward their role in society as functioning, self-actualizing people. By establishing a creative atmosphere and engaging children in creative processes, we can more readily assist children in improving their communication skills, particularly those related to producing writing and speech that is interesting to others.

Integrating the Creative Writing-Creative Speaking Program with the Rest of the School Program

Mr. LeBlanc and Mrs. Edmunds have worked hard as a team to develop a creative atmosphere for their fifty-seven fourth graders. Their aide, Miss Osborn, has a strong motivation to become more creative herself and fits right in. All three of the eduators seem to understand behavior that indicates potential creativity and reward it on those occasions when it is not highly disruptive.

About two hours per day is devoted to specific instruction related to the language arts. Some of the instruction deals with isolated skills such as decoding the VV vowel pattern or spelling irregular spelling demons. But much of the instruction combines two or more of the language arts and often spills over into the social studies, science, art, and music programs.

On one occasion, for example, a small group of children were observed doing the following things during a three-day time span:

1. Reading a story in their basal reader about bears.

2. Reading about bears in their social studies text chapter on Alaska.

3. Talking about what they learned about bears from a trip to a local natural science museum.

4. Making up a story together about two bears who didn't know how to hibernate.

5. Writing individual adventures for the two bears.

6. Sharing their stories with other children.

7. Learning to spell *hibernation, Alaska,* and *grizzly bear* as extra words for the weekly spelling test.

8. Developing a spontaneous dramatic skit about bears who were afraid of hunters.

9. Working on a small mural depicting the life cycle of bears.

10. Beginning the production of a song about "Gretchen the Grizzly"—with the words written together by the children and the music from a John Thompson piano book belonging to one of the children.

11. Learning to take brief notes with the help of the school librarian as they read about bears in reference books.

12. Having individual conferences with Miss Osborn so that she could reinforce those characteristics of interesting writing they had exhibited in their stories.

13. Listening to Mr. LeBlanc read *Gentle Ben.*

14. Warming up for a What If writing assignment by first discussing the question: What if the air became so dirty the sun couldn't shine through it anymore? This was followed by a discussion and then a writing assignment about What if we cut down so many trees there were no more forests for bears to live in?

15. Discussing with Mrs. Edmunds a basal reader lesson involving the CV vowel pattern. In addition to the words *he, go,* and *hotel* suggested in the teacher's guide, Mrs. Edmunds used the word *hi-ber-na-tion* to illustrate the long vowel sound heard in the first and third syllables.

When the two teachers were asked if they were always able to achieve so much integration in the school program, Mrs. Edmunds said, "Oh my no. Integration is a goal which we achieve—oh, say, 40 or 50 percent of the time. Certainly no more than that."

Mr. LaBlanc spoke up, "We'd like to achieve a higher level of integration, of course, because it seems highly motivating to the children and seems to help them retain information better. But it's difficult with all the variables you have to deal with in a classroom setting—kids' different interests and abilities, the demands from parents that their kids learn specific skills no later than yesterday, the available resources, the whole bit. You know what I mean."

When asked how they had managed to develop such a creative, open atmosphere, Mr. LeBlanc replied: "It isn't really that easy. You've got to work at it."

"Especially during the first two or three months," Mrs. Edmunds volunteered.

"We had to be very firm in establishing rules at first," Mr. LeBlanc continued. If you want a creative, open atmosphere you don't just start the year by letting the kids do whatever they want. You have to get them slowly in the groove for taking responsibility and for being creative."

Mrs. Edmunds laughed. "Kids can be as lazy as adults if you let them be. It's a lot easier to be uncreative and disruptive than to be creative and responsible."

Mr. LeBlanc shook his head and smiled ruefully. "That's the truth," he said. "I know when I take a course at night at the university I just want to sit there and let the stuff wash over me like a wave—you know, absorb all that knowledge without really working at it. I resist when the instructor makes me get involved and do all that thinking. I guess kids are somewhat the same way."

"But they love it once they get going," Mrs. Edmunds said.

"And so do I," Mr. LeBlanc admitted. "It's just that inertia you have to overcome. Kids have as much inertia as adults do, I'm convinced of that, especially the television-fed kids of today. But it's wonderful when they snap out of it and begin to enjoy thinking and learning and communicating."

"I agree," Mrs. Edmunds said. "That's what it's all about, helping kids really become skillful in communicating."

More Exercises, Activities, and Games for Creative Writing and Speaking

1. Make a "writer's study" with three sides of a cardboard box taped to a school desk to provide privacy. Use a sign-up sheet or some other means to make the study a privileged place to be.

2. Create a learning center for authors (see Module 12 for ideas).

3. Ask pupils to choose one picture (from a large set of pictures you have collected) to tell or write a story about. Give them a day or two to think about their idea. Then have pupils come one at a time to a quiet corner to tell you the story (or tell it into a tape recorder.) Let child hold picture while telling story.

4. Find pictures that tell a story, e.g., a child crying who is obviously lost. Have children tell or write (or both) what is happening now, what happened just before the picture, and what is going to happen after the picture.

5. Make a "touch book" with a different texture on each page: sand paper, wax paper, silky material, etc. Number each page and pass around the book. When a child has a turn with the book, he or she is to write down the page number and also at least five words that describe how the material feels. The child then hands in the paper to the teacher and passes on the book. (This is an excellent activity for a learning center.) Some children may need help by having a large chart of "touch words" from which to select words for their own lists.

6. Ask pupils to make up one or two sentences which describe you, the teacher. Have fun reading them aloud, while at the same time discussing the kinds of words and phrases that can be used to describe a person's appearance and personality. Using suggestions from your discussion, develop on the chalkboard a model paragraph about themselves.

7. Have the children make up a story or just tell about their own drawings or paintings. Take dictation during the telling or use a tape recorder. Or have them write up their story after telling it.

8. Develop a class story based on an event which occurs during the school day, such as an unusual fire drill or an animal that gets into the room. The teacher takes dictation from the class.

9. Read two or three Dr. Seuss books to the children and discuss the imaginary animals that he created. Have them create their own imaginary animals on paper and tell or write about them.

10. Have the children close their eyes and imagine an imaginary character, such as a strange animal or funny person. Have them describe their characters one at a time and help weave them together into a story as they describe them. You may either stop here or write the characters on the board and have the children make up a story about them. They may use part of the story already created if they wish.

11. Have some of the children bring in toys to explain to the others. Have them pretend they are toy manufacturers and think of ways together of improving the toys. Accept even their wildest impossible ideas; in fact, encourage such ideas. If you wish, you can then have them write a story about a toy maker and how he tried to make the "best toy in the world."

12. Have children read each other's palms. Encourage them to tell exactly what adventures their partners will have, exactly how they will make their fortune, etc.

13. Each person writes a detailed description of a character from a familiar story—one they've all read in class, favorite bedtime

stories, etc. Then each person reads her description and the rest of the class guesses who was described.

14. Make up "balloon adventures" about a helium filled balloon and its travels around the world. An effective "starter" is bringing such a balloon to school and releasing it.

15. Have the children get in groups of four or five. Put several words on the chalkboard that might suggest a story, such as *sailboat, waves, rocks,* and *beach.* Each person in a group starts a story and then passes it on to another person in his group until the teacher says time. When each person has added something to each of the stories, have them read the stories to see how similar and different they are.

16. Pass a newspaper funny with the words cut out to each child. Have them write their own dialogue.

17. Have a class puppet, one that talks to the children every day, telling about an adventure he had (the teacher had) about something he saw one of them doing that he didn't think was such a good idea, about how proud he is of them, etc. Let the children make up adventures for him.

18. After practicing with some What if questions (such as What if all the trees in the world were cut down?) have them write their own What if story.

19. After a period of spontaneous drama, have them write up the story they created.

20. Write a title on the board, such as "The Danger Zone," or "Flying Is for the Birds." Have each person write three sentences as a beginning of a story. Then have them put their names on their papers, fold the papers in half twice, and put them in a large box. They will then blindly pick one from the box and finish the story. Finally they will hand the story to the person who began the story, so that all may see how their story turned out.

21. Give each child five 3 x 5 index cards or other small pieces of paper. Have them write WHO, WHEN, WHAT, WHERE, and WHY on the five cards. After WHO they are to write the name and description of a character they have created. After WHAT they should tell something the character did. After WHEN and WHERE they should tell the time and place of the action. After WHY they should explain why the character did what he or she did (the motive).

For example, WHO: Bill Robertson, a jeweler, age 40, tired looking, graying hair, nail biter. WHAT: stole some of his own jewelry. WHEN: during a summer day when no customers were in the store. WHERE: in his own jewelry store in Chicago in a run-down shopping area. WHY: he wanted to claim he was robbed and collect the insurance money so he could send his daughter to college.

Have the children put the cards in separate boxes: a WHO box, a WHAT box, a WHEN box, a WHY box, and a WHERE box. Mix the contents in the boxes and let the children each select five new cards—one from each box. They are to use their new cards, but only the ones that help them think of a story.

22. Have them create a story from a single Where Sentence. Give each child a sentence on a piece of paper, e.g., I went to the circus, or I went to a farm, or I went to a grocery store. It is all right if several children have the same sentence, but they should all begin with I went to . . . ."

    Show them how to create a "story" from a sentence. Put this sentence on the board: I went to the new shopping mall. Under the sentence write the words: *when, who, what, why.* Then show them how to ask questions that will help them describe their trip. For instance: When did you go? Whom did you see or go with? What did you do there? Why did you do these things?

23. Have them create a story from a single Who Sentence. This is similar to 22. Work with Who Sentences such as I saw Mrs. Twilliger, that lady who sells strange things. Ask questions about where, when, what, and why. For example, where did you see Mrs. Twilliger? When did you see her? What was she doing when you saw her? Why was she doing it?

24. Have them create a story from a single What Sentence, e.g., He was dropping cotton balls from an airplane. Ask who, when, where, and why questions.

25. Have them create a story from a single When Sentence, e.g., It was on a dark, foggy night at the beginning of summer vacation. Ask where, who, what, and why questions.

26. Have them create a story from a single Why Sentence, e.g., She was tired of having those kids tramp across her lawn and pick her flowers. Ask who, where, what, and when questions.

27. Have them create new adventures for their favorite cartoon characters such as Snoopy and Charlie Brown. This is especially good shortly after they have seen a Charlie Brown TV special.

28. Have them create new adventures for their favorite TV character.

29. Have them create a newspaper story about a game they just played on the playground. Be sure to have them include the who, what, when, and where in their story, and the why if it's appropriate.

30. Have the children make up Crazy Titles and put them in a grab box for other children to pick from blindly. An example of a Crazy Title would be: "The Lion Who Ran the People Zoo" or "The Girl Who Walked Backwards."

REFERENCES AND BIBLIOGRAPHY

1. Barron, Frank. "The Psychology of Imagination." In *A Source Book for Creative Thinking,* edited by Sidney J. Parnes and Harold F. Harding. New York: Charles Scribner's Sons, 1962.

2. Biberstine, Richard D. "Response to Personal Writing." *Language Arts* 54 (Oct. 1977): 791–92.

3. Boehnlein, Mary M. "Integration of Communication Arts Curriculum: A Review." *Language Arts* 54 (April 1977): 372–77.

4. Burrows, Alvina K. et al. *They All Want to Write: Written English in the Elementary Schools,* 3d ed. New York: Holt Rinehart and Winston, 1964.

5. Carlson, Ruth K. *Sparkling Words—Two Hundred Practical and Creative Writing Ideas.* Boulder, Colo.: Paladin Press, 1965.

6. Carnegie, Dale. *How to Develop Self-Confidence and Influence People by Public Speaking.* New York: Pocket Books, Division of Simon and Schuster, 1977.

7. Colton, Caleb C. A quotation from *The New Dictionary of Thoughts,* edited by Tryon Edwards. New York: Doubleday and Co., 1961. Chicago, Ill.: Educational Corp., 1961.

8. Cramer, Ronald L., and Cramer, Barbara B. "Writing by Imitating Language Models." *Language Arts* 52 (Oct. 1975): 1011–14.

9. Crandell, S. Judson et al. *Speech: A Course in Fundamentals.* Glenview, Ill.: Scott, Foresman, 1963.

10. Drews, Elizabeth M. "The Four Faces of Able Adolescents." *Saturday Review,* January 19, 1963.

11. Edmunds, Neal R. "Writing in the Intermediate Grades." *Elementary English* 36 (Dec. 1959): 491–501.

12. Flesch, Rudolph, and Lass, A.H. *A New Guide to Better Writing.* New York: Popular Library, 1977.

13. Foshay, Arthur W. "The Creative Process Described." In *Creativity in Teaching,* edited by Alice Miel. Belmont, Calif.: Wadsworth, 1961.

14. Getzels, J.W., and Jackson, P.W. "The Study of Giftedness: A Multi-dimensional Approach." In *The Gifted Student*. Washington, D.C.: Cooperative Research Monograph No. 2, U.S. Department of Health, Education, and Welfare, 1960.

15. Gough, Harrison G. "Imagination—Undeveloped Resource." In *A Source for Creative Thinking,* edited by Sidney J. Parnes and Harold F. Harding. New York: Charles Scribner's Sons, 1962.

16. Graves, Donald H. "Research Update: We Won't Let Them Write." *Language Arts* 55 (May 1978): 635–40.

17. Groff, Patrick. "Does Negative Criticism Discourage Children's Compositions?" *Language Arts* 52 (Oct. 1975): 1032–34.

18. Guilford, J.P., et al."A Factor-Analytic Study of Creative Thinking II. Administration of Tests and Analysis of Results." Reports from the Psychological Laboratory, No. 8. University of Southern California, 1952.

19. _____, and Christensen, P.R. "A Factor-Analytic Study of Verbal Fluency." Reports from the Psychological Laboratory, No. 17, University of Southern California, 1956.

20. Hayakawa, S.I. *Language in Thought and Action*. New York: Harcourt Brace Jovanovich, 1972.

21. MacKinnon, Donald W. "What Makes a Person Creative." *Saturday Review,* February 10, 1962.

22. Maugham, W. Somerset. *The Summing Up*. New York: The New American Library, 1938.

23. May, Frank B., and Tabachnick, Robert B. "Three Stimuli for Creative Writing." *Elementary School Journal* 66 (Nov. 1966): 571–75.

24. Meadow, Arnold, and Parnes, Sidney J. "Evaluation of Training in Creative Problem Solving." *Journal of Applied Psychology* 43 (1959): 189–94.

25. NCTE Commission on Composition. "Composition: A Position Statement." *Elementary English* 52 (Feb. 1975): 194–96.

26. Nelson, Dorothy H. "And Now the Sensuous Writer." *Language Arts* 53 (May 1976): 591–93.

27. Norris, Kay et al. "Creative Classroom." *Teacher* 94 (Sept. 1976): 120–26. One of a series of monthly articles on teaching the basic subjects.

28. Orwell, George. *A Collection of Essays*. Garden City, N.Y.: Doubleday, 1954.

29. Osborn, Alex E. *Applied Imagination*. New York: Charles Scribner's Sons, 1963.

30. Parnes, Sidney J., and Meadow, Arnold. "Effects of 'Brainstorming' Instructions on Creative Problem-Solving by Trained and Untrained Subjects." *Journal of Educational Psychology* 50 (1959): 171–76.

31. Petty, Walter T., and Bowen, Mary E. *Slithery Snakes and Other Aids to Children's Writing*. New York: Appleton-Century-Crofts, 1967.

32. Poincare, Henri. "Mathematical Creation." In *The Creative Process,* edited by Brewster Ghiselin. New York: The New American Library, 1955.

33. Reid, H. Kay, and McGlathery, Glenn. "Science and Creative Writing." *Science and Children* 14 (Jan. 1977): 19–20.

34. Rogers, Carl R. "Communication: Its Blocking and Its Facilitation." *ETC,* Winter 1952.

35. Sessions, Roger. "The Composer and His Message." In *The Creative Process,* edited by Brewster Ghiselin. New York: The New American Library, 1955.

36. Sofell, C. "A Comparison of the Use of Imposed with Self-Chosen Subjects in Conjunction with Elementary Children." Master's thesis, University of Pittsburgh, 1929 (Summarized by Neal R. Edmund in *Elementary English* 36 (1959): 195.

37. Stein, Morris I., and Meer, Bernard. "Perceptual Organization in a Study of Creativity." *Journal of Psychology* 37 (1954): 39–43.

38. Torrance, E. Paul, and Yamamato, Kaoru. "Supplementary Scoring Guide for the Evaluation of Originality and Interest." In *Scoring Manual for Evaluating Imaginative Stories.* Minneapolis: University of Minnesota, Bureau of Educational Research, 1961.

39. Torrance, E. Paul. "Creative Thinking of Children." *Journal of Teacher Education* 13 (Dec. 1962): 448–60.

40. _____. *The Minnesota Studies of Creative Thinking: 1959–62.* Minneapolis: University of Minnesota, Bureau of Educational Research, 1963.

41. _____, and Myers, R.E. *Creative Learning and Teaching.* New York: Harper and Row, 1970.

42. Tripp, Janny G. "The Positive Approach: Response-Evaluation of Children's Writing." *Language Arts* 55 (March 1978): 358–62.

43. Tway, Eileen. "Writing: An Interpersonal Process." *Language Arts* 53 (May 1976): 594–96.

44. Ujlaki, Vilma, and MacDonald, James B. "A Study of Children's Creative Writing in Relation to Various Stimuli." Milwaukee: Research Bulletin No. 62–3. Campus Elementary School, University of Wisconsin—Milwaukee, 1962.

45. Wallas, Graham. *The Art of Thought.* New York: Harcourt Brace Jovanovich, 1926.

46. Witty, Paul, and Martin, William. "An Analysis of Children's Compositions Written in Response to a Film." *Elementary English* 34 (March 1957): 158–63.

Developing Basic Listening Skills

There was a man from Brisson
Who didn't know how to listen.
"It's too much of a chore.
I'd rather be a boor.
And never know what I'm missin'."

Adults in our society spend about two-thirds of their waking day engaged in some sort of communication—either speaking, reading, listening, or writing. The average adult spends about 45 percent of this communication time on listening. About 30 percent of the time is spent on speaking; 15 percent, on reading; 10 percent, on writing. In other words, listening takes up three times as much time as reading and over four times as much time as writing. Listening is truly basic to our mode of life.

Listening is such an important set of skills that most large industrial and business firms include listening instruction in their inservice training programs for employees (4). In the schools, children spend between 50 percent and 80 percent of their school day either listening or pretending to listen (15). At home, they listen to television for another three or four hours before finally going to sleep to prepare their ears and brains for another day's onslaught of words.

This module will look at why listening instruction has been neglected in the schools, even though listening is the primary language art—the major form of communication, the major medium of business transactions, education, politics, religion, advertising, and entertainment. It will also examine the nature of listening skills and how they can be taught. And finally, it will review the principles of motivation and retention to see how these principles can be used to encourage better listening.

Special Prerequisites for Module 7

It is recommended that you complete at least Modules 1–4 before beginning this module. There are no other special prerequisites.

Long-range Outcomes Related to Module 7

This module should help you as a teacher to do the following:

1. Communicate with other professional educators about ways of improving children's listening skills.

2. Incorporate listening instruction into your daily instructional program.

3. Teach children to decode more effectively another person's spoken words.

4. Teach children to notice grammatical signals in other people's speech.

5. Help children use literal and inferential thinking while listening.

6. Motivate children to listen better.

7. Improve children's retention of information gained while listening.

Performance Objectives for Knowledge Level

To give yourself an overview of what is expected of you in this module, you should first scan the objectives and performance standards at all three levels— knowledge, simulation, and teaching. Then use the study guide during your reading of the module. As you find information related to the study guide, write it down in the available blanks or on a separate sheet of paper. Then review this information shortly before your knowledge level examination.

1.1 On a closed-book examination, you should be able to select the best alternative for each multiple-choice question and circle the letter of your choice. The multiple-choice questions (given in the study guide without the alternatives) will be selected from those shown in the study guide. Next to each one write the alternative that you predict will be the correct one on the examination.

1.2 On the same examination, you will be expected to write short, concise sentences in list form, providing the information called for. The information which will be called for is described below in the study guide. Space is provided for you to write in your answers in preparation for the knowledge level examination. Only some of these lists will be selected for the examination.

1.3 On the same examination, you will be asked to match a list of specific listening skills with a list of exercises for improving those skills. The listening skills are listed below in the study guide. Next to each one, write an example of a listening exercise to aid your memory in preparing for the examination.

1.4 On the same examination, you will be presented with samples of teacher behavior in which the teacher is using principles of *motivation* to encourage better listening. After each sample, you will be asked to write the learning principle which the teacher is using the most. To help you prepare for this part of the examination, try writing the four principles of motivation from memory in the space given in the study guide.

1.5 On the same examination, you will be presented with samples of teacher behavior in which the teacher is using principles of *retention* to encourage better listening. After each sample, you will be asked to write the learning principle which the teacher is using the most. To help you prepare for this part of the examination, try writing the four principles of retention from memory in the space given in the study guide.

Study Guide for Knowledge Level Examination

1. What proportion of an adult's waking day is spent on communication?

2. What percent of adult communication time is spent on listening?

3. What percent of the school day do children spend in listening?

4. List three reasons why listening is considered the primary language art.

5. Give an example of how a listening experience can serve as a prerequisite to a learning experience requiring one of the other language arts.

6. How much advertising does a child listen to during a normal week?

7. How much time does the average person spend listening to commercials or political advertisements in a lifetime?

8. List three reasons why listening instruction is neglected in the schools.

9. Give three reasons why listening instruction should not be neglected in the schools.

10. What is listening?

11. What three things does good listening require besides strong motivation?

12. Intelligence accounts for what proportion of a person's listening abilities?

13. What three skills are needed in order to avoid the confusion caused by ignoring phonetic clues while listening?

14. What results should you expect from training in auditory discrimination?

15. How many syllables should a listener hear in a word such as *unsatisfied*?

16. How many morphemes should a listener notice in a word such as *unsatisfied*?

17. What is an example of a "suffix added to modified roots"?

18. What two linguistic tricks do good listeners use unconsciously to help them make good predictions?

19. What kind of word (part of speech) can be substituted for the word *blank* in the sentence, "Mr. Jones was very blank."?

20. What kind of word (part of speech) can be substituted for the word *blank* in the sentence, "The blank is here."?

21. What kind of word (part of speech) can be substituted for the word *blank* in the sentence, "They do it blank."?

22. What kind of word (part of speech) can be substituted for the word *blank* in the sentence, "I blank here."?

23. Using your own words, describe the difference between grammatical context clues and semantic context clues. Give an example of each.

24. List three methods for training children's ability to catch the right meaning of a word when listening to someone talk.

25. Besides listening to phonemes, morphemes, syllables, grammatical context clues, semantic context clues, and the appropriate meanings of words intended by the speaker, what are three other grammatical signals that listeners have to notice?

26. What type of thinking—literal, inferential, critical, or creative—is required by each of these listening skills?

    developing associations or images

    determining main ideas

    following a sequence

    making predictions

    recognizing significant details

27. Studies have shown teachers speak what percent of the words in a classroom?

28. List three ways of adding novelty to children's listening experiences.

29. Write from memory the four principles of motivation. Remember the mnemonic device: Novelty Needs Level Feedback.

30. Write from memory the four principles of retention. Remember the mnemonic device: Involved Masters Practice Transfer.

Performance Standards for Knowledge Level

A. Twenty-five minute time limit on 1.1–1.5 combined.
B. Completion deadline: instructor will notify.
C. Recommended grading standards if grades are used: 96% = A; 92% = A—; 88% = B; 84% = B—; 80% = C; below 80% = incomplete; should be completed at 80% or better before you go on to performance objectives for simulation level. (The instructor may wish to permit a grade of A or B only the first time the test is given in order to encourage more intensive study.)

Performance Objectives for Simulation Level

2.1 As a take-home examination, you should observe a teacher in an elementary school classroom setting. Record in writing how the teacher encouraged or discouraged good listening by employing or violating the four principles of motivation and the four principles of retention.

2.2 (Alternative objective) Same as 2.1 but a video-tape of a teacher may be used.

2.3 (Alternative objective) As an open-book exam, develop a lesson plan for teaching one of the specific listening skills described in the module. The instructor will specify which one at the time of the exam. Long-range outcome and performance objectives are required; also a worksheet that can be used in conjunction with oral directions from the teacher or tape recording.

Performance Standards for Simulation Level

A. For Objectives 2.1 and 2.2 (Recording of Teacher Behavior)
   1. Clear understanding of motivation principles demonstrated.
   2. Clear understanding of retention principles demonstrated.
   3. Report is legible, well-organized, and without spelling or punctuation errors.
   4. Uses numerous examples rather than vague generalities.
   5. Shows awareness of the suggestions in Module 7 for improving motivation and retention.

B. For Objective 2.3 (Written Lesson Plan)
   1. Performance objectives clearly state behavior desired, the conditions under which the behavior is to be performed, and those performance standards which will indicate sufficient mastery of the desired behavior.
   2. Performance objectives relate directly to the long-range outcome; the learning activities relate both to the performance objectives and the long-range outcome.
   3. The teacher-in-training shows a clear understanding of the listening skill which serves as a focus for the lesson plan.
   4. The teacher-in-training shows awareness of the suggestions in the module for teaching the skill.

C. For Objectives 2.1–2.3
   1. Suggested grading standard if grades are used; should be completed at the C level or better before going on to the performance objectives for the teaching level. (Grade based on judgment of instructor and/or peers.)
   2. Time limit and completion deadline: instructor will notify.
   3. Additional standards or modified standards may be developed by the instructor and/or teacher-in-training. It is best to state these standards before the required performance.

Performance Objectives for Teaching Level

> 3.1 In a micro-teaching, observation, student teaching, intern, or supervised teaching situation, teach any listening skill you wish. Lesson plan, worksheet coordinated with spoken directions, and self-critique are required.

Performance Standards for Teaching Level

> A. Uses learning principles effectively; does not violate any of those discussed in Module 3.
> B. Shows a clear understanding of the listening skill being taught.
> C. Has a written lesson plan which meets simulation standards B–1 and B–2.
> D. Lesson plan includes those elements suggested in Module 4.
> E. Self-critique includes those elements suggested in Module 4.
> F. Listens carefully and sincerely to students.

Listening as the Primary Language Art

In the beginning of this module, it was mentioned that adults spend about 45 percent of their daily communication time engaged in listening and that children spend over half their day at school in the same activity. Obviously, then, listening has an important role in most people's lives. In fact, this important role begins in infancy. Listening is the first intelligent language experience for most infants, preceding intelligible speech by several months and intelligible writing and reading by several years.

Listening is the major readiness experience required before reading instruction can take place. Beginning readers have to be able to translate printed words into spoken words and to understand what those spoken words mean. For instance, the printed statement, The dog ate the bone, has to be translated by a beginning reader into speech (or subvocal speech). To understand what he is reading, however, the reader has to have had former experience with dogs, with eating, and with bones. The reader also has to have experiences in listening to the words *dog, ate,* and *bone* (as well as experiences in listening to the grammatical pattern: Noun-Verb-Noun).

Listening experiences are often used by skillful teachers as prerequisites to experiences requiring one of the other language arts: reading, speaking, or writing. Before she teaches children a particular critical reading skill, Mrs. Franklin usually teaches that same skill through listening. If she wishes to improve their ability to distinguish literal statements from figurative statements, for instance, she'll teach them the difference through listening activities first, since listening is an "easier" medium and does not require the translation of print into speech. When Mr. Linoski wants his students to write

Both adults and children in our society spend about one-half of their daily communication time involved in listening.

Haiku poetry, he has them first *listen* to several poems to get the feel of Haiku. To help children pronounce difficult words properly, Miss Janer has them first listen to the pronunciation several times.

For most people, listening is the preferred medium for gaining information. Whether teachers and librarians like it or not, adults and children generally choose a listening activity over a reading activity. This is probably because listening requires less effort than reading, for most people. We can bemoan the fact that much more time is spent listening to television and radio and each other than is spent on reading, but it is unlikely that this state of affairs will change. A more reasonable approach is to teach children both reading skills and listening skills so that they can gain the most from each medium.

Listening is the major medium today by which people are persuaded to buy goods and services, candidates and ideas, and even values. The average child listens to (or is exposed to) 300 minutes of advertising a week on television and radio. For the average person, this means listening to over 1 million minutes of commercials or political advertisements in a lifetime. In addition, the average person will listen to over 4 million minutes of "entertainment"—including sitcoms, dramas, soap operas, news programs, movies, talk shows, and game shows. Such entertainment programs are a major source of new values and reinforced values. They provide modeling behavior for violent acts and kindness, sexual liberation and sexual conservatism, selfishness and altruism, and greed and generosity—to name just a few.

Listening is the major medium of exchange in the business world with its board room conferences, sales meetings, and two-hour work lunches. It's the major medium of the educational world with its lectures and seminars, its conferences and faculty meetings. And listening is the major medium of the political-diplomatic world with its United Nations debates, its cloakroom caucuses, and its endless committee meetings.

The Neglect of Listening Instruction

Listening, in other words, is the primary language art. In spite of its importance in adult life, however, instruction in listening is often ignored or slighted in the schools (7). One reason for this neglect is the assumption that listening can't be taught. Numerous studies have shown that this is not the case (2, 4, 8). Listening abilities can be improved with direct instruction. Another erroneous assumption is that listening is being taught when teachers remind their pupils to listen carefully or pay attention. Usually, however, listening abilities can be improved only with direct instruction (along with positive reinforcement).

Another reason for neglecting listening instruction, particularly in the elementary school, is the time factor. Teachers feel that reading instruction and other types of instruction take up so much time; there is simply no time left over for instruction in listening. Teachers who make this claim have a point: It is truly difficult to find time for everything in a crowded elementary school schedule. It is also true that reading instruction is so complex that it does take more time than most subjects to teach. However, the time spent on direct instruction in listening can pay large dividends in the long run. Once children learn specific listening skills, they can be encouraged to apply them during other types of instruction, thus enabling them to learn in other curriculum areas more readily.

An even more important reason for not neglecting listening instruction is the importance listening has in the development of useful communication skills—skills that can improve people's abilities to make friends, gain important information, and contribute to groups engaged in the process of solving problems.

The Nature of Listening

What is listening? It's certainly more than hearing. Listening is an act of the entire body, not just the ears. At the upper extreme of good listening, the eyes are glued to the speaker, searching for body language that will provide clues on the speaker's attitude and sincerity. The legs are still and not trying to walk out of the room. The hands have ceased their endless quest for something to scratch, poke, or pick. The ears are tuned-in to the words and inflections of the speaker rather than the voices in the corridor, the hot rod down the street, or the sarcastic remarks of a nearby friend. The brain is on red alert, watching for the slightest sign of straying attention, selecting and sifting the incoming information, critically evaluating the information, storing main ideas and details for future use, and creatively applying the information to personal concerns.

At the lower extreme of listening, the eyes are engaged in reading something unrelated to the speaker's topic—a comic book, a handout the speaker was unwise enough to distribute, or a note from a friend. The legs are crossing, uncrossing, and doing everything they can to make an exit. The hands are fiddling, scratching, and writing—notes to friends, grocery lists, and highly elaborate doodles. The ears are tuned only to the soothing vibrations of the speaker's voice—the cello-like buzz or the clarinet-like hum. And the brain? The brain is either asleep or searching for distractions—someone to giggle with, a fingernail that needs cleaning, a bug that "needs" an obstacle in its path.

Between the upper and lower extremes of listening, we have an enormously wide range of alertness, distractibility, motivation, listening vocabulary, and other components of the listening act. Good listening requires strong motivation, a mind free of too many emotional conflicts, a good listening vocabulary, and a host of specific listening skills. Although it is related to intelligence, it is by no means synonymous with intelligence. Some of the brightest people in the world are terrible listeners. Correlations between intelligence test scores and listening test scores range from .22 to .78 (2), which means in effect that intelligence probably accounts for no more than half of a person's listening abilities.

Is a person who is a good reader likely to be a good listener? Not necessarily. The average correlation between reading scores and listening scores is about .57 (2), which means that good readers are sometimes poor listeners and good listeners are sometimes poor readers. Is good listening just good thinking? Not quite. Listening involves more than just thinking. The following list provides a sample of the many specific skills required by the alert listener:

1. Decoding a speaker's words by means of phonetic signals.
2. Decoding a speaker's words by means of morphemic signals.
3. Decoding a speaker's words by means of syllabic signals.
4. Decoding a speaker's words by means of context signals.
5. Recognizing the appropriate meaning of a word used by a speaker.
6. Recognizing common sentence patterns, alterations, and expansions used by a speaker.
7. Differentiating and interpreting pitch variations.
8. Interpreting juncture signals.
9. Performing literal thinking while listening.
10. Performing inferential thinking while listening.
11. Performing critical thinking while listening.
12. Performing creative thinking during or after listening.
13. Performing group problem solving while listening.

Listening to Phonetic Signals

The following dialogue illustrates the confusion that sometimes arises when listeners fail to recognize phonetic clues. (Two sisters, neither of them hard-of-hearing, are sitting and talking on a large front porch.)

ALICE: *I really enjoy gentle riding in the evening.*
BRENDA: *I don't enjoy writing anytime.*
ALICE: *Why not?*

BRENDA: *It's too much like work.*

ALICE: *Why? It's not your back, you know.*

BRENDA: *(puzzled) I know it's not my bag. I just told you I don't like it.*

ALICE: *(looks around) Did the maid bring my cello?*

BRENDA: *You had your Jell-o once today. Why do you want it again?*

ALICE: *You know I have my cello twice a day.*

BRENDA: *Anything you say, dear. I'm going to my bed.*

ALICE: *What do you mean, you're going to your pad. You're in your pad right now.*

BRENDA: *I may act sleepy, but I'm not that bad, am I?*

ALICE: *Brenda, If they had a Miss-Out-to-Sea contest, you'd have my vote.*

BRENDA: *I don't know what you're talking about and I don't want your boat. So good night!*

ALICE: *Good night, Brenda.*

As you can see, ignoring phonetic clues while listening can have amusing results. What skills are needed in order to avoid this type of confusion? Of course, one of the skills is not a listening skill at all, but rather a speaking skill that was discussed in Module 4, namely, enunciation. Sharper enunciation would have avoided some of the problem which Brenda and Alice had. A second skill is that of carefully searching for context clues. Alice said she enjoyed gentle riding in the evening. Brenda ignored the word *gentle* as well as Alice's riding boots and replied that she didn't enjoy writing anytime.

A third skill is called auditory discrimination—the ability to notice the difference between two or more sounds. Some people seem to have much greater auditory discrimination abilities than others, although researchers have yet to come up with a consistent reason for this. Many attempts have been made to improve people's auditory discrimination through training programs. The purpose of these programs has usually been to improve children's *reading* abilities. Although the programs generally have been successful in sharpening children's discrimination powers, they have had inconsistent results in improving children's reading abilities. The reason for this is probably straightforward: reading is a complex set of skills requiring the application and coordination of many discrete visual and auditory skills. Merely improving children's auditory perceptual power does not automatically lead to better reading.

On the other hand, training in auditory discrimination does lead to better auditory discrimination for most people (9). Thus, even though such training will not automatically produce better readers, it may play a small part toward producing better listeners. The following are the types of exercises that may be used to improve children's auditory discrimination. Similar exercises are often used during reading instruction to prepare children for learning a new phonics signal.

Exercises for Improving Auditory Discrimination

1. Have the children close their eyes and listen to pairs of words. Have them keep their eyes closed and raise one finger when

they think the words are the same. [Use pairs of words whose initial consonant phoneme (sound) is either the same or different, e.g., *Jell-o–cello, vote–boat, ship–chip, far–car, head–head, that–bat, hair–dare.*] *Discuss immediately any pairs they have trouble with.* If some are having a lot of trouble, jot down their names and work with them later in a small group.

2. Same as 1 but use pairs whose *final* consonant phoneme is either the same or different, e.g., *bag–back, man–map, run–run, run–rum, bath–bath, match–mash.*

3. Same as 1 but use pairs whose medial vowel phoneme is either the same or different, e.g., *red–rid, pin–pen, sun–sun, here–hair, clip–clap, bad–bed, then–than.*

4. Give children these instructions: "Listen to these three words: *tiger, table, top.* Can you think of some words that begin in the same way?" [Give positive reinforcement for any word which begins with the /t/ phoneme (the t sound). Do other initial phonemes in the same way (see Module 4 for list of phonemes).]

5. Same as 4 but use words whose *final* phonemes are the same (words that end in the same way), e.g., *map–flop–tulip* or *bed–lad–mud.*

6. Same as 4 but use words whose final *phonograms* are the same (words which rhyme), e.g., *hall–ball–install.* Do the same thing for the various vowel sounds (see Module 4).

7. Play this guessing game: "I'm thinking of something in this room that begins in the same way as the word *church.* What is it? That's right; chalkboard." (Do the same thing for other initial phonemes.)

8. Have the children divide a set of objects or pictures into two sets: those which begin in the same way as the word *ball* (or any other word you choose) and those which do not. Do the same for other initial phonemes.

Listening to Syllabic and Morphemic Signals

Besides noticing phonetic differences in a speaker's words, the listener must also notice syllabic and morphemic differences. Trying to decode a speaker's statement phoneme by phoneme would be impossible of course. Most of the time—except for phonemes we don't expect in a sentence—we hear larger units of sound, such as syllables, words, morphemes, familiar phrases, or even entire sentences.

Suppose the speaker, for instance, used the word *redeveloped.* To decipher this word strictly from phonetic clues, the listener would have to receive it this way:

$$/r/ + /\bar{e}/ + /d/ + /\bar{e}/ + /v/ + /\breve{e}/ + /l/ + /\breve{u}/ + /p/ + /t/$$

Instead, the listener is likely to receive it either as four distinct "grunts" called syllables or as three meaningful units called morphemes. The four syllables would be /re/ + /de/ + /vel/ + /upt/. The three morphemes would be re + develop + ed. Each one of the three units is meaningful; removing either the prefix *re* or the suffix *ed* would make a major difference in the speaker's meaning.

In Table 7.1, you will find some of the important elements involved in morphemic listening. You will see, for instance, that a listener has to notice prefixes, three different types of suffixes, contractions, derivatives (*helper* is a derivative of *help*), compound words, and Greek and Latin morphemes such as *tele, phono,* and *graph.*

TABLE 7.1   Some Important Elements Involved in Morphemic Listening

Inflectional suffixes with no root changes	girl*s*, jump*s*, jump*ed*, boy'*s*, high*er*, high*est*, jump*ing*
Compound words	playground, birthday, anything
Contractions	did*n't*, let'*s*, it'*s*, she'*ll*, they'*re*, you'*ve*, he'*d*
Derivative-forming suffixes with no root changes	help*er*, help*ful*, help*fully*, help*less*, quick*ly*, stick*y*, danger*ous*, agree*ment*
Prefixes	*un*lock, *re*paint, *dis*appear, *im*possible, *in*correct, *de*rail, *pre*view, *be*come, *a*like
Suffixes added to modified roots a. Final consonant doubled b. Final *y* changed to *i* c. Final *e* dropped	 rub*bed*, sip*ping*, sit*ter* happi*ly*, hurrie*s*, happi*er*, happi*est* mak*er*, mov*ed*, hop*ing*
Greek and Latin morphemes	tele, graph, phono, photo, port, bi

The following are some exercises that may be used for helping children pay more attention to syllabic and morphemic clues when listening.

Exercises for Syllabic Listening

1. Have the children clap or stamp as they pronounce words presented orally by the teacher.

2. Play a modified game of "Three Steps Off the Mudguard." Usually the leader calls the number of steps which the line of children may take toward her. If anyone takes more than the prescribed number of steps, that person may be tagged—unless he beats the leader to the opposite side. For the modified version, the leader calls a word rather than a number. The children must figure out the number of syllables in that word and take only that many steps.

3. The teacher presents the children orally with three words in rapid succession. The children must remember the words, count the number of syllables in all three words combined, and say the correct number when called upon by the teacher. The first one correct gets to be the leader.

4. To help them gain the concept of syllabic stress or accent, have the children pronounce words that you present to them orally. As they pronounce them, they should clap their hands on the syllable which receives the greatest stress.

Exercises for Morphemic Listening

1. Contractions: The teacher or leader says a sentence which contains a contraction. A child whose turn it is must repeat the sentence immediately, but this time without contracting the words, e.g., "I can't come to your house. . . . I cannot come to your house." If you wish, this can be done in game form by dividing into baseball teams and counting each correct response as a base hit. There are many modifications that can be made of this type of game.

2. Compound words: The teacher or leader says a word which can be compounded easily, such as *some*. A child whose turn it is has five seconds to think of another word to attach to it, thus creating a compound word like *something* or *sometimes*. The lead word can be either the first part of a compound word as in *some*thing, or the second part, as in birth*day*. Other lead words that might be used include *door* (*doorknob*), *cow* (*cowboy*), *thing* (*anything*), etc.

3. Roots and affixes: The teacher or leader says a root word, and the children brainstorm to see how many "family" words they can think of in one minute. For instance, "How many "family" words can you think of for *paint*?" (*paints, painted, painting, repaint, repainted, repainting, unpainted*) How many can you think of for *happy?*

Listening for Context Signals

A large part of listening is predicting. As we listen, we are constantly predicting what word or phrase or sentence or idea will come next. Good listeners unconsciously use two linguistic tricks to help them make good predictions: (1) they listen for grammatical clues; (2) they listen for semantic clues.

If the speaker is saying, "Mr. Jones was very _____, the good listener knows what *type* of word is coming next. It will be a word like *warm, happy, tired, disgusted,* or *fat*. The listener may not even know what an adjective is, but he will know intuitively that an adjective is coming.

If the speaker is saying, "After a long hard day at the office, Mr. Jones was very _____, the good listener knows not only what *type* of word is coming but probably what the exact word will be. The semantic clues, such as *long* and *hard* lead the listener to expect the word *tired* rather than words like *warm, happy, disgusted,* or *fat*.

This ability to predict what the speaker is going to say not only increases the accuracy of the listening experience but also the involvement. When people are engaged in making predictions, they can't help but be involved. And such involvement, as mentioned in Module 3, leads to greater retention of the information being received.

Exercises for Listening to Context Signals

1. The concept of grammatical context can be gained intuitively by children without using formal terminology, such as nouns, verbs, adverbs, and adjectives. Generally, all they need are four types of listening experiences, one for each of the four major parts of speech. For nouns, for example, the teacher would say something like this, "The *blank* is here. What words can you use instead of *blank*? How about *paper*? Can I say, The paper is here? What other words could I use instead of paper?" Later, the teacher would say, "What about swims? Can I say, The swims is here? What about *quickly*? What about *sleepy*? What other words can you think of that will *not* work in the sentence, The blank is here?"

2. For adjectives, the teacher would use a sentence such as this: That thing is very *blank*. Children should come up with words like *funny, slow, ripe,* or *heavy*.

3. For verbs, sentences like these would be suitable: I *blank* here (*am, eat, sleep, sit*). He *blank* it (*hid, ate, found*). She will *blank* (*come, be, stand, run*).

4. For adverbs, you might use a sentence similar to this one: They do it *blank* (*fast, quickly, noisily, here, there, in the house, now, then*).

5. To get students to listen to *semantic* clues as well as grammatical clues, you now should use sentences that are not so open-ended. For instance, the sentence *I blank here* is now too open-ended. Hundreds of words would work: *live, eat, sit, fly,* etc. Now you should provide more semantic clues. For example, John looked at his house and said, "I blank here." Now the most likely word is *live*, rather than *sit* or *fly*.

6. Instead of using That thing is very blank, now use sentences like these: That clown is very blank. That racing car is very blank. That three-week-old banana is very blank.

7. Instead of using The blank is here, now use sentences like these: The blank you wanted for cutting the paper is on the table. The sharp blank is in the kitchen drawer. The blank in the tub is hot. Just outside the bank was the get-away blank. Up the dusty road galloped the outlaw's blank.

8. Instead of using They do it blank, now use sentences like these: When policemen chase speeders, they drive their cars blank. The fat tired man walked up the stairs blank. The ball crashed blank through the window.

Combining Listening Instruction with Reading Instruction

Before going on with other listening skills, it should be pointed out that listening skills are often taught in conjunction with reading lessons. By teaching the use of context signals through listening first, to use just one example, the children can concentrate on that skill and not have to become involved in the more complex process of decoding that reading entails. For instance, if Mrs. Franklin wants her students to notice context clues when they read, she might first have them listen to several sentences for which they have to come up with the missing word. Then she would give them similar sentences to read and fill in the blanks. She would then follow up with the reading of a story in a basal reader, stopping them frequently to look for context clues.

Recognizing Appropriate Meanings

The poor hapless listener of the English language needs all the grammatical clues, semantic clues, and whatever other clues available. The English language is a fluid, creative one, with words changing their meanings and taking on new meanings almost faster than the rise and fall of show business stars. As mentioned earlier, the word *run* has over 200 meanings. The "simple" word *take* has over 100. (What was your take in dollars and cents? I'm gonna take a fall in the third round. What magazines do you take? Take the piece you want. Do you take a dare?)

Three methods can be used to improve children's ability to catch the right meaning when they're listening to someone talk. One method is to teach them how to pay close attention to grammatical and semantic clues. Exercises designed to assist the teacher in teaching these skills were just suggested in the section "Listening for Context Signals."

The second method is to expose the children to numerous books, films, and recordings so that they can acquire through osmosis the various shades of meaning that words can have. While reading aloud to children, it's a good idea to occasionally stop and discuss a word that has an unusual meaning. The third method was mentioned in Module 4, and that is to provide the students with exercises which require them to use several different meanings for words. [1]

Recognizing Other Grammatical Signals

Not only do listeners have to recognize phonemes, morphemes, syllables, grammatical context clues, semantic context clues, and the appropriate meanings of words intended by the speaker, they also have to pay attention to other grammatical signals. They have to recognize, unconsciously, the type of sentence pattern or alteration or expansion that the speaker is using. They have to differentiate among and interpret the speaker's pitch variations, and they have to interpret the juncture signals (pauses) which the speaker makes.

Fritz, a first grader, can understand this sentence: He found his ball there. But Fritz has trouble with this sentence: There he found his ball. He heard each word correctly, but the pattern didn't make sense to him. He wasn't used to hearing words put in that order. Unfortunately, order is what good listening's all about. Good listeners of music don't listen to single notes thumping in their ears one after another. They hear entire musical phrases which gradually

---

[1] These exercises were suggested in detail in Module 4.

evolve into recognizable themes and noticeable variations on those themes. Good listening to people's talk requires listening to broader units than syllables or words.

To really understand another person, you have to sense the way that person arranges words into sentences. This kind of understanding can only come through exposure to a variety of arrangements—to a variety of dialects and idiosyncrasies. It can also come through specific exercises in the kind of creative grammar described in Module 4. You will recall that Module 4 discussed how you can increase children's fluency by teaching them the many ways that sentence patterns can be altered and expanded. This same approach can be valuable in developing the familiarity with sentence patterns required for good listening (see Module 4 for specific exercises).

A listener can hear all the right words but miss the pitch changes, stress, or pauses and thereby miss the entire meaning of a speaker's statement. For example, suppose the speaker said, "Meet *you* at the park? Bring ice cream sandwiches and *pop?* Oh *sure* I will. He may have been speaking sarcastically and had no intention of meeting you. If you ignored his pitch changes and pauses, you would end up at the park waiting all alone with melting ice cream, soggy sandwiches, and warm pop. Module 5 discussed ways of helping children speak, read, and write with expression through the use of stress, pitch variations, and pauses. The exercises discussed at that time will also serve to help children become more aware of such signals when they are trying to listen to someone else.

PerforminG Literal ThinkinG WhilE ListeninG

Receiving the message of the speaker is only half the battle. The other half is *thinking* about what is heard. Good listeners perform literal thinking while they listen. They develop associations or images in their minds. They follow the sequence of the ideas or story. They recognize significant details and store them in their memory as the speaker continues. And they often engage in inferential, critical, and creative thinking as well.

Those children who have trouble comprehending as they listen are often those who have not developed the habit of visualizing while they listen— developing associations between what they hear and their own personal experiences or creating images of what the speaker is describing. For instance, what pictures in your mind would you create if this were read to you? "The bright sails flapped fully in the wind, and the boat shot forward. Jack hung on to the tiller for dear life and desperately steered for shore." Would you picture a sailboat, perhaps some water that is wavy from the wind, sails bulging and flapping, a boy holding tight to a horizontal handle in the rear of the boat, his face tense with anxiety and his eyes searching for the shore? Would you have fleeting memories of your own sailing experiences or other experiences in a boat? The skillful listener develops associations and creates images in order to understand what the speaker is saying. Here are some types of experiences you might use with children to help them develop this skill.

Exercises on Developing Associations or Images

1. Read to the children at least once a day. Children in grades two through eight usually enjoy the Chapter-a-Day plan. Younger children enjoy a picture book read to them each day. Children *need* to listen to well-written language!

2. When reading a story aloud to the children, occasionally have them close their eyes and picture what you're reading. Pause occasionally to discuss their "pictures," or have them describe their picture to a "neighbor."

3. Read a passage to them and then ask them to tell of what personal experience it reminded them.

4. Read a passage to them and have them pantomime while you read.

5. Read a passage to them and have them draw a picture of what you read.

Creating images while you listen is essential for mastering a more difficult literal thinking skill: following a sequence of ideas, events, or directions. The person who is successful at following a speaker's sequence (particularly at the elementary school level) is usually one who has learned to visualize while listening. If the teacher asks Melinda to follow a set of oral directions, Melinda likes to imagine herself following them as she listens. As Oliver listens to a story one of his buddies is telling him, he pictures the action the way it might have been if he'd been in it. Here are some types of experiences you might use with children to help them develop this skill.

Exercises on Following a Sequence

1. Develop children's auditory memory, a highly trainable skill (8) and one which is related to following a sequence. Use exercises such as the following:
   a. Give them a sequence of three numbers and have them repeat them in the same order. Very gradually, over several days, work up to seven numbers. Then play the telephone number game; a child tells his number and calls on someone to repeat it. The person who repeats it successfully gets to be the next leader and gives his number.
   b. Same as a, but use words instead.
   c. Same as b, but use one-word directions instead, such as *stop, go, bend, touch, twist, hop, sit, stand, smile, frown.* Be sure to give at least three in sequence and expect the same sequence from them.

2. Have the children work in pairs. One person reads a set of directions and the other person tries to follow them. Directions can be for making things—paper airplanes, paper doll

costumes, etc. Directions can also be for simple movements, such as putting your finger on the tip of your nose, etc.

3. Read a story to them; then have them decide in what order to place pictures showing events in the story.

4. Read a story to them and then have them pantomime the story in proper order.

5. Divide the class into five groups. First explain a new game to five people; then have those five people act as leaders in explaining the game to the five groups.

6. Read informational material to the children about a sequential process such as the water cycle or the cycle of life for a butterfly or the procedure for making candy bars in a factory. Then have them explain the process to a partner and draw a picture showing the correct sequence.

In addition to creating images and following a sequence, the good listener is searching for main ideas and significant details. When looking for the main ideas of a speaker, we unconsciously select those details which indicate that an idea *is* a main idea, or we look for those details which support a main idea that we have already decided upon. Sometimes, of course, the listener is simply looking for a detail that will answer a specific question in mind, such as, Who left the toad in the teacher's desk? The following are some ideas for helping the students develop the skill of recognizing and recollecting significant details.

Exercises on Recognizing and Recollecting Significant Details

1. Read a story to the children. Have them change it into a brief news report that tells who, what, where, when, and why.

2. Read about an historical event to the children. Have them create a telegram of twenty-five words or less that captures all the essential details. Have them decide what historical person should get the telegram.

3. Have them make up a title for a story that you have read them. Then have them justify the title by recalling details in the story that support the title.

4. Have them listen to a recording, either together or in a listening center, and answer a set of very specific questions requiring one-word answers while they listen.

Performing Inferential Thinking While Listening

Another thinking skill employed while listening is called inferential thinking. This is a somewhat more difficult type of thinking than literal thinking, since it requires creating information that the speaker did not directly provide the listener. Making inferences is not the same as making critical judgments. If the speaker brags about his wife's black eye, we might *infer* that he gave it to her. Or we might infer that his wife goes to karate classes. If we passed critical judgment on the speaker, we might judge him to be a wife beater. Or we might judge him to be a "wife lover"—a person who wants his wife to be able to protect herself. Children should be taught to make inferences and judgments with some caution.[2]

Two other types of inferential thinking are (1) determining main ideas and (2) predicting events, steps, or ideas which logically follow. Exercises which relate to these two skills follow.

Exercises on Finding Main Ideas and Making Predictions

1. Have them make up a new title for a story you have read to them that is "better" than the original title. Have them defend their new title.
2. Have them listen to a tape recording of a news editorial and decide on the main point.
3. Let them make up headlines for stories read to them.
4. Read a story to them. Then have them write a two- or four-line verse or some other form of short poetry which gets at the main idea of the story.
5. After reading a story to them, have them decide whether the theme was (a) people against nature, (b) people against people, or (c) people against themselves.
6. Read a portion of a story to them and have them decide what is going to happen next. Make them defend their ideas, if they can.
7. Read a portion of a story; have them draw or pantomime what is going to happen next.
8. Discuss the main character in a story. Have them predict what influence his characteristics will have on the action in the story.
9. Bake cookies together. Have someone read the directions aloud; stop occasionally to have the rest of the group predict what step will follow.
10. Read an informative passage to them. Stop in the middle and have them predict what you're going to read about next.

Combining Listening Instruction with Reading Instruction

Again, remember that listening exercises are often used as a prerequisite experience before a reading skill is taught. Mrs. Franklin, for instance, might wish to teach some of her pupils to do a better job of predicting events as they read so that they become more involved in their reading and increase their level of comprehension. Before she has them practice this skill with reading selections, she would first have one or more lessons in which she has them listen to selections she reads. During these lessons, she would frequently ask them to predict what is going to happen next. In this way, her pupils can concentrate on the pre-

[2] Exercises related to such caution are described in Module 8.

diction skill without becoming involved in the complexities of decoding the printed words themselves. Once Mrs. Franklin feels the children have learned the skill sufficiently, she would have them apply it in actual reading situations. tions.

Performing Critical Thinking While Listening

All the other types of listening described may be "wasted hearing" if we are slaves to whatever we hear. We may be literally slaves to the spoken word when we do not apply critical judgment to what we hear. And we may be somewhat less than ourselves when we fail to use what we hear as a springboard to our own creativity.[3]

Listening and Motivation

Now that we have discussed some of the many subskills making up the general ability called listening, we need to examine the major factor that influences the quality of listening, namely, the motivation of the listener. Without the motivation to listen, all the listening skills in the world will be of no avail. Good listening, although enjoyable, is hard work. It is so much easier to follow old habits and listen with "half an ear." To get students to want to listen and to want to develop good listening habits requires all of the psychology the teacher can muster.

Module 3 discussed the various principles of learning which would enhance a student's motivation to learn. To motivate a student, you were advised to think of this mnemonic device: *Novelty Needs Level Feedback*. This memory device should help you think of these four principles:

1. Add NOVELTY to their learning experiences.
2. Help them satisfy their basic NEEDS.
3. Teach them at the appropriate LEVEL of difficulty.
4. Provide frequent and specific FEEDBACK.

Add Novelty to Learning Experiences

Let's take the first principle concerning novelty. No one likes to listen to the same voice all day long. No matter how good a voice you may have, children will tire of it. So try to use it sparingly. Studies have shown (12) that teachers speak 50 to 80 percent of the words in a school classroom. Is it any wonder that kids sometimes tune out? To avoid having children tune you out, try some of these "tricks":

[3] Module 10 will discuss in considerable detail the type of listening required in reacting to propaganda and in other situations needing critical thinking.

1. Let children take your place. For example, instead of the teacher always explaining a math problem on the chalkboard, have a child do it. If necessary, go over the explanation with the child before she makes it in front of the class. After a spelling test, let the children write words on the board and spell them out loud. You just stand by and listen. Let an older child come into the room and read to your students, or let one of your own students do the reading. Have a child lead the Pledge of Allegiance. Let one of the children explain how to play the new game for P.E.

2. Make your instructions a game. Challenge them to follow the instructions "after I've told you only once." Praise those who succeed. Those who don't get your instructions should come to your desk for another quiet explanation. Don't force the entire class to listen to your instructions again in a loud, irritated voice.

3. *Sometimes* when you give instructions you can ask children to complete the last word of each sentence. This provides novelty and keeps them on their toes.

4. Pantomime some of your instructions or explanations so that the children actually end up verbalizing them.

5. Explain something to five "leaders"; then divide the class into five groups and let the leaders explain the same things to their group.

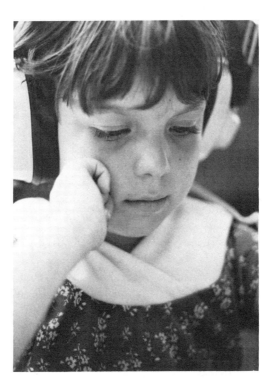

Good listening requires strong motivation to listen.

Help Them Satisfy Basic Needs

Now let's look at the second principle, this one concerning basic needs. One of the physiological needs, you'll remember, is the need for oxygen. Listening is seldom very sharp in a stuffy room full of carbon dioxide. The classroom plants will enjoy such an environment but the children will wilt. Try airing out the room and getting them to touch their toes a few times before asking them to listen.

Help them meet their needs for belonging and status by listening to *them* on a regular basis. One of the best ways to handle this is through a show-and-tell period for young children and a news time for older children. For show and tell, have them sometimes bring their treasures in a paper bag; then have them give hints about what's inside the bag while you and the children listen intently. Praise them for their good hinting and good guessing.

For news time, let the children stay in their seats and tell you and the kids everything newsworthy—how Kevin's dad went through an operation, how the President was nearly assassinated, how Mary had a "close encounter of the first kind." Stand up in front of the class and really listen: showing surprise, asking questions that show you're interested, asking other children if they've had similar experiences or if they heard the same thing on the news.

Teach Them at the Appropriate Level

Children will listen best, of course, when the information they are listening to is at their own level of difficulty. Arranging for this type of listening is not always easy. Children in any group vary a great deal in their ability to listen, in their listening vocabulary, in their motivation to listen, and in their general intelligence. This means that information given verbally to the entire group has to be kept at a fairly simple level, with only occasional side remarks for the "brighter" children. This also means listening experiences need to be arranged that allow for individual differences. This can be done either by dividing the children into listening groups or by using a listening station with tape recorders.

Dividing children into listening groups can be done either by using the teacher's judgment or by relying on listening tests such as those published by Science Research Associates. This type of grouping, of course, is impractical for such things as giving instructions on assignments or other types of procedural explanations. It *is* practical, however, for situations in which children are expected to gain facts and concepts from listening to a tape recording or record. The teacher can then change the pace and the type of discussion for each group.

Listening stations can be set up so that a child can listen at his own pace, stopping and starting the tape recorder whenever something is not clear or whenever instructed to write a response. The number of cassettes now available for classroom listening centers is nearly astronomical. These are often most effective when combined with printed matter that corresponds to the narration on the cassette (Every major publisher of basal readers, social studies texts, and science texts sells such cassettes.)

Provide Frequent and Specific Feedback

Providing children with feedback during listening experiences is perhaps the most neglected motivational device. Good teachers have done it for centuries: "James, why don't you tell the boys and girls what I just said and I'll tell you whether you understood it." If this type of statement is presented as a gentle challenge rather than as an attempt to catch someone napping, it can be a very effective feedback device.

What you're trying to do is provide students with frequent and specific feedback on their listening effectiveness. This means stopping the listening experience every so often and checking on their comprehension. Asking James or Mary to summarize is one way of doing this, but an even more effective way—one which gets more people involved—is to ask a question and then let each person tell one other person the answer. This gives all a chance to verbalize about their listening experiences.

Another way of providing feedback is to hand out a list of short questions before you begin the listening experience. The questions should require either one-word answers or the circling of the correct answer. The order of the questions should correspond to the order of the speaker's presentation. This technique provides specific and immediate feedback on one's listening efficiency. Further feedback may be provided, of course, by going over the answers when the listening experience is over.

Listening and Retention

Next to motivation, your major concern should be retention. The children may be motivated to listen, they may have developed appropriate listening skills, but, naturally, you'd like them to remember what they hear. If we return once more to the learning principles discussed in Module 3, we can see how retention can be enhanced during listening experiences. The mnemonic device suggested was this: *Involved Masters Practice Transfer*. This memory device was to help you remember these four principles:

1. Get everyone INVOLVED at all times.
2. Teach for MASTERY rather than coverage.
3. Provide massed PRACTICE followed by distributed practice.
4. Help positive TRANSFER occur (and watch for negative transfer).

Get Everyone Involved

Let's look at the first principle, concerning involvement. The "trick" here is simply that of making everyone feel responsible for what they're listening to.

You can do this by threatening a test, of course, but this makes the listening experience a negative one. Using a test is not a bad idea, if it's done in the spirit of fun and not used as a grading device. Giving them the test or a worksheet ahead of time is also an effective means of getting everyone involved. A more informal method is simply to list some questions on the chalkboard, either those made up by the teacher or those made up by the students' response to this question: What questions do you think the speaker (record, tape recording, films, or another student's report) will answer for us? What questions do you hope will be answered? If you were talking on this topic what questions would you try to answer for us?

Another way to encourage involvement is to urge students to interrupt with questions during the presentation, recording, or procedural explanation. In a study by Patterson (10), it was found that very few children even think of asking questions when information is not clear to them. It was also discovered that when they were taught to ask questions and were reinforced for asking questions, their listening efficiency improved dramatically. Evidently, many teachers foster the attitude that good listeners are silent listeners and that question asking is disruptive. In actual fact, question asking increases both involvement and retention.

Teach for Mastery

The principle of teaching for mastery is crucial when the medium of listening is used. If students go on to Step 2 or Idea 2 without first mastering Step 1 or Idea 1, the usual result is a sharp drop in the efficiency of learning. This is particularly true when listening rather than reading is the medium. With reading, the student can go back to Step 1 and read it again. With listening, the student is forced to follow the pace of the speaker. Thus, teachers who are using listening as a medium for explaining procedures or concepts need to be highly concerned about mastery.

As you may recall from Module 3, mastery is encouraged when teachers teach with performance objectives in mind and when the material presented is both clear and meaningful. A teacher with performance objectives will stop the listening experience frequently to check for retention. Mr. Hodges, for instance, often stops a student's report (or a recording), asks a question requiring one or two words as an answer, and has the students write down their answer secretly. Then he walks quietly around the room and peeks at the children's answers, praising those who have it right. When he gets back to his desk, he jots down the names of the few children who are having trouble so that he can go over the material with those children later, if necessary. But before the speaker or recording continues, he discusses the right answer and then immediately calls on those who missed it to tell what the right answer is.

The teacher with clarity and meaningfulness in mind will urge students to ask questions, even resorting to a ruse such as this, "Benny, I know you probably understood everything I just said, but to help those who didn't understand, why don't you ask me a question or two." When questions are asked, they are treated with respect no matter how silly they may sound or how much they show that the student really wasn't listening.

The teacher with clarity and meaningfulness in mind will also attempt to determine the prerequisite understandings that will be necessary before the listening experience takes place. Unusual words and concepts will be explained, and a background of information will be provided. Meaningfulness will be enhanced by helping the students see the relevance of the topic to their own lives or to an academic assignment.

Provide Massed and Distributed Practice

The principle of practice is a very common-sense notion. It is surprising how often it is ignored. Because we teachers get in a hurry, we sometimes make the hopeful assumption that just because we have introduced a listening skill to the children, they will be able to use it from then on. Of course, this is no more true with listening skills than it is with multiplication tables. Any skill requires practice, and the best form of practice is massed practice followed by distributed practice. The first time a listening skill is introduced, there should be plenty of practice in order to set the skill in the children's minds and nervous systems. More practice should be provided the very next day before too much "slippage" occurs. After that, the practice should be spaced farther and farther apart. Better yet, it should be applied to more and more daily situations in the classroom.

Help Positive Transfer Occur

And this brings us to the fourth principle, transfer. The whole point in using listening exercises and games is to get children to use the listening skills in everyday classroom situations (and hopefully outside the classroom). If you have provided them with abundant exercises and games on following spoken directions, it is time to require the use of that skill whenever procedures are being taught: procedures for putting away their materials, procedures for solving a math problem, procedures for studying their spelling words. If you have taught them special techniques for following directions (such as imagining yourself doing what the directions call for), be sure to remind them of those special techniques. Don't assume that transfer will automatically take place, because for many children (and adults) it won't. Numerous studies (6) have shown that transfer best takes place when teachers make a conscious effort to help it take place.

Another technique for aiding transfer is to point out similarities that appear perfectly obvious to a teacher but go unrecognized by the students. If they are listening to an explanation of a mathematical operation, for example, point out the specific similarities between this operation and the one described on a previous day.

To avoid negative transfer, try to avoid having them listen to two explanations side by side about similar but different concepts. To take an extreme example, it would be inadvisable to have them listen to explanations of *college* and *collage* on the same day. One term should be reasonably well mastered before introducing the other.

Helping Children with Hearing Problems

It is not unusual to find in a group of thirty elementary school children one or two who are partially deaf. It is also not unusual for the deafness to go unnoticed by the child, the parents, or the teachers. A child may grow up thinking that his hearing condition is normal, that people are inconsiderate in their speech, that there's something wrong with him mentally, and so on.

Some school districts hire an audiologist who periodically tests the children's hearing with an audiometer. If your district does not provide such a service, it would be advisable for you to informally test your children's hearing and to refer children with hearing problems to the principal and the parents so that a physician can examine the child more carefully. Ask a parent or an aide to test each child in a quiet room.

Have the tester hold a watch with a fairly loud tick near the child's ear and move it slowly away. Ask the child to close his eyes and indicate with an upraised finger when he can no longer hear the ticking. This is a very rough measure but is suitable for detecting severe hearing loss. A child who can no longer hear the ticking after a distance of two feet may have a hearing problem.

Once you have identified children with hearing problems, try not to embarrass them by making an issue of it. Talk in your normal voice but directly at their face without anything obstructing their view of *your* face. Talk to them privately about any problems they're having because of their hearing difficulty.

Summary

In this module, we have examined the nature of listening—an act of the "entire body" involving numerous specific skills, a speaking vocabulary, and a reasonably strong motivation. We have discussed methods of teaching the various listening skills and have suggested that the principles of motivation and the principles of retention be used to improve the quality of listening experiences. Listening is the primary language art and the medium for nearly half of people's "communication day." Listening can be taught and should be. Since listening is already an important part of the school day, no large amounts of additional time need be devoted to it. Instead, the *quality* of the listening time needs to be improved.

REFERENCES AND BIBLIOGRAPHY

1. Devine, Thomas G. "Reading and Listening: New Research Findings." *Elementary English* 45 (1968): 346–48.

2. _____. "Listening: What Do We Know After Fifty Years of Research and Theorizing." *Journal of Reading* 21 (Jan. 1978): 296–304.

3. Duker, Sam. "An Annotated Guide to Audiovisual Aids Available for the Teaching of Listening." *Audiovisual Instruction* 10 (1965): 320–22.

4. _____. "Listening." In *Encyclopedia of Educational Research*, edited by Robert L. Ebel et al. New York: Macmillan, 1969.

5. Golden, N.E., and Steiner, S. "Auditory and Visual Functions in Good and Poor Readers." *Journal of Learning Disabilities* 9 (1969): 476–81.

6. Klausmeier, Herbert J., and Goodwin, William. *Learning and Human Abilities, Educational Psychology*. New York: Harper and Row, 1975.

7. Landry, Donald L. "The Neglect of Listening." *Elementary English* 46 (1969): 599–605.

8. Lundsteen, Sara. *Listening and Its Impact on Reading and the Other Language Arts*. Urbana, Ill.: National Council for Teachers of English, 1975.

9. Lyon, Reid. "Auditory-Perceptual Training: The State of the Art." *Journal of Learning Disabilities* 10 (Nov. 1977): 564–72.

10. Patterson, Charlotte J. "Teaching Children to Listen." *Today's Education* 67 (April-May 1978): 52–53.

11. Rankin, Paul. "The Importance of Listening Ability." *English Journal* 17 (1928): 623–30.

12. Russell, David H., and Russell, Elizabeth F. *Listening Aids Through the Grades—One-Hundred-Ninety Listening Activities*. New York: Teachers College, Columbia University, 1959.

13. Tutolo, Daniel J. "A Cognitive Approach to Teaching Listening." *Language Arts* 54 (March 1977): 262–65.

14. Wagner, Guy. *Listening Games*. Perception, 1967.

15. Wilt, M.E. "A Study of Teacher Awareness of Listening as a Factor in Elementary Education." *Journal of Educational Research* 43 (1950): 62–63.

Providing Instruction in
Decoding Written Materials

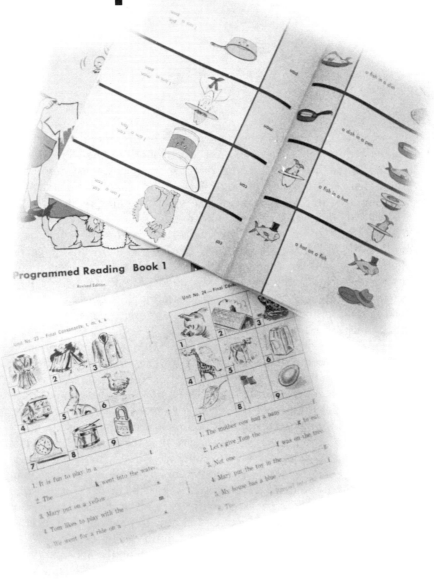

The whole is greater than the sum of its parts . . . .

A teacher who develops a communicative environment is teaching reading. A teacher who establishes a creative atmosphere in the classroom is teaching reading. A teacher who provides direct experiences and vicarious experiences, and a chance to talk about them, is teaching reading. A teacher who teaches speaking, listening, and writing skills is also teaching reading.

Reading skills are highly dependent on other communication skills. When Corrine learns to spell and write, she is working with the same visual media she works with as she reads. When Matthew learns to recognize a speaker's phonological, grammatical, and semantic signals and to think about what he is hearing, he is using the same skills he needs in reading. As Jerome expands his speaking vocabulary and his methods of arranging words grammatically, he is making it easier for himself to translate the printed page into meaningful units of language.

Reading is the interaction of two nearly simultaneous processes— decoding and comprehension. The decoding aspect of reading involves the reader in translating printed words into spoken (or unspoken) words. The comprehension aspect involves the reader in making sense out of the passage by relating it to personal experiences, by relying on his background of concepts and words, and, in general, by thinking about what is being read.

Perhaps by now you can see that reading needs to be taught in the context of the total language arts program (and also the total school program). However, there are times when you will need to teach certain reading skills in a manner which could be described as separate, distinct, and isolated experiences. Just as a budding artist sometimes needs isolated instruction on how to mix paints, how to get perspective, and how to produce various effects, the developing reader also needs isolated instruction at times.

Such isolated instruction is particularly necessary for most children who are learning the decoding skills related to phonic analysis, morphemic analysis, syllabic analysis, and contextual analysis. The purpose of this module, then, is to suggest means of providing such instruction. It is hoped, however, that the teacher will remember that the whole is greater than the sum of its parts; that learning to read is much more than the sum of the isolated exercises related to decoding skills.

The teacher should also remember that this module deals only with decoding skills and not comprehension or critical thinking skills—skills that are more important in the long run than decoding skills. Reading involves the interaction among the decoding, comprehension, and thinking skills. However, for the sake of emphasis, only the decoding skills will be discussed in this module.

Special Prerequisites for Module 8

It would be advisable to complete Modules 1–7 before beginning this module.

Long-range Outcomes Related to Module 8

This module should help you as a teacher to do the following:

1. Communicate with other professional educators about the teaching of decoding skills.
2. Use a variety of methods in teaching phonic analysis.
3. Develop children's structural analysis abilities.
4. Teach contextual analysis skills.
5. Develop children's sight vocabulary.
6. Develop children's readiness skills related to decoding skills.

Performance Objectives for Knowledge Level

To give yourself an overview of what is expected of you in this module, you should first scan the objectives and performance standards at all three levels—knowledge, simulation, and teaching. Then use the study guide during your reading of the module. As you find information related to the study guide, write it down in the available blanks or on a separate sheet of paper. Then review this information shortly before your knowledge level examination.

1.1 On a closed-book examination, you should be able to select the best alternative for each multiple-choice question and circle the letter of your choice. The multiple-choice questions (given in the study guide without the alternatives) will be selected from those shown below. Next to each one write the alternative that you predict will be the correct one on the examination.

1.2 On the same examination, you will be expected to provide information in short concise sentences either by producing a list or completing a list. The information called for is described in the study guide. Only some of the lists will be selected for the examination.

1.3 On the same examination, you will be asked to match terms with definitions, terms with illustrations, teaching methods with teacher behavior, and reading comprehension skills with learning activities related to those skills. The terms, teaching methods, and comprehension skills are described in the study guide.

Study Guide for Knowledge Level Examination

1. Phonic analysis requires three interrelated steps. List those three steps.

2. After each phonic analysis term give either a definition and/or an illustration.

    Word recognition

    Word analysis

    Regular words

    High frequency words

    Sight words

    Phonogram

    Phoneme

    Grapheme

    Consonant letter

    Vowel letter

    Consonant digraph

    Vowel digraph

    Consonant blend

    Diphthong

3. After each teaching method, write an example of teacher behavior that will remind you of the method. The first one has been done for you.

Family method   "Let's write down all the words you can think of that go with *bat, cat,* and *hat.*"

Whole-word phonics method

Rule or pattern method

Substitution method

Linguistics approach

Auxiliary symbols method

4. Write the steps for a remedial lesson on a phonic element. Rely on memory as much as you can. Some of the steps have been completed for you. Be prepared to provide a missing step on the examination.

Step 1   Provide meaningful context for introducing key words.

Step 2

Step 3

Step 4   Introduce auxiliary symbols if they will help.

Step 5

Step 6

Step 7 Provide additional practice with family words.

Step 8

Step 9

5. Relying on memory as much as possible, list the steps involved in teaching syllabic analysis and morphemic analysis and in developing a sight vocabulary. Some of the steps are already listed for you. Be prepared to provide a missing step on the examination.

Syllabic Analysis

1. Introduce sample words in context, visually and orally.

2.

3.

4. Have them develop a generalization and test it.

5.

Morphemic Analysis

1.

2. Help them discover and decode the root words.

3.

4.

5. Provide massed and distributed practice.

Sight Vocabulary

1.

2. Have them create a visual image of each word and then check it.

3.

4. Have them practice decoding the words in isolation.

5.

6.

6. The Basic Sight Vocabulary of Words is composed of irregular words only. What other three things can you say about these words?

7. Next to each reading readiness skill, describe briefly a learning activity which will help you remember how to teach this skill. (This will be a set of multiple-choice items on the examination.)

1. Auditory discrimination   Children close eyes; raise one finger if pair of words are the same.

2. Visual discrimination

3. Letter recognition

4. Left-to-right orientation

Performance Standards for Knowledge Level

A. Twenty-five minute time limit on 1.1–1.3 combined.

B. Completion deadline: instructor will notify.

C. Recommended grading standards if grades are used: 96% = A; 92% = A—; 88% = B; 84% = B—; 80% = C; below

80% = incomplete; should be completed at 80% or better before you go on to performance objectives for simulation level. (The instructor may wish to permit a grade of A or B only the first time the test is given in order to encourage more intensive study.)

Performance Objectives for Simulation Level

2.1 As a take-home exam, develop a lesson plan which will serve as a basis for "teaching" two or more of your peers any reading skill described in Module 8. The lesson plan is for your own use only and is not to be handed in. Hand in, instead, a tape recording of your lesson.

2.2 (Alternative objective to give you practice in team teaching) As a take-home exam, develop with two peers a written lesson plan, a tape of the lesson being taught by one of the team to the other two members, and a worksheet to follow the lesson.

2.3 (Alternative objective) As a take-home exam, compare two commercial reading programs and write up a report on your findings. Imagine you are trying to determine which program you want to use as a basic program with your students. Designate the grade level of your students.

Performance Standards for Simulation Level

A. For Objective 2.1 (Tape of Peer Teaching)
  1. Shows, by her efforts to evaluate the progress of "students" during the lesson, that she has clear-cut performance objectives in mind.
  2. Shows a clear understanding of the reading element being taught.
  3. Uses instructional steps in a defensible order.
  4. Uses learning principles effectively; does not violate any of those discussed in Module 3.

B. For Objective 2.2 (Team Teaching)
  1. The lesson plan has appropriately worded performance objectives which relate directly to the long-range outcome; the learning activities relate to both the performance objectives and the long-range outcome.
  2. The tape shows that the "teacher" is aware of the performance objectives and the long-range outcome and has a clear understanding of the reading element being taught.
  3. The worksheet relates to the performance objectives and long-range outcome and also demonstrates a clear understanding of the reading element being taught.

C. For Objective 2.3 (Evaluation of Commercial Reading Programs)
   1. Makes specific comparisons on specific skill development, e.g., compares method of teaching vowel pattern recognition in the two programs.
   2. Shows understanding of the reading skills being compared.
   3. Compares several different types of skills and how they are developed. Not limited to one or two examples.
   4. Compares up-to-date programs.
   5. No spelling or punctuation errors in report.
   6. Typed (or highly legible handwriting).

D. For Objectives 2.1–2.3
   1. Suggested grading standards if grades are used: should be completed at C level or better before going on to performance objectives for the teaching level. (Grade based on judgment of instructor and/or peers.)
   2. For objective 2.2, the instructor may wish either to give a team grade or to grade one member of the team on the written lesson plan, another member on the tape, and the other member on the worksheet.
   3. Additional standards or modified standards may be developed by the instructor and/or teachers-in-training. It is best, however, to state these standards in advance of the required performance.

Performance Objectives for Teaching Level

3.1 In a micro-teaching, observation, student teaching, intern, or supervised teaching situation, teach a brief lesson (about fifteen to thirty minutes) to two or more students. The subject of the lesson can be any reading skill you wish. Lesson plan, worksheet, and self-critique are required. See Module 4 for what to include.

Performance Standards for Teaching Level

A. Simulation standards A–1 through A–4 should be appropriate.
B. Simulation standards B–1 and B–3 should be appropriate.
C. Additional standards or modified standards may be developed by the cooperating teacher, instructor, supervisor, and/or teachers-in-training. It is best, of course, to state these standards in advance of the required performance.

Word Recognition and Reading

Since reading includes both word recognition (decoding) and comprehension, you won't be able to actually read the sentence below. But you *will* be able to decode it by noticing phonological, grammatical, and semantic clues. What does the following sentence "say"?

> The indefeasible and repathic customs of insabulation have been highly resistant to innumerable endeavors to modify them.

In the process of decoding this sentence, you probably relied on four of the basic word recognition skills. You relied on visual memory (your sight vocabulary) to decode words like *The, and, customs, of,* and so on. You relied on structural analysis when you noticed the affixes *in, ible, re,* and *tion,* and when you unconsciously divided words like *indefeasible* and *repathic* into syllables. You relied on phonic analysis when you decided that the syllable *path* in *re-pathic* probably rhymes with *bath* rather than *bathe*; that the syllable *feas* in *indefeasible* probably rhymes with *please* rather than *face*. And you relied on contextual analysis when you expected a word like *change* or *modify* to occur before *them*. Contextual analysis also told you that *indefeasible* and *repathic* describe the nature of the customs.

If you had used a particular study skill—looking up words in a dictionary—you would have found that *indefeasible* simply means not to be stopped. You would have found that *repathic* and *insabulation* are not in the dictionary (but are imaginary words).

In reality, word recognition and comprehension cannot be separated. Take the following sentence, for example:

> Birch bark is smooth but oak bark is rough.

Sometimes the recognition (decoding) of a word, such as *rough* occurs a split second before the comprehending takes place. For instance, Carla remembers seeing the word *rough* many times before and decodes it from visual memory immediately. Then she realizes that it applies to another word in the sentence. Clarence, on the other hand, might comprehend *rough* a split second before he decodes it (translates it into speech or thought) simply because he expected the word *rough* to occur in the sentence.

In the following material, each of the word recognition skills will be discussed separately although they too operate together in the process of decoding.

Phonic Analysis

Communicating About Phonic Analysis

Phonics is the science of phonetics applied to the act of reading. Phonic analysis is much more sophisticated than just sounding out words. For example, how would you sound out the nonsense word, *cibby?* Should it be pronounced *sĭb by* or *kĭb by?* If you either remember or intuitively use the phonic generalization that *c* before *i, y,* or *e* usually has the soft sound, you'll pronounce it *sĭb by.* Or will you? Perhaps it should be *sī'by,* using a long *i* sound instead of a short *i* sound. No, not if you noticed the consonant pair in the middle of the word, a phonic signal which warns you that the preceding vowel should probably be short. Or perhaps you recognized the first syllable to be *cib,* a VC pattern (vowel-consonant pattern), which signals a probable short vowel sound.

At any rate, you can see that phonic analysis is more than merely sounding out the letters. (Think what a mess you'd have if you merely sounded out the word *knight.*) To be more precise, then, phonic analysis requires three interrelated steps: (1) the recognition of the phonic signals consisting of graphemes and grapheme *patterns,* (2) the translation of graphemes into phonemes, and (3) the blending of the phonemes aloud or silently into a single syllable or word. To get a better grasp of this definition, test it out on the nonsense word *dissabulate.* See if you can detect the three interconnecting steps. (You'll have to do a bit of structural analysis first by dividing the word into syllables.)

One more thing on the definition of phonic analysis: Does phonic analysis simply mean pronunciation? No, it does not. In fact, the purpose of instruction in phonic analysis is *not* to teach children to *pronounce* words. Most children learning to read should already know how to pronounce the words they meet in print; that is, these words should first be made part of their speaking vocabulary. What phonic analysis allows them to do is *translate* the printed words into familiar spoken words.

When teachers share ideas for teaching phonic analysis skills, they use certain terms. These same terms are used (although somewhat inconsistently) by authors of teaching manuals, by remedial reading consultants, and by other people in the profession. Some of the terms will also be useful to you directly in your teaching as you communicate with children. As you study the terms, you will be tested on them to help you remember them better.

Word recognition—The process of decoding printed words by any means available, including visual memory of sight words, sentence context, related pictures, phonic elements and patterns, syllabication patterns, and other structural clues such as prefixes and suffixes, and the diacritical marks and respellings in dictionaries. Terms used as synonyms for word recognition are *word perception* or simply *decoding.*

Some authors use the term *word recognition* to mean both perceiving the word and understanding the concept it represents. Its use in this book, however, will be in reference to *decoding* a word, which is to say, the printed word is translated into its vocal or subvocal equivalent, i.e., it is pronounced aloud or silently, thus transforming the printed symbol into an oral one.[1]

Word analysis—The process of decoding printed words by means of phonic, structural, contextual, or dictionary analysis. Word analysis skills are sometimes referred to as *word attack skills* or *word identification skills.* For all

---

[1] The term *decoding* has become more popular in the profession and may some day supersede the more ambiguous term, *word recognition.* However, it should be again pointed out that *decoding,* to some people, means both the translation of words into their vocal or subvocal equivalents and also the comprehension of the words. *Decoding* is used in this book to refer to the former process of translation only.

practical purposes, the term *word anslysis skills* refers to all those word recognition skills, other than the use of visual memory, which are used for decoding written words.

Regular words—Words which are spelled the way they sound or are spelled according to highly consistent spelling conventions. The word *nation,* for example, is generally considered a regular or phonetic word, because the first syllable is spelled the way it sounds (*nā*), and the last syllable is spelled according to the most common way of spelling the *shun* sound at the end of a word. Other regular or phonetic words are *man, hope,* and *laboratory.* Which of these do you think are regular words—*run, bear, hate, other, that, do, democratic?*[2]

High frequency words—Words which continually reoccur in printed materials. Some of them are regular in their spelling, but many of them are not. An example of a high frequency word that isn't regular is *the.* An example of a high frequency word that is regular is *can.*

Sight words—Words in print that a student can recognize instantly without taking the time to analyze them. Probably every word you are reading in this sentence is a sight word for you. You have seen them so often you do not need to take the time to use your word analysis skills to help you decode them. Some people use the term *sight words* to refer to those irregular words which must be learned by sight (*visual memory*) rather than by phonic analysis. A less ambiguous term for these might be *irregular sight words.*

Before you are overcome by the jargon, let's stop a moment for a brief review of the five terms already introduced. See if you can complete the matching quiz which follows. (Answers will be found at the end of the quiz. You may use more than one letter for some of the answers.)

QUIZ ON PHONICS TERMINOLOGY (PART 1)

_____ 1. Words which continually recur in reading materials for children.

_____ 2. Words in print that are recognized instantly without analysis.

_____ 3. Words which are spelled phonetically.

_____ 4. The process of decoding printed words by means of visual memory, phonic analysis, structural analysis, contextual analysis, and the use of dictionaries.

_____ 5. The process of decoding printed words by means of phonic, structural, or contextual analysis, or by using a dictionary.

a. sight words
b. high frequency words
c. regular words
d. word analysis
e. word recognition
f. word identification
g. word perception
h. word attack

Answers to Quiz on Phonics Terminology (Part 1)

1. b   4. e, g
2. a   5. d, f, h
3. c

[2] If you considered every other word, starting with *run,* to be a regular word, you were right.

Phonogram—From the practical standpoint, a convenient combination of letters used for teaching some of the regular words. The *at* combination, for example, is a phonogram for teaching such words as *at, bat, cat, fat, hat,* and *mat.* What would be a useful phonogram for teaching such words as *bill, kill, chill* and *fill?* (A phonogram is sometimes referred to as a graphoneme.)

Phoneme—The smallest unit of meaningful speech. Over forty phonemes in the English language have been classified, although linguists don't agree on the exact number. Linguists discover the different phonemes in a language by determining what changes in speech sounds indicate changes in meaning. For example, the first phoneme in the spoken word, *bet,* is the *b* sound, represented as /b/. If the first phoneme is changed to /p/, we have a change in meaning, from *bet* to *pet.*

Grapheme—A written symbol used to represent a phoneme. Table 5.1 in Module 5 contains a list of most of the graphemes used in American English. You will remember that sometimes two letters are used as one grapheme to represent a single phoneme, as in the word *chin* which contains only three graphemes—*ch, i,* and *n*—but four letters. Occasionally, more than two letters are used, as in the word *right* which uses *igh* as a single grapheme to represent the long *i* sound.

How many graphemes are used to write the word *this?* How many letters? How many phonemes are used to *say* the word? (Answers: three, four, and three.) How many graphemes are used to write the word *salt?* How many letters? How many phonemes are used to say the word? How about the word *lake?*

Some people mix up the words *grapheme* and *phoneme.* This might be avoided by remembering that *grapheme* comes from the Greek root *graph,* meaning drawn or written. The word *phoneme* has the Greek root *phono,* meaning sound or voice.

Consonant letter—A single letter used to represent a speech sound called a consonant. A consonant is formed by impeding a stream of breath with the lips, tongue, teeth, or palate. Try making the /t/ sound, for instance. What parts of the mouth were used to impede your breath? Some people consider a consonant to be a letter, although strictly speaking this is not correct. (It might help to remember that *consonant* comes from the Latin *sonare,* meaning to sound.) Consonant *letters* include those in our alphabet other than *a, e, i, o,* and *u.*

Vowel letter—A single letter used to represent a speech sound called a vowel. A vowel is made by controlling the size and shape of the mouth cavity with the tongue. To see for yourself how vowels are produced, place an index finger in your mouth almost up to the second knuckle; now rest your teeth on your knuckle and slowly pronounce some of the vowel sounds, such as /ā/, /ē/, /ī/, and /ō/. The vowel *letters* are *a, e, i, o, u,* and sometimes *y.* (Some people include *w* in the list because of the sound made in words like *how* and *show;* the *w* by itself, though, is not a vowel letter.)

Consonant digraph—Two consonant letters used in combination to represent a single phoneme. (The word *digraph* was borrowed from the Greek *di* meaning two and *graph* meaning written.) The word is pronounced (dī /graf) and is often *mispronounced* as (dī/a/graf). Two of the consonant digraphs are *th* as in *this* and *ck* as in *luck.* How many consonant digraphs are in the word *thick?* (Answer: two) Some of the other consonant digraphs include *ch,* as in *church,* and *ph,* as in *phonograph.* What are the digraphs in *chick?*

Vowel digraph—Two vowel letters used in combination to represent a single phoneme. What is the vowel digraph in *boat?* What phoneme does the digraph represent—long o /ō/ or short o /ŏ/? What is the vowel digraph in *cheat?* What phoneme does it represent?

Consonant blend—Two or three consonant phonemes slurred together. What letters represent the consonant blend in *flop?* Notice that the *f* sound and the *l* sound are both heard in the *fl* blend. What letters represent the consonant blend in *spring?* What three phonemes are slurred together? Do the first two letters in *skill* represent a consonant blend or are they a consonant digraph? Since you can hear the *s* sound /s/ and *k* sound /k/ as separate but slurred phonemes, the *sk* represents a blend. The distinction between a consonant digraph and two letters representing a consonant blend is usually easy to make. It is obvious, for instance, in the word *thin* that the /t/ and the /h/ are *not* being blended together. Therefore, the *th* is considered a digraph. Perhaps the only real trouble makers are the *nk* as in *bank* and the *ng* as in *bang,* both of

QUIZ ON PHONICS TERMINOLOGY (PART 2)

Directions: In the blank next to each term write the letter corresponding to the example which illustrates the term.

	a	b	c	d	e	f
_____ 6. consonant letter	u	th	b	cl	oi	oa
_____ 7. grapheme	ill	ight	ch	ed	re	boy
_____ 8. consonant blend	/t/	/sh/	/ght/	/scr/	/at/	/ā/
_____ 9. vowel digraph	i	m	ck	bl	at	oa
_____ 10. useful phonogram	ThrASH	THRAsh	THRASh	tHRASh	Thrash	ThraSH
_____ 11. diphthong	/ē/	/wh/	/n/	/st/	/oi/	/ill/
_____ 12. vowel letter	a	sh	v	sn	oa	oy
_____ 13. consonant digraph	a	oy	p	br	sh	ea
_____ 14. phoneme	/it/	/ing/	/igh/	/bl/	/ē/	/st/

Answers to Quiz on Phonics Terminology (Part 2)

6. c	11. e
7. c	12. a
8. d	13. e
9. f	14. e
10. a	

which are often considered to be digraphs, but some people call them blends. What do you think they should be called? [3]

Diphthong—Two vowels blended together. When two vowels slur together, as in *boil,* you have what linguists call a diphthong, usually pronounced dif´/thong but sometimes pronounced dip´/thong. Linguists do not agree on the exact number of diphthongs, but for reading teachers, the two most important ones are the /oi/ sound and the /ou/ sound. These two sounds are usually represented four ways in print. The /oi/ sound is represented either by *oy* as in *boy* or *oi* as in *toil.* The /ou/ sound is represented either by *ow* as in *cow* or *ou* as in *out.*

Now let's see how well you have learned the last nine terms. Answers will be found at the end of the quiz on page 283. Performance standard for mastery: eight out of nine.

A Warning About Phonics Instruction

Why should phonics be taught? One could learn to "read" merely by memorizing sight words, as long as you always have someone around to say, "That word is *fantastic*" or "this word is *rescue.*" But it would be impossible to become an independent reader without learning phonic analysis or the visual counterpart called the linguistics approach. But phonics is only one tool of the independent reader. The more mature readers become, the less they rely on phonics.

The fact that our spelling system is consistent enough to justify time spent on phonics in the classroom should not lead a teacher either to overemphasize it or go to the other extreme and be overly concerned with the exceptions to phonics rules that are frequently encountered. *Phonics is merely one tool to use in making an intelligent guess as to the oral equivalent of a printed word. In nearly every case, it is best to temper phonic analysis with contextual analysis.*

In other words, the child learning to read needs to be taught to ask these two questions as he employs phonic analysis. What are the most likely sounds in this word? Do these sounds make sense in this sentence? Take this sentence as an example: *Tom went to live with grandmother.* The child who uses phonic analysis and only phonic analysis on the word *live* is in for trouble. Phonic analysis will be quite helpful on the beginning phoneme /l/ and the ending phoneme /v/, but it doesn't work on the middle phoneme /i/ because the VCE pattern (vowel-consonant-final e pattern) in *live* indicates a long vowel sound. Thus, total reliance on phonic analysis would produce /līv/ instead of /lĭv/. Only contextual analysis can get the reader back on the track: /līv/ does not make sense, but /lĭv/ does. Phonics is a probability game. A child should be taught to use phonics in the spirit of a detective playing his hunches on the basis of the available evidence.

As a final warning, it is important to realize that not all children can learn to decode through the use of a phonics approach. Some children have very poor auditory discrimination and auditory memory abilities, abilities which

[3] Some authors find the term *consonant blend* to be one which confuses people, since some use it to refer to sounds and others use it to refer to letters. To avoid this confusion they use the term *consonant cluster* to refer to the letters that represent the consonant blend.

Phonics is only one tool among the many tools of the mature reader.

are necessary prerequisites to the use of phonics. The linguistics approach which emphasizes visual discrimination rather than auditory discrimination is generally the best way to help those children. This type of approach is also quite useful for those children whose home language is not English, such as those who speak Spanish, a language with some phonic elements differing from English.

Methods of Teaching Phonic Analysis

A variety of methods for teaching phonics have been developed over the years, but none of them has been demonstrated to be superior by carefully controlled experimental studies. In fact, it is quite doubtful that method *alone* is the main factor in teaching success. There are probably other important factors, such as teacher enthusiasm, insight into the individual differences of children, the development of children's readiness skills before a method is applied, and so on. As a teacher, you will need to acquire the ability to select that method which is most appropriate for a child under certain conditions. The very least one might expect of a trained teacher is that she is aware of various methods and is flexible enough to try another one if the first one doesn't work.

The Whole Word Phonics Method

This approach is used in many reading programs and probably should be acquired by the reading teacher as one of the basic instructional tools. In its most systematic form, the children are gradually introduced to the most common graphemes and their respective phonemes. Rather than being introduced to them in isolation, however, they are introduced in the context of words and sentences and often in stories as well. For example, for introducing the *ch* grapheme, the children are shown such words as *church, chin,* and *chop.* These words are pronounced by the teacher and then the children. The children are shown, or they discover, that the /ch/ sound is spelled *ch* in these words. Then they are given practice in *hearing* the /ch/ phoneme in words, in *recognizing* the *ch* grapheme in words, and sometimes in *writing* the grapheme. (This method, as well as other methods, will be demonstrated in the next section.)

The Rule or Pattern Method

This technique is sometimes used as an auxiliary method to the whole word phonics method. It is used primarily to strengthen a child's ability to decode several of the vowel graphemes and a few of the consonant graphemes. One of the common rules which children are taught is as follows: In one-syllable words containing two or more vowel letters, the first vowel letter usually represents the long vowel sound and the second vowel letter is silent. This rule often is taught to children this way: When two vowels go walking, the first one does the talking.

Those teachers who feel that verbal rules are inaccurate and too hard for children to remember sometimes teach patterns instead. The rule just stated, for example, would be taught as two patterns: the VCE pattern, as in *cake, ripe,* and *note,* and the VV pattern, as in *rain, boat,* and *beat.* Children are taught to recognize these patterns in unknown words and to predict the long vowel sound for the words. Both the rules and the patterns are subject to many exceptions, of course, but if exceptions are carefully controlled at first and the rules or patterns are treated as probability statements, this approach seems to be quite useful in helping most children.

Several studies have been made on the usefulness or consistency of the many phonic generalizations or patterns which have been taught (2, 9, 13, 15). These studies have made it obvious that only a few of the generalizations are consistent enough or relate to enough words to make them worth teaching. The seven rules related to *c, g, r,* and the major vowel patterns are probably worth teaching (see pages 173–74 in Module 5).

The Family Method

The most common form of this approach is that of using family words, such as *bat, cat, fat,* etc., all of them based on the final phonogram *at.* The use of family words can be very helpful in *introducing* children to letter sounds. By keeping the *at* phonogram constant, for instance, one can expose the learner to several consonant letters and their respective sounds, while at the same time, emphasizing the sound of the final *t* and the usual sound of the *a* in a VC pattern, e.g., *bat, cat, fat, hat, mat, pat, rat, sat,* etc.

This method, along with the linguistics approach to be described later, seems to be particularly useful for children who have difficulty with phonic methods that require a considerable degree of auditory discrimination. Evidently, when the final sound of the one-syllable word is held constant, as in the case of the *at* phonogram, it is easier for them to *see* the difference between words starting in *b* such as *bat* and words starting in *c* such as *cat.* Furthermore, they can concentrate on initial graphemes, such as *b* vs. *c* and essentially ignore the known phonogram, such as *at*. In other words, the need for *hearing* differences is less crucial with this method than *seeing* differences.

Let's compare the family method with the pattern method just described, Henry sees the word *man*. With the pattern method, he would recognize the VC spelling pattern. This would tell him that the *a* has the short *a* sound. He would then recall the sound of short *a*, the sound of *m* and the sound of *n*. He would blend these three sounds together in the proper order and decode the word as /man/. With the family method, he would notice the *an* phonogram and recall that the sound of this phonogram is /an/. He would then recall that the sound of *m* is /m/, and, finally, he would blend the /m/ and /an/ and decode the word as /man/. The major difference between these two methods is that with the family method, Henry didn't have to recall the vowel sound in isolation, a skill which children with auditory discrimination and memory problems seem to have difficulty mastering.

It is important with this method to show children that whereas ending phonograms such as *at* and *ig* have a consistent sound in one-syllable words, they are not as consistent in words with more than one syllable, such as *nation, inflating* and *obliging*.

The Substitution Method

After learning one or more key words by sight (visual memory), the child is taught to use those sight words to unlock new words. For instance, a child is first taught to recognize *dog, dig,* and *dive* by sight and then to "discover" that the *d* represents the same sound for each of them (the whole-word phonics method). He is then taught to make substitutions based on this discovery. "This word is *pen*," says the teacher, pointing to *pen*. Then, pointing to *den*, she asks, "What word is this? It begins like *dog*." Gradually, the child is taught to make more complicated substitutions, such as those required for the word *shake*. By remembering a key word such as *shoe*, he can decode the first grapheme in the word as /sh/. By remembering a key word such as *cake*, he can decode the final phonogram as /āk/. Then he blends the two parts: /sh/ and /āk/. There are many variations of this approach, but its chief element is that of reliance on known words to help one decode new words.

The Linguistics Approach

In its "purest" form, this is a highly visual, substitution approach. Through the use of regular words, such as *can, fan,* and *man*, the child is expected to "discover" how to decode graphemes without the necessity of being taught the sounds represented by letters. In other words, the child doesn't have to be directly taught to associate a given sound with a given letter. The emphasis is on *seeing* the difference in letters rather than hearing their related sounds. Notice these contrasting pairs of words, for example: *man–mat, ant–man, fat–cat*. In all three examples, you will notice a use of *minimum contrast* in the spelling of the words. The word *man* is contrasted with *mat, ant* is contrasted with *man, fat* is contrasted with *cat*. The purpose of the minimum contrast technique is to help the children *see* the difference in graphemes and, thus, see the differences in meaning that are signalled by the differences in graphemes. With the linguistics approach, highly regular words are used whenever possible. The use of highly regular words, of course, makes it easier for the children to accurately predict how words should be decoded.

The Auxiliary Symbols Method

Some early reading programs have been designed with the intent of easing the pain of phonic analysis by introducing symbols which supplement the alphabetical ones. The *Early-to-Read i/t/a Program* (26), for example, uses an alphabet devised by Sir James Pitman, in which the q and x are eliminated, and twenty additional characters are added. This forty-four grapheme system is probably easier to learn than our twenty-six letter system because each phoneme is usually spelled in only one way. In the i/t/a program, for example, the a in *face* is spelled æ , the a in *father* is spelled a, the a in *ball* is spelled au, and the a in *cap* is spelled a, Thus, once the child learns the augmented alphabet, he does not have to guess which sound represented by the letter a should be used in the decoding process. Contrary to a prevalent myth, this approach is not THE approach used in Great Britain, although several experiments with i/t/a have been carried out there, and the i/t/a approach is being used in some parts of both Great Britain and the United States. Research so far seems to indicate that this approach does not cause serious problems, for *most* children, with spelling or with the transition to reading the traditional alphabet. On the other hand, there seems to be no conclusive evidence that it is a superior method to other methods employing systematic instruction in the decoding process (6).

Another auxiliary symbol approach is that of *Words in Color* (18) which provides children with color clues to the correct way to decode certain spelling patterns. Thirty-nine different colors are used, with each color representing a different phoneme. All graphemes used for the same phoneme are shown in the same color band on a wall chart. For example, all the long a spellings—*a, ay, eigh, ea, ey, aigh, ei,* and *ai*—are represented by the same color.

A skillful reading teacher is capable of using a variety of phonics methods.

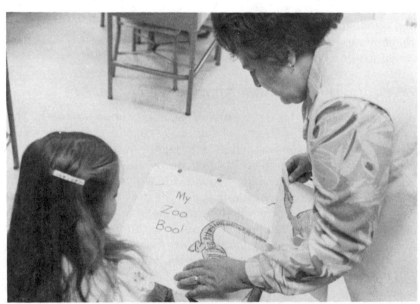

There appears to be no conclusive evidence that this approach is superior to other approaches which incorporate systematic instruction in phonics.

An auxiliary symbol approach in which diacritical marks have been employed has been tested by Fry (16). Long vowels, for instance, were indicated by a macron, as in *hē* and *rēạd*. Silent letters were shown by slash marks. Fry's study compared the reading achievement of those taught with regular materials and those taught with the same materials marked with diacritical symbols. There was no difference in achievement at the end of first, second, or third grades (17).

Sample Phonics Lessons Using An Eclectic Multi-sensory Approach

Now that you've examined a variety of approaches used in teaching phonic analysis skills, let's see how a lesson using "the best" of several approaches might look. First we'll look at how the decoding of a vowel letter might be taught; and then, a consonant letter.

Most teachers prefer to use commercial materials, such as a basal reading program for most lessons. The two sample lessons, therefore, should be considered aids in developing teacher-made lessons for assisting those children who have need of review or remedial instruction.

Sample Phonics Lesson Decoding the Letter A in a VCE Pattern

Long-range Outcome: Decoding printed words via phonic signals.

Performance Objectives:
1. Given words such as *hate, hat, rat, rate,* and *paste* written on the chalkboard, each child will be able to come up to the board during the lesson and circle one word which probably has a long *a* sound in it.
2. Given the worksheet which follows the lesson, each child will be able to do each of the five tasks with no more than one error per task.
3. When I ask each individual to decode out loud five of the words which he has circled on his worksheet and which I point to at random, he will be able to decode at least four of them.

Prerequisite Readiness Skills:
1. Ability to visually differentiate letters in the alphabet.
2. Ability to differentiate the sounds of the letters in the alphabet.
3. Ability to recognize and name most of the letters, digraphs, and blends.
4. Previously demonstrated understanding of the terms *vowel letter, consonant letter, digraph,* and *blend.*

Procedures: [4]
1. (Meaningful context for whole word phonics approach) Put several sentences on the chalkboard or a paper chart. Underline

---
[4]You may not be able to complete all of the steps in one sitting.

those words which demonstrate a long *a* in a VCE pattern, for example:

Bobby went to a *lake* yesterday.

He saw a *snake* in a rocky *place*.

He put it in a jar to keep it *safe*.

When he got home he put it in a *cage*.

2. (Whole word phonics) Read the sentences to the children, moving your hand under the words as you read. Then have the children pronounce each underlined word after you. Ask them what *sound* is the same in each underlined word. Have them make the vowel sound with you. Call it the long *a* sound. Read several words to them. Have them close their eyes and put up their hands whenever they hear a word which has a long *a* sound in it. Some words that might be used are *hate, hat, rat, rate, rope, cap, cape, car, paste, past, man, mane,* and *men.*

3. (Whole word phonics and linguistics emphasis on regular words) Refer to the underlined words in the *sentences.* Ask the children what *letters* are the same in each underlined word. Point out to them that the long *a* sound is often spelled with an *a* in the middle of the word and an *e* at the end. Put other words on the chalkboard or chart (same words used in Step 2) and ask *each* child to come up and circle a word which *probably* has a long *a* sound in it. (Assumption: teacher is instructing a small group rather than the whole class.)

4. (Auxiliary symbols) Ask the children if they can hear the long *a* sound in each of the underlined and circled words. Ask them if they can actually hear the *e* sound in any of the underlined and circled words. Tell them that the final *e* in those words is called a silent letter and draw slash marks through each final *e* in the underlined words. Have a child find the silent *e* in each circled word and draw a slash mark through it. Then show them a way to indicate the long *a* sound by drawing a macron over each *a* in the underlined words, e.g., snākė. Have a child mark the circled words in the same way.

5. (Pattern and rule) Above the underlined words, write the letters VCE to correspond to the last three letters in each word. Remind them that V stands for a vowel letter and tell them that E stands for a final *e*. Ask them what C stands for. (It stands for either a consonant letter, digraph, or blend.) Ask them whether the circled words also have the VCE pattern. Write words like these on the board or chart: *fame, frame, mad, made, hat,* and *hate.* Have children label those which have a VCE pattern. Ask them what vowel sound they hear in the labeled words. Ask them if anyone can make up a rule about the sound of *a* in words having a VCE pattern. Accept anything approximating this: The letter *a* usually has a long vowel sound in words that have a VCE pattern. For contrast, label those words with a VC

pattern and briefly discuss the difference in sound and spelling pattern between words like *mad* and *made, hat* and *hate.*

6. (Substitution) Put word pairs like these on the board or chart: *lice* and *lace, line* and *lane, coke* and *cake, spice* and *space, mote* and *mate.* For each pair, tell the children what the first word is and ask a child what the second one is, e.g., "This word is *lice.* What word is this, Janet?" (Have at least one pair for each child in the small group.)

7. (Family words) Ask children to think of words that rhyme with *lake.* Write them on the board as they say them, placing them in a vertical column so that the VCE pattern is emphasized. When a word has a homophone, such as *brake* and *break,* and you think the child may be referring to the homophone which doesn't fit the VCE pattern, put both spellings on the board, but put the one which doesn't fit the pattern in a separate column.

8. (Practice in context) Put a few sentences such as the following on the board (or better yet, put them on a chart ahead of the lesson):

She *gave* me her (hate) (hat) to wear.

I did not *save* my cake. I (at) (ate) it.

I *have* a (rat) (rate) in a *cage.*

She *came* (paste) (past) the *lake.*

After reading the underlined words with them, ask them if all the underlined words have a long *a* sound in them. Point out that the VCE pattern *usually* indicates a long *a* sound but not always, e.g., *have:* "You have to check to see if the way you say the word makes sense in the sentence." Then, for each sentence have a child go up to the board and circle the word in parentheses which makes sense in the sentence. Have this child read the complete sentence out loud with your help, if necessary.

9. (Individual practice and evaluation) Explain the worksheet which you give them for independent work. For the students, of course, the worksheet will provide additional practice. To strengthen the impact of the practice, be sure the worksheet requires some writing and not just checking or circling. For the teacher, the worksheet will provide information on which students need additional help.

In summary, the nine steps recommended in the first sample lesson were as follows:

1. Provide *meaningful context* for introducing key words.
2. Help them discover the *common phoneme* in each word.
3. Lead them to discover the *common letter* in each word.
4. Introduce *auxiliary symbols* if they will help.

5. Discuss regular *spelling pattern* if it is demonstrated.
6. Use *substitution* technique to provide more practice.
7. Provide additional practice with *family words*.
8. Provide practice in *context*.
9. Explain the *worksheet*.

The order of the nine steps need not be exactly the same as those recommended; nor should exactly the same format be used in every lesson. There are a multitude of play-type exercises which a teacher can use to provide variety. Books which contain such exercises are listed in the bibliography at the end of this module. In the previous lesson, for instance, the children as a group might have been challenged to see how many words rhyming with *lake* they can think of in exactly one minute.[5]

Sample Worksheet for the Lesson Long A in the VCE Pattern

(Note: All directions should be explained to the group before they begin to work individually on the worksheet.)

1. Write four words which rhyme with *came*. The first one is partly done for you. (Teacher reads this and other directions and explains them if necessary.)

   c a m e   b l __ m __   _____   _____   _____

2. Circle the words which probably have a long *a* sound in them. One of them is already circled for you. See if you can say the words that you circle.

   (face)   fast   gate   chase   chair   grade

   cave   snap   take   fat   last   fate

3. For each word that has a VCE spelling pattern, write VCE above it. One of them has already been done . See if you can say the words that you mark.

   VCE
   place   lace   rack   rake   lamb   lame

   mat   mate   bald   bale   trace   chase

4. For any word which has a VCE pattern, put a macron over the *a* and a slash mark through the silent e.[6] One has been done for you. See if you can say the words that you mark.

   wāste   made   mad   scrap   scrape   male

   ball   grass   grace   can   cane   bathe

[5]More ideas on adding variety to lessons were suggested in Module 3. You may also wish to examine the games described in Appendix B.
[6]It is assumed that these terms have already been explained to the children.

5. Circle the word which makes sense in each sentence. One has been done for you. (Teacher reads these before children begin worksheet.)

He wore my (hat) (hate).

My horse is (lamb) (lame).

I (hat) (hate) that bad man.

I went to a candy (salt) (sale).

That is a very (fat) (fate) man.

Sample Phonics Lessons on the Letter P

Procedures: (Objectives, prerequisites, and worksheet have been omitted.)

1. (Meaningful context) Write the Peter Piper jingle on the chalkboard or a paper chart. (It is probably best to use jingles only occasionally and generally to use more meaningful material.) Underline the words which contain the /p/ sound.

   Peter Piper picked a *peck* of *pickled peppers.*

   If *Peter Piper* picked a *peck* of *pickled peppers,*

   Where's the *peck* of *pickled peppers Peter Piper* picked?

2. (Common phoneme) Have children who know the Peter Piper jingle read the jingle with you. Ask them what *sound* they hear in most of the words? Have them make the /p/ sound with you. Try *not* to add a noticeable vowel sound as you demonstrate the /p/ sound. Keep your hand under your chin to remind you not to drop your jaw. (The children can do this too.) All that should be heard is the explosion of air escaping through your lips. (If you find it impossible to say the /p/ sound without distorting it with an added vowel sound, you will have to say something like this: "The sound that the letter *p* stands for is the first sound you hear in each of the underlined words." (This approach, however, makes it difficult for you to correct a child's distortion, which might cause her trouble later in blending phonemes that make up a word.)

   Now read several words to them. Have them close their eyes and put up their hands whenever they hear a word which has a /p/ sound in it. Some words which might be used are *penny, bunny, peach, pear, apple, banana, fun, trip, bear,* and *nap.*

3. (Common letter) Refer to the underlined words in the jingle. Ask them what *letter* is the same in each underlined word. Point out to them that the /p/ sound is always spelled with the letter *p*. Write other words on the chalkboard or chart (same words used in Step 2) and ask *each* child to come up and circle a word which has the /p/ sound in it.

4. (Auxiliary symbols) None are really necessary for the letter *p*, although some teachers like to use a picture to remind the chil-

dren of the /p/ sound. A sketch of Peter Piper, for example, or a picture of a pickle might be used.

5. (Pattern and rule) There is no easily defined spelling pattern associated with the letter *p*, nor is there any verbal rule which might be helpful.

6. (Substitution) Put word pairs like these on the board or chart: *man* and *pan, man* and *map, fail* and *pail, teach* and *peach, tin* and *pin, tin* and *tip, rage* and *page, wide* and *wipe, wipe* and *pipe*. For each pair, tell them what the first word is and ask a child what the second one is, e.g., "This word is *man*. What word is this, Ronny?"

7. (Family words) Ask children to think of words which rhyme with *cap*. Write them on the board or chart as they say them, placing them in a vertical column so that the final *p* is emphasized. You may wish to do the same with *lip*.

8. (Practice in context) Put a few sentences such as the following on the board or chart:

   a. My dog is my (bet) (pet).

   b. I see a (pig) (dig).

   c. He is a (big) (pig) dog.

   d. I can put the cake in the (fan) (pan).

   e. I put the (pack) (back) on my (pack) (back).

   Help the children read each one (with your help when necessary) and select the word in parentheses which makes sense in the sentence.

9. (Individual practice and evaluation) Explain the worksheet which you give them for independent work. Make sure the worksheet provides for some writing and not just checking or circling. Check worksheets to see who still needs help.

Developing Children's Structural Analysis Abilities

Although phonic analysis (or the visual counterpart called the linguistics approach) is necessary for a child who is first learning to read and is sometimes required by the mature reader, it is generally a slow method of decoding. It is especially slow when the reader finds it necessary to decode every letter, digraph, or blend in a word one at a time, e.g., u-n-s-e-l-e-c-t-e-d. Therefore, at the same time that the teacher is giving students a firm foundation in phonics, he should begin to wean them away from an overreliance on phonic signals.

One way of doing this is to gradually introduce them to the concept that a printed word represents larger segments of sound and meaning than mere phonemes. For example, what would be some larger segments of sound and meaning represented by the word *unselected*? In print, this word represents four distinct "grunts." These four grunts, called syllables, are represented by *un, se, lec,* and *ted,* with *lec* being the loudest one. The word *unselected* also represents three meaningful units called morphemes: *un, select,* and *ed.* Each unit is meaningful in that taking it away would *change* the meaning. The difference between *select* and *selected,* for example, is the difference between present and past. The difference between *selected* and *unselected* is the difference between positive and negative.

So what we have, then, is a printed word that represents not only phonemes but morphemes and syllables as well. The task of the teacher is to help the child learn how to translate the printed word into all three types of units, gradually putting more reliance on morphemes and syllables since this usually reduces the time spent in decoding a word.

Teaching children to recognize morphemes and syllables can begin very early in a developmental program. It is possible to introduce the word *cats,* for example, shortly after the word *cat* has been thoroughly learned. After several experiences of decoding singular and plural nouns, the child will learn to recognize the inflectional ending *s* and to realize intuitively that the word *cats* represents two separate morphemes—*cat* and *s* and that the addition or subtraction of the morpheme *s* changes the meaning of the word.

The same type of understanding can be gained about verb changes, such as *jump* and *jumping* or *want* and *wanted,* and also about the effects of adding prefixes and suffixes, as in *happy* and *unhappy, hope* and *hopeful.* Gradually, the child can be taught to recognize familiar inflectional endings and other suffixes, familiar prefixes, and familiar root words.

In addition to an introduction to morphemic analysis, children can also be introduced rather early to syllabic analysis. Words such as *rabbit* and *cotton,* for example, lend themselves to simple clapping or stamping exercises which illustrate the two distinct syllables or "grunts" represented by each word. This type of primitive analysis would eventually lead to a more sophisticated analysis of those particular grapheme patterns which signal a separation of syllables. In the word *rabbit,* for instance, the reader can see two vowel letters separated by a pair of consonants. This pattern, the VC/CV pattern, signals that two syllables should be uttered and that the break in syllables is between the two consonant letters. Having broken the word *rabbit* (or any other VC/CV word) into syllables, the child is then able to look for familiar phonic patterns in each syllable. In the case of the word *rab′/bit,* for instance, it is easy to recognize the VC spelling pattern in the accented syllable, and this would signal a short vowel sound. (The second syllable has a schwa sound in it.)

It should be clear, then, that without some knowledge of syllabic analysis, the reader's ability to use phonic knowledge is limited to one-syllable words. Thus, making children aware of syllables provides them with two benefits: (1) it allows them to gradually escape from an overreliance on phonics by teaching them to perceive larger units than mere phonemes, and (2) it allows them to expand the use of phonic analysis to words of more than one syllable.

Teaching Syllabic Analysis

Now that we have discussed the purposes of teaching morphemic and syllabic analysis—the two components of structural analysis—let's move on to these questions: (1) What elements of both should be taught? and (2) What procedures are helpful in teaching them? With respect to syllabic analysis, children need to learn how to divide words mentally into syllables, which syllables to accent, and what effects the word division will have upon subsequent phonic analysis.

The process of dividing words into syllables, called syllabication, is subject to the same type of limitations that exist with respect to phonic analysis. There are few syllabication rules that one can consistently rely on. As with phonic analysis, one has to "take a chance" and be willing to make mistakes. Therefore, children should be taught to try another method of decoding the syllables if the first one doesn't work. Some syllabication generalizations which are fairly reliable *for decoding purposes* are as follows:

1. Each syllable contains a vowel phoneme, e.g., (pĕn /cəl).
2. The letters *le*, along with the preceding consonant letter, represent a separate syllable when they come at the end of the word, e.g., un/cle, Bi/ble. (/cle pattern)
3. A word may be divided between two consonant letters if they are not a digraph, e.g., dad/dy, bas/ket, fash/ion. (VC/CV pattern)
4. A consonant digraph usually belongs to the syllable of the preceding vowel letter, e.g., crack/er, rath/er, to/geth/er.
5. A word may be divided between two vowel letters only if they are not a digraph or if they do not represent a diphthong, e.g., di/et, be/liev/ing, boil/ing.
6. A consonant letter generally belongs to the syllable of either the preceding or following vowel letter, e.g., ro/bot, rob/in. (Exceptions: words with VCE roots that maintain their final e, e.g., hope/ful, rude/ly.)
7. A prefix normally forms a separate syllable, e.g., pre/view, un/like, re/turn.

Rules for accenting syllables are equally subject to qualification. Two rules that have a fair degree of consistency, however, are the following:

8. For a word having a prefix, usually the first or second syllable after the prefix is accented, e.g., re/gain´, pre/fer´, un/do´/ ing, in/di/ges´/tion.
9. For a two-syllable word without a prefix, usually the first syllable gets the accent, e.g., fa´/ther, run´/ning.

As for the effects that syllabication and accent will have on subsequent phonic analysis, probably only one generalization needs to be taught:

10. The phonic generalizations which apply to one-syllable words generally apply to an *accented* syllable in a multi-syllabic word, e.g., in the word cot´/ton, the accented syllable has the VC spelling pattern and is decoded like a one-syllable word with a short *o*.

Sample Procedures for a Lesson on Decoding Syllables

As with the sample phonics lessons, it is assumed that the vast majority of teachers will wish to use already prepared commercial materials for developmental instruction on syllabic analysis. The following, then, should be considered one type of lesson which might be used for those children whom you have identified as needing extra help. Since you have already developed skill in creating performance objectives, these have not been included in the sample lesson. This lesson is on Generalization 5, which is one of the more difficult rules for children to grasp. Similar steps may be used for the other generalizations.

1. Introduce sample words in context. Put these two sentences on the board:

   The *robin* pulled the worm out of the ground.
   Ron made a *robot* that looks like a man.

   Read them out loud with the students. Ask how many syllables there are in *robin*? How many in *robot*? Clap the syllables if necessary.

2. Show them how to divide and decode some sample words. Put words like these on the board in a vertical column: *robin, robot, cabin, babies, shaving, hotel.* Lead them to discover that all of the words in the list have something in common, i.e., a *single* vowel letter followed by a *single* consonant letter. Show how to divide the first two: *rob/in, ro/bot.* Ask them how the first syllable of *robin* differs from the first syllable of *robot.* Lead them to realize that the first syllable in *robin* has a VC pattern and a short vowel sound; whereas, the first syllable in *robot* has a CV pattern and a long vowel sound. Ask them how *robin* would sound if it were divided like this: *ro/bin.* Ask them how *robot* would sound if it were divided like this: *rob/ot.* (*Note:* in this lesson, avoid using words with VCE roots that maintain their final *e,* such as *hope/ful* or *rude/ly.*)

3. Let them try decoding some sample words on their own. For each of the remaining words in your list, have children come up to the board and divide it both ways, before the middle consonant letter and after it. Each time they divide it, they should decode it out loud, e.g., *ca/bin* (kā′/bən) and *cab/in* (kăb′/ən). Then they should tell which way of saying it makes the most sense.

4. Have them develop a generalizatin or rule. Ask them a question something like this: "What rule can you make up about dividing a word that has a *single* vowel letter followed by a *single* consonant letter. Accept anything similar in meaning to this: It can be divided either before or after the consonant letter. (For an exception to the rule, see Note in Step 2.) Then ask them: "If it's divided *before* the consonant letter, will the vowel letter be long or short?" (long) "If it's divided *after* the consonant letter,

will the vowel letter be long or short?" (short) Have them test their rule on some other words. Ask them to divide and decode words like the following, both before and after the middle consonant letter: *miner, cater, famous, shaping, Robert.*

5. Provide massed and distributed practice. This practice should probably include some form of follow-up worksheet (as part of the massed practice), some more work in context, and, if possible, a bit of novelty.

In summary the five steps that are recommended for teaching syllabic analysis are these:

1. Introduce sample words in context, visually and orally.
2. Show the students how to divide and decode some sample words.
3. Let them try decoding some sample words on their own.
4. Have them develop a generalization and test it on some other words.
5. Provide massed and distributed practice.

Teaching Morphemic Analysis

Whereas syllabic analysis involves the translation of graphemes or grapheme clusters into units of *sound,* morphemic analysis necessitates their translation into units of *meaning.* Let's take the word *revisited* as an example. Syllabic analysis of the word would lead to this: *re/vis´/it/ed.* Morphemic analysis would lead to this: *re-visit-ed.* Morphemic analysis is a quicker, more "mature" form of analysis, but one which generally relies on the visual memory of roots (such as *visit*), the visual memory of suffixes (such as *ed*), and the visual memory of prefixes (such as *re*).

To make this difference between syllabic and morphemic analysis more distinct, let's look at two other examples. Syllabic analysis of the word *unhappiness* would yield *un/hap´/pi/ness.* Morphemic analysis, on the other hand, would yield un-happ(y)-ness, because the reader would recognize the meaningful grammatical units. It's true that she might not recognize *all* the grammatical units; e.g., she might just recognize the prefix and root and have to decode the suffix through phonic analysis. Nevertheless, the goal in teaching morphemic analysis is to help the child eventually develop a sight vocabulary of common roots and common affixes.[7]

As a sample lesson on morphemic analysis, let's take the suffix, *ed.* Suppose you have discovered that certain children know how to decode the *ing* suffix but need help on the *ed* suffix. In order to keep this first review lesson simple, you decide not to use any sample words that require modification before adding a suffix, i.e., you decide *not* to use words such as *hop* or *rake,* which become *hop*(p)*ed* and *rak*(e)*d.* Some steps you might use, then, in the lesson

---

[7]*Affixes* refer to inflectional endings, other suffixes, and prefixes.

are listed below. The answers are easy to discover, so in order to get you more involved, they won't be given.

Sample Lesson on Morphemic Analysis

1. Introduce sample words in context. Put these sentences on the board, and read them with the children:

   a. Fred went walking.
   b. He walked three miles.
   c. Sandy was planting seeds.
   d. She planted them in a neat row.
   e. Betty was mailing letters.
   f. She mailed them to her friends.

2. Help them discover and decode the root words. Ask them what two words in Sentences a and b are almost the same: _____ and _____. Then ask them what part of each word is *exactly* the same: _____. Remind them that this part is called the root word, if they have forgotten the term. Have someone underline and read out loud the root word in *walking* and *walked*. Have other children do the same for *planting* and *planted* and for *mailing* and *mailed* in Sentences c through f.

3. Help them discover and decode the affixes. Ask them how *walked, planted,* and *mailed* are the same. Remind them that *ed* is called a suffix, if they have forgotten the term. Have the children circle the suffixes in *walked, planted,* and *mailed* and read the words out loud. Ask them how the suffix differs for the three words; does it always stand for the same sound?

4. Have them develop a generalization. Ask them what three sounds the *ed* suffix stands for. Have them test their generalization on some other words, such as *jumped, wanted, farmed,* and any others that they can think of.

5. Provide massed and distributed practice. Some of the practice should be with isolated words and some with words in context. For part of the massed practice, for example, provide them with a work sheet that includes a list of words, most of them having *ed* or *ing* suffixes. Be sure not to use words which necessitate root changes before adding a suffix, e.g., words such as *rub(b)ing* or *mak(e)ing*. Have them circle the suffixes, underline the root words, and then read the words out loud to a partner.

In summary, the steps that are recommended for teaching most of the elements of morphemic analysis are these:

1. Introduce sample words *in context,* visually and orally.
2. Help them discover and decode the root words.
3. Help them discover and decode the affixes.

4. Have them develop and test a generalization (if one is warranted).

5. Provide massed and distributed practice.

Teaching Contextual Analysis

As well as being a decoding method in its own right, contextual analysis is the *overseer* of visual memory, phonic analysis, and structural analysis. Visual memory, alone, for example, might lead José to decode *raid* as *rail* in this sentence, *The Vikings came in their ships to raid the coast of England.* But contextual analysis would warn him that *rail* doesn't make sense.

Let's take another example. For the sentence, *Nancy was hoping she could go,* suppose Frances syllabicates *hoping* this way: *hop´/ing.* Then phonic analysis would tell her that the accented syllable has a short *o,* and she would read, "Nancy was hopping she could go." Contextual analysis, however, would get her back on the track, since she would realize that *hŏp´/ing* doesn't make sense but *hō´/ping* does.

To take one more example, suppose Tommy is trying to decode this sentence, *As soon as Bobby shot the ball, the referee blew his whistle.* If he tries to use morphemic analysis on *referee,* he'll end up with re-feree, which would sound something like *re/fur´/y.* Contextual analysis would indicate to him that he needs to try some other way of decoding the word. Suppose he next tries to syllabicate the word and comes up with this: *ref´/er/ee.* Again, contextual analysis would indicate that he's off the mark, but only slightly. Now the word sounds vaguely familiar and probably in less than a second he makes sense out of the word by changing it to *ref/er/ee´.*

We can see, then, that contextual analysis is crucial to the process of decoding words in print. And we can see more clearly now how the various means of decoding words work together. In fact, even contextual analysis must often have help from one of the other decoding methods. Take this sentence for instance:

This poison ivy rash is driving me _____.

Contextual analysis, alone, might lead Wyman to expect a word like *crazy* or *mad.* But suppose he also uses the minimal phonic clue offered by the first letter. That is, suppose he sees the sentence this way:

This poison ivy rash is driving me w_____.

Now the words *crazy* and *mad* probably don't even occur to him. Instead he would be guided by the combination of phonics and context to come up with a word like *wild,* or perhaps *wacky.* And, if he sees the sentence *this* way:

This poison ivy rash is driving me wi_____d,

there would probably be no question in his mind as he reads it; the word is *wild.* It makes sense, and it fits the minimal phonic signals that he has noticed.

Perhaps it is also more clearly seen, now, how decoding and comprehension work together to enable a person to read. We have been treating the process of decoding as if it were separate from comprehension. This has been done, as mentioned earlier, merely to make the process of decoding more understandable. But as we saw in the sentences just used as examples, children must decode properly in order to comprehend, and they must comprehend the sentence or entire passage properly in order to decode through contextual analysis and to provide the proper check on other means of decoding.

It is probably already clear that contextual analysis is a skill that should be developed alongside those of visual memory, structural analysis, and phonic analysis. Every time the teacher asks a child whether a particular word makes sense in a sentence, she is teaching contextual analysis. However, to strengthen and clarify this skill, specific lessons need to be provided—particularly if you have found through diagnostic testing or observation that certain children are deficient in this form of analysis. These lessons should be designed to help the children see that a particular word makes sense in a sentence when it meets three criteria: (1) The word fits grammatically with the rest of the sentence, (2) It fits the meaning of the rest of the sentence, and (3) It fits the phonic clues presented by the word itself.

Sample exercises for teaching contextual analysis were provided in Module 7 on teaching basic listening skills (see pages 255–56). In using this type of lesson for strengthening reading abilities, one needs merely to have the students *read* the sentences rather than listen to them. For example, to help them become more aware of noun signals, the teacher can have them read and respond to the following: Roger is a very good _____. Which of these words can fit in the blank? (*boy, hit, swimmer, his, runs, helper, quickly, here, runner*)

Developing a Sight Vocabulary Through Visual Memory

To become a mature reader, a person has to acquire a large reservoir of sight words. Any other means of decoding words, whether it be through phonic analysis, structural analysis, contextual analysis, or a dictionary, is slow, and even annoying, by comparison. Whenever a person has to slacken the pace to analyze a word according to its graphemes, its morphemes and syllable, its context, or its pronunciation given in a dictionary, both fluency and comprehension tend to suffer.

Sight words are those which are instantly recognized without the use of any type of analysis. They are remembered immediately either because they are highly meaningful words like *mother* or *father* or because the reader has been exposed to them so often. The best way for such exposure to take place, of course, is through abundant reading. For beginning readers, however, the teacher will have to use other techniques for providing frequent exposure. Before we discuss such techniques, let us first look at which words the teacher should concentrate on. After all, with 500,000 words to choose from the teacher must make a decision as to which words should become basic sight words during the early stages of learning to read.

Table 5.2 of Module 5 presented a list of ninety-six "spelling demons" that are basic to children's writing. These same words should be emphasized as a basic sight vocabulary for reading. They meet the following criteria (25):

1. They are high frequency words. They are found frequently in printed materials for adults and children, and they are heard frequently in children's speech.

2. These ninety-six words have appeared on at least two out of eight well-known lists of high frequency words.

3. They all have irregular spelling, thus making the use of visual memory necessary (rather than phonic analysis or some other type of analysis).

4. These words are common to a variety of geographic and socio-economic neighborhoods.

Sample Lessons on Sight Vocabulary

If David is having trouble remembering *regular* words, part of his problem may be insufficient practice, but another part of his problem is likely to be a deficiency in phonic analysis. If, on the other hand, he is having trouble remembering *irregular* words, he definitely needs some guided practice on them. For purposes of helping children who need more practice, whether with regular or irregular words, the following six steps are recommended.

Sample Procedures

1. *Introduce a few of the words in context.* (About three to five words is enough. If you introduce many more it will be difficult to teach for mastery.) For example, the teacher might put these sentences on the chalkboard (using manuscript printing):

   "Who put my ball there?" he said.
   "I want my ball back."

   Then the children can read the sentences with the teacher. After each sentence is read out loud, a child would be asked to frame a particular word with his hands, a word such as *Who, put, there, said,* or *want.* As he frames each word, he should look at it and say it out loud.

2. *Have the children create a visual image of each word.* For each word, have them look at it, close their eyes, and imagine themselves spelling the word on the board, and then check to see if their image was correct (see page 185 in Module 5 for a study method for dyslexic children).

3. *Ask them to write each word from memory.* First, the children should look at the word before the teacher covers it up. Then they should write the word from memory (using manuscript printing), and finally they should provide their own feedback by checking to see if they have written it correctly. Although this is excellent spelling practice, it also augments the visual and auditory experience with a kinesthetic experience. In other words, the eyes, ears, and muscles are all involved in per-

ceiving the word. Regardless of whether such muscle involvement, in itself, makes a difference or whether the writing simply causes the child to visualize a word more accurately, research suggests that writing words "helps the child to commit them to his sight vocabulary" (6, p. 124).

4. *Have them practice decoding the words in isolation.* Using flashcards or a similar device (after completing Steps 1, 2, and 3), have them call out each word as you expose it for a second or less. You may wish to have only one child at a time call the word, but remember to keep them all involved by *not* taking turns in rotation.

5. To ensure that positive transfer takes place, *arrange for them to practice decoding the words in context.* Go back to the sentences you put on the board at the beginning of the lesson and have the children read them without your help, if possible. Then present, either on the chalkboard or preferably in their books, a few more sentences that contain the words you worked on.

6. *Provide massed practice followed by distributed practice.* And while you're at it, why not use another learning principle discussed in Module 3. Add novelty to the learning experiences. There are a variety of ways of making the practice sessions slightly different each time. One simple device, for example, is the "password." Before a child gets to go somewhere—lunch, recess, home—she has to tell you the password, which is the word you flash her on a card.

   In addition to games and exercises that the teacher devises, there are self-instructional machines which make it possible for the child to practice on his own. On one such machine, for example, the child looks at a flashcard, attempts to decode the word printed on it, and then runs the card through a type of tape recorder to hear what the word is.[8] Earphones may be used with the machine so that other children in the room are not disturbed.

In summary, the six steps recommended for teaching sight words are these:

1. Introduce a few of the words in context—visually and orally.
2. Have the children create a visual image of each word and then check it.
3. Ask them to write each word from memory and then check it.
4. Have them practice decoding the words in isolation.
5. Arrange for them to practice decoding the words in context.
6. Provide massed and distributed practice.

---

[8] The *Language Master* (Bell & Howell Co.) or the TTC Magnetic Card Reader (Teaching Technology Corporation) or the *e-f-i Audio Flashcard System* (Educational Futures, Inc.)

Teaching Readiness Skills for Decoding

Reading readiness has at least two different meanings: (1) the skills needed before a person learns to read, and (2) the prerequisite skills necessary before a particular reading skill can be taught. In most cases the same "treatment" is required for both types of readiness, namely, a background of experiences in the other language arts, especially in listening. The person who is about to learn to detect main ideas in reading passages should first have the readiness experience of finding them through listening. The child who is about to learn how to read for the first time needs to have been readied for such an experience by numerous direct experiences, speaking experiences, listening experiences, and (with the language experience approach) even writing experiences.

Readiness for a reading experience sometimes requires a direct experience.

However, there are some readiness experiences which are often emphasized in getting children ready to decode for the first time. Although the presently available research on this matter is inconclusive, it seems likely that six types of learning experiences should be provided to children prior to formal instruction in decoding: auditory discrimination, visual discrimination, auditory-visual discrimination combined, letter recognition, left-to-right orientation, and oral vocabulary.

Exercises for teaching auditory discrimination were suggested in Module 7 on basic listening skills. Experiences for developing oral vocabulary were recommended in Module 4 on fluency. Activities for the other four readiness skills are suggested below.

Exercises for Teaching Visual Discrimination

1. "On the chalkboard are two pairs of words: *happy–happy* and *lazy–sleepy*. Will one of you put a circle around the pair that is

the same? All right. Now here are some more pairs (on the chalkboard or on a worksheet) for you to look at. Circle only the pairs that are the same." (For the pairs that are different use words that have gross differences, e.g., *hope–run, elephant–turtle.*)

2. Same as 1, but for the pairs that are different use words which differ only in the initial grapheme or blend, e.g., *hope–rope, beer–deer, there–where.*

3. Same as 1, but for the unlike pairs use words which differ only in the final grapheme, e.g., *hop–hot, bang–bank, mold–mole.*

4. Same as 1, but for the unlike pairs use words which differ only in a medial grapheme or blend, e.g., *hat–hot, rubber–rudder, master–masher.*

5. Same as 1 but use pairs of *letters* instead of words, starting first with unlike pairs that are grossly different such as *m–p* and moving to unlike pairs that require finer discrimination, such as *m–n,* or *d–b.*

6. Same as 5, but use *cutouts* of letters so that children having trouble making discriminations can try fitting one letter on top of another.

7. Same as 6 but use *dotted* letters and have the children trace over each pair before deciding whether to circle it.

8. "On the chalkboard are a list of words. I'd like you to circle those which begin (or end) in the same way as the first word."

9. Same as 8 but emphasize medial graphemes instead of initial or final ones.

10. Same as 8 but use letters instead of words. "Circle those letters which are the same as the first one."

11. Same as 8, 9, and 10, but have them find the word or letter that is *different* from all the rest.

Exercises for Teaching Auditory–visual Discrimination

It is helpful to use separate exercises on auditory and visual discrimination, as this makes the task easier for beginners. However, once the children have achieved mastery of the skills in isolation, they should work toward mastery of the skills in combination. Exercises which require both auditory and visual discriminations will move the children naturally into the decoding process of translating graphemes into phonemes.

1. "On the chalkboard are three words. These words are *fox, fish,* and *fun.* What do you notice about the beginning sound of these words? That's right, they all begin with the same sound. Now look at the words on the board. What else is the same about these words? Yes, they all begin in the same way. They all begin with the letter *f.* Can you think of some other words that begin in the same way?" (Write down all the words which begin

with *f* in a column. Then have them repeat these *f* words after you. Have them produce the f sound without distortion. Discourage them from saying "fuh"; have them say only the sound heard at the end of *knife*. For difficult consonants such as *b*, have them think of the sound at the *end* of a cue word, such as *tub*. Discourage the exaggerated "buh" pronunciation as this will make it difficult for some to decode words such as *bat* (buh-ahh-tuh) later on. It is best to use exercises such as this one shortly before, or as part of, a regular phonics lesson. In fact, as you may have noticed, this exercise is quite similar to Steps 2 and 3 recommended for a phonics lesson.

2. Most of the previous exercises on auditory and visual discrimination can be repeated in combined form. For example, have pairs of words on the board, some the same, some different. The unlike pairs, let's say, differ only in their initial grapheme, e.g., *hope–rope*. The teacher would pronounce each pair and have the children indicate whether it is the same or different. After each unlike pair, he would have a pupil come up and circle the part of each word in the pair that is different, e.g., (h)o p e –(r)o p e.

Exercises for Teaching Letter Recognition

As you may have already observed, the previous exercises on auditory-visual discrimination provide a natural opportunity for introducing or reviewing letter names. For instance, when developing a list of *f* words, you are essentially introducing or reviewing the name given to the *f* grapheme and the /f/ phoneme. However, in addition to this approach, you will probably wish to use more direct exercises such as the following:

1. Help each child to spell his own name orally and in writing (manuscript).

2. Teach them to write each letter by introducing two or three letters at a time in the context of a word. For example, to teach the letters *s* and *e*, introduce them in the context of the word *see* (*SEE*). After they learn to write the *s* and *e*, both in upper-case and lower-case form, have them write the word in both forms: *see* and *SEE*.

3. Play matching games in which the children match their letter cards to a letter card that the teacher or leader holds up. Be sure to have them *say* the letter name as they match them.

4. Use letter names as a password. Hold up a letter card and have the children name the letter before they can pass from one activity to the next.

5. Put a new letter on the board each day, both in lower- and upper-case. Several times during the day, ask someone to tell what the letter is. Review with flashcards those letters which have been on the board on previous days.

6. Help them to alphabetize anything that seems interesting to them: children's names, favorite authors or titles, favorite television programs, etc.

7. Have a relay race against the clock. The first person dashes up to the chalkboard, writes *A* or *a* (depending on whether you specify small or capital letters), shouts (ay), runs back and hands the chalk to the next person. The next person runs up, writes *B* or *b*, shouts (bee), and so on. Work toward a "world's record."

8. Make an alphabet board by pounding two sets of twenty-six small nails into a piece of plyboard. Purchase fifty-two circular tags with a hole punched near the edge. Write the capital letters on half of them and the small letters on the other half. Hang them on the two sets of nails. Turn some of them around so that the letters cannot be seen and have the children tell you what letters are missing. After a child has said a letter that is missing, she can come up and turn the tag around to see if she was right.

Developing a Left-to-right Orientation

In addition to the three skills already discussed, there is another readiness skill which needs to be developed: the habit of reading from left to right. Most children seem to have no difficulty picking up this habit. However, this is probably because parents and teachers have conditioned the neophytes into expecting words to be decoded that way. After all, it would be quite possible to read from right to left and from bottom to top.

One of the easiest ways for a teacher to condition children to our left-to-right convention is to develop experience charts with them. These are simply sentences dictated by the children and written in manuscript by the teacher on a large piece of paper. The children watch the teacher write the "story" from left to right and from top to bottom. After writing each sentence, the teacher reads it and has the children "read" it with her, passing her hand under the words in a left-to-right direction.

Since the sentences are usually based on children's personal experiences, an experience chart seems to be a meaningful way to develop not only the concept of left-to-right but also the useful concept that "reading is something like changing written words back into spoken words." This concept is extremely important if children are to learn that reading is not word calling but communication.

REFERENCES AND BIBLIOGRAPHY

1. Adams, Marilyn J. et al. "Beginning Reading: Theory and Practice." *Language Arts* 55 (Jan. 1978): 19–25.

2. Artley, A. Sterl. "Phonics Revisited." *Language Arts* 54 (Feb. 1977): 121–26.

3. Austin, Mary, and Morrison, Coleman. *The First R: The Harvard Report Reading in the Elementary Schools.* New York: Macmillan, 1963.

4. Bailey, Mildred H. "The Utility of Phonic Generalizations in Grades One through Six." *Reading Teacher* 20 (1967): 413–18.

5. Baratz, Joan C., and Shuy, Roger W. eds. *Teaching Black Children to Read.* Washington, D.C.: Center for Applied Linguistics, 1717 Massachusetts Avenue, N.W., 1969.

6. Bond, Guy., and Dykstra, Robert. "The Cooperative Research Program in First-Grade Reading Instruction." *Reading Research Quarterly* 2 (Summer 1967): 5–142.

7. Buchanan, Cynthia Dee. "Programmed Reading." In *A Decade of Innovations: Approaches to Beginning Reading,* edited by Elaine Vilscek, pp. 227–33. Proceedings of the International Reading Association, Vol. 12, Part 3, 1967.

8. Burie, Audrey A., and Heltshe, Mary A. *Reading With a Smile: 90 Reading Games that Work.* Washington, D.C.: Acropolis Books, 1975.

9. Burmeister, Lou E. "Usefulness of Phonic Generalizations." *Reading Teacher* 21 (1968): 349–56.

10. Carlin, Philip M. "Teacher Teams in Reading." *Recent Developments in Reading.* Proceedings of the Annual Conference in Reading, University of Chicago, Vol. 27 (1965): 69–72.

11. Ching, Doris C. *Reading and the Bilingual Child.* Newark, Del.: International Reading Association, 1976.

12. Clarke, Louise. *Can't Read, Can't Write, Can't Talk Too Good Either: How to Recognize and Overcome Dyslexia in Your Child.* Baltimore: Penguin, 1974.

13. Clymer, Theodore L. "The Utility of Phonic Generalizations in the Primary Grades." *Reading Teacher* 16 (1963): 252–58.

14. Dykstra, Robert. "Summary of the Second-Grade Phase of the Cooperative Research Program in Primary Reading Instruction." *Reading Research Quarterly* 1 (Fall 1968): 49–70.

15. Emans, Robert. "The Usefulness of Phonic Generalizations Above the Primary Grades." *Reading Teacher* 20 (1967): 419–25.

16. Fry, Edward. "A Diacritical Marking System to Aid Beginning Reading Instruction." *Elementary English* 41 (May 1964): 526–29.

17. _____. *Comparison of Three Methods of Reading Instruction.* USOE Cooperative Research Project No. 3050, 1967.

18. Gattengo, Caleb. *Words in Color.* Learning Materials, 1968.

19. Hall, MaryAnne. *Teaching Reading as a Language Experience.* Columbus, O.: Charles E. Merrill, 1976.

20. Harris, Theodore L. "Reading." In *Encyclopedia of Educational Research,* 4th ed., edited by Robert Ebel. New York: Macmillan, 1969.

21. Jordan, Dale R. *Dyslexia in the Classroom.* Columbus, O.: Charles E. Merrill, 1977.

22. Kavale, Kenneth, and Schreiner, Robert. "Psycholinguistic Implications for Beginning Reading Instruction." *Language Arts* 55 (Jan. 1978): 34–41.

23. Mallett, Jerry J. *101 Make-and-Play Reading Games for the Intermediate Grades.* Center for Applied Research in Education, West Nyack, New York, 1977.

24. May, Frank B., and Eliot, Susan B. *To Help Children Read,* 2nd ed. Columbus, O.: Charles E. Merrill, 1978.

25. _____."A Basic List of 96 Irregular Words for Linguistic Programs." *Reading Teacher* 31 (April 1978): 794–97.

26. Mazurkiewicz, Albert J., and Tanyzer, Harold J. *Early to Read i/t/a Program.* New York: Initial Teaching Alphabet Publications, 1966.

27. Pikulski, John. "Readiness for Reading: A Practical Approach." *Language Arts* 55 (Feb. 1978): 192–97.

28. Russell, David H. et al. *Reading Aids Through the Grades: A Guide to Materials and 440 Activities for Individualizing Reading Activities.* New York: Teachers College Press, 1975.

29. Thompson, Bertha B. "A Longitudinal Study of Auditory Discrimination." *Journal of Educational Research* 56 (March 1963): 376–78.

Teaching Comprehension and Study Skills Related to Listening and Reading

What is not fully understood is not possessed.
                                                    Goethe

Module 8 discussed those decoding skills necessary for translating printed words into spoken (or unspoken) words. In doing this, it was necessary to make an unnatural division between decoding and comprehension skills. As has been pointed out many times in this book, reading involves an interaction among decoding, comprehending, and thinking. (Even the use of three separate words—decoding, comprehending, and thinking—implies a separation that doesn't exist in reality.)

You've also seen that the language arts are difficult to separate in reality. Comprehension of reading materials, for example, depends a great deal on those comprehension skills developed through listening experiences. As Sheila learns to follow a sequence of ideas or directions while listening, she is essentially learning the same skill required for comprehending reading materials. Let's look, for instance, at the following passage:

> When the great white shark goes hunting, it does not bother to circle its prey and wait for the right moment to attack. This twenty-foot monster isn't afraid of anything. It attacks without worrying about enemies. It attacks without any warning!

As Sheila listens to this passage being read to her, she hears the word *when* and unconsciously gets ready for a conditional clause (When the great white shark goes hunting). As she notices the pause after *hunting,* she gets ready for the independent clause that is to follow. (What happens when it goes hunting? It does not bother to circle its prey and wait for the right moment to attack.) As the first sentence is completed, she automatically asks the question "Why?" in preparation for the next statement. (Why doesn't it bother to wait? Because . . . This twenty-foot monster isn't afraid of anything.) As the next sentence begins, she knows that *it* must refer to "this twenty-foot monster: It attacks without worrying about enemies."

Thus, Sheila follows the sequence of ideas and comprehends what she is listening to. This same comprehension skill is used when Sheila is reading the same passage by herself. In addition, of course, she now has to use other comprehension skills and decoding skills in order to translate the printed symbols into spoken (or unspoken) ones.

This module will discuss the various comprehension skills involved in both listening and reading situations. In addition, it will suggest ways of teaching those specialized comprehension skills called study skills—the skills involved in locating information (in both written and oral sources), comprehending information, and recording that part of it which may be useful in the future.

Special Prerequisites for Module 9

It is recommended that you complete Modules 1–3 and 7 before beginning this module. There are no other prerequisites.

Long-range Outcomes Related to Module 9

This module should help you as a teacher to do the following:

1. Communicate with other professional educators about instructional practices related to comprehension and study skills.

2. Provide opportunities for children to use the subskills of comprehension in concert.

3. Use the language experience approach to develop a mental set toward comprehension.

4. Increase children's comprehension of assigned listening or reading selections.

5. Teach study skills necessary for locating, understanding, and recording information available through reading or listening.

6. Help children improve comprehension through a flexible and efficient reading rate.

7. Develop children's skills necessary for using a dictionary.

Study Guide and Performance Objectives for Knowledge Level Examination

To give yourself an overview of what is expected of you in this module, you should first scan the objectives and peformance standards at all three levels—knowledge, simulation, and teaching. Then use the study guide during your reading of the module. As you find information related to the study guide, write it down in the available blanks or on separate paper. Then review this information shortly before your knowledge level examination.

1.1 On a closed-book examination, you should be able to list three subskills related to literal thinking. In preparation for the examination, complete the list below.
1. Developing associations or images.

2.

3.

1.2 On the same examination, you should be able to list three subskills related to inferential thinking. In preparation for the examination, complete the list below.
1. Finding or recognizing main ideas.

2.

3.

1.3 On the same examination, you will be asked to list the three steps recommended by Schwartz and Sheff for training children to read with comprehension. Complete the list below.
1. Posing a problem

2.

3. Verifying

1.4 On the same examination, you will be asked to write a short paragraph explaining the language experience approach and its relationship to comprehension.

1.5 On the same examination, you will be expected to list the four steps useful in increasing children's comprehension of assigned selections. Complete the list below.
1. Provide the experiential background necessary.

2.

3.

4.

1.6 On the same examination, you should be able to list four ways to help children learn the skills involved in locating information. In preparation for the examination, complete the list below.

1. Use discovery-type questions with social studies or science texts.

2.

3.

4.

1.7 On the same examination, you will be given either a graph or a table and asked to interpret its meaning. In preparation for the examination, be sure to study the table and graph shown in this module.

1.8 On the same examination, you will be asked to match the factors related to a slow reading rate with a set of teaching procedures designed to compensate for those factors. Below are a list of factors related to slow reading. To help you prepare for the examination, write in a teaching procedure next to each one. The first one has been done for you.
  1. Vocal or subvocal reading: Child holds pencil between teeth while reading silently.

  2. Materials too difficult:

  3. Reading word by word:

  4. Inadequate word recognition skills:

  5. Insufficient comprehension:

1.9 On the same examination, you will be given a list of subskills necessary for decoding and comprehending a word through a dictionary. You will be asked to provide the missing subskills. In preparation for the examination, complete the list below.
  1. Locate the appropriate section of the pages.

  2.
  3. Determine whether the second letter of the word is before or after the page the student is on.

  4.
  5. Locate the guide words which "enclose" the word the student is looking for.

  6.
  7. Use the diacritical marks to determine the pronunciation of certain graphemes.

  8.

9. Interpret accent marks correctly.

10.

11. Determine whether one of the most common synonyms fits the context of a particular sentence.

12.

13. Select the best definition and apply it to a particular sentence.

Performance Standards for Knowledge Level

A. Twenty-five minute time limit on 1.1–1.9 combined.

B. Completion deadline: instructor will notify.

C. Recommended grading standards if grades are used: 96% = A; 92% = A–; 88% = B; 84% = B–; 80% = C; below 80% = incomplete; should be completed at 80% or better before you go on to performance objectives for simulation level. (The instructor may wish to permit a grade of A or B only the first time the test is given in order to encourage more intensive study.)

Performance Objectives for Simulation Level

2.1 On a closed-book examination, you will be given a choice among a set of skills involving locating, comprehending, or recording information, which need to be "taught" to a fictitious group of children; you may name the age or grade level. The skills will be similar or the same as these:

Using an index to locate information.

Comprehending graphs.

Recording information by developing an outline.

Your simulation task will be that of choosing *one* of the skills to teach and developing a written lesson plan. In this plan you should (a) specify performance objectives, (b) specify special prerequisites, and (c) describe your proposed procedures in detail.

2.2 (Alternative objective) Same as 2.1, except a take-home examination would be given instead of a closed-book one. In this case, the instructor may wish to specify the skill rather than give you a choice.

2.3 (Alternative objective) As a take-home exam, develop a lesson plan which will serve as a basis for "teaching" two or more of your peers any skill of locating or recording information discussed in Module 9 or any skill involving the comprehension of graphs, maps, diagrams, tables, or pictures. The lesson plan is for your own use only and is *not* to be handed in. Hand in, instead, a tape recording of your lesson. (If you and your instructor decide on alternative 2.3, you may wish to discuss the possibility of using peer evaluations in addition to or instead of instructor evaluation.)

2.4 (Alternative objective—to give you practice in team teaching) As a take-home exam, develop with two peers a written lesson plan, a tape of the lesson being taught by one of the team to the other two members of the team, and a worksheet to follow the lesson.

2.5 (Alternative objective) On a closed-book examination, you will be given a children's textbook (social studies or science) and asked to create a worksheet. This worksheet should consist of twelve questions which will help children discover the location and usefulness of different study aids in the book, e.g., two or three questions might be created to guide them toward discovering and using the index.

2.6 (Alternative objective) Same as 2.5, except a take-home examination would be given instead of a closed-book examination.

Performance Standards for Simulation Level

A. For Objectives 2.1 and 2.2 (Written Lesson Plan)
   1. Same as A-1–A-2 of Module 4.
   2. Shows a clear understanding of the skill for which he has developed a written lesson plan.

B. For Objective 2.3 (Tape of Peer Teaching)
   1. Shows by his efforts to evaluate the progress of his "students" during the lesson that he has clear-cut performance objectives in mind.
   2. Uses learning principles effectively; does not violate any of those discussed in Module 3.

C. For Objective 2.4 (Team Teaching)
   1. For the written lesson plan, use Standards A-1–A-2.
   2. For the tape recording, use Standards B-1–B-2.
   3. For the worksheet, use Standard A-2.

D. For Objectives 2.5 and 2.6 (Worksheet on Locating Information)
   1. The teacher-in-training demonstrates by his questions that he has a clear understanding of the skills for which the worksheet was designed to help children learn.
   2. The questions seem well suited to helping children discover the location and usefulness of study aids in the textbook.

E. For Objectives 2.1–2.6
   1. Suggested grading standard if grades are used: should be completed at C level or better before going on to perfor-

mance objectives for the teaching level. (Grade based on judgment of instructor and/or peers.)

2. For Objective 2.4 the instructor may wish either to give a "team" grade or to grade one member of the team on the written lesson plan, another member on the tape, and the other member on the worksheet.

3. (Additional standards or modified standards may be developed by the instructor and/or teachers-in-training. It is best, however, to state these standards *in advance* of the required performance.)

Performance Objectives for Teaching Level

3.1 In a micro-teaching, observation, student teaching, intern, or supervised teaching situation, teach a brief lesson (about fifteen to thirty minutes) to two or more students. The subject of the lesson should be a skill involved in locating or recording information or comprehending graphs, tables, maps, diagrams or pictures. Write up a lesson plan (see Module 4 for what should be included) and develop a worksheet for this lesson. The worksheet should be given to the students, and the results evaluated by the teacher-in-training. Your cooperating teacher, supervisor, or instructor may want to see your lesson plan and worksheet before you interact with the students.

After you have taught the lesson, you should write a brief self-critique, indicating (1) to what extent your performance objectives were met, (2) what might be done to help children who did *not* meet your performance standards, (3) what problems you had, if any, (4) what might have been done to implement your desired long-range outcome more effectively, and (5) what type of follow-up activity might provide useful practice for these students at a later date. Your cooperating teacher, supervisor, or instructor will probably want to see your critique.

3.2 (Alternative objective) Assess the reading rates for several children. For a child with a slow reading rate, assess the factors which may be responsible. Write up a brief report of your investigation. Hand in to your cooperating teacher, supervisor, or instructor.

Performance Standards for Teaching Level

A. For Objective 3.1 (Teaching a Skill)
  1. Standards for A-1–A-2 for the simulation experience may be appropriate.
  2. Uses learning principles effectively; does not violate any of those discussed in Module 3.

B. For Objective 3.2 (Assessing Rates and Slow Reading Factors)
  1. Demonstrates that he is able to use reasonably accurate techniques for assessing children's reading rates.
  2. Uses appropriate techniques for assessing the factors which may account for the slow reading rate of a particular child.
  3. Suggests in the report appropriate means for counteracting those factors which may be causing the slow reading rate.

The Nature of Comprehension

Neither listening comprehension nor reading comprehension are solitary skills. Each of them involves a similar set of subskills. In discussing these subskills, remember that they often act in concert rather than independently. The following is a list of some of the subskills used for comprehending in either a listening or reading situation:

1. Recognizing context signals, both grammatical and semantic.
2. Recognizing appropriate meanings intended for words.
3. Recognizing sentence pattern alterations or expansions.
4. Interpreting pitch variations, stress, and pauses.
5. Performing literal thinking.
  a. Developing associations or images.
  b. Following a sequence.
  c. Recollecting or recognizing significant details.
6. Performing inferential thinking.
  a. Finding or recognizing main ideas.
  b. Making predictions about what is coming next.
  c. Inferring information from what has been implied.
7. Critical and creative thinking.

Since critical and creative thinking, as they apply to comprehension, will be discussed thoroughly in Module 10, they will not be discussed here. Subskills 1–6 were described in considerable detail in Module 7. Several exercises for teaching each subskill through listening experiences were also offered in that module. The same exercises may be used for applying the subskills to reading.

For example, to encourage the act of developing associations or images while listening, teachers can read a story aloud to children, occasionally having them close their eyes to picture what they are hearing. They can have the children describe their "pictures" (images) and discuss the personal experiences they are reminded of (associations). The same thing can be done, of course, while children are reading a story by themselves, either aloud or silently: "What picture in your mind does that sentence give you, Jennie?" "Has anything like that ever happened to you, Jack?"

Providing Opportunities to Use the Subskills in Concert

Similar applications from listening experiences to reading experiences can be made for all the listening exercises suggested in Module 7. Just using isolated exercises, however, is not enough to assure that children will improve in their ability to comprehend what they read or listen to. Since the subskills of comprehension often operate in concert, it is necessary to provide listening and reading experiences which bring the subskills together. Let's go back a moment to the passage about the great white shark:

> When the great white shark goes hunting, it does not bother to circle its prey and wait for the right moment to attack. This twenty-foot monster isn't afraid of anything. It attacks without worrying about enemies. It attacks without any warning!

Notice how the various subskills of comprehension must work in concert in order to achieve understanding of the passage. In the first sentence, what is the *appropriate meaning* for the word *right*? Does the word refer to direction—right vs. left—or does it refer to accuracy? By *recognizing context signals* the reader or listener can infer that the word refers to accuracy rather than direction.

Notice that the first sentence has a dependent clause followed by an independent clause. ("When the great white shark goes hunting" is the dependent clause.) This sentence is an expansion and an alteration of the sentence "The shark bothered" (see Table 4.2 in Module 4). The comprehension of such a complex sentence is based on numerous experiences of *recognizing sentence pattern alterations and expansions,* mostly in listening situations, but also in reading situations.

The first sentence has a significant pause, represented by a comma, after the word *hunting.* Proper *interpretation of this pause* leads the reader or listener to put stress on the word *hunting* rather than *goes* and to realize that the shark is just "hunting" rather than "hunting it."

Nowhere does it mention in the passage that the shark heads straight for its prey when it attacks. However, the reader who comprehends the passage can *infer this information from what has been implied.* Having inferred this, the reader or listener can *develop the image* of a huge shark heading straight for a helpless victim.

Perhaps this is enough to show you how the subskills of comprehension work together to produce understanding when a person listens or reads. The skillful reader or listener uses comprehension skills almost instantaneously.

The inexperienced reader or listener, however, often needs specific training and practice. Schwartz and Sheff (14) suggest a three-step format for this training as children read with the teacher: (1) posing a problem, (2) reasoning while reading, and (3) verifying. In the following dialogue, they provide us with an example of their approach. In this dialogue, the children have been reading about dinosaur fossils.

Posing a new problem

Teacher: Who wants to give us a new idea of what you think they can find out from the skeleton?

Joe: Their shapes, what they look like.

Reasoning while reading and verifying

Teacher: Those are good ideas. Let's read the next sentence to find out exactly.

Keith: "Sometimes the bones show signs that they were broken while the dinosaur was living."

Teacher: That's unusual. I found out something I didn't know. What did you find out? . . .

Lance: The dinosaur's bones are broken.

Posing the next problem

Teacher: A dinosaur's bones are broken! How can a dinosaur's bones get broken? . . .

This same approach can be used for listening experiences by simply stopping the tape recorder in order to pose a problem, reason, or verify. The important idea is that the teacher use the listening experience or reading experience as an opportunity to reinforce or initiate comprehension skills with such questions as the following:

1. What do you think is going to happen next?
2. What do you think they can find out from the skeleton?
3. How can a dinosaur's bones get broken?
4. How does a great white shark attack its victim?
5. What makes you think it attacks straight on?
6. What picture do you now have in your mind?
7. What's the first thing that happens when a shark gets ready to attack? What's the second thing? The third?
8. Which word in the first sentence would you say is the loudest— *goes* or *hunting*? Why?

Comprehension and the Language Experience Approach

As you may recall, the language experience approach includes the technique of having the children dictate a story or a description of a common experience to the teacher. The teacher records the dictation for all to see on a large sheet of paper or on the chalkboard. After the children "write" the story, they are asked to read it. Thus, the children are involved in all four of the language arts: speaking, writing, reading, and listening.

From my observation of teachers using this technique (and from my own use of it with children), it appears that the language experience approach is a natural way to improve reading and listening comprehension. What children have to say about an experience is translated into print. The printed message is then translated back into the spoken message. Listening comprehension is reinforced by the translation into print; reading comprehension is reinforced by the translation back into a verbal message that made sense in the first place.

Perhaps the most important thing that children learn from the language experience approach is that the purpose of the reading act is to derive a message that makes sense, in other words, to communicate—to gain an understanding of what someone else has "said." This mental set of looking for meaning is essential to the development of good readers. The child who doesn't have this set looks at reading as merely decoding words; he can make the right sounds and get approval from the teacher, but he has little concern for the meaning of what he has decoded.

The language experience approach is a natural way to improve reading and listening comprehension.

With the language experience approach, children gradually do more and more of the actual writing themselves, thus producing their own personal reading material. This increase in writing and reading that is personal seems to enhance their mental set toward comprehension (rather than mere decoding) even further.

Lopardo (10) suggests a special way of using language experience charts in order to improve children's mental set toward comprehending what they read. First, the children dictate a story (or a description of a common experience) to the teacher, who transcribes it on an "experience chart" (a sheet of paper or the chalkboard). Before the teacher meets with the children again she rewrites the story on another experience chart, this time deleting approximately every fifth word. The children then read the new version, putting words that make sense in the blank spaces. Finally, they check the two charts to see how well they match. This technique forces the children to think about what they are reading rather than just reading word by word from memory.

As an example of this technique, read the following paragraph and fill in the blanks without looking back at the previous paragraph. Notice how important it is for you to comprehend what you are reading:

Lopardo suggests a special _____ of using language experience _____ in order to improve _____ mental set toward comprehending _____ they read. First, the _____ dictate a story (or a _____ of a common experience _____ the teacher, who _____ it on an "experience _____" (a sheet of paper or the _____). Before the teacher meets _____ the children again, she _____ the story on another _____ chart, this time _____ approximately every fifth word. The children _____ read the new version, _____ words that make _____ in the blank spaces. Finally, _____ check the two charts to _____ how well they match. _____ technique forces the children to _____ about what they are _____ rather than just _____ word by word from memory.

Now compare your paragraph with the original one. How well did you understand the original one?

Increasing Children's Comprehension of Assigned Selections

Students are often asked to listen to assigned selections on tape or to read assigned selections in basal readers, social studies texts, or other books. This is a good time to encourage them to make use of the comprehension skills they have been practicing in isolation. To provide this type of application experience and to encourage better understanding of an assigned selection, the following four instructional steps are recommended:

1. *Provide the experiential background necessary for understanding the selection.* If, for instance, the selection is about a child living in a different culture, you should decide what aspects of that culture need to be "experienced" by your pupils in order to understand the selection. (Remember to use Dale's "Cone of Experience" discussed in Module 4 to help you think of types of experiences that can be provided.)
2. *Discuss those words which seem to be necessary for a good understanding of the selection.* Frequently, teachers discuss

far too many words prior to having the children read. Sometimes this is due to the fact that teachers' editions (in basal readers) list too many. But whatever the reason, it is usually impossible to do justice to more than three or four words in the time available (see Learning Principle 5 in Module 3). Many of the words that teachers "discuss" with the children can be comprehended through context clues; to clarify these words ahead of time is to deprive the children of the opportunity to practice this valuable comprehension skill. Therefore, when selecting words for emphasis, try to choose those which meet more than one of these criteria: (1) those which *cannot* be easily comprehended through the context clues provided in the selection, (2) those which are crucial to Step 1, providing the necessary experiential background, (3) those which are obviously not part of the sight vocabulary of most students involved, and (4) those which may be difficult to decode as well as comprehend.

3. *Provide specific purpose or motivation for completing the selection.* Frequently, this can be accomplished at the same time you are providing experiential background. For example, suppose the selection is about the amazing underground city in New York. During the background session, you may have shown them a diagram or picture of the numerous tunnels under the city. A question that would be reasonably motivational and one that would provide specific purpose for listening or reading would be, "If you were to crawl into those tunnels, what do you suppose you would find?" After a brief discussion, then, during which time they would make their predictions, you would ask them to read or listen to the selection in order to find out how good their guesses were.

4. *Ask questions that will help develop various comprehension skills.* After the children have completed the selection (and often before or during completion), help them to comprehend it more fully by asking questions that encourage some of the comprehension skills discussed previously in this module. For example, you may wish to expand their *vocabulary* by asking them a question about a word in the selection. You may wish to increase their awareness of sentence patterns, alterations, and expansions by asking them about *sentences* in the selection. You might want to help them think about the importance of *expression* by asking them about the meaning of pauses, pitch changes, or punctuation marks in the selection. And you will certainly want to provide them with *thinking* opportunities by asking them questions that require literal, inferential, critical, and creative thinking.

Helping Children Gain Study Skills

A particular set of comprehension skills requiring the acts of locating, understanding, and recording information is often referred to as study skills. Study skills are most applicable to reading situations, but some of them are also appropriate to listening situations (and are often required for speaking and writing assignments). Although the act of locating information is primarily a reading task, the acts of understanding information and recording useful parts of it are appropriate to both reading and listening experiences.

The skill of locating information can be broken down into subskills, such as the following:

1. Examining titles to determine appropriateness of books, tapes, and films.
2. Using a table of contents.
3. Using an index.
4. Using the glossary available in some books.
5. Gaining information from appendixes.
6. Finding appropriate visuals—maps, tables, graphs, pictures, and diagrams.
7. Using the library card catalog.
8. Using encyclopedias and other library reference books.

Whereas most basal reader programs include useful exercises on many of the locational skills, these skills are usually mastered best through actual research projects in which children seek information in trade books, textbooks, encyclopedias, and other library references. Textbooks, though, such as those used for social studies or science, are often handy to use as raw material when the teacher desires to introduce or review locational skills with several students at the same time. Since several copies of a textbook are usually available, each child receiving instruction can look at the same example at the same time. Guided practice should not be limited to textbooks, however, as positive transfer is much more likely to take place when children also employ the locational skills with trade books and reference books which they have found for themselves in the library.

As soon as children begin to use textbooks in science and social studies, they can begin to receive guided practice in "finding the secret treasures hidden within a book." Questions similar to the following are generally useful in helping children discover for themselves the usefulness of indexes, glossaries, illustrations, and so on. (To increase your own involvement and to gain a better understanding of the utility of such questions in aiding discovery, you might try answering these questions as they relate to the book you are reading right now. Feedback can be found at the end of the list of questions.)

1. On what page can you find the beginning of an *alphabetical list* (index) of most of the things talked about in this book?
2. If you wanted to find out something in this book about how to increase children's reading speed, what topic would you look for in the index: children's reading speed? rate of reading? how to increase children's reading speed? reading rate? reading speed? Try those that you think might work and see which one is in the index.

3. On exactly what pages would you find information about children's reading speed?

4. On what pages can you find a list of chapter titles?

5. On what page is there a table that might give you information about graphemes?

6. Between what pages is the module on fluency?

7. On what pages can you find suggestions for other books and articles to read on teaching phonics?

8. Looking only at the *titles* of articles suggested for additional reading on phonics, which one looks like it might lead you to information on the so-called First Grade Studies. (Just indicate the number of the reference.)

9. If you were trying to find the library number of this book, which drawers would you look for in the card catalog? (Use letters)
   a. The _____ drawer if I knew the author's name.
   b. The _____ drawer if I knew the title.
   c. The _____ drawer if I only knew the subject of the book.

10. On what page in this book is the word *articulation* defined?

11. Between what pages is there an appendix of children's writings?

12. If you wanted to find out something about how to teach deaf children to read, which two encyclopedia volumes would be most likely to contain the information you want?
    H   T   D   C   R

ANSWERS: 1. 457; 2. rate of reading; 3. 328, 332–35; 4. v–vii; 5. 172; 6. 100–147; 7. 308–9; 8. 6; 9. M or Ma, T or To, R or Re; 10. 138; 11. 444–48; 12. D (Deafness) or R (Reading).

In addition to the use of discovery questions similar to those just described, a teacher can also get children actively involved as "library detectives." A "detective's badge" or similar token can be given to those children who find all the clues or solve the mystery. In this type of activity, children are usually given clue cards or a list of clues and sent to the library ("the place in which the crime took place") singly, in pairs, or in supervised groups. The following "clues," though facetious in this instance, are the *types* of clues that might be used:

1. The kind of weapon used in the crime was a revolver used by the Barsimians in the War of Tulips. What was the name of the weapon?

2. The main suspect in this case was last seen in the city of Atlantis. In what country is this?

3. The main suspect has the same name (or alias) as the man who wrote *Call of the Tame*. What is the suspect's name?

4. The motive for the crime probably had something to do with narcotics. From what you can find out about narcotics why do

A teacher can get children actively involved as library detectives.

you think the money was stolen, and who else besides the main suspect do you think was responsible for this crime?

A simpler form of this type of activity involves clues which are more direct, though less imaginative. With this form, no "crime" has been committed, and the clues are simply research problems geared to specific locational skills. The following clues will serve as examples:

1. Find in the card catalog the author of *Call of the Tame.*
2. What book in this library tells about the War of Tulips? You'll find it in the subject catalog under one of these topics: War of Tulips, Wars, Battles, or Tulips.
3. Use an encyclopedia to find out the name of the revolver used by the Barsimians in the War of Tulips.

Some teachers also create the necessity for practicing locational skills by requiring children to prepare an oral or written report. Providing certain precautions are taken (see *They All Want to Write* by Burrows, Ferebee, Jackson, and Saunders), this is probably a worthwhile learning experience for most children. However, to require such a report without first providing specific training in locating, comprehending, and recording information, and without providing specific guidance during the preparation of the reports, will generally lead to frustration for the teacher and negative reinforcement for the children.

Understanding the Information That Has Been Located

Now that some ways of teaching children to locate information have been discussed, let us look at the next step—that of *comprehending* it. The following are some of the subskills involved:

1. Interpreting graphs, tables, maps, diagrams, and pictures.
2. Differentiating between facts and opinions.
3. Differentiating between literal and nonliteral statements.
4. Recognizing and selecting significant details.
5. Determining main ideas.
6. Determining accuracy of information.
7. Detecting propaganda and author bias.

Since subskill 7 will be discussed in Module 10, and since subskills 2–6 have already been discussed in Module 7, attention will be directed here to the first one—that of interpreting graphs, tables, maps, diagrams, and pictures.

Harris and Sipay's comment on the interpretation of graphs and tables is probably accurate: "Entirely too many students today have the habit of skipping past anything of this sort with the briefest glance" (6). It is likely, moreover, that such behavior was as common in the recent past as it is today. Yet, a

FIGURE 9.1 An Estimate of Student's Average Reading Rates of Informational Material Grades 1 through College

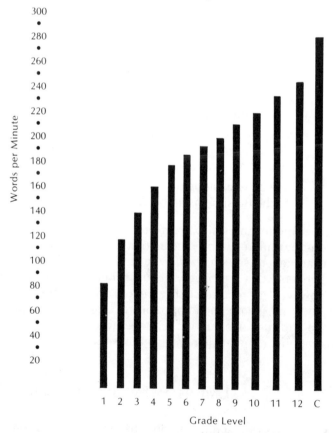

From May and Eliot, *To Help Children Read,* 2d ed. Copyright © 1978 by Charles E. Merrill Publishing Co. Based on information reported by Taylor, Frackenpohl, and Pettee (15).

graph or table offers students something which exposition seldom provides—the chance to get actively involved in "creating" their own information. Take the graph shown in Figure 9.1, for example. See how much information you can "create" without the need of any accompanying test. (Please look at Figure 9.1 before continuing.)

Having "invented" your own facts and generalizations based on the graph in Figure 9.1, perhaps you would agree that graph reading is more fun than exposition like this: "Average reading rates seem to vary almost directly with grade level." Taylor, Frackenpohl, and Pettee (15) found that the average reading rate for first grade was 82 words per minute. For third grade the rate was 138 words per minute, while for fourth grade, the rate was 158 words per minute. For fifth grade . . . " Pretty dull and hard to absorb this way, isn't it?

Now look at Table 9.1 and see what information you can generate on your own. Here too, it can be seen that reading information presented in this manner would probably be more interesting than reading the same information in a long, fact-studded paragraph.

TABLE 9.1 Sex Differences between Boys and Girls in Reading Retardation Measuring One Year or More Retardation

Grade	Percent Boys	Percent Girls
2	9.7	4.2
3	14.7	7.1
4	23.6	12.0
5	25.5	11.6
6	13.7	9.9

From Arthur Heilman, *Principles and Practices of Teaching Reading,* 4th ed. (Columbus, O.: Charles E. Merrill, 1977). Copyright © 1977 by Bell & Howell Company. Reproduced with permission.

Maps can also be a fascinating way for children to gain information. Witness the enthusiasm of children reading the map related to the journey of Bilbo Baggins in Tolkien's *Hobbit.* And so can diagrams and pictures, as shown by the eagerness displayed by children following diagrams for building model airplanes or studying pictures of dinosaurs.

If graphs, tables, maps, diagrams, and pictures *can* be so interesting, why are they often passed over with only the briefest glance? There are probably numerous reasons for this, including the possibility that they take more energy to read than simple exposition. But perhaps the biggest reason is that children have had too few opportunities to discover that reading them *can* be fairly easy and enjoyable.

One way of bringing about such a discovery is through having the children create graphs, maps, tables, diagrams, and informational pictures of their own. As a start, you might wish to have them use simple information that you provide them, such as average winter temperatures in various parts of the world or other such statistical data found in almanacs. But, as rapidly as possible, it is advisable to get them involved in gathering their *own* information and then translating that information into graphic or tabular form. There are almost limitless possibilities for such projects. Here are just a few:

1. A graph comparing the number of children in third grade who prefer vanilla, chocolate, and strawberry ice-cream.
2. A map of the classroom, the school, or the neighborhood.
3. A diagram of "my dream house" or of "how to make a simple glider."
4. A table showing school enrollment during the past ten years.
5. A mural giving a reasonably accurate interpretation of earlier village life of a tribe of Northeast Forest Indians.

All of these projects can be displayed for other children to read and discuss. In this way, some of the guided practice necessary for learning to appreciate and understand visuals can be provided. Also, through the construction of these visuals, the students will be able to discover for themselves the need for some type of scale on maps, graphs, diagrams, and informational pictures; the need for symbols such as color or special lines; and the need for accurate titles and labels.

Recording Information That Has Been Located and Understood

When children read or listen to an informational source, they sometimes may wish to go no further than locating the appropriate material and comprehending it. On certain occasions, though, such as preparing for a report or gathering data for a hobby, children will need to *record* some of the information. This process seems to be a burdensome and cumbersome one to many students. Perhaps this is largely the result of numerous unguided attempts, leading to negative reinforcement and to practicing of clumsy techniques. Many teachers, it appears, ask children to "take notes" on what they read without first giving them the necessary training. As a result, the children usually end up copying information verbatim rather than jotting down its essence. It is not a rare phenomenon to see high school and college students continuing this habit.

There are at least two useful approaches to the training needed in this respect. One of them is the traditional outlining approach, often taught to children in the upper grades. This approach calls for two steps: (1) teaching children the procedure by outlining portions of textbooks with them and (2) having them apply the outlining procedures to the taking of notes. For instance, take the previous portion of this module. The student who had received training in outlining would record the main ideas and important details in a manner similar to the following:

I. Locating Information
  A. Specific skills related to use of:
    1. Titles of books, tapes, films
    2. Table of contents
    3. Index
    4. Glossary
    5. Appendixes

  6. Visuals—maps, tables, graphs, pictures, diagrams
  7. Card catalog
  8. Encyclopedias and other references
 B. Teaching techniques
  1. Basal reader exercises
  2. Social studies or science textbooks
   a. "Secret treasure" for children to discover
   b. Discovery questions leading to use of A-1–A-8
  3. Library detectives
   a. Detective's badge or other token
   b. Clues requiring use of A-1–A-8
  4. Preparation for reports
II. Comprehending Information
 A. . . .
 B. . . .

The outline approach is appropriate when a rather general assignment is given to learn all they can about a topic, or to read certain pages in a text, or when they are preparing for a report on a general topic. However, it is probably more common in out-of-school situations to read or listen to informational sources for a specific purpose—to find the answer to a burning question, to learn how to do a particular thing related to a hobby, and so on. When this is the case, note-taking may be simply a matter of jotting down answers rather than outlining a topic in logical arrangement.

Let's suppose, for instance, that you wished to read for the specific purpose of answering this question, How fast do high school students read? Using the graph in Figure 9.1, your note-taking might look like this:

1. 9th grade—about 214 w.p.m.—avg. for informational material
2. 10th grade " 224 " " " " "
3. 11th grade " 237 " " " " "
4. 12th grade " 250 " " " " "

To take another example, suppose your purpose in reading was to review for a test which requires you to list ways of helping children learn the skills involved in locating information. In this case, rather than outlining or writing down verbatim all that pertains to this objective, one might take notes as follows:

1. Use discovery-type questions to guide them through the use of these skills with social studies or science textbooks.

2. Use exercises provided in basal reader programs.

3. Have children become library detectives; give them clues requiring the use of locational skills.

4. Have them use locational skills in preparing reports.

These two approaches to note-taking—the outlining technique and the specific purpose technique—can both be taught to children as soon as they have demonstrated their ability to decode and comprehend informational materials and to write well enough to read their own writing. For some children, this will be during the third grade or even earlier; for others, it will be much later. It is very doubtful, however, that the teaching of note-taking skills should be reserved for high school, for by this time too many bad habits will have developed.

Increasing Comprehension by Encouraging a Flexible and Efficient Reading Rate

The process of gaining information and pleasure through reading can be enhanced by the development of a flexible and efficient *rate* of reading. Research (13) has shown that many people tend to read various materials inflexibly, at the same speed, even though the content of the materials or their purposes for reading them vary considerably. Research (3) also shows, however, that students can be taught to read nearly all types of materials faster and to vary their speed to match the materials.

Before looking at methods of helping students become more flexible in their reading, let us examine the problem that many children have of reading all materials too slowly. The following is a list of some of the factors which may account for overall slow reading and some suggestions as to what can be done about some of them.

Some Causes of Slow Reading

Materials Too Difficult

This is an obvious cause of some cases of slow reading, although one that is frequently ignored. Several studies in the past (2, 5), for instance, have shown that science and social studies textbooks often require children to read beyond their grade level.[1] This situation can be extremely frustrating to children and teachers alike and one for which there is no easy solution. Some of the "solutions" which teachers have tried are these: (1) refuse to use the textbook entirely, (2) use the textbook for advanced readers and find easier textbooks or trade books for the other children, (3) let the advanced readers read the textbook independently and meet with the others and read the textbook with them, and (4) save the textbook reading for the very end of a unit, at which time the necessary concept and vocabulary development will have been developed through other media. (The fourth approach recognizes the importance not only of providing background preparation for reading but also of presenting concepts through a variety of media.)

Not only are *social studies* and *science* textbooks often too difficult, some teachers try to carry on *reading* instruction with materials that are really at children's frustration level. This can usually be avoided by using some

---

[1] A study by Johnson (8) indicates that publishers are attempting to decrease the readability levels of their texts in social studies (although they are still too difficult for many students).

type of informal reading inventory at the beginning of the school year (and other times when you are in doubt) (see Module 12).

Reading Word by Word

Such behavior for the beginning reader is not at all unusual. However, reading one word at a time can become a habit especially when teachers have put excessive emphasis on phonics rather than balancing this approach with instruction in contextual analysis, sight vocabulary, and reading by phrases and larger thought units.

Inadequate Word Recognition Skills

Children who cannot decode words easily through phonic analysis, structural analysis, visual memory, or contextual analysis will either read very slowly or guess very wildly.

Insufficient Comprehension

As discussed previously, this generally occurs because of an inadequate background of verbal and nonverbal experiences.

Vocal or Subvocal Reading

Vocal reading is simply reading out loud (usually by whispering) when silent reading is called for. This habit is fairly common with beginning readers, but with practice in silent reading, it usually disappears, although it may be more persistent with those children who have not had opportunities for both vocal and silent reading from the very beginning of reading instruction.

Subvocal reading is also quite common among beginners and even among some adults. The most primitive form of subvocal reading is moving the lips. Although this habit may be easily overcome, many people then progress to moving the muscles related to the tongue, throat, and vocal chords.

The disadvantage of these habits, of course, is that they limit one's reading speed to one's talking speed, which is much lower than one can potentially read. Whereas a fast speaking rate is about 200 words per minute, a fast reader can read up to 1000 words per minute, providing he reads every word, and even faster than that if one defines reading as "just getting the gist of what is written."

It is doubtful that teachers of primary grade children should be overly concerned with subvocal reading, although most children by the end of this period of schooling can readily overcome the habits of whispering and lip moving. Generally, all that is needed is to draw their attention to the habits. Some children, however, may find it easier to overcome them by putting their fingers on their lips or by holding something between their teeth while they are engaged in silent reading.

Children in the intermediate grades can be shown how to detect the more subtle muscular movements by having them feel these movements while they are reading. For detecting tongue movements, have them place a finger on the middle of the tongue and read a passage silently. If a child finds it difficult to read at all or feels her tongue tensing, she should be told something like this: "Keep feeling your tongue while you read, but see if you can get your tongue very soft and relaxed. Don't try to hear the words in your head. Try just to see them instead."

Sometimes movements of the tongue, throat, and vocal chords can be detected by having the child place his thumb and forefinger against his "Adam's apple" while he reads something silently. In this case, subvocal reading will be indicated by small muscular spasms or vibrations. Some children will not be successful in detecting muscular movements but *will* report that they hear themselves talking when they read silently.

In any case, the "cure" for subvocal reading seems to require a combination of relaxing the tongue and throat muscles and consciously trying *not* to hear oneself read. This procedure is not easy for many children and should be practiced only with very simple material. Even then, the teacher should not expect very many children to catch on quickly. Too many variables are involved for this to be a one-shot cure. Probably one of the best long-range treatments is a steady diet of fairly easy trade books, particularly fictional accounts that sweep the reader along, causing her to devour books in large gulps. This type of opportunity, along with occasional reminders, are all that many children need.

Subvocal reading, on the other hand, should not be viewed as some sort of disease to be stamped out once and for all. Many of us, if not all of us, who have overcome the habit of subvocal reading, revert back to it when material is hard to comprehend. In fact, sometimes a passage may be so difficult, we'll find ourselves whispering in an attempt to understand it. Perhaps this is only one more illustration of what the linguists call the "primacy of speech."

Children *can* be trained to read faster. But before such training is attempted, the factors just discussed should be considered, and appropriate remedies for each child applied. It does little good, for instance, and may even do harm, to put a child through rate-building exercises when sight vocabulary or word analysis skills are deficient.

Various mechanical devices such as tachistoscopes and pacers have been used for years with the intent of increasing students' reading speed. Results of such practices have been too inconsistent, however, to be very encouraging (although these devices do provide incentive for some children). A simpler approach, and one that seems to work as well, is a three-component program similar to one advocated and tested by Harris and Sipay (6).

The first component is that of diagnosing and treating the more basic reading problems such as inadequate word recognition skills, insufficient comprehension, and so on. The second component is that of encouraging a good deal of voluntary reading of easy trade books in order to develop fluency. The third component is a series of rapid reading exercises, for which the children's words-per-minute and questions-answered-correctly are recorded. Motivation related to these exercises is enhanced by having the children keep a graphic record of both their reading rates and comprehension scores. (Or, you may wish to have them keep only a rate graph, "fining" themselves twenty to thirty words per minute for each comprehension error.) There are numerous commercial materials available for such exercises, including the *Standard Test*

Lessons in Reading (Teachers College Press) for children above grade three. *Developing Reading Efficiency* (Burgess) for children above grade five, and the units called "Rate Builders" in the upper levels of the *SRA Reading Laboratories* (Science Research Associates). For students who can easily read at the sixth grade level, I recommend *Timed Readings* (Jamestown).

Motivating Children to Read Flexibly

Many children who read an abundance of light fictional books find themselves trying to read textbooks or informational books with the same rapid speed, even though they can't understand them very well at this speed. On the other hand, that smaller number of children who usually limit their reading to information materials may attempt to read fiction at the same careful pace.

The task of helping children read more flexibly, however, cannot be successfully tackled until the factors behind the "reading-too-slowly" syndrome have been accounted for. Obviously children can't be truly flexible until they are actually capable of reading at various speeds. Once the teacher has helped them develop such capability he needs to explain to them the virtue of reading different materials at different speeds and to help them establish a *set* for each type of material.

For example, the teacher might compare the importance of reading flexibly to the importance of eating different types of food at different rates: Whereas butterscotch pudding (light fiction) can be gobbled with gusto, one needs to chew raw carrots (informational materials) in a thoughtful manner. Otherwise, digestion (understanding) is seriously hindered. A person doesn't need to chew butterscotch pudding, and she ought not to gobble raw carrots. Such explanations should be supplemented with occasional reminders that help the children establish the proper set before they begin to read. If they are about to read informational material, for instance, they could be reminded that they will now be dealing with "raw carrots" rather than "butterscotch pudding."

Children should learn to vary their reading rate according to their purpose for reading.

A more specific set can be established, however, by discussing with them their *purposes* for reading a particular selection. If Donald's purpose, for example, is simply to find out what an authority has to say about a very specific topic, it is often a waste of his time to read an entire chapter or even entire pages. By using an index and by skimming until he finds a key word related to the topic, he not only saves himself a lot of time but also reads *actively* rather than passively, varying his rate of reading according to his purposes. And this manner of reading, it would appear, is the type of mature behavior a teacher should be encouraging.

The child who reads flexibly, then, is one whose word recognition skills are highly developed, one who has learned to read *some* materials at a speed beyond his rate of speaking, and one who lets his purposes and his desired level of comprehension determine his rate of reading.

Increasing Comprehension Through Use of the Dictionary

Efficient use of a dictionary helps the student both in decoding and comprehending unfamiliar words. A dictionary is necessary in order for children to decode highly irregular words that are not already part of their sight vocabulary— words such as *psychiatrist, pterodactyl, pneumonia, gnome, aisle,* and *fatigue.* It is necessary in order for children to comprehend such words as *dorsal, myrrh, periwinkle, sustain,* and *bedeck*—words that are not common to everyday speech and might not easily be understood through context clues.

In spite of its usefulness, though, most people avoid the dictionary like the plague. For one thing, using a dictionary is the slowest method there is of decoding a word. If the word pops up in the middle of an exciting story, hardly anyone would want to take the time to look it up. In some cases, though, when one is trying to gather information rather than read an exciting story, the dictionary can be the quickest route to knowledge. But still it is avoided. Part of the reason for this may be people's lack of skill in using the dictionary. Such lack of skill results in a trial and error approach for most people—a laborious, painful process that provides negative rather than positive reinforcement.

Teaching Dictionary Skills

The "secret to success" in teaching dictionary skills can be stated negatively: *Avoid* assigning dictionary tasks that are too difficult. Too often children are asked to use dictionaries before they are really ready to use them. That is, the prerequisite skills have not been taught. And this leads to plenty of frustration for both the children and the teacher.

Let's take the word *fatigue,* for instance. Suppose you ask Henry to look up this word and tell the class how to pronounce it. What skills does he need in order to do this quickly and correctly? Assuming he knows where to find the dictionary (an assumption that could easily be erroneous), he should know first of all that since the word starts with *f,* he will need to open the dictionary somewhere in the first part of the book. If he opens it to words beginning with *g,* he must know that he should now go toward the front of the book rather than toward the back. As soon as he finds the *f* pages, he shouldn't look randomly for the word *fatigue;* he should head towards the first *f* pages, since the second letter in *fatigue* is *a.* To put it another way, he should know alphabetical order perfectly. As Henry continues his search, his eyes should only be scanning the top of each page rather than the whole page, for at the top he will find two guide words, which indicate the first and last entry for the page.

Now that he's found the word (take a deep breath), he should study the respelling in parentheses. In this case it's (fə/tēg′), rather than (făt′/ig/yū), which is what he thought it was going to be. Suppose he's thrown by the pronunciation of *fə*, the first syllable. Then he should glance immediately to the bottom of the page at the "Concise Pronunciation Key" to find that ə is equal to *a* as in *alone.* Now, by paying attention to the diacritical mark over the *e,* by noticing the syllabication and the accent mark, and by employing his knowledge of how to translate graphemes into phonemes, he is now ready to tell the class how to pronounce it.

Suppose you ask Henry to tell what the word fatigue *means*. He now has to glance down at the most common synonyms listed under the definitions and decide whether one of them fits the context of the sentence you have written on the board: "The old man felt more fatigue than the young man." If Henry is not sure which synonym is the right one, he has to go back to the definitions and read each of them, before deciding on the one that is most appropriate.

You can see, then, what you've really asked Henry to do! In list form, in order for Henry to decode and comprehend a word through the dictionary, he must be able to do these things:

1. Locate the appropriate section of the pages.
2. Determine whether the first letter of the word is before or after the page he is on.
3. Determine whether the second letter of the word is before or after the page he is on.
4. Determine whether the third or possibly the fourth letter of the word is before or after the page he is on.
5. Locate the guide words (entry words) which "enclose" the word he's looking for.
6. Locate and use the "Concise Pronunciation Key," if necessary, to determine the pronunciation of each syllable.
7. Use the diacritical marks to determine the pronunciation of certain graphemes.
8. Interpret syllabic division correctly.
9. Interpret accent marks correctly.
10. Employ his knowledge of grapheme-phoneme relationships.

11. Determine whether one of the most common synonyms fits the context of a particular sentence.
12. Read some or all of the definitions.
13. Select the best definition and apply it to a particular sentence.

Perhaps it is clear, then, that before we expect children to use the dictionary for decoding a word and for comprehending it better, we had better first teach them the thirteen skills listed. Each of the skills, of course, should be taught for mastery, and practiced on several occasions in a distributed fashion. Some of the skills related to alphabetical order can be taught at an early age, e.g., steps 1, 2 and 3 above. Some of them, however, will have to wait on the developmental program in phonics and structural analysis.

On the other hand, dictionary use can begin even in the first grade by employing simple picture dictionaries that are purchased or made by the teacher, or in some cases, made by the child. Have one page in the dictionary for each letter of the alphabet, in alphabetical order. On each page is a picture the child has cut out to represent an object whose name starts with a particular letter. Usually the name of the object is written under it. Also on each page is the letter, both in lower-case and upper-case format, isolated in one corner.

By the time children reach third or fourth grade, most of them are ready for specific instruction in the use of regular dictionaries that are designed to fit their reading level. Practice exercises to supplement actual dictionary use can be found in most reading workbooks. Many publishers of school dictionaries will provide teachers with free pamphlets on how to provide interesting lessons on dictionary skills.

REFERENCES AND BIBLIOGRAPHY

1. Boehnlein, Mary M. "Integration of Communication Arts Curriculum: A Review." *Language Arts* 54 (April 1977): 372–77.

2. Bormuth, John R. ed. *Readability in 1968*. Urbana, Ill.: National Council of Teachers of English, 1968.

3. Braam, Leonard, "Developing and Measuring Flexibility in Reading." *Reading Teacher* 16 (Jan. 1963): 247–54.

4. Burrows, Alvina, et al. *They All Want to Write*. Englewood Cliffs, N.J.: Prentice-Hall, 1952.

5. Chall, Jeanne S. *Readability: An Appraisal of Research and Application*. Bureau of Educational Research Monographs, No. 34, Ohio State University, 1957.

6. Harris, Albert J., and Sipay, Edward R. *How to Increase Reading Ability*. New York: David McKay, 1975.

7. Heilman, Arthur W. *Principles and Practices of Teaching Reading*. Columbus, O.: Charles E. Merrill, 1977.

8. Johnson, Roger E. "The Reading Level of Elementary Social Studies Textbooks Is Going Down." *Reading Teacher* 30 (May 1977): 901–5.

9. Karlin, Robert. *Teaching Elementary Reading: Principles and Strategies*. New York: Harcourt Brace Jovanovich, 1975.

10. Lopardo, Genevieve S. "LEA—Cloze Reading Material for the Disabled Reader." *Reading Teacher* 30 (Oct. 1975): 42–44.

11. Mattleman, Marciene S., and Blake, Howard E. "Study Skills: Prescriptions for Survival." *Language Arts* 54 (November/December 1977): 925–27.

12. May, Frank B., and Eliot, Susan B. *To Help Children Read*, 2d ed. Columbus, O.: Charles E. Merrill, 1978.

13. McDonald, Arthur S. "Research for the Classroom: Rate and Flexibility." *Journal of Reading* 7 (Jan. 1965): 187–91.

14. Schwartz, Elain, and Sheff, Alice. "Student Involvement in Questioning for Comprehension." *Reading Teacher* 29 (Nov. 1975): 150–54.

15. Taylor, Sanford E. et al. *Grade Level Norms for the Components of the Fundamental Reading Skill*. Research Bulletin No. 3. Huntington, New York: Educational Development Laboratories, 1960.

Encouraging Critical Listening and Reading

Yield not your minds to the passive impressions which others may make upon them. . . .

Tryon Edwards

Critical listening and reading skills may be a luxury in a totalitarian society. In a democracy, however, they are as basic as any of the other basic skills we have been discussing. A democratic society short of critically thinking citizens can too easily be converted to a society manipulated by the elite—democratic in form but not in substance.

Even if such societal demands were to provide insufficient reason for stressing critical listening and reading skills in the schools, there is still another justification: The process of developing critical thinking skills offers one of the best opportunities for refining the more simple basic skills related to speaking, writing, listening, and reading. For in providing experiences in critical thinking, we offer students the controversy and active involvement they often need in order to apply basic skills and in order to understand their importance.

Teachers who ask their students to make personal judgments about what they are listening to or reading usually notice an immediate increase in involvement—involvement which often leads to more speaking, more willingness to read or write, and more interest in listening to what others have to say. In other words, involvement in critical thinking often leads to greater practice of the basic skills related to the language arts.

Teachers who ask their students to engage in propaganda analysis, to take another type of critical thinking experience also notice, for the most part, an increase in involvement and learning. It is easy for students, especially students in the television age, to see the *relevance* to their personal lives of a critical examination of commercials: listening to them, reading them, talking about them, and increasing their understanding of them by writing their own.

This module deals with some of the specific training in critical thinking which teachers can provide children growing up in a language-burdened society. In our society, the language of propagandists badgers us at nearly every turn: "Buy this! Have you tried this? Shoppers: Run to that blinking blue light and save a dollar on something you don't want anyway! Hurry before it's too late. Vote for Stan; he's the man! Kids—get some chocolate covered pebbles for breakfast. Fred Flintstone loves 'em, and you will too!"

This module discusses research which shows that people really are persuaded by such "messages" and suggests tactics which may be taught to children to counteract the suggestions of propagandists. It also looks at other situations in which critical thinking needs to be applied while reading or listening.

Special Prerequisites for Module 10

It is recommended that you complete Modules 1–3 and 6 before beginning this module. There are no other special prerequisites.

Long-range Outcomes Related to Module 10

This module should help you as a teacher to do the following:

1. Communicate with other professional educators about methods of encouraging critical listening and reading.
2. Ask children specific questions during listening and reading experiences which encourage critical thinking.
3. Provide exercises which help children distinguish between factual and nonfactual information.
4. Help children recognize propaganda techniques.
5. Teach techniques of avoiding hasty judgments.
6. Help children evaluate according to definite criteria.
7. Help children evaluate according to logic.

Performance Objectives for Knowledge Level

To give yourself an overview of what is expected of you in this module, you should first scan the objectives and performance standards at all three levels—knowledge, simulation, and teaching. Then use the study guide during your reading of the module. As you find information related to the study guide, write it down in the available blanks or on a separate piece of paper. Then review this information shortly before your knowledge level examination.

In addition, to prepare for the examination, be sure to study the other examples under "Exercises Requiring Deductions," "Exercises Requiring Recognition of Assumptions," "Exercises Requiring Evaluation of Inferences," and "Exercises Requiring Evaluation of Arguments."

1.1 On a closed-book examination, you will be expected to provide information in short, concise sentences either by producing a list, completing a list, or by some other means. The information called for is described in the study guide.

1.2 On the same examination, you will be asked to indicate with a letter whether a teacher's question requires (a) literal thinking, (b) inferential thinking, or (c) critical thinking.

1.3 On the same examination, you will be asked to match a set of critical thinking skills with a set of classroom exercises designed to emphasize those skills.

1.4 On the same examination, you should be able to match a set of propaganda techniques with a set of ads which demonstrate those techniques.

1.5 On the same examination, you should be able to match a set of propaganda techniques with a set of questions which children should learn in order to counteract those techniques.

1.6 On the same examination, you will be asked to solve a set of problems requiring you to evaluate according to logic.

Study Guide for Knowledge Level Examination

1. Distinguishing between factual and nonfactual information is a major type of critical thinking skill. List four other major types.

2. For each type of thinking write either a definition or a sample question:

   Literal thinking

   Inferential thinking

   Critical thinking

3. For each subskill, write a sample classroom exercise. (After each capital letter write in the major type of critical thinking skill—see letter A.)

   A. Distinguishing between factual and nonfactual information

      1) Between literal and figurative expressions

      2) Between fact and fantasy

      3) Between fact and satire

      4) Between factual statements and opinions

      5) Between observations, inferences and judgments

  B. Detecting propaganda techniques

  C.

      1) Withholding judgment during brainstorming

      2) Recognizing stereotypical thinking

  D. Evaluating according to criteria

  E.

      1) Recognizing hidden assumptions

      2) Evaluating premises and conclusions

      3) Determining validity of inferences

      4) Determining strength of arguments

      5) Recognizing the difference between words and things

4. One way of helping children learn to counteract propaganda is to have them study ads in order to recognize the various propaganda techniques. List five other ways.

5. Seven propaganda techniques are discussed in Module 10. Next to each one, write an example of an advertisement that will help you remember the technique when taking the examination.

   a. Referring to Authority:
     "Doctors agree on the effectiveness of this ingredient."

   b. Join the Gang

   c. The Rub-off

   d. Flattery

   e. The Image

   f. Hypnotism

   g. The Fib

6. Next to each propaganda technique write one or more sample questions that children should learn in order to counteract the propaganda.

   a. Referring to Authority: "Who are the experts?" "Is it good for me?"

   b. Join the Gang

   c. The Rub-off

   d. Flattery

   e. The Image

   f. Hypnotism

   g. The Fib

7. Which conclusion logically follows the two premises?

Premise A: All horses have tails.
Premise B: All blimnews have tails.

   Conclusion A: Horses and blimnews are really the same type of animal.
   Conclusion B: Horses and blimnews are biologically related.
   Conclusion C: Horses and blimnews belong to a category of animals with tails.

Performance Standards for Knowledge Level

A. Twenty-five minute time limit on 1.1–1.6 combined.

B. Completion deadline: instructor will notify.

C. Recommended grading standards if grades are used: 96% = A; 92% = A–; 88% = B; 80% = C; below 80% = incomplete; should be completed at 80% or better before you go on to performance objectives for simulation level. (The instructor may wish to permit a grade of A or B only the first time the test is given in order to encourage more intensive study.)

Performance Objectives for Simulation Level

2.1 Teach one of the following propaganda techniques to your peers. (Your instructor may wish to have you do this with one or more partners.)
   a. Referring to authority
   b. Join the gang
   c. The rub-off
   d. Flattery
   e. Image
   f. Hypnotism
   g. Fib

2.2 (Alternative objective) Same as 2.1 but develop a written lesson plan for teaching one of them to children instead.

Performance Standards for Simulation Level

A. For Objective 2.1 (Teaching Peers)
   1. Uses visual images such as a mock T.V. ad or drawings.
   2. Shows clear understanding of the propaganda technique.
   3. Seems to get peers to understand technique better.
   4. Uses learning principles effectively; does not violate any of those discussed in Module 3.

B. For Objective 2.2 (Lesson Plan)

1. The performance objectives clearly state the behavior desired, the conditions under which the behavior is to be performed, and those performance standards which will indicate sufficient mastery of the desired behavior.
2. The performance objectives relate directly to the long-range outcome; the learning activities relate to both the performance objectives and the long-range outcome.
3. Standards A-1 and A-2 would be appropriate.

Performance Objectives for Teaching Level

3.1 In a micro-teaching, observation, student teaching, intern, or supervised teaching situation, teach a lesson related to one of these categories of critical thinking skills *applied to listening*.
A. Distinguish between factual and nonfactual information.
B. Detecting propaganda techniques.
C. Avoiding hasty judgments.
D. Evaluating according to criteria.
E. Evaluating according to logic.
Be sure to limit your lesson to one or two subskills for the category you choose. (See "Nature of Critical Thinking" in this module for list of subskills.)

3.2 Same as 3.1 but teach the subskills as they apply to *reading*.

Performance Standards for Teaching Level

1. Uses learning principles effectively; does not violate any of those discussed in Module 3.
2. Shows a clear understanding of the subskills being taught.
3. Lesson plan includes those elements listed in Module 4 under "Performance Objectives for Teaching Level."
4. Self-critique includes those elements listed in Module 4 under "Performance Objectives for Teaching Level."

Nature of Critical Thinking

Thinking critically about what is being read or listened to requires many subskills. Some of these subskills are as follows:

A. Distinguishing between factual and nonfactual information.
1. Distinguishing between literal and figurative expressions.

     2. Distinguishing between fact and fantasy.
     3. Distinguishing between fact and satire.
     4. Distinguishing between factual statements and opinions.
     5. Recognizing differences between observations and inferences.
     6. Recognizing differences between observations and judgments.
     7. Detecting biases of authors or speakers.
     8. Determining reliability of informant.
  B. Detecting propaganda techniques.
  C. Avoiding hasty judgments.
     1. Withholding judgment until sufficient information is available.
     2. Withholding judgment during brainstorming.
     3. Recognizing and avoiding stereotypical thinking.
  D. Evaluating according to criteria.
  E. Evaluating according to logic.
     1. Recognizing hidden assumptions.
     2. Evaluating premises and conclusions.
     3. Determining validity of inferences.
     4. Determining strength of arguments.
     5. Recognizing the difference between words and things.

    As you can see from the foregoing list, critical thinking differs from literal thinking or inferential thinking (both discussed in Modules 7 and 9). Literal thinking, as you may recall, requires the reader or listener to simply translate information into his own words. Such translation may necessitate following a sequence of ideas, recognizing significant details, or developing images—all of which are important thinking processes—but may not require the reader or listener to go beyond the information given in order to make inferences or judgments.

    Inferential thinking, on the other hand, requires the reader or listener to go slightly beyond the information received by catching the meaning of unfamiliar words through context clues, by predicting what should come next, by determining main ideas, or perhaps just by appreciating the sense of humor displayed by an author or speaker. Information is inferred or guessed at from other information that is actually given.

    Critical thinking involves the reader or listener in making judgments. The critical thinker is removed one step from producing new information through inferential thinking and two steps from merely translating information through literal thinking. The critical thinker is more or less removed from the process of acquiring information in order to make critical judgments about that information.

    Let's return, for a moment, to a passage discussed in Module 9 about the great white shark:

> When the great white shark goes hunting, it does not
> bother to circle its prey and wait for the right

moment to attack. This twenty-foot monster isn't
afraid of anything. It attacks without worrying
about enemies. It attacks without any warning!

Here are some questions about this passage that would require *literal thinking*:

1. About how long is the great white shark?
2. Does the great white shark circle its prey before attacking?
3. Of what enemies is the great white shark afraid?
4. What picture in your mind do you have of the great white shark?

Here are some questions about the passage that would require *inferential thinking*:

1. Does the great white shark attack its prey straight on without hesitation? How do you know?
2. What do you think the word *prey* means?
3. Which is the main idea of the paragraph—the last sentence or the one before it?
4. Since the last sentence in the first paragraph tells us that the great white shark attacks without warning, what do you think this story is going to be about?

Here are some questions about the passage that would require *critical thinking*:

1. What word do you think describes the great white shark best— *strong, mean,* or *fearless*? Why do you think so?
2. Do you think the author would be afraid of the great white shark? Why or why not?
3. Does the author seem to be giving you facts or opinions? What makes you think so?

Teaching Critical Thinking Skills

At least two methods of teaching critical thinking need to be used. The most important method has just been demonstrated—to ask questions during a reading or listening situation that require the various subskills listed in the previous section. The other method is to emphasize each of the subskills by providing children with isolated exercises for each one. Such exercises should always be followed up, however, by helping the children apply the subskills in more extensive and meaningful reading or listening situations. It should be noted, of course, that some of the subskills are too difficult for young children and need to be saved for the upper elementary years. The subskills will be discussed in approximately their order of difficulty.

Distinguishing Between Factual and Nonfactual Information

Even very young children can be helped to see the difference between "real" stories and "make-believe" stories. Often this takes no more than a simple question or two: Could this story really have happened? Why not? As children get older, they can be taught to distinguish between fantasies and realistic fiction and between fiction and nonfiction and to understand the meaning of such terms as *folk tale, science fiction, historical fiction,* and *novel.* Other experiences might include the following:

1. Discuss the meaning of such figurative phrases as "shouting my head off," or "pulling my leg." Have them think of others that they've heard. Have the children picture in their heads or on paper "what the words *seem* to mean and what they *really* mean."

2. Discuss some of the metaphors that are discovered in descriptive passages. Ask what they *really* mean and what they *seem* to mean. For example, in the sentence: "John flew down the hallway to his classroom," what does "flew" *seem* to mean and *really* mean? Have them picture the two meanings in their heads or on paper. Here are some more to try:
   Bill got the *point* of my joke.
   That book is hard to *swallow.*
   Mrs. Smith *plowed* through the papers until she got them all graded.
   What busy little *bees* you are.
   You're a *pig.* Stop eating my cake!
   Hey, that's *groovy,* man. (for older children)
   The world is a *jungle.* (for older children)
   All we are is *dust* in the wind. (for older children)

3. Read out loud to the children the book by Jean Merrill called *The Pushcart War,* a satire which most children in fourth through sixth grade would enjoy and understand. Discuss with them the satirical comparisons that the author makes. Help them grasp the idea that satire is often based on humorous comparisons between something that really exists and something that is imaginary.

4. Read out loud to the children the book by Oliver Butterworth called *The Enormous Egg,* a book which includes satire that most children in fourth grade through sixth grade would enjoy and understand. Ask them to discover how the author satirizes ("makes fun of" or "pokes fun at") advertisers, politicians, and others.

5. Show the children how to distinguish factual statements from opinions by using nonsense statements similar to these:
   a. A snurtzle has two eyes and three fleb pads. (factual)
   b. Snurtzles are very good at swinking. (opinion)
   d. A snurtzle can swink fifty gallons a day. (factual)
   d. It is clear that snurtzles are always flumptuous. (opinion)

6. Present them with a list of statements (either orally or in writing, depending on their reading abilities) and have them indicate which statements seem factual and which seem to be opinions. Discuss their answers with them. The following are sample statements:
   a. Children at Jefferson School are very smart.

   b. Winters are very cold in our town.
   c. The lowest temperature in our town last winter was five degrees.
   d. Jimmy usually gets no more than one wrong on the weekly spelling test.
   e. Jimmy is an excellent speller.

7. Look for opinions in social studies texts, basal readers, library books, newspaper reports, and so on.

8. Have them compare information in two science books, one published recently and one published several years ago; see how many disagreements they can find about a particular topic, such as Mars or atoms. Show them where to find the copyright date in books. Discuss the importance of recency for some information.

9. Have them compare information given in a story with information from an up-to-date encyclopedia. If the information is conflicting, help them find out why it is and which information is probably the most accurate.

10. Have them compare two newspaper reports of the same event to determine how biases influenced the news.

11. Help them learn to distinguish among observations, inferences, and judgments by using three-part statements such as the following:

   Observation: We saw Jimmy Smith take the milk off the porch.
   (Noticing)
   Inference: Jimmy *stole* the milk.
   (Guessing)
   Judgment: Jimmy is a *thief*.
   (Judging)

   Noticing: Jimmy took the milk off Mrs. Jones' porch.
   Guessing: Mrs. Jones asked Jimmy to keep her milk while she was on vacation.
   Judging: Jimmy is a nice kid.

   Noticing: Timmy kicked a dog.
   Guessing: Timmy likes to kick dogs.
   Judging: Timmy's a mean kid.

   Noticing: Timmy kicked a dog that bit him.
   Guessing: Timmy got angry with the dog.
   Judging: Timmy had a right to kick the dog.

12. Present the children with an observation and have them invent inferences and judgments to go with it. For example, have the children write Noticing, Guessing, and Judging on their papers, with a horizontal line next to each word. Then have them fill in something like this for the noticing blank: "Sammy asked Mr. Snell for the ball that crashed through Mr. Snell's window." Have the children work independently and then compare the inferences and judgments about Mr. Snell that they determine.

13. Have a few children put on a spontaneous dramatization of an argument in front of the class. Then have all the children write a newspaper report of the event without using any "guessing" or "judging." Have them exchange papers and circle any time that guessing or judging was used instead of just noticing.

14. Numerous up-to-date science programs for elementary schools can be used to help children understand the difference between observations and inferences.

Teaching Children About Propaganda

Propaganda is the art of telling only one side of the story—the side that benefits the propagandist. Many billions of dollars are spent each year in the United States on that form of propaganda called advertising. (In 1978, one minute of advertising on "Happy Days" cost $212,000.00.) No one really knows how much is spent on the form called political campaigning. We do know, though, that many millions are spent each year on motivation analysis—the science of getting people to buy goods, services, and leaders. And we do know that politicians, or at least their ad people, use many of the same tactics as soap peddlers. In fact, this creates the potential danger, as Hughes (9) points out, of disarmament being discussed on the level of deodorants.

No one would argue with advertising as a necessary means of keeping the economy on the move. In fact, most educators in the United States are probably in favor of a free enterprise system of selling goods and services. But education is a service too. And one aspect of our service should be that of teaching people to differentiate between advertising that educates and advertising that misleads through propaganda.

Those who watch children's shows on T.V. know that propagandists do not aim their arrows only at the adult population. Packard (14) quotes one ad person who advocates an all-out assault on children:

> It takes time, yes, but if you expect to be in business for any length of time, think of what it can mean to your firm in profits if you condition a million or ten million children who will grow up into adults trained to buy your product as soldiers are trained to advance when they hear the trigger words "forward march."

A *Newsweek* survey reported by Packard (14) showed that children are very attentive to commercials and tend to feel a loyalty to the advertised product similar to their loyalty to the program. A study done by Bateman and Remmers (1) demonstrated that even high school students can be influenced quite easily by propaganda. A passage unfavorable to labor unions was read to the students after a pretest dealing with attitudes toward labor unions had been administered. A posttest showed a significant shift toward a less favorable attitude toward labor unions. A second passage, one in *favor* of labor unions, was read and a second posttest was administered. There was a significant change this time toward a more favorable attitude.

Research by Collier (3) illustrates that merely informing students of propaganda techniques is not enough to counteract the influence of propa-

Children can be easily influenced by advertising.

ganda. A group of college students were given two lectures on propaganda techniques and then told to read some Nazi propaganda in the library on their own. Compared to a control group, these students tended to become more favorable toward the Nazi viewpoint, as shown by pre- and posttests.

It appears likely that *intensive* training is necessary to counteract propaganda and allow students to develop the ability to make decisions on a more objective basis. Furthermore, it would seem advisable to provide such training early in life rather than wait until high school or college. Wolfe (19) and Kottmeyer (11) were both successful in teaching intermediate grade children to analyze the techniques of advertisers. My own experience with children suggests that such analysis can begin, on a limited scale, as early as the first grade.

DETECTING PROPAGANDA TECHNIQUES

Although there are dozens of techniques that commercial and political propagandists have invented, only seven which seem most common will be discussed. These have been culled from personal observations and from writings of propaganda analysts (7, 8, 9, 13, 14). The techniques will be discussed in the order which appears to be appropriate for study by children.

Referring to Authority (Expert)

The propaganda technique of referring to authorities or experts has probably been a favorite for several thousands years. It seems almost natural for a child engaged in argument to refer to Mom or Dad or Teacher: "My mom said so," or "If you don't believe me, just ask my teacher." Orators of the Middle Ages usually covered their argument with a quote from Aristotle or from the Bible. It is second nature for many politicians to quote Lincoln or FDR or John F. Kennedy. And advertisements often begin with such clinching phrases as "Doctors agree" or "Four out of five dentists agree."

The following are some other ads that children can analyze for *expert appeal.* Children may also enjoy finding ads in magazines and reporting on ads seen on television.

1. "Michelin's the one that's made radials longer than anyone in the world."
2. Mrs. Olsen, the "expert" from the old country tells the younger woman about Folger's coffee. (even though most coffee is produced in South America)
3. "In his day, Sam Breakstone was one of the most demanding men alive. But if he weren't so demanding, his cottage cheese wouldn't be so good."
4. Tony the tiger says, "They're grrr-eat!"
5. "Sinarest. Created by a research scientist who actually gets sinus headaches."

Here are some questions to teach children to ask themselves when they are confronted by the expert appeal:

1. Is it good for *me*? Even if a thousand doctors or children or firefighters say it's good, is it something that I should have? If two out of three doctors chew sugarless gum, does that make sugarless gum good for me?
2. *Who* are the experts? Which experts were interviewed—the experts working for the company that makes the product? Exactly how many doctors agree? Does two out of three mean two out of *every* three or two out of the three who were given a year's supply of sugarless gum? Did the company do the asking, or did an independent group do it?

Join the Gang

This technique is sometimes referred to as the bandwagon approach. Jump on the bandwagon before it's too late and you're left all alone. It's an appeal to our need for belonging, affection, and love. Like appeals to authority, this gimmick also must have primitive roots. Have you ever been a participant in an argument similar to this one?

FIGURE 10.1 Children Can Be Taught How to Counteract This Form of Propaganda

He uses BEAR aspirin— shouldn't you?

"No, you cannot go to the Red River Slob Dance."
"But, Mother, every kid in school is going to be there."
"Not the kids from respectable families."
"Susie's going. And so are Alice and Bob and Jerry and Lucille. And they all live in our neighborhood."
"Well, I suppose if they're all going. . . . ."

It is conceivable that this type of argument goes far back into the history of human beings. However, it probably occurs much more often today, if Riesman et al. (16) are correct in their observations that the past few decades of rapid population growth have resulted in a rapid rise in "other-directedness." Riesman et al. contend that most Americans are far more concerned today than they used to be about doing what others are doing and believing what others are believing.

A study by Marple (13) illustrates the strength of other-directedness in our society. Several hundred adolescents and adults were asked to express agreement, disagreement, or uncertainty toward seventy-five controversial statements on a variety of topics. One month later, the same subjects were asked to respond to the statements again. But this time one-third of the subjects were first shown how the majority had responded previously (join the gang approach); one-third were first shown how twenty "experts" had responded to the statements, and one-third were shown nothing. With the join-the-gang technique, one-half of those responses which were previously not in agreement with the majority were changed to correspond to the response of the majority. About the same results occurred with the "expert" approach, with very little change occurring among the control group.

This tendency toward other-directedness is grist for the propaganda millers. Their pet serpents are all trained to say, "everybody's doing it!" The propaganda hacks expend their energies thinking of different ways of saying "Jump on the bandwagon!" But it all sounds the same: "More people buy Hupmobile than any other make." "More choose Village Life Insurance: millions

FIGURE 10.2   The Join-the-Gang Technique of Propaganda

"*Everybody loves Maccarilli Pizza*"

more than any other company." "Vote for a winner!" "Forty million people can't be wrong."

Children will learn more about this technique by making up some of their own ads based on the join-the-gang approach. Here are other ads of this type which they may analyze and discuss:

1. "Why do so many want Blatz beer?"

2. "How come Metropolitan Life insures 45,000,000 people and can still keep track of you?"

3. "Scope fights bad breath." "Listerine fights bad breath." (Hidden question: Shouldn't you?)

4. (commercial about a doll and all the things that go with it): "Cindy can be a friend. Pretend she's your very own friend."

5. "Ring around the collar. . . . . My powder didn't work." (Assumption: If I don't do something quick, I won't belong to the good homemaker club.)

6. "I'm a Pepper, he's a Pepper, she's a Pepper, we're a Pepper. Wouldn't you like to be a Pepper too." (Dr. Pepper drink)

7. "Now the world belongs to Charlie." (a perfume)

8. "We're voting for McCloskey. Shouldn't you vote for him too?"

9. "We're selling more and more Brand X cars than ever before."

Here are some questions for children to learn as they analyze ads with the join-the-gang approach:

1. What does *more* mean? "More than any other company that sells the same kind of product" is far more meaningful than just *more*. The term *more* in isolation, can mean "more than we ever hoped to sell of this miserable product" or "more people than last year—thank heavens, we thought we were headed for bankruptcy."

FIGURE 10.3   The Rub-off Technique of Propaganda

2. Do I need or believe the same thing? Do I need the same kind of bicycle, car, or soap that millions of people are using? Will this product do what I need it to do? Even though most of the class wants Fred for president, do I personally think he's the best person for the job?

3. *Why* do more people want it? Because it's cheaper? Because people have discovered it will last longer? Because this company has spent a great deal of money on advertising?

The Rub-Off

A third propaganda device is to get your feelings about something to rub off onto a product or a politician. This technique is probably based on Pavlov's experiments with secondary reinforcement. You remember how Pavlov caused dogs to salivate by presenting them with a piece of meat. At the time of presentation he also rang a bell. Soon the dogs were salivating whenever the bell was rung. The propagandist using the rub-off technique also presents two stimuli simultaneously. In some cases, the original stimulus may be simply a symbol such as a four-leaf clover ("Oh, boy—good luck for me."). The secondary stimulus would be the product he wishes to sell, such as margarine. The propagandist hopes, of course, that the positive feelings toward the symbol will transfer to the product.

Packard (14) describes one experiment which shows how effective this device can be. The makers of Good Luck Margarine gradually increased the size of the four-leaf clover on the margarine package. With each expansion of the symbol, there was a significant rise in sales.

Most politicians are masters of the rub-off technique. If the President comes to town, the local office seekers try to be seen with him as much as possible (coattail politics). When making speeches, politicians will often allude to past glories—how our party saved the country from a depression or kept the country out of war. Or they may attempt to transfer negative feelings by labeling rivals as Communists or Fascists or by bringing up an extinct issue such as the depression of '29 or the Bay of Pigs incident.

Commercial advertisers rely a great deal on the rub-off device in the form of testimonials. Movie stars and other celebrities pick up a good deal of money by mouthing sweet nothings about a product which they may have never tried before and may be content never to experience.

A favorite type of "rub off" is that of labeling a product or a person. By attacking a person as a Communist, a politician can make people's fear of Communism rub off on the politician's rival. By calling a product Zest, the ad person can transfer people's positive feelings about the word *zest* to the product she is trying to sell.

Research shows that transfer through labeling is a very effective device. Sargent (17) selected several words or phrases frequently used in a Chicago paper to describe people or programs that the publisher either liked or disliked. He then presented these words and phrases out of context to a group of people, asking each of them if he liked or disliked or had no feeling about the word or phrase. Sargent felt that these words and phrases were used in the paper as labels which would encourage certain attitudes. He found that the labels used positively by the paper were more often liked than disliked by the subjects and the labels used negatively by the paper were more often disliked.

The following are ads or propaganda techniques which you may wish to use as examples with your students:

1. "Zip is the drink for you."
2. "Please don't take my gusto away." (referring to beer)
3. "I'm a Lipton Tea Lover." (former pro quarterback)
4. "As Mayor of New York City, I'm proud to introduce the next President of the United States."
5. "Ladies and gentlemen, most of you are parents. I'm a parent too. And I say it's time we parents did something about. . . . "
6. A governor took his demand to the Supreme Court to be allowed to lower the U.S. flag at half-mast on Good Friday. Even though he lost, he got a lot of publicity.
7. "Ford wants to be your car company." (famous comedian)

Some questions for children to learn to ask include these:

1. Are the two things really related? Does a four-leaf clover really have anything to do with margarine? Is a super star qualified to make expert judgments on cars, iced tea, or soap? Is the local politician more qualified because she was seen shaking hands with the President of the United States?
2. Is this a dead issue? Does something Abraham Lincoln did have anything to do with what a Republican will do today?
3. Who stands to gain by the association between two things? The super star? The product's company? The politician?
4. Does the label describe a real thing or an imaginary one? Does the soft drink have "zip" in it, or does it contain carbonated

water, sugar, artificial color, and artificial flavor? Is Easy Off really easy off? Are Cheerios really cheery?

FLATTERY

Most of us like to be flattered occasionally and to think that we are special and different, and a person with very high standards too. That may explain why one cigarette company once used the slogan: "Wherever particular people congregate." (They were all smoking the same type of cigarette, of course). It may explain why some ads for women's underwear show a woman admiring her new shape in the mirror. (Women watching the ad are supposed to identify with the woman.) It undoubtedly explains why both political and commercial propagandists talk so much about us—how they care about us, how they think we *should* be treated instead of the shoddy way we're being treated now.

Here are some samples of propaganda using flattery:

1. "I drink Dr. Pepper and I'm proud. I used to be a man in the crowd." (Evidently, if you drink it, you'll be special too.)
2. "I use L'Oreal Hair Color . . . because I'm worth it."
3. "Morris, the cat, is very fussy about his food, but he likes Nine Lives Cat Food." (Hidden message: You were smart enough to get an intelligent cat that is fussy about his food, just the way you're fussy about *your* food. Without a doubt, you will be smart enough to give him the food he deserves.)
4. "I was flat, but I went fluffy. . . . You're going to swear you got more hair." (Prell shampoo)
5. "You've come a long way, Baby." (cigarette ad)
6. "And I know that you good people want something better than that for America." (political speech)

Here are some questions for children to learn to ask:

1. What actual information am I getting? I may be worth it but what have you told me about the worth of the product?
2. Who stands to gain from the flattery?
3. Why do I feel so good about what they're saying?

THE IMAGE

Motivation analysts (usually psychologists who are paid much more to help advertisers than they would get paid to help students or emotionally disturbed people) have discovered that most products and politicians have an image. This is especially true if the product has been on the market for a while and the politician has been around for a while. Prunes, for example, have the image of being a senior citizen's product. A Cadillac has the image of success. A Datsun 280 ZX sports car has a devil-may-care image. Companies, therefore, are very concerned about their image and either attempt to promote the image which their company presently owns or try to change it to a more favorable one.

FIGURE 10.4 The Flattery Technique of Propaganda

*I was flat, but since
I went 'fluffy', boy do I get noticed!*

An image is only useful to a propagandist to the extent that people can identify with it. Thus, a politician will often attempt to develop a father image, a person who will take care of us children, a good shepherd who will watch over his flock. Or he may decide, upon the advice of his advertising agency, to develop the loving son image, the young man for whom all mothers would love to cook dinner and of whom all fathers would be justly proud.

Commercial companies generally have no person for people to identify with; therefore, they have to personalize their products. A particular brand of cigarette takes on the image of virility, strength, and masculinity when big, husky, rugged cowboys are shown lighting up after a hard ride. Another cigarette takes on the image of a workingman's cigarette smoked by "men on the move. Able workers . . . keeping America on the go." A drug company develops an image of protector, of public benefactor, of the dedicated researcher striving unselfishly "to improve man's health throughout the world." A beer producer seeks to build an image of expertise by letting the public become familiar with the company's opinionated brewmaster.

The commercial image makers work hard to maintain the loyalty of customers who are buying the image more than the product. They even go so far as to insinuate that the good guys would "rather fight than switch." Their concern is understandable since studies show that many people can't tell their favorite brand of cigarettes or beer from other brands when the labels are hidden (14). The same thing might happen with politicians if they couldn't be seen and their voices were disguised.

Here are more examples of the image technique:

1. "Strong enough for a man but made for a woman." (a deodorant) Image: Feminine but powerful.

2. "No more ring around the collar." Image: the homemaker's friend.

3. "At MacDonald's we do it all for you." Image: good ol' Mom.

4. "Beautiful, says the man. "The watch or the wrist?" says a breathy, sexy lady. "Isn't it nice to find a quartz watch you can really love?" says a "sincere" narrator. Image: sexy.

5. "I'm just a country boy, but it shouldn't be too hard to run this city better than the city slickers we've had for mayors." Image: just a plain, honest, hard-working person.

6. "Keep 'em home for breakfast with Hostess. . . ." (You, too, can save your family if you provide them with the right dough-nuts in the morning.) Image: just a good wife and mother.

7. "Wheaties . . . breakfast of champions." Image: champion maker.

8. "When the people you care about get dirty. . . ." (soap ad) Image: loving wife and mother.

Here are some questions for children to learn:

1. Do I like the product or the image?

2. Why are they using this particular image? Who will it attract?

FIGURE 10.5   The Image Technique of Propaganda

"If it was good enough for Grandpa, it's good enough for me!"

Hypnotism

Hypnotism has a variety of forms, but the first stage in hypnotizing people is to get them into a state of trance (6). Propagandists use a variety of gimmicks to induce a mild form of trance. One of these is to use a soothing voice; bathe the listener in soft, glowing, bubble-words; say nothing, but say it smoothly, re-sonantly. Don't say, "They're made of mild tobacco." Say, "Aaaannd they are mild." Repetition and rhythm help too. Don't say, "Of, by, and for the workers." Say, "Of the workers, by the workers, and for the workers." Sing with fervor, "I'm a Pepper, he's a Pepper, she's a Pepper, we're a Pepper. Wouldn't you like to be a Pepper too."

But the most common form of trance inducement is the television show. The idea is to entertain the customers and while they're being enter-tained, slip in a few suggestions, such as, "If you're feeling tired it may be because of iron-poor blood . . . a bottle of this contains more iron than thirty rusty nails."

Political propagandists sometimes take advantage of the entertainment trance too. Since 1956 politicians have bought the last few minutes of popular television shows during a campaign. With the viewers already in a mild trance, the propagandists have a susceptible, captive audience (14).

Getting people into various states of trance helps to make them more susceptible to suggestion. But arousal of strong emotions accomplishes the same aim. When feelings such as hatred or pride are aroused, the susceptibility of human beings to suggestion seems to increase (6). That's why some politicians consciously or intuitively try to arouse such emotions. Adolf Hitler, as an extreme example, was a master hypnotist. By scraping on the nerve cells of envy, disillusionment, and fear, he was able to turn most of his weird suggestions into a dogmatic creed followed by millions. It's a rare political campaign in our country which does not attempt at least a touch of Hitlerian hypnosis. As Estabrooks (6) explains,

> the great orator is generally a great hypnotist using direct or prestige suggestion with far more skill than the psychologist employs when he works with hypnotic suggestion. In general, his appeal will be on an emotional, nonlogical basis since this sensitizes the brain and gives his suggestions far greater strength than can be obtained with any logical appeal.

Packard (14) reports that as early as 1955, commercial ad men were considering the use of hypnosis-trained television announcers. An advertisement in 1965 demonstrated how far they went in their thinking. This advertisement for a headache tablet was accompanied by a ticking and swinging pocket watch on a chain, an image of a distressed woman, and a deep, resonating, rhythmic voice intoning the word "Pain . . . Pain . . . Pain."

Today, hypnotic suggestions are employed with a little more subtlety. Here are some examples:

1. (eerie guitar chords; a very deep resonant voice speaking in a very insistent manner) "There's one frozen dish you've never had and it's the one you've been waiting for. . . ." (Morton's frozen steaks)

2. Very attractive person staring directly at you from the page of a magazine. It is difficult to avoid looking at the staring eyes. Once you've been attracted to the page, you realize you're being sold a particular brand of cigarette.

Questions for students to learn to ask include these:

1. What does the hypnotic music have to do with the product?
2. What does the hypnotic voice have to do with the product?
3. Do I like the product or the show I've been watching?
4. Why is the name of the product being repeated so often?
5. Do I like the product or that person's looks?

The Fib

Propagandists usually can't tell a direct lie without getting in trouble. But they can tell a fib, a minor falsehood such as a half-truth or a misleading statement. And they do, over and over again. Political propagandists are well-known for their use of the fib. (Even former Presidents of the United States have been known to use it at times. In fact, it might be hard to find a live person who has never used this technique.) In a West Coast newspaper on November 2, 1964, two days before people were to vote on Proposition 17, an advertisement appeared urging people to "Vote No on Proposition 17." Under a picture of President Johnson in bold type were the words "President Johnson has denounced the promoters of 17." A person reading no further would assume that Johnson was against Proposition 17. But later in the advertisement, in very small type, were the words: "President Johnson has denounced the unauthorized use of his name by the promoters of Proposition 17." In other words, Johnson was probably in favor of Proposition 17 but didn't want his name to be linked with it. The advertisement, however, made it seem that Johnson was against it by telling a half-truth or fib.

Commercial propagandists are fond of the fib too. Many years ago a drug company came up with a claim: "At last, a nasal spray that thinks like a doctor!" Clearly a fib. Everyone knows that nasal sprays can't think like a doctor. (They might be able to think like a perfume dispenser, or an elephant spraying people who won't give him any more peanuts, but never like a doctor.)

Making misleading statements seems to be part of the science of propaganda. Tell people that a nasal spray can think like a doctor. They won't believe it, of course, but the analogy between a doctor and a nasal spray has now been made, and with some people analogies tend to "stick" in the mind.

Or make a statement that implies something else. Take this ad, for instance: "How do husbands react when wives suddenly look years younger? They're a little puzzled at first but they love it, say 9½ out of 10 husbands interviewed." The advertiser then goes on to reason that since a woman's looks depend so much on her hair she should do something about "washing" that gray away with his special shampoo. Two implications are evident, even though buried in soap suds. One is that 9½ out of 10 husbands liked their wives better after they used the advertiser's shampoo; yet the survey had nothing to do with shampoo! The second implication is that the woman does not have to stoop to such a practice as dying her hair; in a very natural way, she merely washes the gray away. It takes a new kind of thinking to understand this part of the advertisement. When you put blue paint over a white wall, you have to say to yourself, "I'm not painting blue over white, I'm painting the white away."

One skin product is advertised as "88 percent moisturizer . . . and 100 percent beautiful." Besides using poor English, the advertisers imply that by giving you 88 percent moisturizer they are giving you something really special, something that will make you completely beautiful. In actual fact, they are giving you nothing more than any other moisturizer gives you—some type of oil to keep the moisture inside your skin from evaporating so rapidly. In other words, they are telling you a fib without telling you a direct lie.

Here are other examples of the fib:

1. (Morton's frozen steaks) "Go ahead. Compare our platter to what you'd get at a steakhouse." (Implication: You'll find our frozen steaks are as good or better than you'll find at a steakhouse. Fact: All they've really said is, "We dare you to compare.")

2. (Hellman's Big H sauce) "It turns your kitchen into the best hamburger place in town."

3. (Prell shampoo) "You're going to swear you got more hair."

4. (Rolaids antacid) "In this test with Rolaid's active ingredient, laboratory acid changes color to prove Rolaids consumes forty-seven times its weight in excess stomach acid." (Does the change in color really prove it?)

5. (Baby-Come-Back doll) Shows doll walking, turning, and returning to delighted child. A half-truth since the doll only works on a smooth floor and won't work on a carpet.

6. (Miracle Whip Salad Dressing) "A sandwich just isn't a sandwich without Miracle Whip."

7. (Charlie, a perfume) "A different fragrance that thinks your way." (Message: Charlie will have a different odor on you than on anyone else. But this is true of all perfumes.)

8. (Westinghouse appliances) "You can be sure if it's Westinghouse." (Sure of what?)

9. (Ford car) "Ford LTD—700 percent quieter." (Than a tank? Than it was fifty years ago? Than what?)

10. (Mouthwash) "Fights bad breath." (Does *fights* mean stops?)

11. (Nestles' cocoa) "Hot Nestles' cocoa is the very best." (Legally this simply means that it is as good as but no better than any other cocoa on the market.)

12. (mascara) "There's no other mascara like it." (True, since no other manufacturer even dreamed of putting in the same strange useless ingredient. What are they really trying to make you think, though, about their product?)

13. (Zenith TV) "Only Zenith has Chromacolor." (Chromacolor is simply a trademark, a legal name that no other company can use for their colored television sets; Admiral has Solarcolor and RCA has Accucolor. What they're really saying is that only Zenith gets to use the word, *chromacolor,* but what do they want you to think they are saying?)

14. "Milk is a natural." (Once upon a time it was what might be called "natural." Now, to protect our health, dairies have to pasteurize it. To give it more protein and less fat, they add a highly unnatural powdered milk. Furthermore, most cows today eat grass that has been sprayed with insecticides and herbicides; the grain they eat has often been sprayed as well and fertilized with unnatural fertilizers such as straight

ammonia. Milk is still probably a good food compared to many others, but natural it is not. Why do the advertisers use the word *natural?* What might they gain by telling this fib?)

Questions for children to learn to ask include these:

1. What is the whole truth? (Does that doll always walk that way?)
2. Is *A* really like *B?* (Is a nasal spray really like a doctor?)
3. Does this "scientific test" really prove anything? (If the acid changes color does that really prove that Rolaids consumes forty-seven times its weight?)
4. Do words like *more* and *better* and *fights* really tell you anything?

Helping Children Counteract Propaganda

Several educational devices can be used to help children counteract the devices of propagandists. Some of them are as follows:

1. Have children study ads in magazines, on radio, and on television after or while learning about the seven propaganda techniques just described.
2. In small groups, have them prepare "television" ads which they can enact for each other and have the rest of the class determine the propaganda techniques used.
3. During a political campaign older children are sometimes capable of analyzing political advertisements or cartoons.
4. Have discussions about how they use some of the seven techniques to persuade their friends and their family.
5. Use some of the seven techniques to sell a product for the class treasury.
6. Help them find ads that "prey" on the normal needs of people for bodily comfort, safety, affection or belonging, and importance.
7. Discuss how we all use these needs to persuade others:
   a. Bodily comfort: "If you don't go with me, I won't give you some of my candy."
   b. Safety: "If you don't go with me, I'll hit you."
   c. Belonging: "If you don't go with me, you can't be my friend —and you can't get in our club either."
   d. Importance: "If you don't go with me, I won't vote for you for class president."
8. For very young children, study only two simple techniques: Join the Gang and Super Star Says So.

9. For older children, teach them to read the ingredients on labels. Invite a pharmacist to the classroom to explain the meaning of some of the strange terms on pharmacy labels.

Teaching Children to Avoid Hasty Judgments

An important skill that is sometimes ignored when teaching children to think critically is the skill of avoiding the premature use of critical thinking. Sometimes, for example, we ask children to carry on debates, panel discussions, or just everyday discussions without first giving them a chance to gather sufficient information. Thus, rather than teach them to withhold judgments until sufficient information has been gathered, we teach them just the opposite.

The problem with critical thinking is this: if we use it too soon we close our minds and block our opportunities to learn. One of the best ways of avoiding this problem is to teach the children to use the "deferred judgment" technique through brainstorming sessions. Brainstorming sessions are initiated by presenting the children with an open-ended question that requires several possible solutions rather than one right answer. Here are some examples of open-ended questions:

1. How can we make this room more attractive?
2. What are some games that can be played during recess?
3. What are some ways of stopping wars?
4. What are some ways of making friends?
5. What are some sources of information we can use for our study of the Spanish explorers?
6. What are different ways of keeping the corridor walls attractive?
7. What are some games we can play at the spring picnic?
8. What different ways of travel might Santa Claus use on Christmas Eve?
9. What are some ways of sharing the playground equipment?
10. How can we make sure everyone learns the multiplication tables?

As the children come up with ideas, the teacher (or one or two children) record them on the chalkboard. As the recording takes place, the teacher makes sure the children follow two simple rules (1) no criticism is allowed until the brainstorming has been completed, and (2) quantity is wanted. Studies by Parnes and Meadow (15) have shown that when these two rules are enforced, not only are *more* ideas generated but also more *high-quality* ideas are produced. (If Peter's idea is criticized as soon as it is offered to the group, his reaction is usually to defend it or to refrain from making any further comment. If this pattern continues within the group, ideas and thinking soon dry up; emotion, apathy, and timidity take over.)

Generally the teacher sets a time limit of five minutes and continually urges the children to come up with more ideas before the time is up. (The greater the number of ideas, the greater likelihood of a few good ones showing up.) When the time is up, the teacher now asks the children to apply critical thinking to the list of ideas. Because the ideas are now up on the board and are not personalized, it is easier to be critical without hurting feelings and without stopping the flow of ideas. Furthermore, the children can learn the importance of withholding critical thinking until creative thinking has been given a chance.

The act of making hasty judgments often leads to stereotyping. We are sometimes in such a hurry to "size up" a person or an idea, we either add or subtract details so we can make a quicker judgment—one that doesn't conflict with our present beliefs. Back in the 1930s, two social scientists (17) demonstrated this phenomenon by showing several Southern white children a picture of an attractive Southern home. Many of the children reported immediately after viewing the picture that they saw a black person in the picture performing a servant's task. Actually, no people were shown in the picture!

Both addition of details and subtraction of details occur in the development of most stereotypes. Cowboy Henry Morgan is seen as "cowboy." If he doesn't seem to have some of the characteristics of a cowboy, we add them to our observations of Henry Morgan. If he has characteristics which conflict with "cowboy," we ignore those characteristics and subtract them from our observations of Henry Morgan.

Children often come to school with their heads full of stereotypes. A group of sixth graders, for instance, were shown a set of photographs of children and asked to select the one they would most like as a friend and the one they would least like as a friend. Nearly all of the girls and some of the boys picked a pretty, well-dressed blond with stylish hair as the one they wanted least as a friend. When asked why, the general answers given were these: "You can't trust a pretty blond," and "She thinks she's better than anyone else," and "She wouldn't be any fun to be with, because she'd always be worrying about her looks." Even though these children were only twelve, they acted like many adults and rigorously resisted the facts that were then given them: that the blond was actually very shy, that she felt insecure about her looks and seldom dressed up for fear of having people notice her, that she was a very sweet person and enjoyed playing all sorts of games. In effect, they responded to the facts with a very strong stereotype: "She's a stuck-up blond."

The following are exercises which may be used to help children understand the process of stereotyping:

1. Cat_1 is not Cat_2. Have each child draw and color a cat doing something that cats like to do the most. Don't allow discussion before they complete their drawings. Have the children show their drawings and describe them briefly. Select two drawings that show cats as quite different creatures. Label one as Cat_1 and the other as Cat_2. Now write some Cat Facts on the board and criticize them together. For example:

   A cat is a yellow animal.
   (Some cats are not yellow.)

Children learn stereotypes at an early age. What stereotypes do you see here? What experiences might teachers provide children to help overcome such stereotypes?

A cat is an animal that catches mice.
(Some cats don't even chase mice; some chase but don't catch.)

Cats like to sit in people's laps.
(Some cats refuse to sit in people's laps; some cats like to sit in laps only sometimes.)

Help them see that Cat_1 is not Cat_2—that cats are different and behave differently under different conditions.

2. Same as 1; use mothers instead of cats. Use Cat Facts about Mothers, such as "A mother is a person who wears a dress," and "A mother is a person who stays home and takes care of the house." (Remind them that Cat_1 is not Cat_2.)

3. Same as 1; use other stereotypes: snakes, cowboys, fathers, teachers, etc.

4. Select three boys in the class. Have other members of the class make up Cat Facts about Boys on the basis of their observations of the three boys, e.g., "A boy is a person with short hair," and "Boys are giggly." Then have the class criticize each Cat Fact as the teacher reads it aloud. Ask them whether this Cat Fact is true whether the boys are ten years old or one. Ask them whether this Cat Fact is just as likely to be true tomorrow as today. Ask them whether Boy_1 is the same as Boy_2. When is Boy_1 not Boy_2, etc.

5. Criticize these Cat Facts together:
   a. Dogs are friendly. (Under what conditions, etc.?)
   b. Boy Scouts are courteous. (Is this a fact or a "supposed to be"?)

    c. The weather is lovely. (What about those suffering from hay
       fever, etc.?)
    d. A good person is one who goes to church each Sunday. (Is
       Churchgoer$_1$ equal to Churchgoer$_2$? Is Good Person$_1$ equal to
       Good Person$_2$?)
    e. Fat people are jolly.

Helping Children Learn to Evaluate According to Criteria

Even in the earliest grades, children can learn to evaluate according to definite criteria. At the end of a story that Mrs. Bracing had read to her second graders, for instance, she asked them the following questions:

1. Do you think it was fair for Mark to go in the boat before Jim? Why do you feel the way you do?
2. Which boy had the smartest plan? Why do you think so?
3. Do you feel that Mark was more honest than Jim? What makes you think the way you do?
4. Which boat was the most beautiful? Why?

Such questions encourage children to evaluate according to particular criteria, such as fairness, intelligence, honesty, and beauty.

Children in the upper grades in the elementary school can learn to develop their own criteria and to make judgments according to those criteria. At the end of a brainstorming session on ways of redecorating their classroom, for example, a group of fifth graders came up with these criteria which they later applied to their list of ideas:

1. Cost (Will it cost too much money?)
2. Time (Will it take too much time?)
3. Space (Will it take up too much space?)
4. Skills (Do we have the skills to do it?)
5. Agreement (Will other teachers, the janitors, the principal, other children, and parents probably agree that it's a good idea?)
6. Equipment and supplies (Can we get what we need to do it?)

As they applied their criteria to the list of ideas they had brainstormed, it became obvious to them that some of their ideas would work and many would not.

Helping Children Learn to Evaluate According to Logic

Although Shotka (18) found that certain logical operations of critical thinking can be taught even at the first grade level, it is likely that intensive training evaluating according to logic will be more fruitful in the upper grades. Evaluating according to logic usually involves a subtlety of thinking which older children can handle much more easily. Exercises for five different logical operations will now be suggested:

Exercises Requiring Deductions

1. Study the following syllogism. Are the two premises true? Does the conclusion logically follow?
   Premise A: All people eat food.
   Premise B: All dogs eat food.
   Conclusion: People are dogs.

2. Study this syllogism.
   Premise A: People like to buy from a company they can trust.
   Premise B: Our company is one that people can trust.
   Conclusion: You should buy from our company.

Exercises Requiring Recognition of Assumptions

1. What assumptions are probably behind this statement? "We will arrive at the airport at 5:00 p.m. Saturday." Explain your answers.
   a. We expect to eat dinner at your house.
   b. No accident will occur on our way.
   c. Airplanes are usually on time.
   d. Saturday is a better time to arrive than Sunday.

2. What assumptions are probably behind this statement? "This rancher's wife knows that Drab is better than any other detergent."
   a. A rancher's wife has to wash very dirty clothes.
   b. A rancher's wife should know what detergent is best.
   c. Drab gets clothes cleaner than any other detergent.
   d. Drab works better than old-fashioned soap.

Exercises Requiring Evaluation of Inferences

After reading each of the following passages, decide which of the inferences are probably true and which are probably false. Are any of them definitely true or false? Explain your answers.

1. In Edwardson School, a poll of the students was recently made. It was found that most of the students like chocolate ice cream better than any other flavor. Over half of the students buy ice cream at the corner drug store at least twice a week. The main ingredients in ice cream are sugar and milk.
   a. Most of the students in Edwardson School would like sweetened chocolate milk if they had a chance to drink it.
   b. Edwardson students like strawberry milk shakes better than chocolate milk shakes.
   c. Most of the students at Edwardson School have a job or receive an allowance from their parents.
   d. The people who made the poll talked to more than half of the students.
   e. No one at Edwardson School likes chocolate candy.

2. Now with new Scotch Boy Walplex, you can roll on new beauty in a single coat. It covers so well, one coat looks like two. New

Walplex is especially made for rollers. That way there's practically no roller marks or splatter. No unpleasant paint odor, either. When you're finished painting, it's a snap to clean up. Soap and water takes all the paint off the rollers and brushes.

    a. This paint has a built-in second coat.

    b. A roller would work better than a brush with this paint.

    c. If you apply this paint with a roller, you'll get no roller marks or splatter.

    d. This paint has no odor.

    e. The paint can be washed off the walls with soap and water.

    f. Even if it takes a week to complete your painting job, you don't have to clean your roller until you're finished painting.

Exercises Requiring Evaluation of Arguments

Which of the arguments for the following statements are good ones and which are poor ones? Why?

1. People should drink milk.
    a. Yes, because we have a lot of cows in the world.
    b. No, because some people used to die from a disease carried in unpasteurized milk.
    c. Yes, because milk contains calcium, which is needed for strong bones.
    d. No, because cream is harmful to some people with heart ailments.
    e. Yes, because milk contains many vitamins.

2. Vote for Pinkston for President.
    a. Yes, he has been a soldier and fought for our country.
    b. No, he has never held any office before.
    c. Yes, he believes in democracy and freedom.
    d. No, he is short, fat, and bald.
    e. Yes, he has been a general and has been a leader of men for twenty years.
    f. No, he disobeyed a former President.

Exercises Requiring Logical Separation Between Words and Things

1. Give several objects in the classroom a new name. e.g., call the chalkboard *wumpa* (or, if this is too hard for the children to remember, *scribble-slate*). Let the children make up names for a few other objects. Have everyone use the new names for a few days. Then discuss the principle of "a word is not the thing." Ask them questions such as these: Can a piece of chalk be used for writing whether we call it *chalk* or *friglew*? Can a chalkboard be used the same whether we call it a *chalkboard* or a *wumpa*? If Nancy calls it *wumpa* and Larry calls it *chalkboard*, will they

have any trouble talking about it? Is it really something to write on, or is it really a chalkboard, or is it really a wumpa? Is this really a pencil or something I call a pencil? Could it be called something else and still do what I want it to do?

2. After a week of using the new names given to classroom objects, make up different names for the same objects used in Exercise 1; use these names for a few days and discuss the principle again.

3. Same as Exercise 1; use a foreign language for purposes of naming objects.

4. Have the children look up multiple-meaning words such as *run* in a large, unabridged dictionary. How many meanings does it have? (*Run* has over 200 in the *Random House Dictionary*.) Why does it have more than one meaning? If I say just the word *run,* will you know what I mean? How will you know what I mean? If two people talk to each other and one person uses the word *run,* will the other person automatically know what the first person has in mind? Start a "50 Meaning Chart" having the students find words with fifty or more meanings and write them on a chart. What does this show us about words and the things they represent? Are they really the same?

5. Discuss the common activity of name-calling. Why does calling some people a skunk or a rat or a dog hurt their feelings? How can a person whose feelings get hurt easily be helped to think about this? Is there something you can tell yourself if someone calls you a rat? What is the difference between a word and a thing?

REFERENCES AND BIBLIOGRAPHY

1. Bateman, Richard M., and Remmers, H.H. "A Study of the Shifting Attitude of High School Students When Subjected to Favorable and Unfavorable Propaganda." *Journal of Social Psychology* 13 (May 1941): 395–406.

2. Boehnlein, Mary M. "Integration of Communication Arts Curriculum: A Review." *Language Arts* 54 (April 1977): 372–77.

3. Collier, Rex M. "The Effect of Propaganda upon Attitude Following a Critical Examination of the Propaganda Itself." *Journal of Social Psychology* 20 (Aug. 1944): 3–17.

4. Dieterich, Daniel, and Ladevich, Laurel. "ERIC/RCS Report: The Medium and the Message: Effects of Television on Children." *Language Arts* 54 Feb. 1977): 196–204.

5. Ennis, Robert H. "A Concept of Critical Thinking." *Harvard Educational Review* 32 (Winter 1962): 81–111.

6. Estabrooks, George H. *Hypnotism*. New York: E.P. Dutton, 1959.

7. Harter, D. Lincoln. "Helping Pupils Understand Mass Persuasion and Propaganda Techniques." In *The Good Education of Youth,* edited by Frederick C. Gruber. Philadelphia: University of Pennsylvania Press, 1957.

8. Hayakawa, S.I. *Language in Thought and Action*. New York: Harcourt Brace Jovanovich, 1972.

9. Hughes, Emmett. "The Impact of TV on American Politics." In *Voice of the People: Readings in Public Opinion and Propaganda,* edited by Reo M. Christenson and Robert O. McWilliams, pp. 365–71. New York: McGraw-Hill, 1962.

10. Hunkins, F.P. *Questioning Strategies and Techniques,* Boston: Allyn and Bacon, 1972.

11. Kottmeyer, William. "Classroom Activities in Critical Reading." *School Review* 52 (Nov. 1944): 557–64.

12. Lundsteen, Sara. *Listening and Its Impact on Reading and the Other Language Arts*. Urbana, Ill.: National Council for Teachers of English, 1975.

13. Marple, C.H. "The Comparative Suggestibility of Three Age Levels to the Suggestion of Groups vs. Expert Opinion." *Journal of Social Psychology* 4 (1933): 176–86.

14. Packard, Vance. *Hidden Persuaders*. New York: David McKay, 1957.

15. Parnes, Sidney J., and Meadow, Arnold. "Effects of 'Brainstorming' Instructions on Creative Problem-Solving by Trained and Untrained Subjects." *Journal of Educational Psychology* 50 (1959): 171–76.

16. Riesman, David et al. *The Lonely Crowd: A Study of the Changing American Character*. New Haven, Conn.: Yale University Press, 1969.

17. Sargent, S.S. "Stereotypes and the Newspapers." *Sociometry* 2 (1939): 69–75.

18. Shotka, Josephine. "Critical Thinking in the First Grade." *Childhood Education* 36 (May 1960): 405–9.

19. Wolfe, Evelyn. "Advertising and the Elementary Language Arts." *Elementary English* 42 (Jan. 1965): 42–44.

Using Children's Literature to Teach Basic Skills

If I were to pray for a taste which should stand me under every variety of circumstances, and be a source of happiness and cheerfulness to me through life, and a shield against its ills . . . . it would be a taste for reading . . . .

Sir John Herschel

It is doubtful that children will acquire a taste for reading through workbook exercises on word analysis and comprehension skills, as important as these exercises might be. It is even doubtful that they will acquire such a taste through assigned reading of stories in basal readers, as useful as basal readers might be.

Children are more likely to acquire such a taste when they are given the freedom to choose some of their own books from the vast supply now available to them; when they are provided with just enough guidance to find books that match their needs, interests, and reading levels; when they are shown how to find answers to their own questions through reading; and when they are given *time* to read, with no strings attached.

Trade books, sometimes referred to as library books, children's books, or children's literature, are often given the role of baby sitter—something for the fast workers to read after finishing their assignments so they'll stay out of trouble. Trade books, on the other hand, can be used by a skillful teacher to provide the flesh to a social studies program limited to a textbook or to a writing program limited to mechanical considerations.

Children's literature can be used to motivate children to learn basic skills and help them practice and retain those skills they are learning. Listening and speaking skills, for example, can be practiced through book sharing and book dramatization. Writing skills can be practiced through a primitive form of author imitation and because of the inspiration to write that books can provide. Reading skills, of course, can be practiced through motivated reading of books that have been selected by children for themselves.

And not without importance is the value of children's literature in providing opportunities for exploring the natural and social environment, thus moving children closer toward the overall school objectives: emotional maturity, social awareness, intellectual vigor, and occupational success. Other values of children's literature and specific ways of using trade books in the classroom will be discussed in this module.

Special Prerequisites for Module 11

It is recommended that you complete at least Modules 1–3 before beginning this module. There are no other prerequisites.

Long-range Outcomes Related to Module 11

This module should help you as a teacher to do the following:

1. Motivate children to read a variety of trade books.
2. Use children's literature as a source of inspiration for children's reading, writing, speaking, and listening experiences.
3. Use children's literature as a model for better writing, speaking, and reading.
4. Use activities related to children's literature that provide practice with basic skills.

Study Guide and Performance Objectives for Knowledge Level Examination

To give yourself an overview of what is expected of you in this module, you should first scan the objectives and performance standards at all three levels—knowledge, simulation, and teaching. Then use the study guide during your reading of the module. As you find information related to the study guide, write it down in the available blanks or on separate paper. Then review this information shortly before your knowledge level examination.

1.1 On the examination, you will be expected to match a set of children's trade book types with a set of book descriptions. For example, the trade book type called outdoor adventure could be matched with this description:
   My Side of the Mountain—a boy proves himself by living on his own in the forest.
   For other examples and a practice test, see pages 384–86.

1.2 On the same examination, you will be expected to list four reasons for having children read trade books. Write them in the spaces below:
   1. Opportunities for personal growth.

   2.

3.

4.

1.3 On the same examination, you will be asked to describe the Newbery Award and the Caldecott Award, i.e., to whom these awards are given and how the winners are selected.
Newbery

Caldecott

How selected

1.4 On the same examination, you will be asked to match a set of ways of fostering children's use of trade books with a set of descriptions of those ways. After each one below, write in a teaching technique related to it. The first one has been done for you.

1. Help them find books that are not too difficult. Use lists such as *Good Reading for Poor Readers* to help you in guiding children.

2. Allow plenty of time for reading

3. Provide a wide choice

4. Suggest books relating to their needs and interests

5. Establish means for creative sharing and reacting

6. Use *some* extrinsic reinforcement

1.5 On the same examination, you will be asked to write a short description of a sharing activity a child or teacher could engage in for each of the five types of book projects described in Appendix B.
Oral project

Drama project

Written project

Arts and crafts project

Demonstration project

1.6 On the same examination, you will be asked to list five ways of using children's literature to motivate children's practice of basic writing, listening, and speaking skills. A sample is given below:

1. After reading a book aloud to them, have them write an additional chapter or a sequel, making sure they maintain the characters' personalities.

2.

3.

4.

5.

Performance Standards for Knowledge Level

A. Twenty-five minute time limit on 1.1–1.6 combined.
B. Completion deadline: instructor will notify.
C. Recommended grading standards if grades are used: 96% = A; 92% = A—; 88% = B; 84% = B—; 80% = incomplete; should be completed at 80% or better before you go on to performance objectives for simulation level. (The instructor may wish to permit a grade of A or B only the first time the test is given in order to encourage more intensive study.)

Performance Objectives for Simulation Level

2.1 As a take-home examination, read at least twenty children's trade books—at least twelve different types—and select or create an idea for using or sharing each book with children (see Appendix B, "Book Projects for Children and Teachers"). These ideas should be written or sketched on index cards and presented to your instructor. On each card put the following: (a) your name, (b) author's name, (c) illustrator's name, (d) title, (e) type of book, (f) a *specific* idea for using or sharing the book with children, and (g) a *specific* idea for using the book as a stimulus for motivated practice of basic language arts skills.

2.2 (Alternative objective) Same as 2.1, except a brief conference with the instructor should be scheduled for discussing some of the books you have read and how you might use or share them with children. The books discussed will be selected at random by the instructor from a list that you hand in.

Performance Standards for Simulation Level

A. For Objective 2.1 (Cards for Children's Trade Books)
 1. Shows evidence of having selected at least twenty books of at least twelve different types.
 2. Selects or creates a variety of ideas for using or sharing the books with children. At least four types of book projects should be represented and each of the twenty cards should represent a different activity.
 3. Has ideas for motivated practice of basic skills that are appropriate to the book.

B. For Objective 2.2 (Conference on Children's Trade Books)
 1. Similar to A-1–A-3.
 2. The teacher-in-training shows evidence of having read thoroughly each book discussed; plot, characterization, setting, and theme, for example, seem to have been understood.

Performance Objectives for Teaching Level

3.1 In a micro-teaching, observation, student teaching, intern, or supervised teaching situation, motivate children's practice of basic skills through the use of children's literature. Lesson plan and self-critique are required (see Module 4 for format).

3.2 (Alternative objective) Select three children's trade books, read them, and then see if you can get some children interested in reading them. Use an oral book project for one of them, an arts and crafts project for another one, and either a written demonstration or drama project for another. Write a brief critique indicating the extent of your success, the problems you had, and how you might do it differently next time. Hand in to your cooperating teacher, supervisor, or instructor.

Performance Standards for Teaching Level

A. For Objective 3.1 (Lesson on Basic Skills)
   1. Uses learning principles effectively; does not violate any of those discussed in Module 3.
   2. Writes complete and appropriate performance objectives.
   3. Selects children's literature appropriate to practice desired.
B. For Objective 3.2 (Interesting Children in Trade Books)
   1. Demonstrates that considerable effort has gone into planning the book projects; obviously well prepared.
   2. Successfully inspires children to read at least two of the books.
   3. Selects books that are appropriate to the age level and interests of the children.
   4. Uses learning principles effectively; does not violate any of those discussed in Module 3.

The Nature of Children's Trade Books

First of all, what is a *trade book,* as this term applies to books for children? Which of the following definitions would you select?

   1. A library book.
   2. A textbook
   3. A book that is *not* part of a series of graded instructional books.
   4. A book that is considered "literature."
   5. A book designed to inform.

The only "wrong" answer would be 2, a textbook. Of the remaining answers, perhaps the most accurate one is 3, a book that is *not* part of a series of graded instructional books, although this definition applies more to children's books than to trade books for adults. At any rate, those books designed to provide pleasure and information but *not* designed to provide basic instruction in a school subject will be discussed here.

A basal reader, of course, is a textbook. A book such as *Tom Sawyer,* or *Little Women,* or *An Introduction to Birds* is a trade book. Trade books, particularly if they are fictional or biographical, might be classed as literature, but here we are dealing with a word that is often value-laden. What is literature to some is trash to others. While I urge you to foster children's reading of "good" literature, I rely on your wide reading of children's books to provide the meaning for you of the word *good*. In the references at the end of this module, you will find lists of books that others consider to be good (2, 3, 12, 17).

Selecting Trade Books for Children

In many libraries across the United States, the juvenile circulation accounts for at least one-half the total circulation. This is a distinct rise from 1939, when the juvenile circulation accounted for only one-third of the total circulation (12). Part of this increase probably comes about as the result of the vast growth in the publication of juvenile titles—from 852 new titles in 1940 to over 3000 new titles a year today (12). Along with this quantitative growth has come an increase in the variety of children's books available. The ever-popular mysteries and fantasies now must compete for shelf space with fictional stories of ever-increasing realism, with informational books on nearly every conceivable subject, and with a host of other types.

Teachers who wish to foster children's growth through reading should be aware of these various types of trade books, so that they may participate in the process of getting the "right" book to the "right" child at the "right" time. To test your awareness, try the matching exercise which follows: see if you can find the type of book that a child needs. (Feedback and reinforcement can be obtained by checking the answers at the end of the exercise.)

The Type You Will Look For When

_____ 1. A fiction book which portrays people coping with the universal problems of life as these problems exist in modern times.

_____ 2. A fiction story which concentrates on finding clues and discovering why and how an incident took place.

_____ 3. A book of short selections, most of which describe the essence of something—sometimes in rhyming or rhythmic patterns of words.

_____ 4. A book in which the story is told or information given in two ways—both at the same time. One way is through words and the other way is through numerous illustrations.

_____ 5. A fiction story of an adolescent coping with the universal problems of love.

a Child Needs or Wants a

a. picture book

b. book of folk tales

c. sports story

d. biography

e. historical fiction book

f. science fiction book

g. realistic fiction book

h. mystery story

i. animal story

j. fantasy

k. informational story

l. outdoor adventure story

m. teen-age romance story

n. book of poetry

o. humorous story

p. book of plays

The Type You Will Look For When   *a Child Needs or Wants a*

_____ 6. A book of legends, fables, tall tales, epics, myths, old fairy tales, or any other traditional stories formerly handed down by word of mouth.

_____ 7. A fiction story in which sitations or characteristics— usually of a realistic nature—are exaggerated to the point of amusement.

_____ 8. A fiction book in which an animal, such as a dog or horse, becomes a heroic figure in a realistic way.

_____ 9. A fiction book based on principles or possibilities of nature and often involving future times, space travel, and other worlds.

_____ 10. A nonfiction book about a noteworthy person.

_____ 11. A fiction story in which success in an athletic game is an important element of the conflict and is generally related to the game of life.

_____ 12. A book of fiction stories written in drama format— nearly all dialogue.

_____ 13. A nonfiction book which explains natural and social phenomena or suggests experiments, activities, or procedures.

_____ 14. A fiction book which emphasizes historical settings and usually historical characters or events.

_____ 15. A fiction story involving considerable danger, courage, and a struggle with the natural elements.

_____ 16. A fiction story (created in writing rather than handed

The Type You Will Look For When   a Child Needs or Wants a

> down orally) in which the
> events are not only improb-
> able but seem to be impos-
> sible, e.g., talking animals,
> magic wands, tiny people,
> events conflicting with
> scientific knowledge.

Answers

1. g	3. n	5. m	7. o	9. f	11. c	13. k	15. l
2. h	4. a	6. b	8. i	10. d	12. p	14. e	16. j

If you got twelve or more correct, you should probably celebrate this event in some way, for these sixteen categories and their descriptions are slightly ambiguous and rely upon subtle distinctions. Some teen-age romance stories, for instance, might be classified as realistic fiction books. Some science fiction books might be classified as fantasies. Precisely how one decides to classify a particular book, of course, is not very important. What is important is that you become familiar with the various types of books that are available to children at various age levels.

If you're teaching second graders, you might be able to forget about the teen-age romance stories, but all of the other types have been published for children of this age. The teacher of children in the intermediate grades will want to become familiar with all sixteen types—even the picture books, many of which have been published for children beyond the primary grades.

The best way to become truly familiar with children's books is *not* to read anthologies or reviews, but to read and enjoy the books themselves. Included in one of the simulation objectives for this module is the pleasant task of reading a small number of children's books. Hopefully this will get you started (if you haven't already) on a life-long "trip" with children's books—one which will not only enhance your relationships with children but provide you with excellent bedtime reading.

In your reading of children's books, it is hoped that you will keep four things in mind:

1. *Read books for a wide range of age levels.* Remember that children at any grade level vary tremendously in their reading abilities and interests. Carolyn Haywood's books, for instance, (*B Is for Betsy, Eddie and His Big Deals,* etc.) are excellent for the average reader in grades two and three. But some children at this grade level will be reading fourth and fifth grade books, such as *Henry Huggins* by Beverly Cleary or *Little House on the Prairie* by Laura Ingalls Wilder, while others will be reading simple picture books like *Where the Wild Things Are* by Maurice Sendak or *Millions of Cats* by Wanda Gag.

2. *Read a variety of book types.* In this way, you can be more helpful to the child who is looking for "a real scary mystery" or "something really true to life" or even "a real good sports story."

Teachers need to be aware of the great variety of trade books available to children today. What types do you see here?

3. *Read them with a sense of involvement from cover to cover.* Skimmed books are as bad as poorly digested meals. Only by reading books thoroughly can you prepare yourself to share them honestly with children.

4. *Start by reading several that are considered by many to be of "good" quality.* Then when you come across poor quality books, you will recognize them almost instantly; thus, you will avoid wasting your own time and be able to recommend high quality books to children.

In the suggested references (and in Appendix C) at the end of this module, you will find sources listed (2, 3, 12, 17) that will help you decide which books are likely to be worthy of your time. The following list is for those who somehow cannot obtain one of these sources. It should be remembered, though, that this list is merely a starter and is biased by my concept of "high" quality. It is also somewhat weighted with books for intermediate grade children with the expectation that you will get more emotionally involved in reading them than you would with books for younger children. It is also weighted with books that seem to be perennial favorites of both children and adults.

Picture Books

Stone Soup, Marcia Brown
Mike Mulligan and His Steam Shovel, Virginia Lee Burton
Goggles, Ezra Jack Keats
Burt Dow, Deep-Water Man, Robert McCloskey
Abraham Lincoln, Ingri and Edgar Parin d'Aulaire
Thirteen, Remy Charlip and Jerry Joyner (a wordless picture book)
The Great Cat Chase, Mercer Mayer (a wordless picture book)

Folk Tales

The Merry Adventures of Robin Hood, Howard Pyle
The Cow Tail Switch and Other West African Stories, Harold Courlander and George
    Herzog
Thunderbird and Other Stories, Henry Chafetz
John Henry, An American Legend, Ezra Jack Keats
The Three Billy Goats Gruff, P.C. Asbjørnsen and Jorgen E. Moe

Realism

The Dead Bird, Margaret Wise Brown
The Big Wave, Pearl Buck
Durango Street, Frank Bonham
The House of Sixty Fathers, Meindert DeJong
The Noonday Friends, Mary Stolz
Berries Goodman, Emily Neville
It's Not the End of the World, Judy Blume
Trouble on Treat Street, Anne Alexander
Steffie and Me, Phyllis Hoffman
Me Day, Joan Lexau
Ronnie, Eileen Rosenbaum

Outdoor Adventure

Island of the Blue Dolphins, Scott O'Dell
Boomerang Hunter, Jim Kjelgaard
My Side of the Mountain, Jean George
Call it Courage, Sperry Armstrong

Biography

Amos Fortune, Free Man, Elizabeth Yates
Peary to the Pole, Walter Lord
Abraham Lincoln, Clara Ingram Judson
Daniel Boone, James Daugherty
The Columbus Story, Alice Dalgliesh
Freedom Train, The Story of Harriet Tubman, Dorothy Sterling
The Mel Ott Story, Milton J. Shapiro

Historical Fiction

The Courage of Sarah Noble, Alice Dalgliesh
The Witch of Blackbird Pond, Elizabeth Speare
The King's Fifth, Scott O'Dell
The Matchlock Gun, Walter D. Edmonds
Johnny Tremain, Esther Forbes
The Little House in the Big Woods, Laura Ingalls Wilder
Walk the World's Rim, Betty Baker

Fantasy

The Enormous Egg, Oliver Butterworth
Rabbit Hill, Robert Lawson
The Hobbit, J.R.R. Tolkien
The 500 Hats of Bartholomew Cubbins, Dr. Seuss
Mary Poppins, Pamela L. Travers

Science Fiction

A Wrinkle in Time, Madeleine L'Engle
The Space Ship Under the Apple Tree, Louis Slobodkin
The Boy Who Discovered the Earth, George Felsen
Miss Pickerell Goes to Mars, Ellen MacGregor
The Wonderful Flight to the Mushroom Planet, Eleanor Cameron

Humor

Homer Price, Robert McCloskey
Henry Huggins, Beverly Cleary
"B" Is for Betsy, Carolyn Haywood
Mrs. Piggle-Wiggle, Betty MacDonald
Mr. Twigg's Mistake, Robert Lawson

Poetry

The First Book of Poetry, Isabel J. Peterson
The Monster Den, John Ciardi
The Peaceable Kingdom, Elizabeth Coatsworth
Peacock Pie, Walter De la Mare
Like Nothing at All, Aileen Fisher
Wind Song, Carl Sandburg

Information

Ashanti to Zulu: African Traditions, Margaret Musgrove
How Far Is Far? Alvin Tresselt
A Tree Is a Plant, Clyde Robert Bulla
The Story of Ants, Dorothy Shuttlesworth
101 Science Experiments, Illa Podendorf
The Game of Baseball, Sam and Beryl Epstein
The Courtship of Animals, Millicent E. Selsam
Knights, Castles and Feudal Life, Walter Buehr
Eskimo Family, Moreau S. Maxwell

Animal

Blaze Finds the Trail, C.W. Anderson
The Incredible Journey, Sheila Burnford
Along Came a Dog, Meindert DeJong
Old Yeller, Frederick B. Gipson
King of the Wind, Marguerite Henry
Gentle Ben, Walt Morey

Mystery

Secret of the Emerald Star, Phyllis Whitney
The Alley, Eleanor Estes
The Witch's Daughter, Nina Bawden
The Mystery of the Hidden Hand, Phyllis A. Whitney
The Mysterious Christmas Shell, Eleanor Cameron
The Case of the Cat's Meow, Crosby Bonsall

Sports

All American, John R. Tunis
The Trouble with Francis, Beman Lord
Rookie First Baseman, Cary Paul Jackson
Little League Amigo, Curtis Bishop
Basketball Sparkplug, Matt Christopher

Teen-Age Romance

The Boy Next Door, Betty Cavanna
Fifteen, Beverly Cleary
The Innocent Wayfaring, Marchette Chute

Plays

100 Plays for Children, Edited by A.S. Burack
Plays, The Drama Magazine for Young People
Short Plays for Children, Helen Louise Miller

Reasons for Having Children Read Trade Books

High quality trade books have much to offer children: (1) opportunities for personal growth, (2) enrichment of the social studies and other areas of the curriculum, (3) esthetic experiences, and (4) motivated practice of the basic skills related to the language arts. Let's look briefly at each of these potential virtues.

Opportunities for Personal Growth

Psychologists tell us that one of the chief ways in which people develop values, ambitions, and a self-concept is through emotional identification with another person—by imagining ourselves to be that person or by actually becoming similar to that person. Trade books, particularly biographies and fiction, offer infinite opportunities for such identification.

A single book, of course, is not likely to provide as powerful a model as, say, a likeable teacher or an admired parent. Yet, if you will think for a moment about your own experiences with books, you'll probably remember the times that books made a difference in how you felt about yourself, about human behavior, about animals perhaps, or about beliefs or prejudices you once had. Even if one is unwilling to accept the possibility that a book could cause any permanent change in behavior (a possibility I readily accept), it would be hard *not* to believe that a book can at least reinforce one's developing values or make one question those values.

Enrichment of the Curriculum

Without the use of trade books, it would be nearly impossible to achieve some of the objectives of the newer social studies and science programs. In the social studies area, for example, the teacher is usually trying to help children identify with the problems, values, and life styles of different people. Simply reading about these people in a textbook will not accomplish this aim.

Social studies and science textbooks, because of their wide coverage, tend to be somewhat shallow, intellectual, and difficult. It is often hard for children to identify with the people talked about in social studies texts, and it is hard for them to find enough meaningful associations and examples in

Children's literature offers infinite opportunities for personal growth through identification.

science texts. More emotional involvement, more examples, and simpler explanations are often needed.

Films and other audio-visual media help a great deal, but trade books—fictional, informational, biographical—offer vital opportunities for emotional involvement and intensive study. Furthermore, because there are usually a variety of books at a variety of levels on a single topic, it is often possible to find just the right book for a particular child.

Esthetic Experiences

Some of the best writing and graphic art today can be found between the covers of children's books. (And probably some of the worst as well, it should be admitted.) Marguerite Henry's *King of the Wind,* for example, is rich in beautiful prose, sensitive characterization, and subtlety of plot development. To read a book such as this is to achieve that intangible something called an esthetic experience. One feels better for having experienced it, and perhaps that is enough justification for reading any book.

Then, too, there is the esthetic experience provided by the superb illustrations found in many picture books and other children's books today. Offset printing has made it possible for artists to use freely and creatively any graphic media they wish. A look at some of the books illustrated by Ezra Jack Keats, Symeon Shimin, Leo Lionni, and Marcia Brown will offer the reader the opportunity to test this assertion.

Two coveted awards have been associated with, and perhaps partly responsible for, the esthetic quality of children's books. One of these is the John Newbery Medal, presented each year to "the author of the most distinguished contribution to American literature for children." The book whose author will receive the award is selected by a committee of the Children's Services Division of the American Library Association. This committee selects the book which it considers to be the best one published the previous year, and also a number of runner-up books for that same year. A list of the winners since 1922 may be found in Appendix C. It should be emphasized that not all of the award-winning books are enjoyed by children, and some of them are better read aloud by the teacher because of their difficulty.

The other highly coveted award is the Caldecott Medal, presented each year to "the artist of the most distinguished American picture book for children." The winning book and illustrator, along with several runners-up, are selected by the same committee that selects the winner for the Newbery award. A list of the winners since 1938 may be found in Appendix C.

To limit one's selection of books, however, to the winners and runners-up for the Caldecott or Newbery awards, is to make the error of attributing some god-like power to the committee of human beings who make such awesome decisions each year. On the other hand, it is probably wise to read several of them to sharpen one's own awareness of those qualities that make certain books seem great and others mediocre.

Motivated Practice of Basic Reading Skills

Trade books provide motivated practice for those comprehension and decoding skills which the teacher wants the children to acquire. The practice is "motivated" because Tommy is reading a book of his own choice; and, if the book is the right choice for him, it is giving him pleasure. In other words, the reading experience is its own positive reinforcement and leads to the desire for more reading.

Even in the first grade, children can experience such practice, since several series of hard-bound "real" books are now available for children of this age. One of these series is the *Beginner Books* series, which includes the first one in the series, entitled *The Cat in the Hat* by Dr. Seuss. This series also includes such delightful books as *Are You My Mother* by P.D. Eastman, *The Bears' Picnic* by Stan and Jan Berenstain, and many others.

For the true neophyte, there's the accompanying series called the *Bright and Early Books for Beginning Beginners*. One of the books in this series—*Bears on Wheels* by Stan and Jan Berenstain—has only fourteen words, and surprisingly enough, is fun for both children and adults to read. Other books in this series include *Great Day for Up* by Dr. Seuss, *I'll Teach My Dog 100 Words* by Michael Frith, and many others.

Another important series is the *I Can Read* books, including *Frog and Toad are Friends* and *Frog and Toad Together*—the first of which was a Caldecott Honor Book and the second of which was a Newbery Honor Book. A companion series is called the *Early I Can Read* series and includes a book on a favorite children's topic, *Dinosaur Time*.

Allow Time for Reading

There are several ways of encouraging children to read trade books. One of these is simply to allow plenty of *time* for them to read. In spite of the hustle and bustle of a modern classroom, it is often a better place in which to read than the home. At home, remember, reading must frequently compete with the omnipresent "big eye," with its tempting tidbits of instant culture and instant action.

Many teachers sincerely believe that they do offer their students enough time to read trade books during the school day. When pressed to define what they mean by "enough time," though, some of them answer like this: "I let them read all during the day. Whenever they get their assignments done, they're supposed to get out a library book and read quietly." What this generally means in practice is that the same three or four students who always get their assignments done early are doing about 90 percent of the reading. Most of the others either spend all their time on the textbook-workbook assignment or, if they do finish early, they have so little time to read before the next assignment befalls them, they usually decide not to bother.

A first year teacher wanted to know why his fifth grade students didn't seem to want to read. When he was asked how much time they had for free reading, he said, "Well, whenever they finish their other assignments—and sometimes I give them a ten-minute free reading period before lunch." It was suggested to him that he try something for two weeks—giving them two thirty-minute periods a week for free reading. In two weeks' time, he had changed his mind about most of his students: "It takes some of them five or six minutes to get started, but once they get going, I can't tear them away from their books." (Who knows? Perhaps this is what a few teachers are afraid of.)

Fader and McNeil (15) recommend a timed approach in which, during the first week, only five minutes a day is set aside for intensive reading. This time is gradually increased until the children are reading intensively for thirty to forty minutes per day. In their book, they explain how this intensive reading may be encouraged. Their success with this approach leads them to advocate it for those children who are reluctant to read.

Some may wonder where all that time will come from. But if "the *reading* child" is a long-range outcome we desire, it seems imperative that the time be found and that time spent on less important outcomes be whittled down. Perhaps it will be conceded that an hour a week is not too much time to allow for the major objective of reading instruction. (It should be pointed out, of course, that a thirty-minute block of free reading time is too long for many children below the third grade. But unless one allows at least fifteen minutes, some children won't make the effort to get started.)

Provide a Wide Choice

A second way to encourage children's use of trade books is to provide them with a wide choice. This can usually be done in various ways, depending on the school and municipal facilities. Many schools today have their own libraries. Some teachers take their children to nearby municipal libraries to check out a collection which they then take to the classroom. A vast number of teachers encourage their students to purchase their own paperback books at a reasonable price from one of the well-known book clubs. These books, and other paperbacks available from bookstores, are usually printed from the same plates as the original hardbound copies, and the quality of selections is generally high. Some publishers have come out with fairly large classroom collections of paperbacks designed for "free reading" times. School libraries, municipal libraries, county libraries, state libraries, book clubs, book stores, publishers—some way can be found by resourceful teachers to provide their students with a variety of trade books.

Find Books of Appropriate Difficulty

Another way of encouraging trade book reading is to help children find books that are not too difficult. A child can easily become discouraged if one book after another offers little more than frustration. Teachers who make it a habit to read children's books themselves have little trouble offering children guidance in this respect. There are also numerous lists of easy reading books for those children whose interests are beyond their reading skills. One of the most complete lists is the paperback book by Spache, entitled *Good Reading for Poor Readers* (17), which has been frequently revised to keep it up-to-date. In offering suggestions to children about what they might want to read, whether it be reading just for fun or reading related to a social studies report, etc., it is advisable, of course, to avoid any approach which will make them feel inferior. Imagine, if you will, a well-meaning teacher in a crowded library offering a child a book with these endearing words: "Here, Ronnie, this picture book is about right for you!"

Teachers who read children's books themselves find it easier to be book advisors to children.

Select Relevant Books

A fourth way to foster the habit of reading trade books is to suggest books to children which seem to relate to individual needs and interests. Gradually during a school year, a teacher can get to know the pupils' interests, hobbies, and personal problems—through informal conversations and observations, and sometimes through a formal interview or questionnaire.

The teacher who also becomes familiar with children's books is in the enviable position of being able to suggest specific books to specific children for particular interests or problems that they might have. Perusal of book reviews is also helpful to the teacher in this respect. Sources of book reviews (18) can be found at the end of this module. *Reading Teacher,* the monthly journal of the International Reading Association, publishes an annotated list each year of "Classroom Choices: Children's Trade Books." This list is comprised of books that are selected primarily by children and includes annotations that tell how each book fits into the school curriculum.

Share Books

Still another way to promote trade book reading is to establish means for sharing books or reacting creatively to them. As mentioned in Module 6, many people feel inspired by good books to either share them in some way with others or to react to them in a personal, perhaps creative, way. The old-fashioned book report, it goes without saying, doesn't generally meet this need. A better approach, one that many teachers have found to be much more successful, is to encourage various types of sharing and creative projects following the completion of a book. In Appendix B you will find over seventy "Book Projects for Children and Teachers," which you can modify to fit the age level and interests of your particular students. The vast majority of these have been tested in classrooms (including the author's) and appear to be interesting and worthwhile to children.

Of course, the guidance the teacher offers is often the key factor in making the projects interesting and worthwhile. Simply passing out a list of projects is not terribly motivating. Probably the most effective form of guidance is that of reading children's books and carrying on some of the projects yourself. For instance, one of the oral projects suggested is to put on a puppet play about one part of the book. You can imagine what an inspiration your sharing a book in this way could be for children to read your book or to share theirs in a similar fashion. Don't make your presentation so awe-inspiring, though, that they'll be afraid to emulate you. Use a simple scene and puppets which the children could easily make themselves.

Along with the more creative approaches, just chatting a bit about a book you have read will usually encourage many in the class to read the same one. In addition to guiding by showing, however, the teacher can occasionally meet with individuals for a few minutes to talk about books they have recently read and ways they might share them with others. (Incidentally, sometimes a child would prefer to simply share her book with you alone.)

Although the oral projects, the arts and crafts projects, and the drama projects listed in Appendix B are usually carried on by the children with great enthusiasm, teachers report that the written projects are often greeted at first with something less than spontaneous joy. Here again, the teacher's leading the way will sometimes help immensely. A special bulletin board or "class book" for written projects is generally a must. Here the teacher's and children's written projects can be seen by the other people in the class (providing they *want* them to be seen). Again, however, don't overawe them with your writing powers, or yours will be the only one there. For children below the fifth grade, special praise in front of the class may also work in inspiring some children to take the "writing road to fame."

Use Extrinsic Reinforcement

A final way of instigating the trade book habit is to use extrinsic forms of positive reinforcement. We've already talked about intrinsic forms, such as finding books that are easy enough, making a wide choice available, and providing avenues for sharing and reacting creatively. All of these are directly involved with the act of reading itself. But sometimes this isn't enough, and some type of symbolic or even tangible reward may have to be used. This is a bit dangerous, of course, because if you're not careful the extrinsic reward might become more important to some children than the intrinsic reward of pleasurable reading. For reluctant readers, however, it is probably worth the risk.

One form of extrinsic reward is simply that of having the children keep personal records of the books they read. By checking these records with the children every few weeks and by praising them for the quality or variety or, in some cases, the *quantity* of reading they have done, you can often spur children on to further reading. Some teachers like to add a bit of spice to the record keeping by providing small rectangles (about one-half inch by three inches) of colored paper which represent book spines. On each slip of paper, the child writes the title and author of the book he has just finished; then the slip of paper is pasted on a dittoed "shelf," and the ditto sheet is placed in his folder or notebook.

Along with an individual record scheme, such as the one just described, you may wish to keep a class record of "Books We Have Read." However, note that this does *not* refer to a competitive form of record, such as a chart of names with so many stars after each name. Such a record may easily do more harm than good, since the slowest readers have no chance to "win the race," *and* because many children will falsely claim to have read certain books just to win it. What *is* being referred to is a cooperative record similar to the thermometer graph so often used for community chest drives or blood bank drives. Or you may wish to construct a "class book shelf," using different colored paper for different types of books. For this type of project, you can have the children put the title and author on the front of the piece of paper and their name on the *back*; these "books" can then be returned in an envelope to each child at the end of the year.

Some teachers give symbolic tokens for books that children say they have read; some prefer to give them only for books shared through projects. Whatever tactic teachers use, though, they shouldn't defeat the purpose by becoming too serious or demanding about it. Encourage rather than nag, inspire rather than require, help them cooperate rather than compete; these should be the mottoes of a teacher who desires to foster the reading of trade books and the motivated practice of reading skills.

Motivated Practice of Basic Writing Skills

As a model and inspiration for children's own creative writing, it is hard to beat children's literature. I have never had such interesting, highly motivated writing occur in my classrooms as that which follows the conclusion of books I have read aloud. Numerous teachers have had the same experience. If the teacher has helped the children become aware of an author's use of words, the

Children's literature often provides inspiration for children's own writing.

characters' personalities, and the subtleties of the plot, many children will be bursting with ideas for extending the story, changing its ending, or even writing a sequel. A similar type of enthusiasm, although not always as strong, often follows the conclusion of a book they have read by themselves.

In Module 6, specific exercises were suggested for helping children understand and recognize the various ways they can make their writing or speech more interesting—via clarity, conciseness, energy, flexibility of style, imagery, naturalness, inventiveness, and insight into human nature. Once the exercises on these eight characteristics have been completed, children's literature can be used to further illustrate the characteristics. As teachers read aloud to their children, they can stop occasionally to point out the imagery, inventiveness, or some other characteristic of interesting writing that is clearly illustrated. Some of the children can be given a library book project of finding illustrations of the characteristics in their book.

Mrs. Norwood, who teaches fourth grade in an economically depressed area, uses children's literature as a stimulus for what she calls "noncreative writing." "Sure," she says, "I'd like to get my kids to use more imagery and inventiveness in their writing, but first I've got to get them to write. If I push creativity at them, they freeze up and don't write at all. So what I do is read them a chapter a day from a good children's book. Then once a week after I read a chapter, I have them write it in their own words. Of course theirs is seldom more than a page long but what I'm after are the main events of the chapter. Can they remember the main events and put them in the right order?"

Mrs. Norwood is asked how she reinforces the correct sequence and the selection of main ideas. "I have some of them stand up and read their version of the chapter. This usually leads to a debate among the kids about which ideas were the most important and which order was correct. You'd be surprised how involved they get in this."

Mrs. Norwood then tells us how she uses their chapter summaries to teach handwriting, spelling, and punctuation. "Sometimes I have them proofread their own papers with a red pencil. Sometimes I have them proofread each other's papers. And sometimes I proofread them myself. . . . No, they don't seem to mind. Not like kids do when you criticize their really creative writing. They seem to recognize it as a writing exercise to improve their writing. They don't treat it as a personal affront, as kids often do when you proofread their creative, personal writing. Sometimes I even make an overhead projector acetate with some of their papers and we proofread them together. I hide the names, of course. . . . Oh, sure, if I notice some imagery or inventiveness in their summaries, I'm quick to point it out and praise them for it. But mainly I just praise them for very practical things like clarity, handwriting, good spelling, and good punctuation."

Mrs. Mendoza has a group of fourth graders who she feels are "verbally bright." "I really lucked out with this group," she says. "Most of them love to write and debate and play with words. My biggest job is finding new ways to capture their enthusiasm. I use their own library books a lot for this. I give them special tokens every time they do a book project that requires writing."

Mrs. Mendoza shows some of the book projects on one of the bulletin boards. Janice has written a letter to a friend urging her to read the book she has just finished and telling her all the reasons she should read it. Mark has developed a new table of contents for his book, inventing his own chapter titles. David has produced a magazine ad for his book. Sally has described an event in her book as if she were a newspaper reporter who was there at the time of the event. Jake has written a letter to one of the characters in the book, telling him how his own life is different.

When asked why these papers are so free of spelling and punctuation errors and why the handwriting is so legible, Mrs. Mendoza says, "No perfect copy—no token. I help them clean them up, of course, but they have to do a lot of their own proofreading. . . . The tokens? They use them to buy a paperback children's book. I have a large collection. A few I've paid for myself. The rest I've accumulated from the bonus books given to teachers by Scholastic Book Clubs."

Motivated Practice of Basic Speaking and Listening Skills

Does reading children's literature improve children's speaking skills? This question poses a complicated and perhaps impossible measurement task. Cohen (8) did find that reading selected trade books to children and using related follow-up activities resulted in greater vocabulary growth and reading comprehension for the experimental group than for the control group. Although experimental research on this question is meager, there is a strong probability that children do expand their own speaking-writing vocabularies and learn new ways of express-ing themselves by experiencing children's trade books, particularly if these books are read aloud to them. As children and teachers share books in this way, a "touch of grandeur" lingers on, for a while at least, as children try out phrases and words of their favorite characters. (This same phenomenon often occurs with adults after they've watched a Shakespearean drama or listened to poetry read aloud.)

In addition to direct improvement of children's speaking and listening skills through children's literature, there is also the possibility of using children's literature indirectly. Mr. Filene uses children's book projects for this purpose. One of the projects is the game called "Twenty Questions." "It's a simple game," Mr. Filene says, "but it teaches them to listen carefully and to remember what they've heard. It also helps them learn to ask clear, accurate, and sharply defined questions. . . . How does it work? Well, a kid who has just finished a book gets up in front of the class. He gives them twenty questions to guess what object or person in his book was very important. The only clue he gives them is to tell them whether it's animal, vegetable, or mineral. Let's sup-pose the object that's very important in the story is a leather hat. Okay, a leather hat is made from an animal, so he says, 'Animal.' Now, if the kids are on the ball they don't ask whether it's a bear or a cat or a leather belt. They ask questions that eliminate huge areas of possibility like, 'Is it made from an animal?' or 'Is this a live animal?' or 'Is it something people wear?' . . . Yes that's right, the questions have to be the kind that can only be answered Yes or No."

"It's amazing," Mr. Filene continues, "how hard you have to listen in this game, and how hard you have to think in order to come up with good, precise questions. And the kids love it. They'd play it all the time if I'd let them. But I only let them play it after they've finished reading a book. And I only let a child use this project for every fourth book. In other words, he has to do three other types of projects before he can play Twenty Questions again."

In addition to Twenty Questions and other oral book projects, Mr. Filene encourages numerous drama projects related to the library books the children are reading. When two or more children have read the same book, for instance, he will have them develop a brief skit depicting one of the important scenes from the book. Sometimes the skit is tape recorded and presented as a radio play, while other times it is presented live or as a television play.

As you can see, then, children's literature provides many opportu-nities for stimulating growth in the basic skills related to the language arts. Some of these opportunities come through direct reading of the trade books, them-selves. Other opportunities come through activities stimulated by teachers' reading of trade books to the children. Still other opportunities come through book projects which children engage in after completion of a library book.

REFERENCES AND BIBLIOGRAPHY

1. Aasen, Helen B. "A Summer's Growth in Reading." *Elementary School Journal* 60 (1959): 70–74.

2. Arbuthnot, May H., and Sutherland, Zena. *Children and Books.* Glenview, Ill.: Scott, Foresman, 1972.

3. _____. *Children's Books Too Good to Miss.* Cleveland: Press of Case-Western Reserve, 1971.

4. Artley, A. Sterl. "But—Skills Are Not Enough." In *Reading and the Elementary School Child,* edited by Virgil M. Howes and Helen Fisher Darrow. New York: Macmillan, 1968.

5. Ashley, L.F. "Bibliotherapy, etc." *Language Arts* 55 (April 1978): 478–81.

6. Cacha, Frances B. "Book Therapy for Abused Children." *Language Arts* 55 (Feb. 1978): 199–201.

7. Chambers, Dewey W. *Children's Literature in the Curriculum.* Chicago: Rand McNally, 1971.

8. Cohen, Dorothy H. "The Effect of Literature on Vocabulary and Reading Achievement." *Elementary English* (Feb. 1968): 209–13, 217.

9. Comer, Dorothea. "Using Literature to Extend Children's Experience." *Elementary English* (Jan. 1959): 28–29.

10. Crosby, Muriel, ed. *Reading Ladders for Human Relations.* Washington, D.C.: American Council on Education, frequently revised; look for the latest edition.

11. Greenlaw, M. Jean. "Information Please! Books and their Many Uses." *Language Arts* 55 (April 1978): 498–500.

12. Huck, Charlotte S. *Children's Literature in the Elementary School.* New York: Rinehart and Winston, 1976.

13. Martin, Sue Ann. "Techniques for the Creative Reading or Telling of Stories to Children." *Elementary English* 45 (1968): 611–18.

14. Moss, Joy F. "Learning to Write by Listening to Literature." *Language Arts* 54 (May 1977): 537–42.

15. Moss, R.H. "Luring the Non-reader." *National Education Association Journal* 50 (1961): 14–16.

16. Russell, David H. "Identification through Literature." *Childhood Education* (May 1949): 397–401.

17. Spache, George D. *Good Reading for Poor Readers*. Champaign, Ill.: Garrard, 1974, frequently revised; look for latest edition.

18. Styer, Sandra. "Biographical Models for Young Feminists." *Language Arts* 55 (Feb. 1978): 168–74.

Individualizing Through Learning Centers and Other Means

We can teach a child but not children.

It is axiomatic that students have different styles and rates of learning. Some learn best through listening; some, through reading; some, by interacting with others in group discussions or projects; some, through manipulating physical objects or intellectual variables in a problem-solving situation. Teachers who wish to help children acquire basic skills must plan their instruction to take account of such individual differences.

Part 1 of this book discussed three strategies of language arts instruction: (1) planning for basic skills instruction by using long-range outcomes and performance objectives, (2) recognizing the effects that the environment has had (and continues to have) on children's language skills development, and (3) relying on learning principles to guide your instruction. By employing all three of these strategies in their language arts program, teachers are going a long way toward individualizing their teaching.

By using performance objectives whenever appropriate, you are saying in effect, "I want each child to achieve at a certain level of mastery, and if he doesn't achieve at that level I will arrange for the extra individual help that each needs." By becoming aware of each child's environmental past and present it becomes easier to determine the nature of the individual help that each child needs. By using learning principles as instructional guides, we can remember to plan for the effects on motivation that such things as appropriate level of difficulty, individual feedback, and satisfaction of individual basic needs can have. We can remember to plan for the effects on retention that such things as individual involvement and individual mastery can have.

Module 12 looks at three additional means of individualizing your language arts instruction—three additional means of making it more likely that your students learn the basic skills related to the language arts. One of the means is that of using diagnostic tests and other assessment devices to determine the specific strengths and weaknesses of each child. Another means is that of grouping children within a classroom, team-teaching "pod," or school in order to provide instruction that is at the appropriate level of difficulty. The third means is that of developing and using learning centers in order to allow for differences in rate and style of learning.

Special Prerequisites for Module 12

It is recommended that you complete Modules 1–3 before beginning this module. There are no other special prerequisites.

Long-range Outcomes Related to Module 12

This module should help you as a teacher to do the following:

1. Communicate with other professional educators about the processes of individualizing language arts instruction.
2. Administer an informal reading inventory.
3. Administer an informal word recognition inventory.
4. Prepare and use informal check lists pertaining to writing, speaking, and listening skills.
5. Individualize your instruction through various grouping procedures.
6. Prepare multi-sensory single skill learning centers.

Study Guide and Peformance Objectives for Knowledge Level Examination

To give yourself an overview of what is expected of you in this module, you should first scan the objectives and performance standards at all three levels—knowledge, simulation, and teaching. Then use the performance objectives for the knowledge level as a study guide during your reading of the module. As you find information related to each performance objective, write it down in the available blanks or on a separate sheet. Then review this information shortly before your knowledge level examination.

1.1 On a closed-book examination, you should be able to select the best alternative for each multiple-choice question and circle the letter of your choice. The multiple-choice questions (shown here without the alternatives) will be selected from the following. Under each one write the alternative that you think will be the correct one on the examination.

Set A: The Informal Reading Inventory

1. How long should the selections be?
   About 100–200 words.
2. Select your portion from what part of the book?

3. What kind of atmosphere for testing should you establish?

4. At what level should you usually start a child reading?

5. What types of words should you circle?

6. What types of words should you not circle?

7. When should you stop the testing?

8. How do you mathematically determine the instructional level?

9. What percentage usually indicates instructional level?

Set B: Other Diagnostic Assessment Devices

1. What is the purpose of the "baf test"?

2. Why is diagnostic assessment not used as much with the other language arts as it is with reading?

3. What information may be used for developing check lists for speaking and listening skills?

Set C: Individualizing through Grouping

To prepare for this set of multiple-choice questions, complete the following. After each characteristic listed below, write the letter of *each* program that *usually* incorporates that characteristic.

Programs

a. Small group basal
b. Joplin
c. Individualized reading
d. Language experience
e. Open concept
f. Performance based

1. Individual conferences on library books   c, e
2. Heavy use of programmed materials
3. Self-selection of reading materials
4. Somewhat permanent grouping
5. Immediate feedback to learner
6. Integration of the language arts
7. Group membership changes frequently
8. Trade books used as major instructional material
9. Sequence of learning steps planned by reading specialists
10. Homogeneous grouping
11. Small sequential steps in the learning process   a, b, f
12. Strong relationship between reading and writing
13. Self-pacing (Hint: should have four answers here)

14. Grouping by *general* reading ability
15. Students work individually most of the time
16. Children may go to another classroom for instruction
17. Children plan much of their day
18. Most of the learning occurs in groups
19. Uses large variety of books for instruction
    (Hint: only one answer)
20. Sequence of observing-discussing-writing-reading

1.2 On the same examination, you will be asked to provide information in the form of lists
   1. List four learning principles related to the use of learning centers:

      Level of difficulty

   2. List four examples of single skills or single concepts that are appropriate for the Multi-sensory Single Skill Approach.

      Maintaining a consistent slant in handwriting.

   3. List the five usual parts of an M-Triple-S learning center.

      Programmed lesson

   4. List six advantages of using a multi-sensory single skill approach.

      Children tend to favor different modes of learning.

   5. List three criteria for a successful M-Triple-S learning center that pertain to motivation.

6. List three criteria for a successful M-Triple-S learning center that pertain to retention.

7. List three criteria for a successful M-Triple-S learning center that pertain to independence.

Performance Standards for Knowledge Level

A. Twenty-five minute time limit on 1.1 and 1.2 combined.

B. Completion deadline: instructor will notify.

C. Recommended grading standards if grades are used: 96% = A; 92% = A—; 88% = B; 84% = B—; 80% = C; below 80% = incomplete; should be completed at 80% or better before you go on to performance objectives for simulation level. (The instructor may wish to permit a grade of A or B only the first time the test is given in order to encourage more intensive study.)

Performance Objectives for Simulation Level

2.1 As a take-home examination, select one of the single skills or concepts listed in Module 12 (or one equally specific) and develop a M-Triple-S learning center for any grade level you choose. The learning center should have five parts in it, as described in Module 12.

2.2 (Alternative Objective) On an open-book examination, you will listen twice to an audio-tape of a child reading several passages, each at a higher reader level than the preceding one. On a transcribed copy of the passages, you will be asked to circle the appropriate miscues and compute the word recognition score as a percentage. You will then be asked to indicate in writing the appropriate instructional level for the child.

Performance Standards for Simulation Level

A. For Objective 2.1 (Learning Center)
   1. The center meets the twenty-three criteria listed at the end of Module 12.
   2. The concept or skill is specific enough to lend itself to the M-Triple-S Approach.

B. For Objective 2.2 (Informal Reading Inventory)
   1. Time limit of forty-five minutes.
   2. Agreement with instructor as to exact grade level for instruction.
   3. No more than 1 percent difference with instructor on word recognition score.
   4. At least 90 percent agreement with instructor on exact words circled.

C. For Objectives 2.1 and 2.2.
   1. Completion deadline: instructor will notify.
   2. Should be completed at C level or better before moving on to teaching level.

Performance Objectives for Teaching Level

3.1 Same as Simulation Objective 2.1 but use your learning center in an actual classroom. Prepare a self-critique of this experience, using the twenty-three criteria as a guideline.

3.2 Same as Simulation Objective 2.2 but work with an actual child instead of a tape recording. Prepare a brief report and a self-critique.

Performance Standards for Teaching Level

A. Uses learning principles effectively; does not violate any of those discussed in Module 3.

B. Follows steps and/or criteria discussed in Module 12.

C. Additional standards or modified standards may have to be developed by the cooperating teacher, instructor, supervisor, or teachers-in-training. It is best, of course, to state these standards in advance of the required performance.

Individualizing Through Diagnostic Assessment

Diagnostic assessment is commonly applied to the problem of determining which materials should be used for teaching children to read and what specific difficulties children are having in learning to read. For a variety of reasons, similar energy is seldom spent in assessing children's levels and difficulties with respect to other language arts. Let us first look at diagnostic assessment as it applies to reading and then examine the possibilities of using similar assessment techniques with the other language arts.

In a typical group of fifth graders, the level of reading ability would range from second grade through eighth grade. A typical group of first graders would contain children who are already reading at the first, second, and even third grade levels, some who are just beginning to read, and some who need considerable help in developing reading readiness skills.

Obviously, reading instruction cannot be successfully implemented with the same reading material for all children. The most accurate and practical method for determining which children are to be instructed with which materials is to administer an informal reading inventory to each child early in the school year. Some of these inventories are quite elaborate and provide a means for miscue analysis as well as for determining reading levels. To prepare and administer the simplest form of the IRI (informal reading inventory), the following procedures are recommended:[1]

1. Reproduce portions (about 100–200 words) from basal readers you have available for your reading instruction unless these are already available from the publisher. You will need a short selection for each reading level, preprimer, primer, first reader—possibly on up through grade six or further. Select your portion from the middle of each book, as this is probably most representative of that level. The pupil can read from the book while you follow along with your dittoed copy.

2. Before "testing" the pupil, try to develop a relaxed atmosphere. Make the examination informal but explain your purpose.

3. Start the child reading at the preprimer level unless you have an estimate of his instructional level. It's better to start too low than too high.

4. Circle every word that the child has trouble with, i.e., that he repeats, mispronounces, substitutes another word for, omits, or "reverses."

5. If the child inserts a word, write that word and circle it.

6. Ignore those "mispronunciations" that are caused by a nonstandard dialect rather than a reading problem.

7. Stop the testing when the child has finished a selection which has been obviously frustrating.

8. Don't circle words in the title or any proper nouns.

[1]See *To Help Children Read* (15) for a more complicated form of the IRI that provides the teacher with more information.

9. Determine the instructional level by subtracting the number of circles from the number of words in the passage and then dividing by the number of words in the passage. For example, if the passage has 100 words and the child has four miscues, you would divide 96 by 100, which would give you .96 or 96%. A good instructional level for a selection is between 94 and 97 percent. If Nathan gets a score of 98 percent on a fourth grade selection, a score of 95 percent on a fifth grade selection and a score of 92 percent on a sixth grade selection, you would be able to estimate the following:

a. His reading instruction should be carried on with fifth grade material.

b. Sixth grade material would probably be too frustrating for him and cause him to develop negative attitudes towards reading.

c. Fourth grade material would be too easy for him and would not provide sufficient challenge for instructional purposes.

If you would like to determine not just the child's *level* of reading but also the specific difficulties she might have, there are several diagnostic reading inventories available through commercial publishers. Some teachers, however, prefer to use parts of the "Word Recognition Inventory" developed for teachers by May and Eliot (15). This inventory may be reproduced by teachers for noncommercial use without breach of copyright. The three most widely used parts are reproduced for your convenience in Figure 12.1.

Using Diagnostic Assessment with the Other Language Arts

The major reason that diagnostic assessment is not used with the other language arts as much as it is with reading can be described with two words: grouping logistics. Teachers, rightly or wrongly, use diagnostic assessment primarily to enable them to form small groups of children with similar instructional needs. Those children whose reading levels seem to fall within grades 2.0 to 2.5, for instance, are placed in the same instructional group. Or, those children who have decoding troubles with the same vowel pattern, for example, are placed temporarily in the same instructional group.

Although children are often placed in instructional groups according to assessed *reading* level, it usually becomes impractical to regroup the children for every other subject in the total curriculum: Susan might be in Group C for reading, Group F for spelling, Group A for math, Group D for social studies, and so on.

Whatever the grouping procedures used in the school, however, teachers can carry on informal assessment of children's abilities in writing, speaking, listening, and other areas. By doing this, they can become more aware of skills that need to be emphasized with the entire class, skills that could be strengthened through temporary small group instruction, and skills that can be developed with individual instruction and projects.

FIGURE 12.1   Word Recognition Inventory

WORD RECOGNITION INVENTORY

The purpose of the following inventory is to enable a teacher to achieve a greater degree of individualization in his or her reading instruction. By determining the specific word recognition problems which each student has, the teacher should be able to use temporary grouping and individual instruction to help students overcome their difficulties.

Although the first three parts of the inventory must be administered individually, all of the other parts may be administered as group tests. After half or more of the school year has passed, it would be advisable to administer the inventory again to determine the type of instruction which is still necessary.

Although this inventory, developed by the authors, is copyrighted (as are all parts of this book), permission is hereby granted to teachers to reproduce the inventory for use with children. Reproduction of the inventory for commercial use, however, is *not* permitted without the consent of the authors and publishers.

PART I:* CONSONANT LETTERS, DIGRAPHS, AND BLENDS

(For those whose *instructional* level is at least "Primer")

This part of the inventory should be administered individually. You will need to reproduce a copy of this page for each child. The children should be encouraged to try decoding each nonsense word without your help. If they miss one, simply circle it and have them continue. *Be sure to pronounce the first one for them (ăf) and have them pronounce it correctly before they continue.*

Name of Student _____

Directions to be Read or Told to the Student

"These words are nonsense words. They are not real words. I'd like you to think about what sounds the letters have; then read each word out loud without my help. Don't try to go fast; read the list slowly. If you have any trouble with a word, I'll just circle it and you can go on to the next one. The first word is băf. Now you say it . . . All right, now go on to the rest of the words in row 1."

A	B	C	D	E	F	G
			Consonant Letters			
baf	caf	daf	faf	gaf	haf	jaf
kaf	laf	maf	naf	paf	raf	saf
taf	vaf	waf	yaf	zaf	baf	bax

* This part and Part II, in combination, have been dubbed by the authors as "The BAF Test."

FIGURE 12.1 (cont.)

A	B	C	D	E	F	G	H
			Consonant Digraphs				
chaf	phaf	shaf	thaf	whaf	fack	fang	fank
			Consonant Blends				
blaf	braf	claf	craf	draf	dwaf	flaf	fraf
glaf	graf	fand	plaf	praf	quaf	scaf	scraf
skaf	slaf	smaf	snaf	spaf	splaf	spraf	squaf
staf	straf	swaf	thraf	traf	twaf		

PART II: VOWEL LETTERS, VOWEL DIGRAPHS, AND VOWEL BLENDS

(For those whose *instructional* level is at least "Primer")

This part of the inventory should also be administered individually. You will need to reproduce a copy of this test for each child. The children should be encouraged to try decoding each nonsense word without your help. If they miss one, simply circle it and have them continue. *Be sure to pronounce the first one for them (băf) and have them pronounce it correctly before they continue.* Note that for 3G (boof), the children should be asked to pronounce it two ways; circle it if they cannot. The same is true of 5B (bufe).

Name of Student _____

Directions to be Read or Told to the Student

"These words are nonsense words. They are not real words. I'd like you to think about what sounds the letters have; then read each word out loud without any help. Don't try to go fast; read the list slowly. If you have any trouble with a word, I'll just circle it and you can go on to the next one. The first word is băf. Now you say it. . . . All right, now go on to the rest of the words in row 1."

A	B	C	D	E	F	G
baf	bafe	barf	baif	bawf		
bef	befe	berf	beaf			
bof	bofe	borf	boaf	bouf	boif	boof
bif	bife	birf				
buf	bufe	burf				

FIGURE 12.1 (cont.)

PART III: BASIC SIGHT VOCABULARY—IRREGULAR WORDS ONLY

(For those whose *instructional* level is at least "primer.")

This part of the inventory should also be administered individually. You will need to reproduce a copy of this page for each child. Start the student randomly at any one of the 16 rows. Circle any word which the children do not recognize instantly. Even a self-correction should be considered an error. If they can complete three rows with no more than one error, you probably need not continue. If they make more than one error, you may wish to check them on all 96 of the words. If they miss more than ten of the words, they probably should be given special assistance on those words that they missed.

Name of Student _____

Directions to be Read or Told to the Student

"I would like you to read each of these words without my help. Many of these words are hard to read. If you don't know a word right away, I'll just circle the word and you can go on to the next one. All right, I'll point to the row where you should start."

A	B	C	D	E	F
anything	give	great	Mrs.	says	very
a	could	group	night	should	want
because	do	have	nothing	some	water
again	does	head	of	something	was
almost	done	knew	brother	the	were
another	door	heard	on	sometimes	wanted
always	buy	know	off	their	what
any	enough	light	one	they	where
are	four	only	long	who	thought
been	from	dog	other	there	father
both	friend	many	own	through	goes
brought	full	might	people	to	work
house	don't	money	put	together	you
city	live	mother	right	today	would
come	gone	Mr.	said	two	your
year	they're	school	our	there's	once

An informal check list may be devised by using the lists of long-range outcomes for the language arts shown in Module 1. A check list for writing skills, for example, might look like Table 12.1.

TABLE 12.1   Check List of Writing Skills

Student's Name _____

Degree of Instruction Required

	High	Moderate	Low
1. Vocabulary—appropriate word selection			
2. Sentence complexity			
3. Grammatical constructions			
4. Standard English			
5. Overall interest appeal			
a. Clarity			
b. Conciseness			
c. Flexibility of style			
d. Imagery			
e. Naturalness			
f. Inventiveness			
g. Insight			
6. Proper sequencing of ideas of events			
7. Overall handwriting legibility			
a. Letter formation			
b. Alignment			
c. Spacing			
d. Slant			
e. Size			
8. Overall punctuation			
a. Commas			
b. Full stops			
c. Quotation marks			
9. Overall spelling			
a. Regular words			
b. Irregular words			
c. Capitalization			

Individualizing Through Grouping

As mentioned earlier, grouping is very common for reading instruction and far less common for instruction in the other language arts. Let us now look in on four different teachers to see how they have grouped children for reading instruction and how the other language arts fit into their grouping schemes.

The Track Basal Approach

Mrs. Alberts has a self-contained classroom of twenty-seven children in the third grade. She teaches all of the subjects except music to these children. At the beginning of the school year, she gave her students an informal reading inventory to determine their approximate reading levels. By looking at the results of this inventory and other information found in the cumulative folders, she was able to divide the class into three manageable reading groups—an advanced, average, and remedial group. Her children have named their groups "The Rockets," "The Star Warriors," and "The Astronauts."

At 9:00 she explains a workbook and worksheet assignment to the Rockets and Star Warriors and then meets with the Astronauts. At 9:30 she explains a proofreading assignment to the entire class and then meets with the Star Warriors. She suggests that the Astronauts complete their worksheet before starting on the proofreading assignment. At 10:00 she checks to see that everyone understands their assignments and then meets with the Rockets. At 10:25 she takes the entire class outside for recess.

At 10:45 Mrs. Alberts' class works on spelling. From 11:00 until 11:45 they all work on mathematics. At 11:45 Mrs. Alberts engages the children in a listening game until it's time to go to the cafeteria. During the lunch period, Mrs. Alberts is asked about the basal readers she is using for reading instruction.

"We have nothing but old textbooks," she explains, "so we use the old-fashioned track system. Those kids in the remedial group are supposed to use a reader from the Lippincott series, only one grade lower. In other words, my third grade remedial readers are supposed to use a second grade reader from the Lippincott series. . . . The average group uses a third grade reader from the Scott, Foresman series and my advanced group uses a fourth grade reader from the Ginn series.

"Why use readers from three different publishers? Well, what you're trying to do is to avoid having children read the same basal reader twice. Suppose, for instance, a kid is placed in the *average* group in grade four and is reading the fourth grade reader in the Scott, Foresman series, okay? Now, suppose in fifth grade he is placed by a different teacher in the *remedial* group. This would mean, if you were only using one series, that he would again have to read the fourth grade reader in the Scott, Foresman series. Do you see what I mean?"

From 12:50 till about 2:00, Mrs. Alberts' children work on a combination of social studies, art, and language arts projects. The projects include a film on "Indians of the Past," a discussion of the film, and a language-experience chart developed about the film. Later, in small groups they work on a mural, an adventure story a few children are writing, and some Indian headbands.

From 2:00 to 2:30 is physical education time. "I work, hard on getting them to follow verbal directions during P.E. time," Mrs. Alberts says. "They know if they don't follow them correctly they may end up sitting on the bench instead of playing."

The final hour of the day is spent on science projects, finishing assignments, and listening to Mrs. Alberts read a chapter from a library book. Reading, writing, speaking, and listening skills are all put to good use during this hour as children follow directions for a science experiment, complete worksheets, record observations in their science notebooks, listen to a story, and discuss plans for tomorrow with Mrs. Alberts.

After the children leave for home, I ask Mrs. Alberts what she feels is the main advantage of using basal readers in her reading program. "Oh, it's the structure, I suppose," she says. "As children move through a series, more and more new words are introduced. This gives them a chance to build their reading vocabulary gradually. Also, word recognition skills are introduced gradually through the workbooks and the suggested learning activities in the Teacher's Edition. It's a highly organized approach, and the children usually like the stories. It's true that the children learn to perceive themselves as advanced, average, and remedial readers, but I don't know any good way to avoid that kind of social stigma."

I then ask Mrs. Alberts about free reading of materials other than basal readers. "Oh, yes, they all read library books," she says. "Every Friday afternoon I give them at least a half hour. And they're all expected to read a library book whenever they have their assignments finished. . . . Do I do any grouping for any of the other subjects? Oh my no. I don't think I could handle it. I know my program isn't perfect, but it works pretty well, and it fits my personality. A teacher has to be who she is. You have to find an approach that fits you and do the best you can."

I agree with Mrs. Alberts and thank her for showing us what can be done with limited materials toward individualizing through grouping. Now we move on to Lincoln School to observe in Mr. Baldwin's class.

The Joplin Plan

Mr. Baldwin also has a classroom of twenty-seven children in the third grade. His daily schedule and learning activities are strikingly similar to those of Mrs. Alberts. Two differences are observed, however. Mr. Baldwin groups his children for handwriting instruction, for one thing. "My advanced group is already well into cursive," he says. "My average group is just beginning to learn cursive. And

With the track approach, the teacher works with one group while the other children work independently.

my remedial group—well, my remedial group has not really mastered manuscript yet. I'm working hard with them to get them to form their letters correctly, to use a consistent slant, and so on."

The second difference between Mrs. Alberts and Mr. Baldwin is that Mr. Baldwin uses the Joplin Plan rather than the self-contained approach used by Mrs. Alberts. "All of the teachers in the building are involved in the plan," Mr. Baldwin says. "That's the secret to success if you want to use the Joplin Plan. It doesn't work too well if just the third grade teachers use it. You need a lot of teachers involved, so you can have groups of kids whose reading level is very similar.

"If only the third grade teachers use the plan, then one teacher gets all the fourth grade readers, one teacher gets all the third grade readers, and one teacher gets all the second grade readers. That's still too much spread in one group. If you get all the teachers in the school to participate, you can have one group whose test scores showed a range of say, 2.0 to 2.4; another group could have test scores from 2.5 to 2.9, and so on. The Joplin Plan requires cooperation from the principal and all the teachers.

"When do we have reading instruction? At 9:00 a bell rings and the children disperse throughout the building to their reading teachers for an hour and ten minutes. What group do I have? I have twenty-five kids whose reading scores ranged from 3.9 to 4.5. They all use the same basal reader, but I group them anyway into three instructional groups so I can give them more individual attention.

"When do they read library books? They're supposed to be given two half-hour periods for this in their homeroom each week. . . . . Yes, theoretically a kid could change from one reading group to another during the year. This is seldom done, though, because we usually feel it's more important for the teacher to get to know the child. If a kid is falling behind, we give him special help. If Mary is getting ahead, we give her special projects and special reading materials."

The Performance–Based Approach

Move on now to Jefferson School, where we observe Miss Carpenter and Mrs. Dagmar team teaching with sixty first and second graders. They are assisted by their teacher-aide, Ms. Enright. I am surprised by the similarity of their schedule and learning activities to those of Mrs. Alberts and Mr. Baldwin. By the end of the day, however, I've discovered some differences. The Carpenter-Dagmar-Enright team has the class in permanent spelling and handwriting groups, but the reading groups are temporary and change frequently, depending on the difficulties children experience.

Basal readers are not used by this team. "We rely mostly on the Sullivan materials," Miss Carpenter says. "These materials include programmed workbooks which kids finish at their own pace. After they finish so many pages, we meet with them either individually or in small groups to make sure they understand the pages they've just done or to give them a brief mastery test. You see, they all have a series of performance objectives to meet at the 80 percent level of mastery before they go on to other performance objectives—or until they go on to one of the short hard-bound books that go with the Sullivan materials."

I ask Mrs. Dagmar why so many children are "plugged into" headsets during the reading period. "That's one of our auxiliary reading programs," she explains. "Some of our children are working beyond the Sullivan program— or at least beyond the point that we want them to work on. Other children need extra help or practice in order to master the performance objectives. So they are following instructions that are recorded on cassettes.

"When do we meet with the children? Oh, quite often. We meet with them individually or in small groups to give them short diagnostic tests related to the workbook pages they have completed. We meet with them to prescribe new learning activities for them. We meet with them to hear them read or discuss what they've been reading in their Sullivan hard-bound books. We meet with kids who are already into library books to share experiences and work on comprehension skills."

I ask Miss Carpenter why she likes to use programmed workbooks. "Because of the immediate feedback the kids get every few seconds. They know whether they're reading something right by whether they're getting the correct answer or not. The whole idea of the performance-based approach is to make sure that each child proceeds in very small steps at his own rate and that he masters each step before going on to the next one."

The Open Concept Approach

At Horace Mann School, I am led to Pod 3, where Mr. Federici and Mrs. Grossman are team teaching with a third-fourth grade combination. When I arrive, the children and teachers have evidently just finished their morning planning session. There are all kinds of names and activities listed on the chalkboard. Some lists refer to group meetings the children will be attending during the day for specific instruction, e.g., "Handwriting: Bobby E., Danny F., Jennie C." Some of the lists evidently refer to the activities the children are now engaged in.

One small group of children is preparing a large illustrated book about "Indians of the Past." One group is painting a mural. One group is working with Mr. Federici to construct an Indian tepee. "They'll all get a turn at it before it's completed," he informs me. Mrs. Grossman is giving a lesson to some children on the difference between the vowel sounds in VC and VCE patterns. "These children have obviously not picked up the difference yet and need special instruction," she says.

All around the large room we see children reading, writing, talking, listening—most of them with apparent purpose and a few of them seemingly lost in the industrious hubbub. There are several learning centers in the classroom. One of them provides instruction (in five different ways) on the spelling and meaning of particular homonyms. One of them is a music center with xylophones and rhythm instruments along with some charts urging them to try certain melodies or rhythms. A listening center provides six headsets and numerous cassettes on a variety of subjects, including social studies, reading, creative writing, and science.

Around 10:00, two parent aides come in and begin to interact with the children, listening to some of them read, helping some with math problems, helping the "lost" ones find purpose again. A quarrel among three children playing a reading game develops and one of the parents helps settle the argument. As the day continues in this fashion, I begin to wonder when the formal instruction will begin. By the time the day is over, I realize that informality is "the name of the game."

When the children leave, I ask whether children can actually learn through the open concept approach. "Frankly," Mr. Federici says, "some research studies say *yes* and some say *no*. I guess it all depends on the teachers. Our classroom may look like complete chaos to an observer, but we have a pretty good idea what's going on most of the time. What the observer doesn't realize is that we have records on all these kids—papers that show what weaknesses they have in writing and spelling, scores from short diagnostic tests that look just like activities to the kids, anecdotal records from our parent helpers. We have a pretty good idea of what kind of help each kid needs. That's why we can steer them into certain kinds of activities, or if that doesn't work, we just sit them down and teach them directly."

I ask about the schedule for the day. "It changes from day to day," Mrs. Grossman says. "Essentially each kid plans his own day, although he or she has to get in his 'Musts' sometime during the day. . . . What are the 'Musts?' These are those lists on that chart over there that tell each kid what lessons or activities he *must* complete during the day whenever he can squeeze them in. . . . If he doesn't get them done, he has lost his freedom of choice for the next day. He *must* do them before doing anything else. . . . Yes, it does teach them to take responsibility for their own learning, we think."

"What is the open concept approach?" I ask.

"It's different things to different teachers," Mr. Federici replies. "To us, it means open ended. There are few mixed boundaries. Each child is encouraged to be creative, self-motivating, and curious. . . . What materials do we use for reading instruction? Lots of language experience charts, stories they write themselves, some simple graded booklets, and the school library."

"We're pretty heavy on the language experience approach and the individualized reading approach," Mrs. Grossman says. "By using the language experience approach, we recognize the fact that listening, speaking, writing, and reading skills are interdependent and mutually reinforcing. The kids learn that what they have to say is worthwhile and can be put into print. And they learn that what they've said and written can be read and listened to."

"By using the so-called individualized reading approach," Mr. Federici says, "we recognize the fact that children are motivated to read by making their own choices of library books rather than being forced to read an assigned story from a basal reader. Children are proud of their ability to read to us from a book they have chosen, and they don't seem to mind too much when we give them a reading lesson right on the spot—you know: Johnny, you read that word as *bath*; let me show you why it should be *bathe*."

As I get up to leave, I ask them whether all teachers could use their approach to language arts instruction. "Definitely not," Mrs. Grossman says. "It is only for those who enjoy watching children learn in what we consider to be a natural, although somewhat chaotic, manner."

With the open concept approach, the children often read library books or stories they have written themselves.

We have seen four different approaches—and there are many more—toward arranging the most appropriate learning experiences for each child so that learning really does take place. Some teachers attempt to do this by getting children into more homogeneous groups. Some attempt to do it by providing materials that let children proceed at their own pace; some by permitting more choice of reading materials; some by using performance objectives; and some by working with fewer children at one time. Some teachers individualize by using the child's own language as a basis for producing her own reading material. And some believe that true individualization can only occur when the classroom atmosphere is open and free. But perhaps the most masterful, artful teachers of all are those who have learned a *variety* of ways of individualizing their instruction.

The following are summaries of the different approaches discussed. It is hoped that you will be able to select those elements of each approach which are suitable to your teaching style and to the needs of your students.

Summaries of the Different Approaches

The Track Basal Approach

1. The children are divided at the beginning of the year into about three ability groups—advanced, average, and remedial. These groups are for reading instruction only.

2. The same teacher teaches all three groups but at different times during the day.

3. Each ability group uses a different basal reader, each one at a different reading level.
4. The teacher works with one group while other groups work on workbooks, assignments, or projects that require no teacher supervision.
5. The sequence of learning is generally determined by the gradually increasing difficulty of the selections in the basal readers.
6. Free reading in library books is provided about once a week and whenever the children have spare time.

The Joplin Plan

1. The children's reading levels are determined by tests and teachers' judgments.
2. Once the range of reading levels and the frequency of each reading level are established, the teachers are assigned to teaching the various levels. The range of levels assigned to each teacher is dependent upon the frequency of each score and the number of teachers in the plan.
3. Each day when it is time for reading instruction, the children disperse to their reading teachers. After the reading period is over, the children return to their regular homeroom activities.
4. Reading of library books is done in the homeroom.
5. Children who get behind or ahead of their reading group may theoretically move to another group anytime during the year.
6. Other procedures are similar to the track basal approach.

The Individualized Reading Program

1. Children select their own reading materials, usually from a large collection of library books, and read them at their own speed.
2. A conference is held with each child at least once a week.
3. The teacher diagnoses children's problems through tests, through listening to them read, and through discussing with them what they have read.
4. Both the teacher and the children keep records of progress and difficulties.
5. Actual instruction is given during the individual conferences and in small temporary groups made up of children with similar skill deficiencies.
6. Children share their books in ways that motivate others to read and in ways that extend their own language skills.

The Language Experience Approach

1. Listening, speaking, writing, and reading skills are viewed as interdependent and mutually reinforcing.

2. Children's transcribed dictation or their own writing are the major reading materials until they learn enough sight words and word attack skills to read published books. Their own writing and the writing of their peers, though, continues to be an important reading material.

3. Grouping is flexible, temporary, and used for sharing and for learning skills several children are ready for at the same time.

4. This approach is used primarily with beginning readers, but it can be used to advantage with older children, particularly those with a lack of motivation to learn.

THe PerformANCE–BASeD ApproAch

1. There is a carefully sequenced set of performance objectives which children master in small steps at their own rate.

2. There is frequent use of brief diagnostic tests followed by teachers' prescriptions for each child.

3. There is an extensive use of programmed materials which provide immediate feedback without the necessity of constant teacher presence.

4. Recordings and individual headsets are used to present some of the procedural and instructional information to children.

5. Detailed records are kept on each child's progress. With some programs, much of this record keeping is handled by computers.

6. Small group sessions are held for practice on oral reading and comprehension skills.

THe OpEN ClAssRoom ApproAch

1. The children are actively engaged in planning the nature and sequence of their activities for the day.

2. Learning to read is considered to be a random, loosely structured process for most children.

3. There is an emphasis on self-motivation, creativity, learning as "play," and on the child as a "natural" learner.

4. Instruction in reading is incidental and can be obtained through center activities, games, reading to the teacher, and abundant exposure to graded readers, trade books, and labeled objects.

5. The language experience approach is usually incorporated into the open classroom approach.

IndividualiziNq ThrouqH LearninqCenters

A learning center is simply a place in a classroom designed to inspire children to fulfill a specific purpose by thinking and by engaging in one or more of the language arts. Suppose that on a small carpet in a classroom is a tray containing a bar magnet and several iron and noniron objects—paper clips, buttons, etc. Veronica sits down on the carpet in front of the tray and reads the "Directions Card" on it: "What things will this bar magnet pick up? What are those things made of?" Veronica begins touching the magnet to the various objects. Now we have a person using a designated space with a specific purpose. Now we have a learning center with a person using the processes of thinking and reading in that center.

The use of learning centers is one of the best ways of offering children an opportunity to learn at their own rate and *level of difficulty*. It is a way of providing *distributed practice* after a concept or skill has been introduced, thus assuring greater *mastery* of that concept or skill. And it is a way of assuring a high degree of individual *involvement*.

There are many types of learning centers, but this module describes a special kind of center called a Multi-Sensory Single Skill Learning Center. The development of these centers is referred to as the M-Triple-S Approach. This approach is one alternative to the "busy-work approach" used by some teachers.

The Busywork Approach Toward Learning Centers

For a sample of the busywork approach toward the use of learning centers, let's look in on Mrs. Radcliff's third grade classroom. Although Mrs. Radcliff has a self-contained classroom with four solid walls and a closed door, she has made an admirable attempt to employ some of the ideas usually incorporated in an open concept building. Mrs. Radcliff "believes" in learning centers. She has learning centers all over the classroom and tells everyone who will listen to her that she has an open classroom.

It is now "learning center time" in Mrs. Radcliff's room, and she makes sure that every child gets to the learning center he is scheduled to "attend." In the "Sewing Center" the children pull bits of cloth out of a box. Two of them are already fighting over the best scissors. One child begins to thread a needle, gives up, and heads for Mrs. Radcliff. Mrs. Radcliff is busy and tells him to go back to the Sewing Center and wait for her to come to him.

In another center, the children are banging in random fashion on small xylophones. Above the banging xylophones is a sign that reads ironically: "Music Center." In another center, children are building a castle with Cuisenaire Rods. Above the builders is a sign that says, "Math Center." In the "Artists' Corner," children can be seen dabbing paint on large easels. Frankie can be seen dabbing paint on Margie's left ear. Meanwhile, in the "Science Center" a child who is supposed to be testing for sugar in liquids is showing his buddy how to make "nitro-glycerine" so they can "blow up the whole school!"

Mrs. Radcliff is not satisfied with her use of learning centers and asks a friend for advice. Her friend advises her to have the children go to the learning centers when they are finished with more basic assignments. "That way," her friend says, "you can be working with some of the kids on reading and math, and those who are finished with an assignment can keep busy in one of the centers."

This makes sense to Mrs. R. so she tries out the new approach. She notices immediately that she has lost the carnival atmosphere which she didn't care for, so she sighs with relief. While working with a reading group, however, she finds one kid after another coming to her for an explanation of what to do in a particular learning center. This makes it impossible to teach the reading group, so she calls a halt to learning center activity for the day and waits till dismissal time to figure out what went wrong.

It occurs to her that the directions for each learning center are not always clear. It also occurs to her that some children can't read too well, and, therefore, the directions are like Egyptian hieroglyphics to them. She rewrites the directions for the centers in much simpler language, using diagrams and pictures to help make them easier to follow. But she's not satisfied. Over the weekend, she makes a tape recording for one of the centers that the children are having so much trouble with. In that way, the children can listen to the directions before they attempt the activity. Just to be on the safe side, she explains each one of the centers to the children on Monday before they start their other work. She also establishes rules with them as to how many can be in each center, which child will be asked for advice if they can't figure out the directions, and what the level of noise must be if they are all going to work in the same room.

This time she feels satisfied. In fact, she feels satisfied for two whole weeks. But there's something still bothering her, and she's not sure what it is. The children seem to enjoy most of her learning centers, but most of the children go through a center as if they were wine tasters in the basement of an old French monastery. A sniff here . . . a taste here . . . not much more. No serious learning seems to be taking place.

"Maybe I'm just old-fashioned," she reasons. "Maybe I'm just too hung-up about kids learning something all the time. Maybe I just need to relax and let things go the way they're going." Which she does, but the doubts continue. Over the Christmas vacation, Mrs. R. tries to erase her doubts by determining what each of her learning centers must be teaching. "Let's see," she says to herself. "This one where they make a frog puppet out of a paper bag, what does it teach? It teaches them how to use scissors and paste, but they already know how to do that. . . . I wonder what concept or skill it teaches. . . . Wait a minute. . . . I know. . . . " Mrs. Radcliff writes down what she considers to be the concepts it teaches:

1. People can communicate through different media (including puppets).
2. Sounds of animals can be imitated by people.
3. Movements of animals can be acted out.

In spite of the impractical nature of such "concepts," Mrs. R. is at last satisfied. As far as she's concerned, she has an "open classroom," she has a lot of enjoyable learning centers, and she can justify every one of them.

We have no real argument with Mrs. Radcliff. She's come a long way from the dreary, lifeless classroom she once had before she began using learning centers. The children are happier in her room than they've ever been before, and Mrs. Radcliff is happier.

There are *alternatives,* however, to Mrs. Radcliff's approach—alternatives which maintain the enjoyable aspects of learning centers but also insure that more learning actually takes place. One of these alternatives is that of the Multi-Sensory Single Skill Approach, or the M-Triple-S Approach.

The Multi-sensory Single Skill Approach (M-Triple-S Approach)

With the M-Triple-S Approach, teachers do not start with a learning center activity and then try to dream up skills or concepts which it might teach. They start, instead, with a single skill or concept that they want to emphasize in their classroom. It might be a skill or concept that most of the children are having trouble with, or it might be one which the teachers have decided ahead of time needs emphasis at a particular grade level.

Suppose, for instance, that Mrs. Snelling wants her students to have a better idea of how to add fractions. With the M-Triple-S Approach, she first decides what specific single skill needs the most emphasis. Should she have a learning center just on fractions? That's much too broad; there are dozens of single skills related to fractions. Should she have a learning center on addition of fractions? Still too broad. What do they have the most trouble with? What do they need the most practice on? Addition of fractions with unlike denominators? If so, that's the single skill which will serve as the focus for the learning center.

What about learning centers for the language arts? Mr. O'Leary is concerned about his pupils' spelling abilities. Should he have a learning center on spelling? Much too broad. What do his students have the most trouble with? Mr. O'Leary decides they have the most trouble with homophones and also with words with the VV vowel pattern (e.g., spelling *coat* as "cote"). So he develops two different learning centers to help children on their spelling.

The Need for Specificity (and the Limits of the M-Triple-S Approach)

How specific does a learning center have to be? It needs to be specific enough to allow the teacher to determine quickly whether a child has mastered the skill. Obviously a learning center on spelling does not meet that criterion; whereas, one on changing the *y* to *i* does.

Do all learning centers have to be that specific? No, only if you wish to have children master a particular skill. If your aim, instead, is to just broaden their experiences in something like creative writing, then you will probably not even want to use the M-Triple-S Approach for that particular center.

The following are some examples of single skills that are appropriate for the Multi-sensory Single Skill Approach:

Handwriting

1. Maintaining a consistent slant.
2. Mastering the cursive letters: *b, d, p,* and *q.*
3. Maintaining consistent spacing.
4. Mastering the cursive letters *a, c, o,* and *u.*
5. Maintaining alignment.

6. Mastering the manuscript letters *b, d, p,* and *q.*
7. Maintaining a consistent size.

Spelling

1. Common homophones (e.g., *there, their, they're*).
2. The *-ght* words (such as *night, fight, weight*).
3. Words for relatives (*mother, father, sister, brother, uncle, aunt,* etc.).
4. Some VV words often misspelled with the VCE pattern (e.g., "cote" for *coat,* "tode" for *toad*).
5. Changing the *y* to *i* (e.g., *happy, happier, happiest, happily*).
6. Doubling consonant to maintain VC pattern (e.g., *hopped* rather than *hoped, stopped* rather than "stoped," *daddy* rather than "dady," *hopping* rather than *hoping*).
7. Dropping *e* before *ing, er, ed,* and *est* (e.g., *saving, saver, saved, bravest*).

Creative Grammar

1. The Noun + Linking Verb + Adjective pattern (e.g., The girl was happy.).
2. The present perfect alteration of the transitive verb pattern (e.g., The boy ate the apple. . . . The boy has eaten the apple.).
3. The relative clause expansion of the transitive verb pattern (e.g., The boy ate the apple. . . . The boy who wore a blue jacket ate the apple.).

Study Skills

1. Using guide words in a dictionary.
2. Using a pronunciation key in a dictionary.
3. Finding topics in an encyclopedia.
4. Using the subject card catalog.
5. Reading and making bar graphs.
6. Reading and making line graphs.
7. Reading a key for a physical relief map.
8. Making an outline.
9. Making a picture dictionary.

Reading (Word Recognition)

1. The hardest words from the "Basic Sight Vocabulary of 96 Irregular Words."
2. The VCE vowel pattern.
3. The VC vowel pattern.

4. The VV vowel pattern.
5. Common suffixes.
6. Common prefixes.

Inferential and Critical Thinking (via Listening or Reading)

1. Differentiating between facts and opinions.
2. Detecting propaganda devices.
3. Differentiating real-life stories from fantasy.
4. Determining main ideas.
5. Making deductions from premises.
6. Differentiating observations from inferences.
7. Evaluating arguments.

Listening

1. Auditory discrimination (determining which sounds are alike and different, particularly phonemes).
2. Auditory memory (remembering sequences of sounds, such as telephone numbers, letters in a name, etc.).
3. Listening to directions (following them accurately and in the right order).
4. Learning new words through context clues.
5. Listening to descriptions (matching oral descriptions with pictures, etc.).

Children's Literature

1. *Charlotte's Web* (use learning center when finished with the book; deepens understanding of the plot, characterization, setting, and theme).
2. Any other book that children commonly read at a particular grade level.

Writing

1. Detecting and writing passages with vivid imagery.
2. Detecting and using a flexible writing style.
3. Detecting and using inventiveness in plots and characters.
4. Detecting and writing passages with clarity.

Vocabulary

1. Understanding the meanings of words with such Greek roots as *photo, phono, tele, graph, phone,* etc.
2. The many words for colors, such as *aquamarine, indigo, azure, chartreuse, emerald, turquoise, crimson, ruby, maroon.*

3. Some of the many meanings of the word *run.*

4. The meanings of common affixes: *un, anti, pre, re, sub, dis, ful, less, ness, proof.*

5. Words that describe feelings, e.g., *irritated, puzzled, bewildered, lonely, disheartened,* etc.

6. Words for baby animals, such as *kids, cubs, foals,* and so on.

Making the Single Skill Center a Multi-sensory One

Having decided on the single skill you are going to use as a focus for a learning center, the next step in the M-Triple-S Approach is to prepare about five multi-sensory activities that teach that skill. The advantages of using a multi-sensory approach (with about five activities instead of one) are these:

1. Children tend to favor one modality in their learning. Some learn best through sight, some through sound, some through manipulation.

2. Using sight, sound, and manipulation rather than just one of these tends to increase retention.

3. Using a variety of modalities increases motivation because of the novelty effect.

4. Practicing a skill in five different ways increases mastery.

5. Three of four children can use the same learning center without having to do the same thing at the same time (providing the activities are not put in sequence but are made independent of each other).

6. Several different layers of the cognitive domain may be utilized; some activities can require sheer knowledge; some, comprehension; some, application or analysis.

The five parts of a multi-sensory single skill learning center are usually as follows (this will vary with different learning centers):

Programmed Lesson. This is an audio-tape accompanied by a brief booklet of two to five pages. The tape is simply a reading of the booklet, enabling the child to read along with the tape. The booklet and tape teach the skill (or concept) sequentially in *very small* steps. After each step, the student is asked a question; the student writes or thinks the answer and then checks immediately to see whether the answer was correct.

Visual Manipulative Aid. This is a learning activity that teaches the selected skill (or concept) by involving the students' eyes and hands. It requires them to manipulate one or more objects in such a way that the skill or concept may be taught by discovery, if it has not already been learned.

Puzzle, Problem, or Directions for Construction. This is an activity in which the student is challenged to solve a problem, complete a puzzle, or construct an object related to the skill or concept.

Game.   This is an actual game (and not an activity) for two or more people. Materials for the game are provided to the students, along with instructions of the object of the game (how one wins the game), procedures for playing and scoring, and procedures for determining who goes first. The game must teach the skill or concept.

Practice Exercises.   This is a worksheet with a series of exercises or questions. The questions generally start with something the students already know and gradually lead to the skill or concept they don't know.

Now that you've had an overview of the five subcenters, let's look at an example of each. Frank Meile, a fourth grade teacher, has prepared a M-Triple-S center on "How to Read Abbreviations." The center is spread out on a large round table in one corner of his classroom. There are enough chairs for four children at the center. In the center of the table is a large plastic cube—the kind usually used for photographs. Mr. Meile has dubbed this "The Force." Inside the cube are numerous words and their corresponding abbreviations.

"The cube is there," he says, "to help those who don't know an answer. I could have just put a sheet of paper there, but I thought a cube would be more attractive and less easily damaged."

The five parts of the center are spread out on the table so there is plenty of room for everyone. A can of pencils is in the center of the table next to a stack of "response sheets." (A sample response sheet can be seen in Figure 12.2.) The children know they are to fill out a response sheet and leave it in the "mailbox" before they leave the center. The mailbox is an attractively decorated cereal box with a picture of Snoopy lying inside a country mailbox.

Next to a programmed booklet is a small tape recorder and a set of earphones. As I turn on the tape recorder, I hear Mr. Meile giving directions: "Take a response sheet and a pencil. . . . Put your name on the paper. . . . Find a part of the response sheet that has a picture of a booklet and a tape recorder. . . . You will find the numbers one through eleven there. . . . Be sure to write on your response sheet and not on the booklet. . . . Find the pink cover slip so you can cover the answers while you are writing down your own answer. . . . Be sure to check each answer right after you write it. Just move down the pink cover slip until you find the number of the question you are answering. . . . Now turn to page one and read the booklet along with me. . . .

Mr. Meile's Programmed Lesson on Abbreviations

ANSWERS

"Days of the week like *Monday* and *Tuesday*—and other special words like *Doctor* and *Mister*—are often written in a short way. The short way is called an abbreviation. The abbreviation for *Monday* is *Mon.* (Mr. Meile reads "M-O-N-Period.") Abbreviations always have a period at the end.

Monday   1. What does *Mon.* stand for?

Sometimes we use the first letter of each word as an abbreviation. An *M.D.* is a *Medical Doctor.* A *District Attorney* is also called a *D.A.*

FIGURE 12.2 Response Sheet for Center on Abbreviations

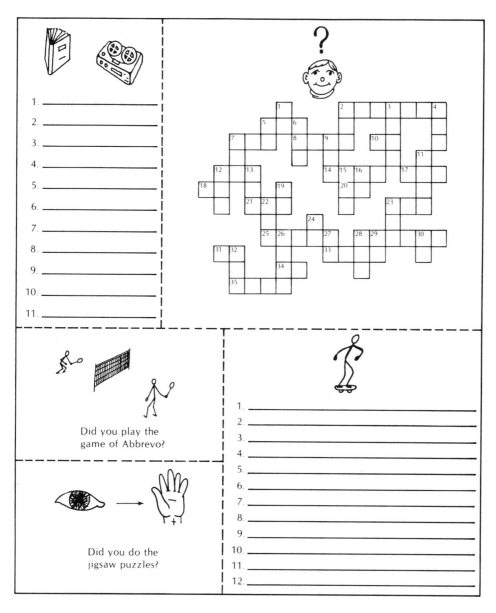

M.D.   2. What is the abbreviation for a *Medical Doctor?*

Sometimes we use the first and last letters of a word for the abbreviation. *Doctor* is usually written *Dr.* because *D* is the first letter and *r* is the last. *Mr.* means *Mister.*

doctor   3. What does *Dr.* mean?

More than two letters from a word are sometimes used for an abbreviation. The abbreviation for *Manager* is *Mgr. Bldg.* stands for *Building.*

Mgr.   4. What is the abbreviation for *Manager?*

Some units of measure use the first three letters for an abbreviation. *Dozen* is written *doz*. *Gal*. stands for *gallon*.

doz.   5. What is the abbreviation for *dozen*?

Some units of measure use the first and last letters. The abbreviation for *foot* is *ft*. *Yd*. stands for *yard*. A *quart* is written *qt*.

yard   6. *Yd*. is the abbreviation for what?

Sometimes we do not use the letters found in the word. The abbreviation for *pound* is *lb*. The abbreviation for *ounce* is *oz*.

pound   7. What does *lb*. stand for?

People often use abbreviations for addresses. The abbreviation for *Street* is *St*. *Ave*. stands for *Avenue*. The abbreviation for *Road* is *Rd*. *Apt*. stands for *Apartment*.

Ave.   8. What is the abbreviation for *Avenue*?

Days of the week are easy to abbreviate. For most of the days, we use the first three letters. *Sat*. means *Saturday*. The abbreviation for *Sunday* is *Sun*. For *Monday* we use *Mon*.

Wed.   9. What do you think the abbreviation for *Wednesday* is?

It is fun to learn abbreviations. For *teaspoon* we use *tsp*. For *tablespoon* we use *tbs*. *Hr*. stands for *hour*.

min.   10. What do you think the abbreviation for *minute* is?

pt.   11. The abbreviation for *quart* is *qt*. What do you think the abbreviation for *pint* is?

Next to the tape recorder and the programmed booklet is the next part of the learning center. Here there is a large envelope with a picture of an eye and a hand at the top. "The eye and hand stand for visual-manipulative aid," Mr. Meile says. "When the kids see the eye and hand, they know they should find the eye and hand on the response sheet so they can write something there. In this case, all they have to write is yes in the blank where it says, 'Did you do this part of the learning center?' For the programmed lesson you just looked at, they had to write their answers out in the eleven spaces that were provided. On the response sheet was a small picture of a little booklet and tape recorder so they'd know where to write their answers."

On the outside of the envelope are directions for using the visual-manipulative aid.

1. Remove the pieces from the large envelope.

2. Spread them out with the words and abbreviations up.

3. Each jigsaw puzzle has two pieces—one for a word and one for the abbreviation of that word. For example, one piece will have *Mister* on it, and the other piece will have *Mr*. on it.

4. Put the twenty-four jigsaw puzzles together. If you have trouble, use the plastic cube called "The Force."

5. When you finish, write yes on your response sheet in the blank next to the eye and hand. Put the pieces back in the envelope.

When the jigsaw puzzles are put together, they look like Figure 12.3.

FIGURE 12.3   Mr. Meile's Jigsaw Puzzles for Abbreviations

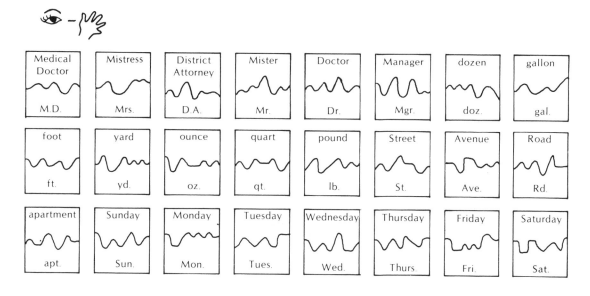

We notice that each puzzle, when put together properly, not only matches a word with its abbreviation but also puts Snoopy back together again. Since we're not as artistic as Mr. Meile we decide we would have cut out pictures for our abbreviation puzzles.[2]

Next to the visual-manipulative aid is a table game called Abbrevo (see Figure 12.4). The rules have been written on a separate sheet of tagboard:

1. Two to four players may play.

2. Take the foam die from the can (a cube of foam with a different number of dots on each side).

3. Now each person should choose one of the colored disks from the can to use as a marker.

4. Throw the die on the game board to see who goes first. The one who throws the highest number goes first.

5. The one who goes from Start to Finish first wins the game.

6. The first player throws the die and slides that number of spaces from Snoopy's doghouse.

7. If there is an abbreviation on that space, you must say what it means in five seconds. If you're right, you stay there. If you're wrong, you move back five spaces.

8. Correct or incorrect answers are decided by the other players, who use the Abbrevo answer sheet lying face down next to the game board. Be sure to return it *face down* after each person's turn.

9. If you land on the word *SWITCH,* you must change markers.

[2]In actuality, each of Mr. Meile's puzzles put together a picture of Snoopy. For copyright reasons, Snoopy could not be reproduced here.

FIGURE 12.4 Mr. Meile's Abbrevo Game

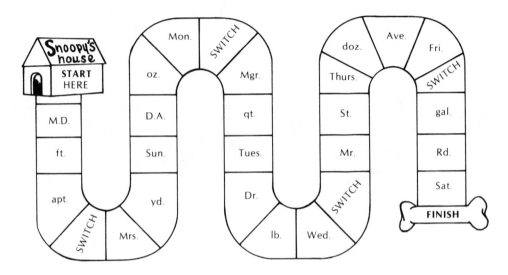

and places with the person on your left. (Only two people switch.)

10. To finish you must roll the exact number on the die. For instance, if there are two spaces between you and the finish, you must throw a three.

11. If you land on the space where another player is, that player must move back five spaces.

 EXAMPLE: John rolls a six and moves from Snoopy's doghouse to the abbreviation *yd.* He says "yard" and stays there. Mary rolls a five and moves from Snoopy's doghouse to *Mrs.* She says "Misses" and stays there. John rolls a six and lands on *Mgr.* He says "margarine" instead of *manager* and has to move back five spaces to *Sun.* Mary rolls a six and lands on *SWITCH.* So Mary and John switch markers and places. Mary is now on *Sun.* where John was. John is now on *SWITCH* and ready for his next turn.

12. When the game is over, put the die and the markers back in the can and write yes in the blank on your reponse sheet next to the picture of the badminton game.

After playing Abbrevo, we move to the crossword puzzle. "Sometimes I use crossword puzzles," says Mr. Meile, "but other times I use a tricky problem or maybe a set of directions on how to make something. In this one over here, for instance, they have to make a color wheel with color words written on them—hard color words like *chartreuse* and *crimson.* In this one over here on map skills, they have to solve a problem by using directions and the key to a physical relief map. The problem has to do with finding a treasure chest of diamonds."

To solve the crossword puzzle in front of me, I am allowed to refer to "The Force"—that magical answer cube. I notice that the puzzle has been reproduced in miniature on the response sheet so I can write my answers there (see Figure 12.5).

Since I don't have time to finish the fifth part of the center, I put my response sheets in the mailbox for safekeeping. "That's what I have the kids do," Mr. Meile says. "They're too likely to lose it otherwise." The next day when I return to Mr. Meile's room, I find the partition opened between his room and Miss Friel's room. "We team it about half of each day," he says. "That way we can share each other's learning centers and also do some special grouping of the kids for reading and math."

Before I look at other learning centers, I decide to look at the fifth part of the center on abbreviations. A child is already working on that part so I ask him if I can glance at it while he's finishing it. The fifth part is a set of "practice exercises" which require the use of the answer cube ("The Force"). Jamie reads each sentence to himself, noticing the words that are underlined. He then rewrites the sentence on his response sheet, using abbreviations for the underlined words. Some of the abbreviations he seems to know already, but others he has to look up on the answer cube. When he is all finished, he turns over the practice sheet and compares his answers with the teacher's.

Here's what the practice exercises look like:

1. Doctor Reed will come on Monday or Tuesday to our house on Bull Road.
2. Michael buys a foot long hot dog every Sunday.
3. Manager Jones lives on Grant Avenue in Apartment 7.
4. On Thursday, the District Attorney bought a new home on Pacific Street.
5. Sue went to the store on Saturday to get a gallon of milk and a pound of nuts.
6. On Wednesday, Mary bought a yard of material to make the Medical Doctor a tie.
7. Sally uses an ounce of tea every Friday.
8. Mister Smith's wife is often called Mrs. Smith.
9. In a three quart bowl, mix the oatmeal and the peanut butter.
10. In a two quart pan, mix together four tablespoons sugar, two teaspoons cocoa, and one pint milk.
11. Bring to a boil. Boil one minute. Add one teaspoon vanilla.
12. Let cool about one hour. It makes two dozen cookies.

Criteria for Successful Multi-sensory Single-skill Centers

Now that we've seen an example of a successful M-Triple-S center, let's develop a list of criteria which will serve as a check list in the production of such centers. To develop a M-Triple-S center we need to be concerned about five things.

FIGURE 12.5 Mr. Meile's Crossword Puzzle on Abbreviations

Across

2. sport in which you roll a ball
5. Friday (abbr.)
7. Apartment (abbr.)
8. home for a bird
10. opposite of down
12. place where you sleep
14. title of a person
17. dozen (abbr.)
18. District Attorney (abbr.)
20. Road (abbr.)
21. Saturday (abbr.)
23. Manager (abbr.)
25. Thursday (abbr.)
28. something you look through
31. yard (abbr.)
33. Tuesday (abbr.)
34. pound (abbr.)
35. an oak or a fir

Down

1. Doctor (abbr.)
2. used in baseball
3. what you kiss with
4. gallon (abbr.)
5. foot (abbr.)
6. used in a pen
7. Avenue (abbr.)
9. Sunday (abbr.)
11. part of a house
12. opposite of good
13. Doctor of Dental Science (abbr.)
15. part of a body
16. Medical Doctor (abbr.)
19. quart (abbr.)
22. subject that uses crayons
23. Monday (abbr.)
24. Mister (abbr.)
26. opening in ground
27. Street (abbr.)
28. Wednesday (abbr.)
29. yesterday he *was*, today he _____
30. ounce (abbr.)
32. a tiny spot

Motivation

1. Have you thought of the introductory learning experience presented by the teacher which must precede your learning

center? Many learning centers require a previous lesson or explanation by the teacher before children are permitted to use them. In Mr. Meile's case, he simply explained the center on abbreviations to his students and gave them a few examples of abbreviations. Abbreviations was not a new topic to the children: it was simply something they were having trouble with. If it had been a new topic or skill, Mr. Meile would have provided one or more lessons on it before introducing the children to the learning center.

2. Does your learning center attract through color, design, and novelty? Mr. Meile had used inexpensive felt pens on white tagboard to achieve a bright, colorful appearance for his center on abbreviations. His use of Snoopy cartoons was very eye-catching and amused the children as well. His game board for Abbrevo looked like one you'd purchase and was very popular with the children. Several of them played the game more then once.

3. Does the center challenge, excite, or interest the student? Abbrevo was especially exciting because of the SWITCH places on the board. The programmed tape and booklet offered the pleasure of immediate feedback on their own answers and ended with two questions for which information had not already been given, thus providing them with a minor challenge. Using an answer cube instead of an answer sheet provided novelty; labeling it "The Force" reminded the children of the movie, "Star Wars" and offered a positive association.

4. Have you included both easy and difficult experiences in each part? Each one of the five parts in the abbreviations center began with fairly easy problems and gradually led up to more difficult ones. Even the Abbrevo game used simpler abbreviations for the first several spaces. The level of difficulty never seemed to be too high or low for fourth graders.

5. Does each part provide feedback to the student? The practice sheet on abbreviations had answers on the back. The programmed booklet had answers right next to each question. The student simply hid the answer until he had written it down on the response sheet. The game had an answer sheet face down next to the game. The visual manipulative aid had jigsaw puzzles which wouldn't fit together unless they were correct. The crossword puzzle had the answers on the back, although this wouldn't always be necessary since most crossword puzzles can't be completed unless the answers are correct.

Retention

6. Does each of the five parts teach the same skill or concept? Mr. Meile's programmed lesson, game, visual-manipulative aid, puzzle, and practice sheet all stuck to the same "mini-topic" or skill. In each part, the children were involved in reading abbreviations; most of the abbreviations were the same in each part.

7. Have you separated the information or directions into small, easily "digested" pieces? Mr. Meile's programmed booklet and tape provided very small bits of information followed by a specific question and specific feedback. There was little opportunity for the child to get lost. The instructions for each part were given in short, easily understood sentences.

8. Is there a source of information readily available for the student? Mr. Meile's answer cube provided all the information necessary for a successful experience at the learning center. Instead of an answer sheet or answer cube, some teachers simply provide an example or two at the beginning of each part of the learning center; this is particularly true if the learning center is serving mainly as a review rather than a new learning experience.

9. Does each part help the student attain mastery of the skill or concept? This is very likely to happen if each part teaches the same skill or concept. The positive transfer from one part of the center to every other part almost guarantees initial mastery. More permanent mastery, however, can only be attained if practice is distributed throughout the school year. Active involvement by the student and the use of very small, easily digested pieces of information also assures initial mastery.

10. Is your center free from inaccuracies, misspellings, grammatical errors, and misleading punctuation? All of these are not only distracting influences, but they also can lead to negative transfer and, thus, to a lack of mastery. When something is learned incorrectly the first time, it becomes more difficult to teach it in its correct form.

Independence

11. Is each part independent of the other parts, so that a student does not have to complete one part before going on to another? If each part is dependent on a previous part, every child must follow the same sequence. This makes it necessary for children to wait for other children in order to move into the center. Thus you get the "bus line effect" with children waiting in line or fidgeting restlessly while they wait for a child to complete a part of the center. With five independent parts, three or four children can be allowed to visit the center at the same time. The other advantage of independent parts is that each part reinforces the same level of skill or concept, and mastery is more easily attained.

12. Does each part start off consistently at about the same level of difficulty? If one part is much more difficult than the others, you have not really created five independent parts. The easier ones will have to be completed first, thus negating the advantages mentioned earlier for five independent parts.

13. Are your directions simple, clear, and complete? Obviously if they're not, children are not going to be able to complete each part without assistance from the teacher or another child.

14. Do your directions have specific examples? As clear as the directions may seem to the teacher, without examples, many children can't follow them.

15. Have you sequenced your information or directions in such a way that each statement leads directly to the next one in a natural or logical order? Without such order, the children will become confused and require assistance.

16. Can the learning center be used by the students without your assistance so that you can be working with other students? The answer to this question is largely dependent upon your answers to the last three questions.

Physical Utility

17. Is your learning center portable and designed for easy storage? Mr. Meile kept each of his learning centers in a large thirteen-by-fifteen-inch envelope. Even the game boards were designed to fold and fit into the envelope.

18. Is each part coded so that setting up your center is fast and easy? Mr. Meile kept small pieces in envelopes that were coded according to the topic of the center and the part of the center. The visual-manipulative pieces, for instance, were stored in an eight-by-ten-inch envelope that was labeled "Reading Abbreviations" and had a picture of a face with a question mark above it—his code for puzzles and problems. Some people would have coded each piece of the jigsaw puzzle, but Mr. Meile decided it wasn't necessary.

19. Is each piece durable enough to last for several years? Since making a M-Triple-S center takes time, Mr. Meile wanted his centers to be used again and again. Therefore, he laminated each piece. Other teachers use transparent "contact paper." The tagboard he selected was stiff enough to discourage bending. Since the teachers of the same grade level shared learning centers, he was particularly concerned about durability.

20. Does the size of your manipulative pieces fit the dexterity level of your students? Students can easily become frustrated with pieces that are too small or too thin to handle easily.

21. Does each manipulative piece fit well and move easily? Spinning dials that always stick, jigsaw puzzles that don't really fit together, poorly designed materials, in general, distract the learner and decrease the value of the learning center.

Evaluation

22. Do you have some way for each student to record her responses so that you can determine which students have completed each part? Students who need the practice the most may avoid your learning centers, preferring instead to use the time for gossiping, doodling, or teasing. It is probably a mistake to think that every student will rush to the learning center with a burning desire to learn. Some form of accounta-

bility needs to be instituted. The other advantage of using response sheets of some sort is that it gives students a feeling of accomplishment and recognition.

23. Do you have a "mailbox" or some other means of collecting the response sheets easily and conveniently? Some teachers check the mailboxes at the end of each day in order to record the progress of each student.

Here is a summary of the criteria we have been discussing.

Questions to Ask Yourself about
Your M-Triple-S Learning Center

_____ 1. Have you thought of an introductory learning experience to precede the learning center?

_____ 2. Does your learning center attract through color, design, and novelty?

_____ 3. Does the center challenge, excite, and interest the students?

_____ 4. Have you included both easy and difficult experiences in each part?

_____ 5. Does each part provide feedback to the student?

_____ 6. Does each of the five parts teach the same skill or concept?

_____ 7. Have you separated the information or directions into small, easily digested pieces?

_____ 8. Is there a source of information readily available for the student?

_____ 9. Does each part help the student attain mastery of the skill or concept?

_____ 10. Is your center free from inaccuracies, misspellings, grammatical errors, and misleading punctuation?

_____ 11. Is each part independent of the other parts?

_____ 12. Does each part start off at about the same level of difficulty?

_____ 13. Are your directions simple, clear, and complete?

_____ 14. Do your directions have specific examples?

_____ 15. Have you sequenced your information or directions in a natural or logical way?

_____ 16. Can the learning center be used by the student without your assistance?

_____ 17. Is your learning center portable and designed for easy storage?

_____ 18. Are the parts coded so you can set up your center quickly and easily?

_____ 19. Is each piece durable enough to last for several years?

_____ 20. Does the size of your manipulative pieces fit the dexterity level of your students?

_____ 21. Does each manipulative piece fit well and move easily?

_____ 22. Do you have some way to determine which students have completed each part?

_____ 23. Do you have some way of conveniently collecting the response sheets?

Although the M-Triple-S Approach has been described as one which uses five different activities in a center at the same time, in some cases, the teacher may wish to sequence the activities and use them as five different centers at five different times. While the M-Triple-S approach is not always the appropriate approach toward the development of a learning center, it is one which can help students thoroughly master basic skills and concepts related to the language arts.

REFERENCES AND BIBLIOGRAPHY

1. Beck, Isabel L., and Bolvin, John C. "A Model for Non-Gradedness: The Reading Program for Individually Prescribed Instruction." *Elementary English* 46 (Feb. 1969): 130–35.

2. Blitz, Barbara. *The Open Classroom: Making it Work.* Boston: Allyn & Bacon, 1973.

3. Breyfogle, Ethel et al. *Creating a Learning Environment: A Learning Center Handbook.* Goodyear, 1976.

4. Davidson, Tom et al. *The Learning Center Book: An Integrated Approach.* Goodyear, 1976.

5. Feeley, Joan T., and Rubin, Blanche. "Reading in an Open Classroom." *Language Arts* 54 (March 1977): 287–89.

6. Floyd, Cecil. "Meeting Children's Reading Needs in the Middle Grades: A Preliminary Report." *Elementary School Journal* 55 (Oct. 1954): 99–103.

7. Frankell, Jill C. "Learning Centers for Reading in Junior High." *Journal of Reading* 19 (1975): 243–46.

8. Gilbert, Jerome. "Tesla School Breaks the Lock Step." *Elementary School Journal* 64 (March 1964): 306–9.

9. Goodman, Kenneth S. "A Linguistic Study of Cues and Miscues in Reading." *Elementary English* 42 (Oct. 1965): 639–43.

10. Gross, Ronald, and Gross, Beatrice. "A Little Bit of Chaos." *Saturday Review* (May 16, 1970): 71–73.

11. Harris, Albert J. "Grouping in the Teaching of Reading." *Reading Teacher* 5 (Sept. 1951): 1–3.

12. Johns, Jerry L. et al. *Assessing Reading Behavior: Informal Reading Inventories.* Newark, Del.: International Reading Association, 1977.

13. Lopardo, Genevieve S. "LEA—Cloze Reading Material for the Disabled Reader." *Reading Teacher* 30 (Oct. 1975): 42–44.

14. Marshall, Kim. *Opening Your Class With Learning Situations.* Learning Handbooks, 530 University Avenue, Palo Alto, California 94301, 1975.

15. May, Frank B., and Eliot, Susan B. *To Help Children Read,* 2d ed. Columbus, Ohio: Charles E. Merrill Publishing Co., 1978.

16. Osmon, Fred L. *Patterns for Designing Children's Centers.* Educational Facilities Laboratories, 850 Third Avenue, New York, 10022, 1971.

17. Pflum, John, and Waterman, Anita H. *The New Open Education: A Program for Combining the Basics with Alternative Methods.* Washington, D.C.: Acropolis, 1974.

18. Resnik, Henry S. "The Open Classroom." *Today's Education* 60 (Dec. 1971): 16–17 and 60–61.

19. Schwartz, Judy I. "Standardizing a Reading Test." *Reading Teacher* 30 (Jan. 1977): 364–68.

20. Silberman, Charles E., ed. *The Open Classroom Reader.* New York: Random House, 1973.

21. Stewart, William J. "Teaching Children and Not Subjects in the Language Arts." *Reading Improvement* 13 (Summer 1976): 71–73.

22. Veatch, Jeanette. *Individualizing Your Reading Program: Self Selection in Action.* New York: Putnam, 1959.

23. Weintraub, Samuel. "Programmed Reading Materials." In *Recent Developments in Reading.* Proceedings of the Annual Conference on Reading, University of Chicago Press, 1965.

Appendix A

SAMPLES OF CHILDREN'S HANDWRITING, PUNCTUATION, AND SPELLING ERRORS

Sample 1

About Safety you are
not supose to go near someone
you don't now. and if someone
ask you for a ride never go
unless you now them. And never
take candy from strangers.
And when it is Halloween never
go in the persons house.

Sample 2

rallbit

My favorite rallbit is a boy
and my sister as the mother and I have
The father. And my sister is rallbit
is going to have a baby. And two
more are goingtwo have baby

Sample 3

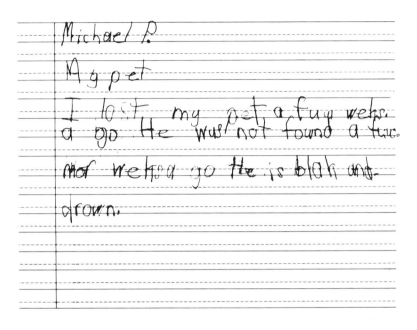

Sample 4

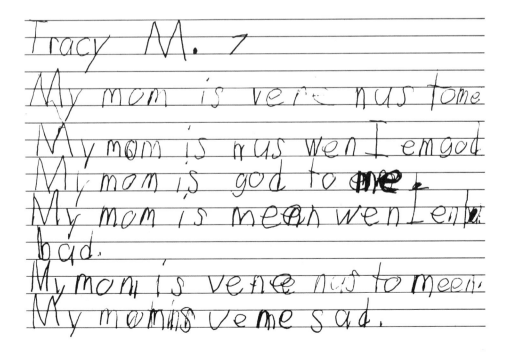

Sample 5

My favorite show

My favorite show is. Starsky and Hutch.
They are kind of cute. They are good
detectives. Starsky owns a red car
with a white stripe
  Starsky's name is - Paul Michelle Glaser
  Hutch's name is - David Soul
  Hutch is the cutest.

Sample 6

About a Book

The Frist day a little girl took me. I said
to myself were are you taking me.
I was afaid and she open the book and she
being to read the book and when she finish to book.
She threw me down the stair and I had a
big pain.
She pick it up and put me in the drawn.
And she went to sleep.
And I had a nap.
In the mraning she took me and I said again to my
self. were are you taking me
She took me were I belong in the libary

Sample 7

Mother's Day

Mother's Day is a day to renber..
for mother's my mother likes
mothers day. My mother gets alot
of cards and flowers and candy
and she gets breakfast in bed on
Sunday I like mothers Day becouse
I can make thing for her and I bry
plants and I make cards we have
a pemny sale at school and you
can bry anything your want if its
there there is alot of nice stuff
Mothers Day is nice it is a Day
for loving and giving to your Mom
Mothers Day is
Nice

Appendix B

BOOK PROJECTS FOR CHILDREN AND TEACHERS

Oral Projects

1. Try to interest others in a book you have read by reading an interesting part to the class. Practice before you read to them.

2. Read an exciting part to the class. Stop reading right in the middle of the action. Practice before you read to them.

3. Tell about one character in the book. Tell why he is such an interesting person. Make the others in the class want to know more about him.

4. Show on a globe or map how you would get from your home to where the story took place. Tell how you would travel there. Then tell something about this place. Tell a little bit about why it was important in the story. Make the others in the class wish they could go there.

5. Pretend you are one of the characters in the book. Describe yourself and tell one or two things you do in the story. If others have already read the book, ask them to guess who you are.

6. Find an object which is important in the book you just read. Show it to the class and have them guess what it is and why it might be important in the story. Give them a few hints but don't tell them too much.

7. Play Twenty Questions with the class. Have them think of the object or person you have in mind that was important in the story. First tell them whether it is "animal, vegetable, or mineral." After the game, give them some hints as to why the object or person was important, but don't tell them too much.

8. Tell the class some interesting facts that you have learned about a country you read about. Then ask them three or four questions to see what facts they can remember.

9. Tell how you would have done something differently than the way a person in the story did it.

These projects are designed to provide practice on basic skills.

10. Prepare and present a T.V. commercial of your book. Try to interest others in "buying" your book.

11. Read to the class two or three poems from a book of poems you have read. Be sure to practice several times before you do this. You may wish to use the tape recorder for practicing.

12. Find someone else who has read the same book of poetry. Together read to the class two or three poems. You might try different arrangements as with a song. For example, one person could read the first verse, the other person read the second verse, and then read the third verse together.

13. See if you can recite from memory a favorite poem from a poetry book you have just read.

14. Dress up as a character in the book and tell something about yourself—or about one of the adventures you had.

15. After reading a book of folk tales, see if you can learn one of the stories well enough to tell to the class.

16. Look up the author in *Something About the Author, The Junior Book of Authors,* or *More Junior Authors* (in the reference section of the library). Tell the class a few interesting things about him or her.

17. Make up another adventure for one of the characters. Tell the adventure.

18. Make up a new ending for the book. Tell your ending to the class after you first tell a little bit about the beginning and the middle. Don't tell them the real ending, though.

19. Have a panel discussion about a book that three or four of you have read. Tell how you agree and disagree about some of the characters or about part of the story.

20. Tell about an adventure you had that was similar to one a character in the book had.

21. Meet in small groups to chat about books you have read.

Drama Projects

1. Pantomime a scene from your book. Have the class guess what you were doing. Tell them only enough to get them interested in the book.

2. Plan so that you and a friend read the same book. Then prepare and present a skit on a part of the book. You may have to make up some of your own dialogue, or you can say what the characters said in the book.

3. Tape record a skit based on the book. You may have to make up some of your own dialogue and make your voice sound like several different people. Play the tape recording to the class.

4. Put on a puppet play about one part of the book.

5. Play Meet the Author. Find someone who has read the same book. One person pretends to be the author and the other interviews him. The interviewer asks questions about the book, about the author's life (if you can find information about his life), etc.

6. Pretend you are the author of the book and you are trying to get someone to publish it. Tell the "publishing staff" (your class) why it would be a good book to publish. Let them ask you questions.

7. Play charades with the class. Act out each word of the title. See how long it takes for the class to guess the title.

8. If several others have read this book, pantomime a scene from the book—by yourself. Then ask the class to guess the *title* of the book. See if they can also guess the author.

9. Pretend you are a character in the book you have read. Find someone who will pretend he is a character in a different book *he* has read. Carry on in front of the class a conversation between the two characters. You might tell each other about some of your adventures or about some of the people you know (those described in the books).

10. Put on a play by yourself in which you play two or three parts. Make name cards for each character. Each time you switch parts hold up one of the cards.

11. Find some dolls that can be used to represent characters in your book. Put on a doll play about one part of your book.

12. Put on a play with one or two others. Have the class guess the title and author of the book.

Written Projects

1. Write an advertisement for the book you have read. Put the ad on the bulletin board. Be sure to tell where the book may be found and a few things about why it's a "marvelous" book.

2. Write a letter to a friend and try to persuade him to read the book you just read.

3. Make up a new table of contents for your book. Use your imagination to invent chapter titles which would interest someone else in reading the book.

4. Read two or three chapters of the book. Then write down what you think will happen in the next chapter. Draw a line under what you have written and read the next chapter. Then write briefly about how close you were with your guess.

5. Make a brief outline of your book. Use roman numerals for the chapters, and so on. See example below:

Tom Sawyer
I. Tom plays, fights, and hides
   A. Tom tricks Aunt Polly
   B. Siddy gets Tom in trouble
   C. Tom fights with a new boy
   D. Tom returns home late at night
II. The glorious whitewasher

6. Write about something that happened in the book in the same way a newspaper reporter would describe it. A reporter tries to answer these questions: Who? What? When? Where? Why? Don't forget to make up a snappy headline for your newspaper article.

7. Write a pretend letter to a character in the book. Tell him how his life is the same or different from yours.

8. Write a real letter to the author of the book. Send the letter in care of the publisher.

9. Make a short diary for one of the characters in the book. Describe three or four days as if you were the person in the book.

10. Pretend you are one of the characters in the book. Write a letter to another character in the book.

11. Add another chapter to the book. Tell what happened next, or what adventure was left out.

12. Write an ending to the book which is quite different from the one the author wrote.

13. Write about *two* books you have read that are on the same topic. Tell how the books are similar and different.

14. See how good your memory is. Describe the important details in one chapter. Draw a line under your description. Then reread that chapter. Write down any important details you left out.

15. Write about an adventure you had that was like an adventure a character in the book had. Tell how the two adventures were alike and different.

16. Read in an encyclopedia or in another factual book about a person, place, or thing described in your book. Write down some of the things you learned this way that you did *not* learn from the book itself.

17. Try to make a list of all the characters in the book from memory. List both their first and last names. Draw a line under your list. Now skim through the book to see if you remembered all of them. Write down any you didn't remember. How good was your memory for names?

18. Write about the character in the story that you would most like to have for a friend. Tell why he would be a good friend. Also write about the character that you would *not* like to have for a friend. Tell why.

19. Write about how you would have solved a problem a different way from the way a character in the book did.

20. Pick two characters from the story. Write about how they were alike and how they were different.

21. Make a list of words or phrases in the story that helped you to almost see or hear or smell or feel or taste something described in the story.

22. Write a poem that tells about one adventure in the book.

Arts and Crafts Projects

1. Make clothes for a doll to match a character in the book. Display it for the rest of the class to see. Make sure you have a card by it with the name of the book, the author, and your name.

2. Make an object which is important in the book you just read. Have the class guess what it is and why it might be important in the story. Give them a few hints but don't tell them for sure.

3. Make a flannel board or bulletin board display about your book.

4. Make a comic strip about one of the scenes in your book. Put it on the bulletin board.

5. Make a diorama (a small stage) which describes a scene in the book. Use a cardboard box for the stage. Make the objects and people in your scene out of clay, cardboard, pipe cleaners, papier mâché, or any other material.

6. Make a mobile representing five or six of the characters in the book.

7. If the book doesn't have a book jacket, make one for it. Be sure to put a picture on it and all the necessary information. A used manila folder might be good to use.

8. Make a "movie" of one scene in your book. Use a long piece of butcher paper. After you draw a sequence of several pictures, roll the butcher paper. Then ask two people to unroll it as you describe the scenes to the class.

9. Make a picture of one scene in the book. Put it on the bulletin board. Underneath it put the title and author and two or three questions about the scene. Try using crayon, chalk, or charcoal.

10. Same as 9. Use tempera or water color.

11. Same as 9. Use collage materials: bits of paper, cloth, or other materials.

12. Study the illustration in the book. What kinds of techniques did the artist use? See if you can make an illustration of a part in the book that was not illustrated. Try to use some of the same techniques as the artist did. Put your illustration on the bulletin board. Be sure to name the illustrator that you imitated.

13. Make a time line of the story. Use main events rather than dates. Draw pictures to illustrate the main events.

14. Read half or more of the book. Then draw three pictures to show three different ways the book might end. Put them on the bulletin board, along with a card giving the title, author, your name, and "Three Ideas on How This Book Might End."

15. Make a scrap book of things related to the book. Be sure to label what you put in your scrap book.

16. Make a map to show where the characters went in the story.

Demonstration Projects

1. Demonstrate a science principle you learned from your book by performing an experiment in front of the class.

2. Show the class how to make something you learned how to make from reading your book.

3. Show the class how to do something you learned how to do from reading your book.

NEWBERY AND CALDECOTT AWARD BOOKS

Newbery Award Books

1922 *Story of Mankind* (van Loon)—Liveright
1923 *Voyages of Dr. Doolittle* (Lofting)—Lippincott
1924 *Dark Frigate* (Hawes)—Little
1925 *Tales from Silver Lands* (Finger)—Doubleday
1926 *Shen of the Sea* (Chrisman)—Dutton
1927 *Smoky the Cowhorse* (James)—Scribner's
1928 *Gay Neck* (Mukerji)—Dutton
1929 *Trumpeter of Krakow* (Kelly)—Macmillan
1930 *Hitty, Her First 100 Years* (Field)—Macmillan
1931 *Cat Who Went to Heaven* (Coatsworth)—Macmillan
1932 *Waterless Mountain* (Armer)—McKay
1933 *Young Fu of the Upper Yangtze* (Lewis)—Holt
1934 *Invincible Louisa: Anniversary Edition* (Meigs)—Little
1935 *Dobry* (Shannon)—Viking
1936 *Caddie Woodlawn* (Brink)—Macmillan
1937 *Roller Skates* (Sawyer)—Viking
1938 *White Stag* (Seredy)—Viking
1939 *Thimble Summer* (Enright)—Holt
1940 *Daniel Boone* (Daugherty)—Viking
1941 *Call It Courage* (Sperry)—Macmillan
1942 *Matchlock Gun* (Edmonds)—Dodd
1943 *Adam of the Road* (Gray)—Viking
1944 *Johnny Tremain* (Forbes)—Houghton
1945 *Rabbit Hill* (Lawson)—Viking
1946 *Strawberry Girl* (Lenski)—Lippincott
1947 *Miss Hickory* (Bailey)—Viking
1948 *Twenty-One Balloons* (du Bois)—Viking
1949 *King of the Wind* (Henry)—Rand McNally
1950 *Door in the Wall* (de Angeli)—Doubleday

1951 *Amos Fortune, Free Man* (Yates)—Dutton
1952 *Ginger Pye* (Estes)—Harcourt
1953 *Secret of the Andes* (Clark)—Viking
1954 *And Now Miguel* (Krumgold)—Crowell
1955 *Wheel on the School* (de Jong)—Harper
1956 *Carry on, Mr. Bowditch* (Latham)—Houghton
1957 *Miracles on Maple Hill* (Sorensen)—Harcourt
1958 *Rifles for Waitie* (Keith)—Crowell
1959 *Witch of Blackbird Pond* (Speare)—Houghton
1960 *Onion John* (Krumgold)—Crowell
1961 *Island of the Blue Dolphins* (O'Dell)—Houghton
1962 *Bronze Bow* (Speare)—Houghton
1963 *Wrinkle in Time* (L'Engle)—Farrar
1964 *It's Like This, Cat* (Neville)—Harper
1965 *Shadow of a Bull* (Wojciechowska)—Atheneum
1966 *I, Juan de Pareja* (de Trevino)—Farrar
1967 *Up a Road Slowly* (Hunt)—Follett
1968 *From the Mixed-up Files of Mrs. Basil E. Frankenweiler*
      (Konigsburg)—Atheneum
1969 *High King* (Alexander)—Holt
1970 *Sounder* (Armstrong)—Harper
1971 *Summer of the Swans* (Byars)—Viking
1972 *Mrs. Frisby and the Rats of NIMH* (O'Brien)—Atheneum
1973 *Julie of the Wolves* (George)—Harper
1974 *Slave Dancer* (Paula Fox)—Bradbury
1975 *M.C. Higgins, The Great* (Hamilton)—Macmillan
1976 *Grey King* (Cooper)—Atheneum
1977 *Roll of Thunder, Hear My Cry* (Taylor)—Dial
1978 *Bridge to Terabithia* (Paterson)—Crowell
1979 *The Westing Game* (Raskin)—Dutton

Caldecott Award Books

1938 *Animals of the Bible* (Lathrop)—Lippincott
1939 *Mei Li* (Handforth)—Doubleday
1940 *Abraham Lincoln* (d'Aulaire)—Doubleday
1941 *They Were Strong and Good* (Lawson)—Viking
1942 *Make Way for Ducklings* (McCloskey)—Viking
1943 *Little House* (Burton)—Houghton
1944 *Many Moons* (Thurber & Slobodkin)—Harcourt
1945 *Prayer for a Child* (Field & Jones)—Macmillan
1946 *Rooster Crows* (Petersham)—Macmillan
1947 *Little Island* (MacDonald & Weisgard)—Doubleday
1948 *White Snow, Bright Snow* (Tresselt & Duvoisin)—Lathrop
1949 *Big Snow* (Hader)—Macmillan
1950 *Song of the Swallows* (Politi)—Scribner
1951 *Egg Tree* (Milhous)—Scribner
1952 *Finders Keepers* (Nicolas)—Harcourt
1953 *Biggest Bear* (Ward)—Houghton

1954 *Madeline's Rescue* (Bremelmans)—Viking

1955 *Cinderella* (Brown)—Scribner

1956 *Frog Went A-Courtin* (Langstaff & Rojankovsky)—Harcourt

1957 *A Tree Is Nice* (Udry & Simont)—Harper

1958 *Time of Wonder* (McCloskey)—Viking

1959 *Chanticleer and the Fox* (Cooney)—Crowell

1960 *Nine Days to Christmas* (Ets & Labastida)—Viking

1961 *Baboushka and the Three Kings* (Robbins)—Parnassus

1962 *Once a Mouse* (Brown)—Scribner

1963 *Snowy Day* (Keats)—Viking

1964 *Where the Wild Things Are* (Sendak)—Harper

1965 *May I Bring a Friend* (de Regniers)—Atheneum

1966 *Always Room for One More* (Leadhas & Hogrogian)—Holt

1967 *Sam Bangs & Moonshine* (News)—Holt

1968 *Drummer Hoff* (Emberley)—Prentice

1969 *Fool of the World and the Flying Ship* (Ransome)—Farrar

1970 *Sylvester and the Magic Pebble* (Steig)—Simon

1971 *Story, a Story* (Haley)—Atheneum

1972 *One Fine Day* (Hogrogian)—Macmillan

1973 *Funny Little Woman* (Mosel)—Dutton

1974 *Duffy and the Devil* (Zemach)—Farrar

1975 *Arrow to the Sun* (McDermott)—Viking

1976 Why Mosquitoes Buzz in People's Ears (Aardema)—Dial

1977 *Ashanti to Zulu: African Traditions* (Musgrove)—Dial

1978 *Noah's Ark* (Spier)—Doubleday

1979 *The Girl Who Loved Wild Horses* (Goble)—Bradbury

Index